Police Violence

Police
Violence

Understanding and Controlling
Police Abuse of Force

Edited by

William A. Geller

Hans Toch

Yale University Press

New Haven and London

Published with assistance from the Louis
Stern Memorial Fund.

The research and writing of this book were
supported by grant 91-IJ-CX-0027 from the
National Institute of Justice to the Police
Executive Research Forum. The opinions and
recommendations are those of the authors and
do not necessarily represent those of the U.S.
Department of Justice or the membership of
the Police Executive Research Forum.

Designed by James J. Johnson and
set in Stemple Garamond type by
Tseng Information Systems, Inc., Durham,
North Carolina. Printed in the United States
of America by BookCrafters, Inc., Chelsea,
Michigan.

*Library of Congress Cataloging-in-Publication
Data*

Police violence : understanding and
controlling police abuse of force /
edited by William A. Geller, Hans Toch.
p. cm.
Includes bibliographical references and index.
ISBN 0-300-06429-2

1. Police misconduct—United States.
2. Police psychology—United States.
3. Police training—United States.
4. Police—United States—Attitudes.
I. Geller, William A.   II. Toch, Hans.
HV8141.A72 1996
363.2'3—dc20   96-33939

A catalogue record for this book is available
from the British Library.

10 9 8 7 6 5 4 3 2 1

Contents

Preface

Sadly, the subject of this book is topical. An earlier version of the book (Geller and Toch 1995) appeared in the wake of Rodney King's beating, and of the trials, riot, commentaries, retrospectives, and commission reports that ensued. The televised image of King's recumbent body, and of batons swishing through the night air, have begun to fade from the public mind. But newer images and new voices have reached the public of late, calculated to reawaken its concerns. The most alarming of the voices the public has heard is that of a retired detective named Fuhrman boasting of brutal acts he claimed to have routinely perpetrated. And there have also been voices—very angry voices—that have reminded us that to many among us Fuhrman and those like him typify American policing in action.

Though the prevalence of police-citizen conflict has in fact diminished in recent decades, it appears no less true today than it was in the days of the 1968 Kerner Commission that "the abrasive relationship between the police and minority communities has been a major—and explosive—source of grievance, tension and disorder" (National Association for the Advancement of Colored People, 1995, p. xv).

The suggestion that a police officer's use of force has been excessive typically triggers a zero-sum game in which somebody, the police or the complainant, must lose for the other to win. The possibility of a win-win scenario, in which the legitimate concerns of *all* interested persons are acknowledged and dealt with justly, probably seems fanciful to most police and community leaders. To us it seems feasible (but difficult), and this volume attempts to suggest why.

Who cares about police abuse of force? Around any given controversial episode the communities of interest are many and diverse: the individual civilian and officer participants in the violent encounter and their friends and families; representatives of groups who particularly trust or distrust the police; the community at large; police managers and their legal, strategic, and tactical advisors; rank-and-file officers and their bargaining agents and lawyers; civil liberties groups; police oversight officials (police boards, misconduct review panels, etc.); crime victims' advocates; elected and appointed officials; the news media; and others.

This volume is designed to speak to the concerns of most if not all of these stakeholders in the problem of police misuse of force. Chapter after chapter acknowledges that there are legitimate concerns on the part of every one of these interest groups. The chapters represent neither partisan attacks on nor defenses of the police. In tone and substance, their aim is problem solving—seeking to clarify what is known and what still needs to be learned to better understand, prevent, and remediate police abuse of force. We are not looking for villains. It is neither political correctness nor co-optation that dissuades us from adopting a tone in this volume that is particularly critical of police or their critics. We just do not believe that assessing blame is conducive to enlisting the support of the key interest groups with the capacity to help ameliorate police abuse of force. In the words of a Japanese corporate philosophy enunciated in the 1993 film *Rising Sun*, our orientation in this book is to "fix the problem, not the blame." And we cannot hope to fix it if we don't understand it in its complexity. Minimally, that understanding must be built on consideration of how the problem looks from many diverse perspectives. The contributors to this volume bring a rich diversity of talents and perspectives to their assigned topics. Among them are scholars (criminologists, criminal justice professors, social psychologists, lawyers, and public administration specialists), former police managers, a police union leader, men and women of different races and ethnicities, civilian oversight agency administrators and analysts, civil liberties advocates, police litigation expert witnesses, and media commentators. They represent constituencies that often do not sit down and talk civilly with one another, especially about topics as sensitive as police abuse of force.

We also had the benefit early in this project, when we were considering which chapter topics to include, of advice from an esteemed group of leaders in the civil rights, civil liberties, police (management and labor), municipal governance, victims' rights, academic, and legal communities. Their input helped us a great deal; the result, naturally, is our own responsibility and does not necessarily represent an official position of any of the organizations our advisors so ably lead, of the Police Executive Research Forum, or of the State University of New York. Nor do the views expressed on these pages necessarily reflect the views of the National Institute of Justice or the U.S. Department of Justice, whose generous support made this work possible.

Contributors

WILLIAM A. GELLER is associate director of the Police Executive Research Forum.

HANS TOCH is Distinguished Professor at the School of Criminal Justice at the University at Albany, State University of New York.

KENNETH ADAMS is associate professor and assistant dean for graduate programs in the College of Criminal Justice at Sam Houston State University.

DAVID H. BAYLEY is dean of the School of Criminal Justice, State University of New York at Albany.

MARY M. CHEH is professor of law at the National Law Center, George Washington University.

TIMOTHY J. FLANAGAN is professor of criminal justice and dean of the College of Criminal Justice at Sam Houston State University.

JAMES J. FYFE is a professor of criminal justice at Temple University.

J. DOUGLAS GRANT was formerly director of research for the California Department of Corrections and president of the Social Action Research Center.

JOAN GRANT has conducted research and evaluation projects on school crime, delinquency prevention, and police organization.

GEORGE L. KELLING is professor in the College of Criminal Justice at Northeastern University and a research fellow in the Program in Criminal Justice at the Kennedy School of Government, Harvard University.

WAYNE A. KERSTETTER is professor in the department of criminal justice, University of Illinois at Chicago.

ROBERT B. KLIESMET is past president of the International Union of Police Associations, AFL-CIO, and the sheriff of Milwaukee County, Wisconsin.

CARL B. KLOCKARS is professor of sociology and criminal justice at the University of Delaware.

DAVID LESTER is executive director of the Center for the Study of Suicide in Blackwood, New Jersey.

HUBERT G. LOCKE is professor and former dean of the Graduate School of Public Affairs at the University of Washington (Seattle).

WILLIAM KER MUIR is professor of political science at the University of California at Berkeley.

DOUGLAS W. PEREZ is on the faculty of Trinity College of Vermont.

MICHAEL S. VAUGHN is assistant professor in the department of criminal justice at Georgia State University.

ROBERT E. WORDEN is assistant professor of criminal justice and of public policy at the University at Albany, State University of New York.

Police Violence

CHAPTER ONE

A Theory of Excessive Force and Its Control

CARL B. KLOCKARS

Whatever vestigial significance attaches to the term "lawful" use of force is confined to the obvious and unnecessary rule that police officers may not commit crimes of violence. Otherwise, however, the expectation that they may and will use force is left entirely undefined. In fact, the only instructions any policeman ever receives in this respect consist of sermonizing that he should be humane and circumspect, and that he must not desist from what he has undertaken merely because its accomplishment may call for coercive means. We might add, at this point, that the entire debate about the troublesome problem of police brutality will not move beyond its present impasse and the desire to eliminate it will remain an impotent conceit, until this point is fully grasped and unequivocally admitted. In fact, our expectation that policemen will use force, coupled by our refusals to state clearly what we mean by it (aside from sanctimonious homilies) smacks of more than a bit of perversity. (Bittner 1975a, first published 1970)

No one knows what excessive force is. If that point is true, and I believe it is as true today as when Bittner made it in 1970, it follows that all the talk of wanting to reduce or eliminate it is largely meaningless.

This chapter seeks, with considerable guidance from Bittner's pioneering work in *The Functions of the Police in Modern Society*, to define precisely what is, has been, and should be meant by police use of "excessive force" and to explore the consequences and implications of those definitions for mechanisms appropriate to its control. If no one knows what excessive force is, empirical research that accurately measures it or its reduction is also nonexistent. This theoretical effort is a necessary first step toward changing that situation.

Toward a Definition of Excessive Force

What defines police, what distinguishes them from other citizens, is that we give them the very general right to use coercive force when they believe the situation calls for it.[1] They are in this respect like other professionals (e.g., doctors), to whom we give special rights to do things (cut people open, give them dangerous drugs, examine their private parts, etc.) that we permit no other persons to do. Moreover, the police officer's freedom to use force is far broader and more varied than the physician's freedom to use medicine to fight disease. The police need not invoke the law to use force, though they may decide to use force to invoke "the law"; they need not obtain the consent of a complainant nor of the person on whom it is used; there are few, if any, occasions in which anyone has a legal right to re-sist police use of force, even if police use it improperly; and police use of force is rarely reviewed or evaluated.

The enormous range of the legitimate authority of the police to use force is at the heart of the problem of defining and controlling its excessive use. At present, three of the major mechanisms that appear to do so are *criminal law*, which says that an officer's use of force shall not be so excessive as to constitute a crime; *civil liability*, which says that an officer's use of force shall not cause such an injury to a person that the person or heirs should be awarded compensation for the offi-cer's misconduct; and *fear of scandal*, which says that an officer's behavior shall not be of such nature as to embarrass his employer. Each of these mechanisms for controlling excessive force by police embodies a form of definition of it.

Criminal Law and Excessive Force

With rare exceptions, the force used routinely by police to take suspects into custody, restrain belligerents, handcuff, use or discharge lethal or nonlethal weapons at persons, as well as threats to use such force, would constitute a criminal offense if used by persons who are not police. Although the typical state law makes all of these activities criminal for all citizens, it normally exempts police officers in the definition of the particular offense or in a general disclaimer to the effect that none of these laws "shall apply to any law enforcement officer or his agent while acting in the lawful performance of his duty" (e.g., Del. Code, Title 11, s. 542).

Such exemptions, in whatever form, should not be understood to mean that police officers cannot be found guilty of murder, manslaughter, offensive touch-ing, assault, battery, terroristic threatening, and other criminal acts while on duty. However, what must be demonstrated, and in a criminal prosecution demon-strated beyond a reasonable doubt and to a moral certainty, is that the commission of the alleged offense by the police officer cannot be justified by reference to a legitimate performance of the officer's duty. In practice, such laws tend to be ap-plied to police officers only when they are clearly off duty (for example, when they assault a spouse in a domestic argument), though even under such circumstances fellow officers are likely to attempt to handle such offenses informally, if it is possible to do so without scandal.

In addition to those laws that expose police officers to criminal liability in the same way they do other citizens (*if* the officer cannot demonstrate a reasonable relationship between his acts and his duty), most states and the federal government subject police officers and other public officials to laws that provide criminal penalties for intentional abuse of office. The federal law—Title 18 of the U.S. Code, section 242, "Criminal Liability for Deprivation of Civil Rights"—provides for a penalty of a fine of up to $1,000 and one year imprisonment or, if death results, imprisonment up to life for any person who, "under color of law, statute, ordinance, regulation or custom wilfully subjects any inhabitant of any state, Territory, or District to the deprivation of any right, privileges, or immunities secured or protected by the Constitution or laws of the United States."

It is by no means unusual for arrestees to express an interest in filing criminal charges against arresting officers, but court commissioners, magistrates, and justices tend to regard such complaints with suspicion. In many jurisdictions they are prohibited from accepting such criminal complaints against police officers unless they have first passed review by a prosecutor. These are not the only obstacles to employing the criminal law as a mechanism for controlling excessive force. There is also the greater credibility likely to be attached to a police officer's account of an incident as opposed to that of an accused criminal, the reluctance of witness officers to testify against fellow officers, and the public's unwillingness to punish police with penalties normally reserved for criminals (see Geller and Scott 1992: 292-95).

Successful criminal prosecutions of police officers for the use of excessive force are extremely rare. Petrillo (1990) reports, for example, that the San Diego County district attorney's office absolved San Diego police officers of any criminal liability in all of the 190 officer-involved shootings that occurred from January 1, 1985, through December 20, 1990. Similarly, criminal charges were filed in only one of 477 shooting incidents in which deputies of the Los Angeles County sheriff's office were involved (Katz 1991). Kobler (1975a) estimates that during the 1970s, criminal prosecutions were initiated in only one out of every 500 cases of shootings by police (see also Waegel 1984a; Hubler 1991; Levitt 1991; and Blumberg 1989: 458-59). While these studies of the use of the criminal law have examined only situations involving control of deadly force, it is likely that the rates at which the criminal law is used to control nondeadly force are even lower. However, even if the rates for the use of the criminal law to control nondeadly force are roughly equivalent to those for deadly force, criminal law is unlikely to have anything but the most marginal influence on controlling police use of excessive force in the line of duty.[2]

Civil Liability and Excessive Force

Although criminal prosecutions of police officers for use of excessive force in the line of duty are rare and convictions rarer still, civil actions against police for use of excessive force are common.[3] From the point of view of persons alleging injury, they are preferable to criminal action for several reasons:

1. Proof need only be offered at a level of the "preponderance of evidence" rather than "beyond a reasonable doubt."
2. There is a substantial economic incentive for attorneys and their clients to pursue such suits.
3. Initiation of such suits may not be prevented and need not pass prior review by police, prosecutors, magistrates, grand juries, or other traditional gatekeepers of the criminal process.
4. Rights of discovery, including the capacity to compel possibly culpable testimony from the defendant, are far more generous than in criminal actions.
5. The plaintiff and the plaintiff's attorney are free to choose the form and forum in which the action is brought.
6. The cost of defending oneself against such an action is so high and the risk of a devastatingly high damage award is substantial enough to make financial settlements of even marginally credible civil suits a reasonable defense alternative.

Police officers are exposed to civil liability for the use of excessive force in a variety of forms and forums. Three federal statutes—sections 1983, 1985, and 1981 of Title 42 of the U.S. Code—each create police liability in a slightly different manner. Section 1983 creates civil liability that is virtually identical to the criminal liability described above in Title 18, section 242. Section 1985 provides liability for conspiring to interfere with civil rights. For example, if two officers decide to beat an arrestee, they can be held liable individually under section 1983 and for conspiring to do so under section 1985. In addition, section 1981 imposes liability for interference with the exercise of certain specific civil rights, but does not, as 1983 and 1985 do, limit that liability to persons acting under the color of law. Thus it includes but is not limited to public officials acting in the line of duty.

Civil actions may also be brought against police under a variety of state laws. They include private wrongs alleged in tort actions as well as actions brought under state civil rights laws. Such laws are similar to the above-mentioned federal laws that allow claims for deprivation of rights guaranteed by the state or federal constitution. For a variety of tactical reasons—including more liberal discovery rules, explicit provision for attorney's fees, more expeditious resolution, and, often, trial venues preferable to those offered in state courts—Federal section 1983/1985 actions are most frequently chosen for seeking civil redress for alleged police use of excessive force (see chapter 13).

Although civil actions offer plaintiffs numerous advantages not available in criminal actions, civil actions also offer police defendants two major defenses and a powerful tactical device that are not available in criminal actions. The first is qualified immunity. Police officers enjoy immunity from liability in most state tort actions (but not in section 1983 actions) if it can be demonstrated that the officer was performing a discretionary act. If, for example, an agency leaves to officers the choice of the type of nonlethal force an officer may use to restrain a resistant suspect, the officer enjoys immunity from state tort liability for that decision.

A second, allied defense, available in both state tort actions and section 1983 cases, offers individual police officers but not police agencies immunity from liability if it can be demonstrated that the officer was acting "within the scope of employment." In determining whether an act meets this criteria the court will "consider whether the act in question is of a kind he was hired to perform, whether the act occurred within the authorized time and space, and whether the employee was motivated, at least in part, by the desire to serve his employer" (*Stanfield v. Laccoarce*, 284 Or. 651 [1978], quoted in del Carmen 1991: 58).

Third, a tactic available to police is widely used to thwart civil actions in cases alleging excessive force. It is standard police practice to arrest and charge any person on whom significant force is used with one or more criminal offenses, typically resisting arrest, disorderly conduct, assault or assault and battery on a police officer, plus whatever offense the person may have been involved in that prompted police attention. The U.S. Supreme Court in *Town of Newton v. Rumery*, 480 U.S. 386 (1987), has held that, if the agreement is voluntary, police agencies may negotiate the dismissal of the criminal charges in exchange for a release of the agency and/or officers from civil liability (Kreimer 1988).

Before May 15, 1989, the definition of excessive force that most federal appeals courts applied in section 1983 actions derived from the 1973 Second Circuit Court of Appeals decision in *Johnson v. Glick*, 481 F.2d 1028 (2nd. Cir.), *cert. denied*, 414 U.S. 1033 (1973). The *Glick* decision established four criteria to be considered before a plaintiff could obtain redress for abuse of force in a section 1983 suit:

1. the need for the application of force;
2. the relationship between the need and the amount of force used;
3. the extent of injury inflicted; and
4. whether the force was applied in a good faith effort to maintain or restore discipline or maliciously and sadistically for the very purpose of causing harm.

In the decision that overturned *Glick*—*Graham v. Connor*, 490 U.S. 386 (1989)—the Supreme Court found that the *Glick* standard, based on substantive due process, ultimately embodied a "shocks the conscience" standard. For force to be excessive under *Glick* it not only has to produce severe or substantial bodily injury but also must be the product of malicious or sadistic action by police. In *Graham* the court replaced the *Glick* "shocks the conscience" standard with a standard based on "reasonableness" under the Fourth Amendment. Inasmuch as the Fourth Amendment guarantees citizens the right "to be secure in their persons . . . against unreasonable seizures," the Court declared that henceforth a Fourth Amendment standard for whether force was excessive would apply. The "objective reasonableness" of a police officer's use of force would be "judged from the perspective of a reasonable officer on the scene rather than with the 20/20 vision of hindsight."

Graham appears to make it easier for plaintiffs to challenge excessive force in that it abandons the necessity to demonstrate that the use of force was maliciously or sadistically employed for the purpose of causing harm. However, at least one Circuit Court has found no grounds for a violation of section 1983 when no serious physical injury occurred. In that case, a "deputy sheriff was escorting the plaintiff from Florida to Texas to stand trial when the plaintiff escaped from his custody. When Deputy Sheriff Kennard found the plaintiff he 'handcuffed him, pressed his service revolver against Wisniewski's mouth, and told Wisniewski to open his teeth or Kennard would blow them out. Kennard had the hammer on his service revolver pulled back. In addition, the defendant allegedly threw the defendant by his hair into a truck and punched him in the stomach three times' " (*Wisniewski v. Kennard*, 901 F.2d 1276 [5th Cir.], *cert. denied*, 111 S. Ct. 309 [1990]).

Likewise a Texas Federal district court found no section 1983 liability when an "off duty officer dressed in a bathing suit and wielding a pistol stopped [the plaintiff] for speeding. When the plaintiff tried to escape, the officer shot and hit the plaintiff's car. After commandeering a truck, the officer was able to block the plaintiff's escape and pulled him out of his car at gunpoint" (*Palmer v. Williamson*, 717 F. Supp. 1218 [W.D. Tex. 1989]). (Both cases above are quoted from Brown [1991: 1285].)

Even under the *Graham* standard of "objective reasonableness," section 1983 actions apparently still require that the injury sustained by the plaintiff and the actual amount of excessive force used rise to some unspecified status of a "serious" violation of constitutional proportions. In the words of a leading expert on police civil liability, "Mere words, threats, a push, a shove, temporary inconvenience, or even a single punch in the face does not necessarily constitute a civil rights violation. Nor does Section 1983 apply to cases of false testimony, simple negligence, or name calling . . . though the use of excessive force to compel a suspect to confess constitutes a clear and serious violation of a constitutional right" (del Carmen 1991: 39).

Fear of Scandal and Excessive Force

It is obvious from the above discussion that police can engage in all sorts of objectionable behavior without transgressing criminal or civil definitions of excessive force. If one adds to the problems of legal definition the related obstacles imposed by qualified immunity, necessary standards of proof, juror sympathy for police and hostility to criminals, and the availability of arrangements that permit police to drop criminal charges in exchange for releases from civil liability, the fact remains, as Bittner stated in 1970, that all "the frequently heard talk about the lawful use of force by police is practically meaningless." And, of course, because severe financial judgments sometimes follow such meaningless talk, police agencies are quite concerned with it, even if they are understandably unsure about what to do about it.[4]

There is, however, a definition and a mechanism beyond the criminal and civil law that may also exert some influence on police use of force. It is the fear of the charge of brutality and the scandal such a charge may inspire. Because police depend to one degree or another on community support and their wages and budgets are the product of negotiations with politicians who are elected to represent those communities, police are sensitive to their public image and normally seek to avoid incidents that might damage it.

What citizens mean by "police brutality" differs substantially from the concept of "excessive force" (see, generally, chapters 2, 5, and 6). What citizens commonly understand by "police brutality" is any behavior that in their judgment treats them with less than the full rights and dignity owed to citizens in a democratic society. According to Reiss (1968a), popular conceptions of brutality include:

1. the use of profane and abusive language;
2. commands to move on or get home;
3. stopping and questioning them on the street or searching them and their cars;
4. threats to use force if not obeyed;
5. prodding with a nightstick or approaching with a pistol;
6. the actual use of physical force or violence itself.

Although every one of the above behaviors can be abusive of the rights or dignity of a citizen of a democratic society under certain circumstances, under other circumstances every one may be wholly appropriate and necessary police behavior. The real difficulty is, however, that in many circumstances police behavior is *both* abusive of the rights or dignity of citizens *and* necessary and appropriate police conduct.

There is no definition of excessive force that automatically renders it a form of brutality and escalates it to the status of a scandal. There are many cases of excessive force that satisfy a "shocks the conscience" standard and prompt internal investigations, civil suits, settlements, damage awards, and officer discipline and dismissals but do not become scandals. Scandals require an incident of dramatic excessive force with features that merit publicity and sustain press and popular interest.

While it is true that police are interested in avoiding such scandals, it should be remembered that the extent to which an excessive-force scandal damages the reputation of and erodes community and political support for any specific police agency depends on the role that scandal plays in forming the overall image of that agency. The unfavorable press brought by a scandal is always viewed alongside whatever favorable publicity that same police agency has been able to generate. While some excessive force scandals may become serious enough to bring down a police chief, many police agencies and chiefs have large enough treasuries of good will and achievement to weather even fairly major scandals.

At present, meeting these three standards with respect to the use of excessive force—avoiding punishment under the criminal law, escaping the costs of civil liability, and averting public scandal—are all that is expected of police and all that police, in practice, expect of themselves. None of these standards is sufficiently high for the kind of policing necessary in a modern democratic society. We would not find the behavior of a physician, lawyer, engineer, teacher, or any other professional acceptable merely because it was not criminal, civilly liable, or scandalous, and it is preposterous that we continue to do so for police.

Beyond Crimes, Civil Penalties, and Scandals

It is necessary to move beyond the impasse of these three defining standards in order to make practical progress in controlling the excessive use of force by police. If policing is to move beyond these three standards, it must go to the same source where every other profession finds standards: within the skills of policing itself, as exemplified in the work of its most highly skilled practitioners. The proper standard by which excessive force should be defined, therefore, is not crime, scandal, objective unreasonableness, or shocking behavior. Force certainly need not result in serious physical or mental injury to be deemed excessive. Moreover, it need not (and usually will not) be the product of malicious or sadistic behavior. It can spring from good intentions as well as bad, mistakes and misperceptions, lack of experience, overconfidence, momentary inattention, physical or mental fatigue, experimentation, inadequate or improper training, prejudice, passion, an urge to do justice or demonstrate bravery, misplaced trust, boredom, illness, a specific incompetence, or a hundred other factors that might influence an officer to behave in a particular situation in a less than expert way. *Excessive force should be defined as the use of more force than a highly skilled police officer would find necessary to use in that particular situation.*

Properly understood, this definition of excessive force imposes the highest possible standard on the conduct of police. It leads to findings of excessive force far more frequently than any other reasonable definition and does so in many instances where criminal, civil, commonsense, and even less than expert police understandings would find no excess whatsoever. Consider two straightforward examples.

An officer responds to a report of domestic disturbance called in by a neighbor of the quarreling couple. He knocks on the door of the apartment in which he can hear a loud argument proceeding. A man, smelling strongly of alcohol, answers the door with the greeting, "What the fuck do you want?" In response, the officer explains that he has received a complaint about the noise. The man steps back from the doorway, leaving the door open, and points to a woman in the room saying, "If there's a problem, it's that nigger bitch's fault!" Infuriated by the remark, the woman, who seems to be drunk or high, grabs a cast-iron ashtray and charges at the man, who jumps behind the officer for cover. The officer draws his baton and knocks the ashtray out of the woman's hand, breaking a bone in her thumb as he does so. Upon seeing "his woman" struck by the officer, the man becomes outraged and, from behind, knocks the officer to the floor with a roundhouse right. On the floor and dazed from the blow, the officer looks up to see that the woman has retrieved the baton he dropped when the man knocked him to the floor. She strikes the officer once on the hip, and when she brings her arm back for a second hit the officer draws his pistol, screams for her to stop, and shoots her in the stomach as she brings her arm down with another blow. He then points the pistol at the man, who backs off, and holds him at gunpoint until an ambulance and reinforcements arrive.

A call is received that a group of teenage boys have built a clubhouse on public property where they drink and carouse. It is also reported that they have guns at the site. Two officers in separate vehicles respond to the call; one brings a shotgun to the wooded site. They find two male teens in homosexual intercourse inside the plywood shack. The officers are both amused and disgusted by their discovery and order both boys to get dressed, watching them as they do. As soon as the boys are dressed and stand up, one officer moves forward to handcuff them. Terrified, both boys break for the door of the clubhouse. The first officer grabs one boy as he passes him, forces him to the ground, and proceeds to handcuff him. The second boy gets by the first officer, but the second officer knocks him to the ground with a blow to the ribs with the barrel of the shotgun.

Why, under the "highly skilled police officer" standard, are both of the above scenarios examples of excessive force? In the first case, every forceful act of the officer, from knocking the ashtray from the rushing woman's hand to shooting her in the stomach was an act of self-defense. Moreover, it is doubtful that a lesser degree of force would have been effective. The problem with the way the officer handled the call is that he attempted to handle a domestic disturbance complaint by himself. No skilled officer would attempt to do so. Had he waited until a second officer arrived to handle the call, it is likely that no one would have been injured and very little if any force would have been needed. It is no defense of the officer's behavior to contend that perhaps no second officer was immediately available to support him in handling the call. He ought to have waited, no matter how long it took, for a second officer to assist him. His failure to wait resulted in not only an avoidable use of force but injury to himself, death to another, felony criminal charges to a third person, and, depending on whether the case against the man goes to court, whether the officer needs medical treatment for his injury, and whether the officer is placed on inactive status pending the outcome of the investigation of the shooting, anywhere between a week and one month of police time consumed in investigation, paperwork, processing, and prosecution.

In the second case the excessive force springs directly from the second officer's error in carrying a shotgun to the scene of the incident. Occasions when it is advisable to bring a shotgun on a call are rare, because carrying a shotgun severely compromises the officer's ability to use minimal and intermediate levels of force. An officer with a shotgun in his hands is of almost no help in grabbing, restraining, or handcuffing; he or she is seriously compromised in any apprehension that involves a foot pursuit; and, for all practical purposes, he or she surrenders the option to use a baton. Given the nature of the complaint, bringing a shotgun was a mistake because it limited the officer carrying it to using a degree of force that was too severe under the circumstances.

The officer's error in carrying the shotgun is further exacerbated by his choice to use it as an impact weapon. Doing so risks the possibility of an accidental discharge. A skilled police officer in that predicament would have let the boy run by. Even grabbing him with one hand while holding the shotgun in the other would risk a fight in which the officer was limited to the use of one hand. Such a fight could well escalate to a struggle over the shotgun or the officer's service revolver. The escaped boy's accomplice probably would identify him under questioning, and, even if he refused to do so, it would not be difficult to determine his identity and take him into custody at a later time.

While skilled police work would have greatly reduced the degree of force used or eliminated altogether the use of force in these incidents, it is doubtful that either case would prompt meaningful criticism in the overwhelming majority of police agencies in the United States. Neither case, for example, would qualify as an excessive or unnecessary use of force under the classification criteria adopted in the major studies by Black and Reiss,[5] and Ostrom, Parks, and Whitaker.[6] Likewise, both would qualify as a proper use of force if one applied the escalation-deescalation-ladder type analyses that seek to define proper and excessive uses of force by balancing levels of resistance or aggression against levels of severity of force (Desmedt 1984; Connor and Summers 1988; Americans for Effective Law Enforcement 1988; Clede and Parsons 1987; Connor 1991; Graves and Connor

1992; Geller and Scott 1992: 308–13).[7] Such analyses are routinely included in modern police force policies and structure much of what is taught about the appropriate or inappropriate use of force in police academies.

Because the definition we propose for excessive force is fundamentally different from previous legal, popular, research, or police conceptions,[8] we should like to offer, in concluding this section, five brief arguments for it.

The first argument is ontological. It maintains simply that in any definition which employs the concept of "necessary," whatever is alleged to be necessary should be, in fact, necessary. Force that a highly skilled police officer would not find necessary to employ in a given situation is not necessary force.[9]

The second argument is personal. It asks individual citizens of a democratic society to reflect on how they would want to be treated by the police that they employ with their taxpayer dollars. Would they be personally willing to accept a use of police force on *themselves* that was any greater than a highly skilled police officer would find necessary to use? Only a masochist could logically opt for a less demanding standard.

The third argument is professional. It maintains that in policing, as is the case with every other profession, the standards for proper and improper conduct of practitioners must be set in terms of the skilled practice of that profession. It is foolish to maintain that all one should require of a physician, lawyer, engineer, or police officer is the behavior of a "reasonable" person.

The fourth argument is administrative. It maintains that if police administrators wish to keep police officers in their employ from use-of-force behavior that is criminal, civilly liable, or scandalous, the way to do so is to develop and require a standard for officer performance that is so far above those minimal standards that, for all practical purposes, police officers and police agencies need not be concerned with them.

The fifth and final argument appeals to utility. The above discussion illustrates that all sorts of learned and well-meaning people, including judges, lawyers, researchers, citizens, police officers, and police administrators, have formed, explicitly or implicitly, conceptions and definitions of excessive force. Our rejection of these conceptions as too crude and our suggested definition based on the standard of a highly skilled police officer are driven by a concern for utility. The usefulness of any definition of excessive force must be measured by its potential to help control abuses of authority. All the previous definitions of excessive force were developed within systems that sought to define police use of excessive force in such a way that police officers or police agencies could be punished for it, criminally, civilly, politically, or administratively. The ambition to punish police use of excessive force stimulated definitions that were limited to egregious examples and ignored the ordinary use of excessive force that occurs regularly as a consequence of unskilled police practice.

There was a time when it was valuable to establish the rate at which police officers engaged in aggravated assault, decided to "kick ass," behaved in ways that shocked the conscience, provoked scandal, incurred civil liability, or were unreasonably violent. Mechanisms to punish such behaviors are already in place and, despite their defects, to one degree or another, have been for many years. It is doubtful that the capacity of such mechanisms to control extreme cases of excessive force can be meaningfully increased.[10]

Describing such extreme incidents, establishing their rates of incidence, and discovering conditions under which they occur have few theoretical or practical implications for efforts that might reduce the police use of excessive force. It is time to move on to a new definition of excessive force, a new generation of study of it, and new mechanisms through which it may be controlled.

Controlling Excessive Force: An Administrative Agenda

Once one defines excessive force as more force than a highly skilled police officer would find necessary to use in a given situation, it is possible to configure an administrative apparatus that is specifically designed to respond to that definition. Such an administrative apparatus would work differently from a mechanism designed to discover and control criminal misconduct, unreasonable violence, or behavior that risks civil liability or scandal. The design and comments offered here are based on two years of development and experimentation with just such a system in one police agency. It is premature to claim that the specific apparatus we designed or an administrative approach of the type we describe below will be effective in reducing excessive force. However, given that such systems seek to control a level of excessive force that previous systems did not even acknowledge exists, the effort holds considerable promise. Below we attempt to identify what appear to be some necessary components of a genuine excessive force control apparatus, highlighting potential obstacles to successful implementation and emphasizing how such a system differs from conventional excessive force control mechanisms.

It is convenient to think of any administrative control mechanism as composed of two parts: a policy, goal, or objective, and an organizational apparatus through which to realize it. The control mechanism outlined here is composed of a policy that requires police officers to work in ways that minimize the use of force and an administrative arrangement that encourages them to do so.

Force Policy

A comprehensive statement of policy on police use of force can be stated in a dozen words: *Police officers shall work in ways that minimize the use of force.*[11] The difficulty is not in declaring such a statement to be agency policy, but in getting police administrators to believe that such a policy is important and to take it seriously.

At top administrative levels such a policy is likely to face a variety of practical obstacles. The most important is probably the absence of any serious pressure to support it. Although there is pressure to control criminal, civilly liable, or potentially scandalous officer conduct, the kind of excessive force that results from unskilled policing typically goes unnoticed and is not likely to stimulate complaints; if it does, such complaints can be rather readily diffused and dismissed. The people who are most likely to be victims of excessive force are persons who are the least likely to complain and least likely to be believed if they do. In short, excessive force of the kind that regularly occurs as a consequence of unskilled police work is not normally understood to be a problem in police agencies, and moving to address it must compete with an array of everyday demands, concerns, and "real" pressures on top police.

This is not to suggest that top police administrators cannot be persuaded that a policy seeking to raise officer performance to skilled levels in the use of force is desirable. It simply emphasizes that adopting a policy that discovers excessive force in officer behavior that was previously regarded as acceptable may require substantial and persistent efforts at persuasion. Such efforts may succeed with innovative and imaginative chiefs on the merits of the arguments, but timing those arguments to be offered in the wake of an egregious excessive force scandal and/or civil judgment against the agency will enhance their reception (see Sherman and Bouza 1991a, 1991b). The case for prevention is ironclad, but in the real world wheels must often wait for grease until they squeak.

The Technology of Controlling Excessive Force

Assuming that a police agency commits itself to making its officers work in ways that minimize the use of force, what must it do to realize such a policy? At minimum, it must do three things: monitor the use of force, evaluate the skill with which it is used, and educate officers in its skilled use.

MONITORING THE USE OF FORCE. Because the question of whether or not a use of force is excessive cannot be determined without review of the circumstances of its use, any police agency that seeks to control the use of excessive force should ideally collect information on *every* occasion on which force of any kind or degree is used. The decision to collect this information involves answering three questions: What should constitute a reportable use of force, what information should such a report contain, and who should be made responsible for preparing such a report?

Defining a Reportable Use of Force

While many use-of-force incidents should obviously be reported—including those that cause death or bodily injury or involve the use of such police equipment as firearms, batons, chemical irritants, stun devices, and attack dogs—the overwhelming majority of occasions of police use of force inflict little or no physical injury to the person on whom they are used. Police use very low levels of force in almost every custodial arrest. Grasping a person by the arm or shoulder, grabbing a shirt or a belt to hold a suspect, twisting arms to apply handcuffs, tightening handcuffs until they fit, and pressing a head down to protect it in the course of sitting an arrestee in the back seat of a vehicle all constitute uses of force. The same is true of the use of force in accident and rescue situations, restraining friends and family of victims, steadying and transporting the sick, the injured, the infirm, and the delirious, and controlling crowds. Although on all of these occasions police use force, it is impractical to require a report of such uses.

At the same time it must be said that every one of the above-mentioned low-level uses of force can be done in a manner or under circumstances that a skilled police officer would find excessive. It is possible to choke a person with a twisted shirt, strain a back or break a rib with a hard enough pull on a belt, twist arms into a handcuff position in a manner that dislocates shoulders, tighten handcuffs to painful and punitive levels, and force heads down so firmly that they hit knees. Although there is no hard evidence, the vast majority of occasions on which police use excessive force are likely to be instances of low-level use, if for no other reason than the vast majority of all police uses of force are of low levels.

I know of no wholly satisfactory way to solve the problem of requiring the report of potentially excessive uses of low-level force without paralyzing police by requiring the report of all such uses. Tentatively, and fully subject to revision based on research, I propose two rules to govern when a low-level use of force that does not produce injury should be reported: whenever anyone gives any indication or suggestion of any dissatisfaction with the officer's use of force, or any occasion on which any officer involved in the incident believes for any reason that a use-of-force report would be desirable. Both rules are admittedly imperfect but extend the scope of force monitoring beyond instances causing injury.

Describing a Use-of-Force Incident

Police are skilled at writing accounts of incidents of many types, and an account of a use of force should be taken as seriously and with about as much detail as a report of a routine traffic accident. It should contain standard information: date, time, and place the use of force occurred; names and addresses of all persons who witnessed or were involved in the incident; a detailed description of the type and amount of force used; a description of the incident and relevant events that led up to and followed it; and a description of injuries sustained by any parties.

In preparing the account of the incident, all witnesses, including the officer and the person on whom force was used, should be interviewed for their version of the incident, and, should they wish to offer explanations or rationales for acting as they did, these should be included in the report.

Responsibility for Preparing the Use-of-Force Report

Having said this much about what a use-of-force report should contain, we may now move to the question of who should prepare it. It is not uncommon to find police agencies that require the officer involved in the use of force to submit the use-of-force report. For reasons ranging from the appearance of conflict of interest to the potential compromise of interviews with witnesses and the person on whom force was used, such a practice is unacceptable.

An alternative approach involves assigning responsibility for the preparation of all use-of-force reports to an independent internal affairs investigator. While doing so is advisable in incidents where criminal or civil action against the officer or agency may be anticipated (force incidents resulting in death, disfigurement, or severe injury), occasions of low-level use of force do not require the special skills and independence of an internal affairs investigator. Assigning the responsibility for routine use of force review to internal affairs would be likely to provoke an understandably defensive posture on the part of police officers and allow them to invoke the range of defenses and due process guarantees to which they are entitled in any internal affairs investigation.

No such rights arise for officers in routine supervisory review of their conduct, and for that reason in particular, police supervisors should be charged with producing use-of-force reports as a routine supervisory responsibility. Immediate supervisors are also the preferred choice because they know the officers who work for them and are usually skilled, experienced police officers themselves. Assigning supervisors the responsibility for preparing use-of-force reports has a third advantage: it offers an extra incentive for supervisors to encourage their officers to work in ways that minimize the use of force. Doing so will save the supervisor from the work of preparing a report on it.

EVALUATING POLICE SKILL. From the point of view of controlling the excessive use of force, it is pointless to report a use of force without evaluating it. There are, of course, many options for evaluation. Particularly in the wake of scandal and in efforts to reform, many agencies have adopted some form of outside civilian review (Walker and Bumphus 1991; American Civil Liberties Union 1991; chapter 11). Historically, American police officers have resisted outside review of their conduct on the grounds that "civilians" do not understand what police work requires. They are right, in the same way a physician would be right in insisting that a layperson would not have the knowledge to evaluate skilled medical practice properly. The problem with outsider review of police or medical practice is not that laypersons would demand too much of police or physicians but that they do not possess the knowledge of options and alternatives that would permit them to demand more (Kerstetter 1985; chapter 11). The only individuals who have the detailed knowledge necessary to distinguish good policing from that which is merely not criminal, civilly liable, or scandalous are highly skilled police officers.

The breakthrough in controlling excessive use of force by police will come about only when skilled officers are willing to apply their knowledge and expertise to identifying uses of excessive force and specifying alternatives that would minimize its use. That must be the engine of any second-generation effort to control the use of excessive force. Three obstacles stand in the way. The first is "the code," the usually unspoken agreement among police officers which calls upon them to go to extreme lengths to protect one another from punishment (Muir 1977, chapter 11). The second is the "cover your ass" syndrome. Endemic in police agencies, "CYA" calls upon all police to behave in ways that will not expose them to criticism. The third is the view, widely held among line officers and among many supervisors, that the "good" supervisor is the one who will "back up" an officer when he or she makes a mistake. Under such conditions supervisors—skilled, experienced police officers—will resist offering the kind of evaluation of the use of excessive force that is necessary to reduce it.

Each of these obstacles springs from a single source: the fundamentally punitive orientation of the quasi-military administrative apparatus of American police agencies. From the point of view of working police officers, the administrative structure of the agencies that employ them is little more than a collection of hundreds and in some cases thousands of rules and regulations, the violation of which can lead to punishment (see chapter 10). Under such conditions it is not merely likely that "the code" and the CYA syndrome flourish; it is inevitable. Under such conditions supervisors do not supervise; instead, they "discipline," or, if they are "good" supervisors, gain the loyalty and support of those who work for them by covering for those who run afoul of the rules.

In the face of the occupational culture and punitive administrative environment of police agencies, under what conditions might police supervisors become willing to apply their skills and knowledge to the identification of excessive force and teach alternatives to it? Some supervisors, for reasons ranging from their own lack of skill to opposition to reducing the use of force on people who they believe deserve it to categorical refusal to second guess the field decisions of a fellow police officer, will refuse to do so under virtually any conditions. Others may be made willing to apply their skills and knowledge under three conditions. They are:

1. They be clearly and specifically required to do so.
2. They be held accountable for doing so by having their evaluation of each use-of-force incident reviewed by persons who are equally expert.

3. They be permitted to offer their evaluation under circumstances in which
the normal punitive and disciplinary orientation of police administration is
suspended.

A force review process that meets the above requirements might operate as
follows. After preparing a use-of-force report, the supervisor responsible for preparing it is required to reach one of three conclusions: 1. the use of force was
necessary and appropriate; 2. the use of force was legitimate, but an alternative
approach might have made it unnecessary; or 3. the use of force may constitute
a violation of agency policy—refer to internal affairs. After the first-line supervisor completes the use-of-force report and makes an evaluation, it is passed up
the chain of command. In small agencies it may be passed directly to the chief. In
larger agencies, if, for example, a sergeant prepares the report, the report should be
reviewed by a lieutenant and, after that, by a captain. Both of them in order should
also be required to reach one of the evaluative conclusions. In reaching their
evaluations each of them is not only evaluating the conduct of the officer involved
in the use of force but also the assessment of the previous supervisor. A supervisor
can "cover" for an officer and fail to find that an officer worked in a manner that
did not minimize the use of force, but that supervisor does so in peril of his or her
own reputation as a supervisor before his or her superiors. The idea is to mobilize
the same sentiments on the part of police supervisors that exist among judges who
do not want to have their decisions reversed by judges in a higher court.

Such a mechanism will work only if the person at the top of the review ladder is prepared to mobilize the "highly skilled officer" standard defining excessive
force and thus set the expectation that supervisors down the chain of command
do the same. Although there are certain disadvantages to a centralized, hierarchical command structure, the capacity of such a structure to articulate a uniform,
agency-wide standard of officer conduct is one of its great strengths. It is precisely
what gives police chief executives the capacity to exercise real leadership (Goldstein 1977; Reiss 1985; Napper 1985).[12]

After the review process is complete, and it should normally be completed
within forty-eight hours of the use-of-force incident, the use-of-force report and
evaluation by three supervisors should be returned to the officer. A finding that
the use of force was necessary and appropriate requires no further comment, but
a letter complimenting the officer for handling the incident with a high level of
police skill would not be out of order. A reference to internal affairs will inform
an officer that the incident is under further investigation and punishment of some
form may follow, pending its outcome. But a finding that the officer's behavior
was legitimate (i.e., that it did not constitute criminal, civil, or scandalous misconduct) but that an alternative approach might have made it unnecessary should
prompt an occasion in which a senior skilled and experienced police officer explains to a fellow officer in detail how that officer might have conducted himself

in a way that might have avoided the need to use force or minimized its actual use. No discipline or punishment should follow such an advisory session, but supervisors must make clear that the officer will be expected to work in ways that minimize the use of force in the future.

EDUCATING POLICE OFFICERS IN THE SKILLS OF MINIMIZING THE USE OF FORCE. This analysis of the concept of excessive force and the consequences that spring from alternative constructions of it concludes that *only* from such instruction, from skilled supervisors taking seriously their obligation to supervise and to teach the skills of good police work, will real progress be made in controlling excessive use of force by police. To some unknown degree such teaching already takes place in many police agencies. It is done by some field training officers, by some senior police officers who mentor young officers, and by some skilled supervisors. It happens for the most part sub rosa because identifying publicly a use of excessive force triggers almost automatically an assumption on the part of someone that it should be punished. Willful, malicious, sadistic, conscience-shocking, unreasonable uses of force certainly should be reprimanded. However, the just outrage that such violence provokes has had the effect of suppressing the identification, discussion, and development of alternatives to everyday uses of excessive force that are often the product of nothing more malevolent than a lack of skill. The irony in defining excessive force at a point which merits punishment is that all sorts of unnecessary force will be deemed acceptable up to that point and police behavior will continue to flirt with legal liability and scandal. As long as that lack of skill is denied, tolerated, hidden, or otherwise removed from administrative control in sympathetic efforts to shield well-meaning officers from punishment, no real progress will be made in controlling the police use of excessive force.

Not all uses of excessive force by police should be punished. Understanding excessive force in the way I have argued that it should be understood, most uses of excessive force should not be punished, any more than should all mistakes in diagnosis or unsuccessful treatment by doctors. Every trial lawyer of experience has lost cases that a more skilled attorney might have won. Engineers continually develop approaches to solving problems that reveal defects in previously accepted engineering strategies and render them unacceptable. Progress in medicine, law, and engineering and the development of skilled physicians, lawyers, and engineers have occurred largely when their mistakes are identified by fellow professionals of the highest skills and are reviewed candidly, and when efforts are made to avoid them in the future. Progress will come in control of excessive force when the same can be said of police.

An Overview

The efforts to control the abuse of force by police have, to date, consisted largely of employing devices—criminal and civil law, scandal, and the quasi-military administrative order—which sought to reduce the abuse of force by threats to punish it. Use of these devices to control the use of force by police required the development of a definition of excessive force that set a standard of acceptable use of force so low that any use of force not meeting that standard warranted punishment.

Criminal and civil law, scandal, and the quasi-military administrative order succeeded in providing a technology for controlling the most egregious abuses of the police monopoly of the general right to use coercive force. However, that technology of punitive control offers disincentives to both individual police officers and police agencies to raise in any way the standard by which excessive use of force by police might be identified. Resistance to raising standards for the use of force is at the root of "the code," the ethic of CYA, line-officer distrust of administration, and administrative antipathy to the press and public. It is a nearly sacred tenet of police organizational culture. Police officers and police agencies respect and perpetuate it out of rational self-defense. To put it bluntly: what foolish police officer or police agency would wish to enlarge the scope of behavior for which they may be punished?

As long as the concept of excessive force identifies a level of force beneath which punishment is threatened, none of this will change. Such a conception of excessive force limits both what police may be asked to impose on themselves and what society is prepared to impose on its police.

To move beyond this impasse requires a fundamental reconstruction of the idea of excessive force. That restructuring must make it possible to discover and discuss the use of excessive force freed from the threat or fear of punishment. The reconstruction proposed in this chapter advances a concept of excessive force based on police skill. It finds "excessive" any force that a police officer of the highest skill might find a way to avoid.

There are a variety of virtues to reconceptualizing the idea of excessive force in this way. The most important is that it makes possible the collegial discussion of excessive force removed from threats to punish it. In doing so it breaks the silence required by "the code," undermines the need for CYA, and enables skilled supervisors to supervise. At the same time that it makes excessive force a matter of collegial discussion and professional opinion, it invites research. It welcomes inquiry into what the skill of policing might consist of and how that skill might be measured, organized, enhanced, and taught.

NOTES

The author would like to acknowledge valuable comments on previous drafts of this essay from Egon Bittner, James Fyfe, William Geller, David Klinger, Peter Manning, and Robert Worden.

1. Throughout this essay, *force* and *coercive force* are used interchangeably. Both terms should be understood to mean the application of physical strength for coercive purposes, including on occasions when the use of that strength is multiplied or amplified by weapons. Force is distinct from authority, power, and persuasion and does not include verbal or non-verbal threats, pleadings, warnings, or commands, all of which are of a wholly different order of means of domination and control. For emphasis, displaying a snarling police dog, pounding a baton on a suspect's car hood, and brandishing the electric arc of a stun gun during a confession are not examples of force. They are coercive threats, a variety of persuasion. They, unlike force, appeal in one form or another to the will of the person being coerced. In and of itself, force makes no such appeal, although the person on whom it is applied, as well as others, may reflect on its use and alter behavior in response to it (see Arendt 1973; Klockars 1985).

This approach to the definition of the police role follows Egon Bittner's systematic destruction of all norm-derivative approaches to defining the police in *The Functions of the Police in Modern Society* (1975a), which seeks to define the police role by reference to the ends it is supposed to achieve. The most popular of such defective definitions finds police to be an agency of law enforcement. Bittner defines police as a "mechanism for the distribution of non-negotiably coercive force deployed in accord with an intuitive grasp of situational exigencies" (1975a: 46). In "Florence Nightingale in Pursuit of Willie Sutton: A Theory of Police" (1974: 40) he observes that, although force is the core of the police role, the skill of policing consists in finding ways to *avoid* its use. In Klockars (1985: 12) *police* is defined as "institutions or individuals given the general right to use coercive force by the state within the state's domestic territory."

2. Despite the fact that criminal prosecutions of officers for the use of excessive force are extremely rare, it is common practice for internal affairs investigations of excessive force complaints to proceed under rules of criminal evidence collection. Under such conditions officers are accorded a range of rights that are not available in administrative review. If the net effect of the threat of criminal prosecution is to impede the discovery of facts in such investigations, a mechanism for the early waiver of that threat—a decision to waive criminal prosecution—may be one of the most powerful investigative devices.

3. Although there is no reliable national count of the number of suits against police, according to a survey by McCoy (1987) the majority of police chiefs of agencies serving populations of 100,000 or more report that they not only have been sued but expect to be sued in the future. These same chiefs report that the most common claim made in suits against them or their agencies is excessive force.

4. In a nationwide survey of police agencies conducted in late summer and early fall 1990 (seven months prior to the Rodney King incident), concern with civil liability was identified, after changes in the law, as the factor most often responsible for initiating police research. In the same survey, 65 percent of the 477 agencies responding to the survey were engaged in revising their agency force policies (Klockars and Harver, 1992).

5. Reiss (1968a) employed six standards to define unnecessary force: "1. If the policeman assaulted a citizen and then failed to make an arrest; proper use involves an arrest. 2. If the citizen being arrested did not by word or deed, resist the policeman; force should be used only if it is necessary to make the arrest. 3. If the policeman, even though there was resistance to the arrest, could easily have restrained the citizen in other ways. 4. If a large

number of policemen were present and could have assisted in subduing the citizen in the station, in booking, and in interrogation rooms. 5. If the offender was handcuffed and made no attempt to flee or offer violent resistance. 6. If the citizen resisted arrest, but the use of force continued even after the citizen was subdued." While Reiss's approach to defining "unnecessary force" falls far short of what we advance as an appropriate definition, Reiss's criteria 1 and 2 appear to this author specifically defective. As to the first criterion, use of force on a citizen need not involve an arrest. It is routine for police to use force on mentally or physically ill persons who resist necessary medical attention. Arresting such people who lack *mens rea* is probably illegal and possibly unjust, though it is frequently done to protect officers against civil liability. Concerning Reiss's second criterion, while resistance by "deed" sometimes justifies the use of force, it is hard to imagine a case in which mere resistance by "word," unaccompanied by any passive or active resistant act or deed, would do so. Finally, as I discuss below, defining precisely the amount and nature of force that must to be used to qualify as a recordable instance of force is a tricky practical problem. A push or shove, scuffle, pin, wrench, press, grab, tackle, come along, or lock hold all qualify as uses of force under my definition and, under certain circumstances, can be excessive. Reiss limited his study to instances when a "policeman struck the citizen with his hands, fist, feet, or body, or where he used a weapon of some kind, such as a nightstick or pistol."

6. According to Worden (see chapter 2), observers in the Ostrom, Parks, and Whitaker study were instructed to classify force as unnecessary or excessive in instances where the observer judged that the officer was "kicking ass."

7. The defect in ladder-type analyses that approve escalation and de-escalation of levels of officer use of force in correspondence to levels of citizen resistance is that such analyses lack a sufficient temporal dimension and are silent on crucial strategic and tactical issues that in the majority of cases structure the situation in ways that ultimately promote or reduce the possibility that force may be used. As long as force incidents are treated narrowly as split-second decisions they will leave little room or time or sympathy for efforts to reduce the use of excessive force by police. Consider in this vein Bayley and Garofalo's conclusion, after some 2,000 hours of field observations of evening shift New York City patrol officers: "Anticipating problems before they arise is probably more important in avoiding unnecessary and injurious use of force than being clever after the encounters begin" (1989: 20; see also Scharf and Binder 1983; Fyfe 1989a; and Geller and Scott 1992: 323–35).

8. James J. Fyfe's work in Miami-Dade (Fyfe 1988b), as well as some of his early work in New York City, is premised on mobilizing police expertise in the reduction of the use of force. It is highly consistent with the conception of excessive force and prospects for its control advanced in this paper. We are, however, far less sanguine than Fyfe (see, e.g., Fyfe 1986; Skolnick and Fyfe 1992: 200–05) about the value of enlarging the role of civil liability as an excessive-force control mechanism.

9. In a review of an earlier draft of this chapter, a colleague whose contributions to the study of police use of excessive force are enormous warned that the "highly skilled police officer" standard for identifying excessive force would prove to be a point of contention. He phrased the challenge to this standard with the question: "What other profession uses its *stars* as the yardstick for detecting malpractice?" No profession does so and neither, of course, should police. This chapter advances no such argument. The problem of defining a level of police use of force that can be judged malpractice is quite a different problem from that of defining excessive force. Identifying malpractice requires a standard of minimally acceptable behavior. That standard must be set so low that any behavior less than that minimum merits punishment. The criminal and civil law have already done, in my opinion, a quite adequate job at that. By contrast, defining excessive force by the highly skilled police officer standard is based on a vision of what policing at its best might be. It is a vision based

upon the premise that the skill of policing consists in finding ways to minimize the use of force. It does not seek to punish officers or agencies who fall short of that standard but to encourage aspiration to it and raise it whenever possible. That is, I think, the role of "stars" in any profession.

10. According to every measuring device available, occasions on which police use excessive force (as the term has been historically understood) are so rare that any true changes in the frequency of excessive force are likely to be indistinguishable from random variations. The average officer in the Los Angeles Police Department, a department in which police brutality is alleged to be nearly rampant (Skolnick and Fyfe 1993: 12–14), provokes a complaint of excessive force about once every *12 years*. Admittedly, LAPD procedures for receiving complaints may discourage some people from reporting them, but the LAPD rate is barely distinguishable from that of Atlanta, San Francisco, Seattle, or Baltimore County and requires powerful magnification to see it at all. In fact, the frequency of complaints of excessive force in almost every major U.S. police agency is so tiny that it only becomes visible when expressed in multipliers such as the number of complaints per thousand officers per year (see also Pate and Fridell 1993).

An alternative approach to assessing the level of use of (traditionally defined) excessive force that might be reduced by some type of intervention is to identify a group of chronic offenders. The problem is that there are very few of them and the frequency with which citizens accuse them of using excessive force is not particularly high. In fact, according to the Christopher Commission (Independent Commission on the Los Angeles Police Department 1991: 37), the officer with the highest rate of complaints against him in the entire 8,450-officer department, a rate twice as high as the officers in second place, had an average of three complaints filed against him per year.

There is not enough excessive force around for us to learn if any effort to reduce it failed or succeeded. In the wake of Rodney King, this is neither the prevailing popular nor academic definition of the "problem" of excessive force. I believe, however, it is exactly the problem and that stating it in this fashion suggests the only real solution. In order to reduce excessive force, we must first discover (or create, through setting higher standards) a great deal more of it.

11. The word *policy* is used here to mean the general standard that guides relevant conduct in an agency and from which subordinate rules and procedures are ultimately derived. The policy I propose would, for example, be a predicate for defense-of-life shooting rules and rather strict vehicle pursuit regulations.

12. An alternative to a hierarchical review process would be one composed of peers, similar, perhaps, to the strategy devised by Toch, Grant, and Galvin (1975). In *Agents of Change*, the confidential, peer-review strategy managed one essential element of mobilizing police skill: a nonpunitive educational environment. However, it did so at a cost of displacing supervisory responsibility for teaching police skill, placing that burden upon peers who compete for the same scarce rewards a police agency has to offer, and sacrificing agency control and review of the substance of that education.

CHAPTER TWO

The Causes of Police Brutality:
Theory and Evidence on Police Use of Force

ROBERT E. WORDEN

Every serious prescription for controlling police brutality rests at least implicitly on some theory of police behavior.[1] Fortunately, over the past twenty-five years social scientists have given considerable attention to some forms of police behavior and have made some headway in developing theories that account, at least in part, for these behaviors. The exercise of officers' authority to make arrests has been analyzed in a number of studies, as has the use of deadly force, and a substantial (but still inadequate) body of empirical evidence has accumulated. Unfortunately, little social scientific evidence has accumulated on the use and abuse of nonlethal force, and faint effort seems to have been made to consider whether the theories applied to other forms of behavior apply to the use of nonlethal force.[2]

This chapter seeks to connect theories of police behavior with new evidence on the use of force by police. First, I briefly review the theories of police behavior, along with the evidence that bears on those theories, drawing principally on empirical analyses of arrest and of deadly force. I then consider the handful of studies that have examined the use of nonlethal force and evaluate the data—collected through in-person observation of police officers—on which most of these analyses are based. I then turn to the new empirical evidence on the use of force, which is also based on an analysis of observational data. I conclude by discussing how further research may contribute to the development of theory and to the deliberation about reform.

Theories of Police Behavior

Existing research on police behavior reflects the diverse training and backgrounds of those who study the police—sociologists, political scientists, psychologists, and others. Even so, much of this research can be subsumed within three explanatory rubrics: sociological, psychological, and organizational.

Sociological Theory

One prominent sociological approach to understanding the behavior of police officers is based on the premise that police behavior is influenced by the social dynamics of police-citizen encounters. For example, Donald Black's sociological theory of law holds that the "quantity of law" is influenced by the social attributes of concerned parties—victims and suspects, or plaintiffs and defendants, as well as the agents of social control themselves (see especially Black 1976).[3] According to this theory, police officers are least likely to take legal or other coercive action against lower-status persons—especially the poor and racial and ethnic minorities—whose accusers are also of low status, but more likely to take such action against lower-status persons whose accusers are of higher status (Black 1980: ch. 1). Somewhat more generally, this line of inquiry has directed analytical attention to the structural characteristics of the situations in which officers and citizens interact: the social class, race, and gender of complainants and their dispositional preferences—i.e., whether or not they want offenders arrested; the social class, race, age, gender, sobriety, and demeanor of suspects; the seriousness of the offense (if there is one); the nature of the relationships between complainants and suspects; the visibility of the encounters (whether they transpire in public or private and whether bystanders are present); the numbers of officers at the scene; and the character of the neighborhoods in which encounters take place. From this theoretical perspective, these "situational" factors (Sherman 1980a) are the cues on which officers form judgments about how incidents should be handled (Berk and Loseke 1980–81). Bittner formulates perhaps the most comprehensive and succinct statement of this explanatory approach: "The role of the police is best understood as a mechanism for the distribution of non-negotiably coercive force *employed in accordance with the dictates of an intuitive grasp of situational exigencies*" (Bittner 1970: 46; emphasis added).

Most empirical research that is grounded in this theory has examined the use of arrest powers (e.g., Black 1971; Lundman 1974; Smith and Visher 1981; also see Sherman 1980a: 77–85). This research has consistently shown that arrest is influenced by the demeanor of suspects—arrest is more likely if the suspect is antagonistic or disrespectful to police (but cf. Klinger 1994; also see Lundman 1994; Worden and Shepard 1996)—and by the preferences of complainants (if any)—arrest is more likely if complainants wish to press charges and less likely if complainants prefer informal dispositions. This research has also produced somewhat inconsistent findings. For example, some analyses indicate that nonwhite suspects are more likely to be arrested than white suspects (Lundman 1974; Smith and

Visher 1981), whereas others show that the relationship between race and arrest is either null (Berk and Loseke 1980–81; Worden and Pollitz 1984; Smith and Klein 1984; Worden 1989) or spurious—that black suspects are more likely to be arrested because they are more frequently disrespectful and that race has no independent effect (Black 1971; Sykes and Clark 1975; but cf. Black 1980: ch. 5; Smith, Visher, and Davidson 1984).[4] Overall, research of this genre has demonstrated that officers' arrest decisions are influenced by situational factors, but fails to explain at least half of the variation in arrest.

Research on the use of deadly force has dwelt on one hypothesis that is quite compatible with this theory, namely that minorities are more likely to be shot at by police. As Locke notes in chapter 6, the empirical evidence confirms that minorities are, in fact, overrepresented among the human targets at which police shoot, relative to their numbers in city populations, but it also indicates that minorities are overrepresented among those whose actions precipitate the use of deadly force by police (see Milton et al. 1977; Fyfe 1980a, 1981b; Blumberg 1981; Geller and Karales 1981; Alpert 1989; see, generally, Geller and Scott 1992). Insofar as this alternative explanation for these racial disparities is captured in the available data (e.g., on felony arrests), this hypothesis—that minorities are more likely to be the objects of police deadly force merely because of their race—has received support in only a few analyses (Meyer 1980; Geller and Karales 1981: 123–25; Fyfe 1982).

Psychological Theory

A second approach to understanding the behavior of police officers is psychological. This approach highlights variation among officers in their behavioral predispositions, variation that is obscured by the sociological approach. This perspective directs attention to the outlooks and personality traits that presumably produce different responses to similar situations by different officers. This perspective also underlies many suppositions about behavioral differences related to officers' race, gender, and educational background, inasmuch as black officers, female officers, and college-educated officers are expected to have outlooks that differ from their white, male, less-educated colleagues, and these differences in attitude are presumed to manifest themselves in officers' behavioral patterns. Hypotheses that link attitudes and behavior have intuitive appeal, but social psychological research has shown that, in general, people's behavior is often inconsistent with their attitudes; one review of this research concluded, "in most cases investigated, attitudes and behaviors are related to an extent that ranges from small to moderate in degree" (Schuman and Johnson 1976: 168).

Psychological theory (or some version thereof) is reflected in portions of the report by the Christopher Commission (Independent Commission on the Los Angeles Police Department 1991), which identified a small group of "problem officers" who were disproportionately involved in incidents in which force was used or allegedly misused. Although the commission focused on what management could and should do after the fact, once these problem officers were identified, it implicitly presumed that the outlooks or personalities of these officers were at the root of their seemingly distinctive behavioral patterns.[5]

One more specific hypothesis might be that officers who are predisposed to use force have "authoritarian" personalities (Balch 1972; more generally, Adorno et al. 1950). Research on the personality characteristics of police has been concerned primarily with whether officers are psychologically homogeneous and, moreover, different as a group from the general public. These efforts to establish a modal (and pathological) "police personality" have been inconclusive (Balch 1972; cf. Lefkowitz 1975). Moreover, such analysis is misguided if one seeks to account for behavioral variation among officers. The findings that officers as a group are not authoritarian do not refute the proposition that those officers who score high on indices of authoritarianism are also those who use force with unusual frequency. Officers' authoritarianism or other personality traits should be examined as characteristics that vary among officers, and that may covary with officers' use of force.

The richest discussions of psychological hypotheses about police behavior can be found in studies that have constructed fourfold typologies of police officers (White 1972; Muir 1977; Broderick 1977; Brown 1981), each typology being based on two (in one case, three) attitudinal dimensions. For example, Muir (1977) classifies officers according to their outlooks on human nature and their moral attitudes toward coercive authority. Although these four studies together define sixteen categories of officers, a careful comparison of the types of officers described in these studies shows that five composite types can be isolated (Worden 1995). These types do appear to differ in their propensity to use force.

One type of officer, for which I have borrowed White's (1972) label of the "tough cop," is perhaps the most likely to use force improperly. Tough cops are cynical, in the sense that they presume that people are motivated by narrow self-interest. They conceive of the role of police in terms of crime control, focusing especially on serious crime, and they see themselves as a negative force in people's lives. They believe that the citizenry is hostile toward police, and they identify with the police culture. They believe that experience and common sense are the best guides in dealing with the realities of the street, and that curbstone justice is sometimes appropriate and effective.

By contrast, "problem-solvers" (also White's term) have what Muir (1977) calls a "tragic" perspective: they recognize that people's actions are influenced by complex sets of physical, economic, and social circumstances, and not simple self-interest. They conceive of the role of police as one of "offering assistance in solving whatever kind of problem . . . [their clientele] face" (White 1972: 72), and thus they see themselves as a positive force. They are skeptical of traditional police methods, as they are unable to reconcile the use of coercive measures with their moral codes. This type of officer is probably the least likely to use force improperly (or at all).

The descriptions of these and the other types of officers suggest that, if there are officers with pronounced propensities to use force, they share several outlooks that distinguish them from other officers.[6] Officers who are the most likely to use force could be expected to (a) conceive the police role in narrow terms, limited to crime-fighting and law enforcement, (b) believe that this role is more effectively carried out when officers can use force at their discretion, and (c) regard the citizenry as unappreciative at best and hostile and abusive at worst (also see chapter 9).

The few efforts to systematically test these hypotheses have produced little or no support. Brown's (1981: ch. 9) analysis, based on officers' responses to hypothetical scenarios, indicates that—as expected—there is more variation across than within categories of officers in the ways that they handle common incidents (such as family disputes and drunk driving). But it also shows that officers' behavior is affected by the organizational context in which they work; behavior is not a simple extension of attitudes, as organizational and other social forces can attenuate the impact of attitudes on behavior. Snipes and Mastrofski (1990) undertook a small-scale examination of hypotheses derived from Muir's framework, by conducting in-depth interviews with and observations of nine officers in one department; they found little consistency between officers' attitudes and behaviors and little consistency in each officer's behavior from one incident to the next. My own analyses (Worden 1989) indicate that officers' attitudes are only weakly related to their discretionary choices in the initiation and disposition of traffic stops, in the initiation of field interrogations, and in the disposition of disputes. The results of these studies do not constitute sufficient evidence to reject psychological hypotheses, however, and none of these studies examined the use of force. But these findings suggest that the connections between officers' attitudes and behavior are probably more complex (and perhaps more tenuous) than many have supposed.

A larger body of evidence has accumulated on the relationship of officers' behavior to their background and characteristics—race, gender, length of police service, and especially education. Officers' educational backgrounds have been the subject of a number of studies, and although this research has shown that education bears no more than a weak relationship to officers' attitudes (e.g., Weiner 1974; Miller and Fry 1976; Hudzik 1978; Worden 1990) and no relationship to the use of deadly force (Sherman and Blumberg 1981), it also indicates that college-educated officers generate fewer citizen complaints (Cohen and Chaiken 1972; Cascio 1977). The reason for this difference is not clear.

Similarly, the most systematic comparison of male and female officers shows small or no differences in attitudes other than job satisfaction (Worden 1993). Other research reveals some behavioral differences—in the frequency with which men and women initiate encounters and make arrests—but on most behavioral dimensions the differences are negligible (Bloch and Anderson 1974; Sherman 1975; cf. Grennan 1987).

One study of the effects of officers' race on behavior (Friedrich 1977: 307–19) found that black officers patrol more aggressively, initiate more contacts with citizens, are more likely to make arrests, and more frequently adopt a neutral manner toward citizens of either race. Other research has found that black officers are more likely than white officers to use deadly force, on duty (Geller and Karales 1981) and off as well (Fyfe 1981a), but these differences can be attributed to black officers' duty assignments and to where they choose to live (also see Blumberg 1982).

Finally, analyses of officers' length of service indicate that less experienced officers are more active in that they patrol more aggressively, initiate more contacts with citizens, and are more likely to make arrests, write crime reports (Friedrich 1977: 280–90; Worden 1989), and use deadly force (Blumberg 1982; cf. Alpert 1989).

Organizational Theory

Some approaches to understanding the behavior of police officers emphasize features of the organizations in which officers work. A theory that highlights organizational properties as influences on police behavior would seem to hold the greatest potential as a guide for police reform, as organizational factors are more readily altered than are the demeanors of suspects or the outlooks of officers. However, organizational analyses of police are seldom undertaken, probably because of the expense and difficulty of collecting comparable data on multiple police agencies. Thus organizational theories of police behavior are not well supported by empirical evidence.

One theory emphasizes the influence of the formal organizational structure on police officers' behavior, especially the system of incentives and disincentives and the content and application of rules and regulations. The principal statement of this approach is by Wilson (1968), whose exploratory research formed the basis for the delineation of three organizational styles of policing—the legalistic, watchman, and service styles—and for hypotheses that these styles can be attributed to the orientations of chiefs, which influence officers' behavior through the medium of organizational structure. While Wilson acknowledges that the capacity of police administrators to shape officers' behavior is constrained by the nature of police tasks, he seems to see the glass of managerial influence as half (or partly) full rather than half (or partly) empty. Wilson's study has more to say about the use of the law than about the use of physical force; however, it suggests that improper force is more likely to be used by officers in watchman-style departments, usually in response to perceived disrespect for police authority. Some research has tested hypotheses derived from Wilson's framework (Gardiner 1969; Wilson and

Boland 1978; Smith 1984) with generally supportive results, but only Friedrich (1980), whose study I discuss below, tested hypotheses about the use of force.

Some research on the use of deadly force has shown rather convincingly that administrative controls can have salutary effects on the frequency with which officers use their firearms. Policies that set clear boundaries around the use of deadly force and that provide for effective enforcement (by, say, establishing review procedures) have reduced the number of shootings (Fyfe 1979b, 1982; Meyer 1980; Sherman 1983), especially the more discretionary or "elective" shootings (Fyfe 1988a: 184–87). Whether such controls are, by themselves, as effective in controlling the use of nonlethal force is an open question. But there is good reason to be skeptical; the use of deadly force is a more visible act—or, more precisely, an act with more visible outcomes—which probably makes this form of behavior more susceptible to administrative controls.

Another theory emphasizes the limitations of formal structure in directing and controlling the behavior of patrol officers and the importance of the informal organization or peer group, i.e., the police culture (see chapter 10). According to this perspective, the formal, more obtrusive controls on police—rewards and punishments, rules, regulations, and standard operating procedures—extend to the more observable and, for the most part, more mundane aspects of police work, such as the use of equipment, reports, and officers' appearance (Manning 1977; Brown 1981; more generally, see Prottas 1978). At the same time, the application of unobtrusive controls on police in the form of socialization and training is governed by the work group. Analyses of the socialization process are quite scarce, but the available evidence indicates that new officers learn the police craft on the job (not in the academy) from more senior officers, especially their field training officers (FTOs) (Van Maanen 1974; Fielding 1988). Rookies are quickly led to believe that their academy experience was merely a rite of passage, that the training they received there is irrelevant to the realities of policing, and that they will learn what they need to know on the street. Thus, according to this line of argument, the police culture is not only the primary reference group for officers but also the principal mechanism of organizational control (to the extent that control is exerted at all) over the substantive exercise of police discretion.

One must be careful not to confuse what has been called the police culture with the cultures of police organizations. "The" police culture is an occupational culture, consisting of outlooks and norms that are commonly found among patrol officers in police agencies. This culture emphasizes the danger and unpredictability of the work environment, the consequent dependence of officers on each other for assistance and protection, officers' autonomy in handling situations, and the need to assert and maintain one's authority (Westley 1970; Skolnick 1975; Brown 1981; Manning 1989). The police culture does not prescribe the substance of officers' working styles so much as it protects officers from administrative scrutiny and sanction and insulates them from administrative pressures for change (Reuss-Ianni 1983); thus it allows officers the latitude to develop and practice their own styles.[7]

One may find variation in the *organizational* cultures of police departments, even while one finds consistency in the elements of the *occupational* culture. Wilson maintains that the administration of police departments produces differing styles both directly, by shaping the calculus on which officers' choices are based, and indirectly, by cultivating a "shared outlook or ethos that provides for [officers] a common definition of the situations they are likely to encounter and that to the outsider gives to the organization its distinctive character or 'feel' " (1968: 139). Officers in both legalistic and watchman departments might subscribe to a norm of loyalty, but, according to Wilson's analysis, they would differ in their beliefs about the nature of the police role and about the proper use of police authority. Brown (1981) disputes this argument, finding officers with different styles within each of the three departments he studied. These arguments can perhaps be reconciled, inasmuch as any organization that is differentiated by task and authority might well develop multiple subcultures (Reuss-Ianni 1983; Worden and Mastrofski 1989; Jermier et al. 1991), and even where multiple subcultures exist, one may predominate. Unfortunately, the distinction between the occupational culture of police and the organizational culture of a police department is seldom made; most previous research has attended to the former but ignored the latter.

The report of the Christopher Commission makes reference to both of these theories. The commission identified the LAPD's "assertive style of law enforcement" as a reason for "aggressive confrontations with the public" (p. 97), and traced this style of policing to a " 'professional' organizational culture" that has been cultivated by the LAPD administration through training and the incentive structure. Officers in the LAPD are rewarded for hard-nosed enforcement that is likely (occasionally) to produce arrests and (often) to bring police into conflict with citizens. The commission further found that the administration of the LAPD fails to discourage the improper use of force, in that (a) the complaint intake process discourages citizens from filing complaints, (b) many complaints that are filed are not substantiated as a result of inadequate resources and procedures for investigating complaints, and (c) the sanctions imposed on officers against whom complaints have been substantiated have been too light, both as a deterrent and as a message that such behavior is inappropriate. Like Wilson (1968), the commission concluded that the LAPD's incentive structure influences officers' behavior directly and that there is a link between the (formal) administrative structure and the (informal) organizational culture. The implications for administrative practice are fairly straightforward: reduce the incentives for hard-nosed enforcement and increase the sanctions for the improper use of force.[8]

But the commission also acknowledged the limitations on the formal structure in controlling police conduct, reporting that "perhaps the greatest single barrier to the effective investigation and adjudication of complaints is the officers' unwritten 'code of silence,' [which] consists of one simple rule: an officer does not provide adverse information against a fellow officer" (p. 168). From this conclusion one cannot easily draw practical implications, and the commission's recommendations do not address this barrier. Because this culture originates to a significant degree in the nature of the work itself and is not unique to the LAPD or even to policing (see Gouldner 1954), it is not likely to be altered by traditional organizational reforms (Van Maanen 1974; Toch 1976).

The LAPD depicted in the Christopher Commission report may represent an extreme and unrepresentative case, where formal and informal organizational forces tend to reinforce each other in producing an aggressive style of policing and an elevated probability of the use of force. Most American police departments are smaller, less bureaucratic, and less insulated from the communities they serve;[9] as a result, the formal expectations in such departments might be less unambiguously crime-control oriented, and the potentially restraining influence of administrative controls might be greater. Any characterization of the problem of police brutality must take this variation among departments into account. So too must research on police brutality, because if large departments can be structured to simulate the relevant conditions that prevail in smaller departments, there is much to be learned by studying small and medium-sized police departments.

Internally, one might expect that in smaller police departments, which typically have fewer levels of hierarchy, administrators could more closely monitor and supervise street-level performance by taking advantage of the less distorted information that flows through the shorter formal channels of communication, and of the greater amount of information that flows through the wider informal channels of communication (Whitaker 1983). In principle, managers in smaller agencies could more directly and hence effectively communicate their priorities and expectations to street-level personnel. In addition, as they need not rely so heavily on statistical summaries of individual performance, managers can base their evaluations of officers' performance on a richer and probably more accurate base of information; consequently, patterns of problematic behavior are likely to be more readily detectable, and the incentive system need not emphasize quantifiable, enforcement-related activities at the expense of the more qualitative aspects of police performance. Brown's (1981) analysis confirms the expectation that administrative controls are more palpable in smaller departments, where Brown found that officers are more reluctant to take the risk of administrative sanction that they would run by practicing an aggressive style of patrol. Furthermore, insofar as work groups are more stable in smaller departments, immediate supervisors could be expected more frequently and effectively to play an instrumental role in the development of subordinate officers' judgment and moral outlooks (see Muir 1977).

Externally, one might expect that smaller agencies would be subject to closer oversight both by the public and by its representatives. Insofar as smaller municipalities are more homogeneous and their residents are in greater agreement about the delivery of police services, public officials have less latitude in setting policy and priorities (Wilson 1968). Citizens in smaller municipalities also might take a more active part in local affairs (Dahl 1967), so that municipal officials might better apprehend citizens' preferences regarding municipal services. In smaller municipalities public officials—including councillors, mayors, and city managers—may play more active roles in policymaking and oversight (Mastrofski 1988), and inasmuch as aggressive policing could be expected to generate political friction from which the department is not insulated, internal administrative influences may tend toward restraint rather than aggressive enforcement.

Theory and Research on the Use of Force

Reiss (1968a) points out, "what citizens mean by police brutality covers the full range of police practices," including the use of abusive language and seemingly unjustified field interrogations, but "the nub of the police-brutality issue seems to lie in police use of physical force." Some of the problems with which police deal may require the use of force, and under many circumstances the line between proper and improper force is rather unclear; where force is necessary, judgments must be made about the amount of force that is reasonable. Whenever such decisions must be made, some misjudgments are probably inevitable; such cases of *excessive* force involve the use of more force than is reasonably necessary. Other cases of improper force, however, involve the use of force where none is necessary; these are instances of *unnecessary* force.

Although the distinction between the use of *excessive* force and the use of *unnecessary* force rests on overt and thus observable behavior, it is admittedly an elusive one. Officers not only respond to situations but also help to create them; sometimes, officers' choices early in police-citizen encounters can contribute to the emergence of circumstances that require the use of force (Binder and Scharf 1980; Bayley 1986; also see chapter 1). Insofar as these two forms of behavior can be distinguished, we may find that they are sufficiently distinct phenomena that each is influenced by a different set of situational, individual, and organizational factors. We may also find that interventions intended to reduce excessive force, like (re)training officers, have little effect on the incidence of unnecessary force and, conversely, that disincentives have a greater effect on unnecessary force than on excessive force (but cf. chapter 8).

Most empirical research on the use of nonlethal force by police is based on data collected through the observation of officers on patrol. Generally, observation of police enables one to collect data on forms of behavior that can not be reliably measured by other means. These forms of behavior, such as field stops or the resolution of disputes, often result in no official record and thus are least visible. Observation also generates data on the setting of police action; even when such information is contained in officers' reports, it is frequently incomplete or of dubious validity. Analyses of observational data make unique contributions to our understanding of police use of force, since observation by independent observers enables one to enumerate, describe, and analyze instances in which force is used, whether or not they result in citizen complaints or departmental disciplinary actions. Like survey data on victimizations, which uncover unreported crime, observational data on police behavior reveal unreported instances of police use of force (see chapter 3).

Observational data are not without shortcomings, as they may be biased as a result of "reactivity" when officers refrain from the use of force in some instances due to the presence of observers. But efforts to assess the bias introduced by reactivity suggest that the validity of observational data, in general, is quite high (Mastrofski and Parks 1990); moreover, the relationships between some forms of police behavior and other variables (such as characteristics of the situation) are unaffected by reactivity (Worden 1989: n. 8). As Reiss (1971b: 24) observes, based on the results of one observational study (to be discussed below), "the use of force by the police is situationally determined by other participants in the situation and by the officer's involvement in it, to such a degree that one must conclude the observer's presence had no effect" (Reiss 1971b: 24; also see Reiss 1968a, 1968b). At a minimum, the bias in observational data is no greater and probably less than that in archival data.

The first large-scale observational study of police was undertaken by Black and Reiss (1967) for the President's Commission on Law Enforcement and Administration of Justice. This research was conducted during the summer of 1966 in Boston, Chicago, and Washington, D.C. Observers accompanied patrol officers on sampled shifts in selected high-crime precincts. "In the data collection, emphasis was placed upon gaining detailed descriptions of police and citizen *behavior.* . . . The social and demographic characteristics of the participants as well as a detailed description of the settings and qualities of the encounters were also obtained" (Black and Reiss 1967: 15; emphasis in original).

Reiss (1968a, 1971a) applied a sociological approach to understanding police brutality. He describes the incidents in which officers used undue force in the following terms:

> Seventy-eight percent of all instances where force was used unduly took place in police-controlled settings, such as the patrol car, the precinct station, or public places (primarily streets). Almost all victims of force were characterized as suspects or offenders. They were young, lower-class males from any racial or ethnic group. Furthermore, most encounters were devoid of witnesses who

would support the offender. In general, persons officers regarded as being in a deviant offender role or who defied what the officer defines as his authority were the most likely victims of undue force. Thirty-nine percent openly defied authority by challenging the legitimacy of the police to exercise that authority, 9 percent physically resisted arrest, and 32 percent were persons in deviant offender roles, such as drunks, homosexuals, or addicts. (Reiss 1971a: 147–49)

Reiss also points out, however, that "many instances where the citizen behaved antagonistically toward the police officer and many encounters with deviants did not involve uncivil conduct or misuse of force by the police" (1971a: 149) and, more generally, that police-citizen encounters do not follow a rule of reciprocity in incivility—"whenever incivility occurs in an encounter, the chances are only 1 in 6 that the other party will reciprocate with incivility" (1971a: 144).

In a 1980 article, Robert Friedrich reviewed the problems with then existing research on police use of force and outlined three approaches to explaining police use of force—"individual," "situational," and "organizational"—that correspond, respectively, to the psychological, sociological, and organizational theories discussed above. From each approach, he pointed out, one can derive a number of specific hypotheses about the use of force; using the Black-Reiss data, Friedrich tested some of those hypotheses to produce what was at that time the most thorough and sophisticated analysis of the phenomenon.

Friedrich found, first, that physical force was used only infrequently by police, and that the use of excessive force was still less frequent. Force was used in 5.1 percent of the 1,565 encounters that involved suspected offenders (and in only one of the remaining 3,826 incidents that involved no suspects). "Excessive" force was used in 1.8 percent of the encounters with suspects, or in no more than twenty-nine incidents.[10]

Friedrich further found that situational, individual, and organizational hypotheses were, with few exceptions, unsupported by the data. Bivariate and multivariate analyses showed that characteristics of the police-citizen encounters bore the strongest relationship to the use of force, which was more likely if the suspect was antagonistic, agitated, intoxicated, or lower-class, if the offense was a felony, or if other citizens or officers were present. Yet situational characteristics together had no more than modest explanatory power. The characteristics of officers— their length of service, attitudes toward the job, race, and (among white officers) attitudes toward blacks—accounted for little of the (limited) variation in the use of force. Differences across departments were of marginal significance and did not conform to Friedrich's expectations. The incidence of the use of force overall and of improper force in particular was, as Friedrich hypothesized, somewhat lower in the "professional" department (Chicago) than in the "traditional" department (Boston), and, contrary to Friedrich's hypotheses, lowest in the "transitional" department (Washington, D.C.).[11]

Other analyses of the use of nonlethal force tend to corroborate Friedrich's findings. Analyses of other observational data have shown that force is used infrequently. Sykes and Brent (1980, 1983), who analyzed sequences of interactions between officers and citizens, concluded that officers "regulate" or control their interactions with citizens primarily by asking questions or making accusations and secondarily by issuing commands; they found that "coercive regulation [including threats as well as the actual use of force] is rare" (1980: 195). Bayley and Garofalo (1989), who conducted a smaller-scale observational study under the auspices of the New York State Commission on Criminal Justice and the Use of Force, found that, even in encounters that qualified as "potentially violent mobilizations," police used force in only 8 percent of these situations and that the force "consisted almost exclusively of grabbing and restraining" (p. 7).

Croft (1985) analyzed reports of the use of force filed by officers in the Rochester (N.Y.) Police Department from 1973 through 1979, along with a comparison sample of arrests in which no force was used. Like Friedrich's, Croft's analysis indicates that the use of force was infrequent—2,397 reported uses of force and 123,491 arrests during the period—and was typically prompted by citizens' actions like threatening or attacking officers and/or other citizens or attempting to flee. Croft's analysis also suggests that many citizens against whom force was used were antagonistic and/or uncooperative, either verbally abusing officers or disobeying officers' commands.[12] Neither gender nor race bore the expected relationship to the use of force. Furthermore, Croft found that some officers were much more likely to use force, even after controlling for officers' "hazard status," that is, the risk of "being exposed to police-citizen incidents having a potential for use of force" (p. 160); 119 of 430 officers selected for analysis were classified as "high force" officers, who used force in 6.1 percent or more of the arrests they made. However, "high force" officers could not, for the most part, be distinguished from "low force" officers by their background characteristics; officers' use of force was related only to their age and length of service and was unrelated to their gender, race, education, prior military service, or civil service test ranking. Nor did the two groups differ in their arrest productivity or numbers of citizen complaints, internally initiated complaints, or disciplinary charges. Thus this analysis of official police records yields results that mirror those based on observational research.

Analysis of the Police Services Study Data

Data collected for the Police Services Study (PSS) afford another opportunity to analyze police use of force based on systematic observation. The PSS was funded by the National Science Foundation and conducted by Elinor Ostrom, Roger B. Parks, and Gordon P. Whitaker. The study was designed to examine the impact of institutional arrangements on the delivery of police services. The second phase of the PSS provided for the collection of various kinds of data about twenty-four police departments in three metropolitan areas (Rochester, N.Y., St. Louis, Mo., and Tampa–St. Petersburg, Fla.); attention focused in particular on sixty neighborhoods served by those departments. During the summer of 1977, trained observers accompanied patrol officers on 900 patrol shifts, fifteen in each of the sixty neighborhoods. Observers recorded information about 5,688 police-citizen encounters in field notes and later coded that information on a standardized form; in many cases, narrative accounts of the encounters were also prepared. In addition, the observed officers (and samples of other officers) were surveyed. These data form the principal basis for the analyses reported below.

Compared with the Black-Reiss data and other observational data, the PSS data are broader and deeper. The Black-Reiss study focused on high-crime precincts in three major cities. The departments included in the PSS are more representative of American police agencies; they range in size from 13 officers to more than 2,000, serving municipalities whose populations range from 6,000 to almost 500,000. Within jurisdictions, neighborhoods were selected with explicit reference to racial composition and income to ensure that different types of neighborhoods were represented. The departments and neighborhoods provide a rough cross-section of organizational arrangements and residential service conditions for urban policing in the United States. Thus the PSS data provide a much firmer basis for generalizing about police practices in American metropolitan areas (and not only in urban, high-crime areas).

The Use of Force

While they were observed for the PSS, officers used no more than reasonable force to restrain or move a citizen in thirty-seven encounters.[13] In twenty-three encounters, officers used force that the observer judged to be unnecessary or excessive; in three of those, officers hit or swung at citizens with a weapon.[14] This analysis will focus on these two categories of behavior, i.e., the use of reasonable force, and the use of improper (unnecessary or excessive) force. According to the coded data, reasonable force was used in less than 1 percent of the encounters, and improper force was used in less than one-half of 1 percent; in encounters with suspects, who one would presume to be the most likely targets of police force, reasonable force was used in 2.3 percent, and improper force in 1.3 percent. Even so, incidents in which improper force was used represent a substantial proportion of the incidents in which any force (reasonable or improper) was used (see chapter 3).

This division of officers' behavior into the categories of no force, reasonable force, and improper force for present analytic purposes should be recognized for what it is: a simplification. Officers' use of force can be conceived of (if not precisely measured) as a continuum, say from minimal force to even deadly force;

these differences of degree are largely lost in this trichotomy. Moreover, this conceptualization of officers' behavior also obscures differences in the use of improper force, but the PSS data do not reliably differentiate the use of excessive force from the use of unnecessary force.[15]

The Effects of Situational Characteristics

Bivariate analyses of PSS data indicate that the use of reasonable force and the use of improper force are more likely in encounters that involve (a) violent crimes, (b) automobile pursuits, (c) at least four bystanders (increasing with ten or more bystanders), and (d) more than one officer (increasing with at least five officers).[16] Further, use of reasonable force and the use of improper force are somewhat more likely (a) if the citizen is black, male, and over eighteen, (b) if the citizen exhibits signs of drunkenness or mental disorder, (c) if the citizen has a weapon (still more likely if the citizen attempts to use a weapon), and (d) if the citizen is hostile or antagonistic, especially if the citizen fights with the officer(s).[17]

Multivariate analysis, using suspects as the units of analysis, permits one to impose statistical controls and thus to estimate the independent effects of these variables; it also provides an estimate of the extent to which these variables together account for the use of force. The results of a multinomial logit analysis show that several variables have statistically significant effects on the use of both reasonable and improper force.[18] Whether reasonable or improper, force is more likely in incidents that involve violent crimes and against suspects who are male, black, drunk, antagonistic, or physically resistant to the police. Physical resistance has by far the greatest effect on the use of force. But even when the effects of physical resistance are statistically controlled, suspects' demeanor has significant effects on the use of force. And even when the effects of physical resistance and demeanor are statistically controlled, suspects' race has significant effects on the use of force. That officers are more likely to use even reasonable force against blacks might suggest that officers are, on average, more likely to adopt a punitive or coercive approach to black suspects than they are to white suspects.[19] Such an approach is illustrated in this narrative written by a PSS observer:

> Shortly after midnight we received a call of disturbance and [the observed officer] proceeded to the scene without delay. We were the first to arrive and noticed two older women and a man standing on the south side of the street and a large group of younger women standing on a porch on the north side of the street. There was no disturbance upon arrival. [The observed officer] pulled up by the smaller group of people and asked them if they had called the police. They said that they had not. The [officer] apparently assumed (correctly) that the man in the group was the source of trouble, for he told the man that some-

one had called the police about a disturbance and that it would be necessary for them to go inside. The man (black, 30) said that there was no problem and stood his ground. At this point another [officer] and a friend of the man walked up to our car. [The observed officer] said that whether there was a problem or not they would have to get off the street. One of the women (the man's mother) told him to go inside but the man began muttering about how no one was going to tell him what to do. It was then that I realized that he was very drunk. [The observed officer] said that if the man didn't get off the street and the police got another call to come out he would be arrested. The man didn't like this at all and began raving about how there was no problem and about how the police were just trying to hassle him. The friend pleaded with the man to come inside but the man would not move and continued his muttering. [The observed officer] got out of the car and placed himself very near the man. He began saying something about not going anywhere and [the officer] told the man that he was under arrest. [The second officer] helped handcuff the man who was being very uncooperative. His friend told him that he was ignorant and asked the [officer] if he could go to the station with them. [The officer] said yes. They placed the man in the back seat of our car and we drove to the station, all the while being accused of harassment and racism. The man threatened to kill us and [the officer] said he would have his chance when we got to the station. When we arrived [the officer] took him out of the car but the man started pulling away. [The second officer] grabbed him by the hair and [the observed officer] said that he had originally planned to let the man go when they got to the station but since the man was being such an ass he was going to book him.

In this case, the officer's actions early in the encounter—ordering the man to get off the street and then confronting and challenging him—were, arguably, precipitous and ill-advised, making it all the more likely that force would later be used.

Several additional variables have statistically significant effects on the use of reasonable force but not on the use of improper force.[20] The likelihood that reasonable force will be used rises with the number of bystanders. The use of reasonable force is also more likely if the encounter involves a nonviolent crime or if there is some evidence that the citizen has a mental disorder. Curiously, the use of reasonable force is *less* likely if the citizen uses a weapon.

The effect of bystanders, and perhaps even of mental disorder, may reflect some officers' judgment that such encounters are best handled with dispatch. The following narrative illustrates this approach:

We were on routine patrol when flagged down by an [officer] waving a flashlight. He was out of breath from chasing a "mental," a black woman about 22 years old. We noticed an ambulance in the parking lot of an apartment complex, and [the observed officer] decided to check it out. The first officer explained that the young woman had been drinking heavily and had put her head through a plate glass window, sustaining minor (but bloody) injuries. Her mother had called both the police and the ambulance because the woman had a history of drinking and mental disorder and might abuse her two children. When the police arrived, the woman ran away, covering about two blocks before the police and her mother caught her. When we arrived, the woman was having a heated discussion with her mother about whether or not she should go to the hospital. A third [officer] arrived. Two National Ambulance attendants were also trying to persuade the woman to go along. She became more and more distraught, and began yelling and cursing the attendants and officers. Lights began appearing in apartment windows, and several people began filtering out toward the confrontation. The woman kept screaming, "Momma, you done me wrong." Suddenly, [the observed officer] and the first [officer] grabbed the woman by the arms and began dragging her, kicking and screaming, to the ambulence. She was rather large, and put up a good struggle. The third [officer] and an attendant each had to grab a leg. They threw her on a stretcher. [The observed officer] sat on her legs while the other two officers held her arms and the attendants tied her hands and feet to the stretcher. She cursed and spit at the officers. [The observed officer] bounced on her legs and grinned. (She was wearing a bathrobe and underwear, and the bathrobe lost its effectiveness in the struggle. [The observed officer] mocked the woman, saying that her spit was 100 proof. The mildest epithet used was "Get your white ass offa me, motherfucker." An attendant put a pillow over her face to keep her from spitting.) . . . In reflecting on the case as we patrolled, the [observed officer] mentioned that he had stopped even though there were two officers on the scene because both were young and sometimes indecisive. He said that the officers let the situation drag on too long, that people were beginning to come out of their apartments, and that he had to act.

This officer apparently believed that the encounter was better resolved before a large crowd formed and altered the dynamics of the encounter, as Muir (1977: ch. 7) illustrates in his discussion of "the crowd scene."

Two variables have statistically significant effects on the use of improper force, but not on the use of reasonable force. Improper force is more likely if the encounter involves a car chase, even controlling for physical resistance by the suspect. One reason may be that pursuits are emotionally and physiologically intense experiences that are in some cases or for some officers "catalytic" (see chapter 4). Another reason may be that suspects' flight is another form of disrespect for police authority, as is a hostile or antagonistic demeanor, which (sometimes) prompts officers (unduly) to assert their authority. Either explanation could account for the following incident.

At about 18:05, we were sitting in the car in a parking lot on the corner of B
and LK [streets] talking to a patrol supervisor, when a Lilliput [a pseudonym
for another municipality] police car went by chasing a motorcycle. Both the
patrol car and the supervisor took off after the bike, which had turned onto
LK Avenue. We chased him down LK to S, where he turned right and onto LT
and back into Lilliput. By the time a Lilliput car and our car stopped him, two
other Lilliput cars and another Metro [another pseudonym] car had arrived.
Two Lilliput officers and a Lilliput detective jumped out of their cars, tackled
the suspect, roughed him up a bit, and handcuffed him. . . . The suspect was
frisked and loaded into the back of a Lilliput patrol car.

The likelihood of improper force also rises with the number of officers at
the scene. This finding is also open to (at least) two interpretations (Friedrich
1977: 93). One is that an officer is more likely to use force when other officers are
there to provide physical and social psychological reinforcements. Another is that
incidents in which force is used are also those to which other officers come (or are
summoned); according to this interpretation, the presence of other officers is an
effect rather than a cause. Unfortunately, the analysis cannot rule out either interpretation.

In some respects these results parallel Friedrich's, who found that "police use
of force depends primarily on two factors: how the offender behaves and whether
or not other citizens and police are present" (1980: 95). In particular, Friedrich
shows that the use of force is affected by the citizen's demeanor and sobriety. This
analysis of the PSS data corroborates these findings: drunkenness, a hostile demeanor, and especially physical resistance all make the use of force more likely.
But Friedrich's analysis indicated that the use of force is unaffected by other characteristics of citizens, including race and gender. The results of the analysis in this
chapter indicate that the use of force *is* affected by race as well as by gender.[21]

The explanatory power of situational factors can be assessed in terms of the
success of the model in predicting the use-of-force outcomes of these encounters; the proportion of cases that are correctly classified can be compared with the
proportion that one could correctly classify based on knowledge only of the frequencies of the outcomes. Given that the use of force is so uncommon, however,
predictions based only on the frequencies would be quite accurate. Indeed, one
could correctly classify more than 97 percent of the cases if one predicted that
force was never used; if one randomly classified cases to reproduce the frequencies, one could correctly classify 94.6 percent. Overall, the model has no more
than a 5.7 percent potential improvement in predictive success over random classification. In fact, the model's predictions correctly classify 97.7 percent of the
cases, a 3.3 percent improvement over chance. A fairer assessment of the model,
perhaps, is its success in classifying cases in which force was used; random clas-

sification would result, on average, in 2 percent correct (one of forty-nine cases), while the model yields 24.5 percent correct. Furthermore, this analysis also suggests that these situational factors taken together predict the use of improper force more accurately than they do the use of reasonable force. Five of thirty-five cases (14 percent) are correctly classified as those in which reasonable force was used, whereas seven of fourteen cases (50 percent) are correctly classified as those in which improper force was used.

The Effects of Officers' Characteristics

Bivariate analyses indicate that the two forms of force bear modest relationships to officers' attitudes. First, officers who said that police should not "handle cases involving public nuisances, such as barking dogs or burning rubbish," were more likely to use force, as were officers who said that "police should not have to handle calls that involve social or personal problems where no crime is involved." Thus officers who conceive their role in narrow terms are somewhat more likely to use force. Second, officers who said that "if police officers in tough neighborhoods had fewer restrictions on their use of force, many of the serious crime problems in those neighborhoods would be greatly reduced" were more likely to use force, as were those who said that "when a police officer is accused of using too much force, only other officers are qualified to judge such a case." Finally, officers who said that "the likelihood of a police officer being abused by citizens in this community is very high" were more likely to use force, as were officers who disagreed with the statement, "most people in this community respect police officers." However, judging from the percentage differences alone, the strength of these relationships is as weak as their direction is consistent with expectations.[22]

Multivariate analyses, using officers as the units of analysis, form a better basis for assessing the impacts of officers' characteristics on their use of force. For such an analysis, one may measure officers' use of reasonable and improper force, respectively, as number of occasions on which each officer was observed to use force, or as a dichotomy—whether or not each officer was observed using force. As it turns out, the results are the same regardless of the measure and the statistical technique used.[23]

Only three variables (other than the amount of time for which officers were observed) have significant effects on one or both forms of force. First, officers' attitudes toward citizens—i.e., citizens' respect for police and the perceived likelihood that officers would be abused by citizens—have significant effects both on officers' use of reasonable force and improper force;[24] officers with more negative attitudes toward citizens are more likely to use either kind of force. Second, the effect of officers' attitudes toward the use of force on their use of improper force is of marginal statistical significance (at the .10 level with a one-tailed test);

officers with more positive attitudes toward the use of force tend to use force improperly with greater frequency.[25] Third, the effect of officers' education on their use of reasonable force is statistically significant (at the .07 level in the OLS regression and at the .05 level in the Poisson regression); in particular, officers with bachelor's degrees are more likely to use reasonable force.

Overall, then, officers' characteristics contribute very little to an explanation of the use of reasonable or improper force in these data. In OLS analyses, these variables explain less than 3 to 4 percent of the variation in officers' uses of force. In logit analyses, this set of variables has practically no predictive power; all officers were classified as having not used force. Furthermore, even these modest relationships are problematic to some extent, as officers who are assigned to the more active, violent, socially disorganized police districts, in which the use of force is more frequently necessary, might as a result have more negative attitudes toward citizens; those officers might also have less seniority, and thus be younger, less experienced, and more highly educated. When officers' characteristics are included with situational factors in an analysis using suspects as the units of analysis, only one of these three variables—officers' attitudes toward citizens—has a statistically significant effect, and only on the use of reasonable force. Psychological hypotheses about officers' use of force find little support in these analyses of the PSS data.

The Effects of Organizational Characteristics

As one might expect, given the infrequency with which force was used in the observed encounters, the incidence of force varies little across the twenty-four departments. In eleven departments there were no observed uses of force; in each of five other departments there was only one observed case of reasonable force; and in each of five other departments observers recorded two or three uses of force. In each of the remaining three departments, observers recorded 10, 16, and 19 incidents, respectively, in which force was used. These raw numbers are potentially misleading, however, as these remaining three departments were not only the largest departments but also those in which the largest numbers of shifts were observed. Taking into account the varying amount of observation across departments as well as the frequency with which officers in the respective departments encountered suspected offenders, the incidence of improper force in three smaller departments equals or exceeds that in the largest departments. But even when the use of force is standardized across departments for the duration of observation, these estimates of the use of force as an *organizational* property rest on a narrow foundation of data collection; in the smaller departments, observation extended over only fifteen to thirty shifts, or approximately 120 to 250 hours.

Rather than use the departments as the units of analysis, one can include the theoretically relevant characteristics of the departments with situational factors in the same model, using suspects as the units of analysis. This approach has the advantage of controlling for the frequency with which officers in different departments confront situations whose characteristics (examined above) make the use of force more likely. Three characteristics of the departments, which are featured in organizational theory, can be measured with PSS data.

First, the bureaucratization of the departments can be measured in terms of their size (the number of full-time employees), their levels of hierarchy or vertical differentiation (the number of separate ranks), their degree of specialization (the number of separate units, such as traffic, juvenile, etc.), and the extent to which the departments are civilianized. These characteristics can be analyzed as individual variables, or they can be combined to form a single index of bureaucratization.[26] In either case, bureaucratization is conceived as a continuum, rather than as a dichotomy (or as a synonym for organization).

Second, the priority that the executives of the departments place on law enforcement and crime-fighting can be gleaned from in-depth interviews with the chiefs and other high-ranking police administrators. Respondents' answers to one or more of three questions in these interviews provide some clues to their priorities:

1. Would you characterize the department's emphasis as being one of primarily providing service to residents, as primarily trying to suppress crime, or as something in between?
2. Are there any specific departmental policies regarding patrol style or emphasis?
3. What kinds of reports do you [does the chief] get on day-to-day operations of your patrol officers? (Probes: What things get brought to the chief's attention immediately? What kinds of indicators does the chief think are important regarding patrol?)

On the basis of these interview data, three departments appear to have a decidedly "legalistic" or "professional" orientation (Wilson 1968) in the sense that their chiefs place the primary emphasis on fighting crime. One chief, for example, told the PSS interviewer that "the department's first priority was the suppression and prevention of crime, and its second priority was responding to calls for service. The respondent felt that the department receives many trivial or 'bullshit' calls for service. . . . The department does what it can to respond to all calls, but such calls as these take low priority." Furthermore, administrators in that department monitored patrol officers' performance through time sheets, filled out by each officer, "indicating how much time he spent on a variety of activities and various production measures: hours on patrol, hours traffic control, hours accident investigation, hours special duty, hours court, hours office duty, hours writing reports, hours approved overtime, sick leave, number of field interrogation reports filed, number of miscellaneous investigations conducted, number of complaints investigated, number of accidents investigated, number of nontraffic arrests, number of traffic arrests, number of accident arrests, number of warrant arrests, number of juvenile arrests, number of warnings issued." This chief's express priority on crime-fighting was reinforced by the department's information system.

Predictably, not all chiefs' answers revealed an unambiguous and well-ordered set of priorities. Some chiefs may have been reluctant to tell interviewers that "service" was secondary to suppressing crime; they may have shared the orientation (but not the candor) of other chiefs whose departments have been coded as legalistic. But it is equally or more likely that ambiguous answers reflected unclear priorities. For better or worse, police administrators typically are not compelled to establish clear priorities among the multiple and sometimes competing goals and functions of the police; the LAPD under Chief Daryl Gates may have been exceptional in the clarity of its priorities. Be that as it may, priorities can be communicated, even unwittingly, in the form of activity report categories, criteria for evaluation, reasons for sanctions, orders, memoranda, and the like. The PSS interviews with police administrators are not sufficient to measure priorities established in these ways, but the measure based on these data represents an improvement over those available for previous research (e.g., Friedrich 1980).[27]

Third, survey data on patrol officers in each department can be aggregated to measure some features of the informal cultures of the departments. In addition to the observed officers, the survey included all or a sample of the other officers in each department.[28] Their responses to seven questionnaire items, described above for the analysis of officers, reveal wide variation in the collective attitudes of the departments. For example, the proportion of respondents who agreed that police should not have to handle social or personal problems ranged from 6.3 percent in one department to 62.5 percent in another. The proportion of respondents who agreed that fewer restrictions on the use of force would reduce the serious crime problems in tough neighborhoods ranged from 14.3 percent in one department to 69.2 percent in another.

When these variables—bureaucratization, the priority placed on crime-fighting, and the collective attitudes of patrol officers—are added to situational factors in analyses of the use of force, the estimated effect of one organizational characteristic achieves statistical significance: the likelihood that reasonable force will be used increases with the bureaucratization of the department.[29] The effect of bureaucratization on the use of improper force does not achieve a customary level of statistical significance (although it too has a positive sign), and the estimated effects of the other organizational variables are negligible. The inclusion of organizational factors modestly improves the explanatory power of the model: 28.6 percent of the cases in which force was used are classified correctly, compared with 24.5 percent correctly classified based only on the situational factors.

It would seem, then, that compared with officers in more bureaucratized departments, officers in less bureaucratized departments are less likely to use force when it would be justified, seeking instead to handle problems in other ways, or are less likely to take actions early in an encounter that make it more probable that force will be necessary later. These results may offer some support for the proposition that in smaller, less bureaucratic departments, administrators can more effectively monitor the performance of officers, and perhaps that immediate supervisors can more frequently attend to the development of their subordinates' judgment. These are long inferential leaps, to be sure, but they are consistent with the quantitative results.

These conclusions find some additional support in the interviews with administrators. The chief of one department pointed out that his "is a small enough department to allow [him] to read each crime report every day or two." When asked about the reports that are used to get a feel for day-to-day operations, another chief, whose department was relatively small (with twenty-seven full-time patrol officers), said (as summarized by the interviewer), "Just listening to the radio . . . is a good way to tell how things are going. And he pointed out that he can tell by the tone of voice of the officers, the way they are answering calls, whether there is anything wrong, and he said that listening to the men talking around the department is also a good way to keep track of daily operations. He emphasized that not anyone can do this; one has to know the individual officer's personality to be able to tell if the person is quieter than usual." The chiefs of larger departments are scarcely in a position to take advantage of these sources of information. Larger, more bureaucratic agencies tend to rely on quantitative measures of performance, both of individuals and of the agency as a whole, and the less quantifiable aspects of police performance may thus receive too little attention. Indeed, the chief of one larger department (with 381 full-time patrol officers) "mentioned that a big problem in law enforcement was an overwhelming concern for statistical measures of performance, such as arrest rates, clearance rates, crime rates. [The chief] indicated that many of the statistics are misleading, but that nearly all professional departments use them, people come to expect their use, and it is difficult to come up with other more meaningful comparative measures of police performance."

Quantitative indicators of performance are useful primarily for measuring officers' productivity in enforcement; they reveal little about officers' performance of other police tasks, or even some aspects of their enforcement activities, such as the judiciousness with which they use force. Police administrators are not blind to this problem. But as the Christopher Commission's analysis suggests, a higher incidence of the use of force may be one consequence of relying too heavily on such performance measures. A decentralized administrative structure, which would permit mid-level managers to monitor officers' performance through a more complete range of information channels, might enable the subunits of a large department to capture some of the managerial advantages of smaller departments (see Brown 1981: ch. 10; Whitaker 1983). An explicit and vigorous commitment to addressing the problems of the community, as the community defines them, might also be a step in the right direction, insofar as it underscores both the multiplicity of the functions that police perform and the legitimacy of citizen preferences in shaping police policy.

Conclusions

Analyses of the Black-Reiss data and the PSS data, as well as other data, show that physical force is infrequently used by the police and that improper force is used even less. Is police brutality, then, "rare"? The incidence of the use of improper force is rare in the sense that aircraft fatalities are rare: it is infrequent relative to the large volume of interactions between police and citizens, just as deaths in aircraft accidents are infrequent relative to the large number of passenger-miles flown. That these events are rare does not, of course, mean that no effort need be devoted to making them more rare. Both types of events are inevitable to some degree. But as we extend our understanding of how best to structure and regulate human behavior, we may expect that the frequency of both events can be further reduced.

Analyses of the Black-Reiss data and the PSS data also show that to some extent the use and abuse of force by police is influenced by characteristics of the situations in which officers and citizens interact. It would be surprising to find that the use of force is distributed randomly across police-citizen encounters; that officers are more likely to use force against suspects who offer physical resistance is hardly startling. That officers are more likely to use force—and especially improper force—against suspects who are inebriated or antagonistic (other things being equal) is, if not unexpected, at least cause for concern. That officers are more likely to use improper force against black suspects (other things being equal) is cause for grave concern. These results are open to different interpretations. For example, one might interpret the effect of race simply as the behavioral manifestation of hostile police attitudes toward African-Americans. A somewhat different interpretation was offered by one chief of police (in a private communication with the author), who thought that some of his officers were especially fearful of black suspects; the unstated implication is that those officers might use force preemptively (and unnecessarily) or act (unwittingly) in such a way that provokes resistance to which they must respond with force. These varying interpretations, moreover, would seem to have different implications for the form and likely efficacy of managerial interventions. In general, a sociological approach to *explaining* police use of force may not suffice for *understanding* the use of force.[30] Further research on the dynamics of police-citizen encounters in which force is used, with a view toward how those dynamics may be affected by—and the ways in which officers interpret—specific situational factors, may improve our understanding of these results (Worden 1989; Mastrofski and Parks 1990).

Neither this analysis nor previous analyses demonstrate that officers' characteristics or attitudes have a substantively (rather than merely statistically) significant effect on the use of force. Such results are consistent with the disappointing results of recruit screening (see chapter 7). Even so, this analysis offers some weak support for psychological hypotheses. The most prudent conclusion at this juncture may be that, if officers' propensities to use force are affected by their backgrounds and beliefs, then those effects are probably contingent on other factors, including the characteristics of the police-citizen situations and the characteristics of police organizations. The effects may also be interactive rather than additive— that is, officers' propensities to use force may be affected by a constellation of outlooks rather than by each individual perspective. For example, the officers who are most likely to use and abuse force might be those who define the police role exclusively in terms of crime-fighting *and* who are inclined to bend or break rules that regulate their authority in order to bring about outcomes that they consider desirable *and* whose (formal and informal) training has provided them with few alternatives to the use of force. Such officers might be more likely to use force if they work in (more) bureaucratic agencies that emphasize hard-nosed enforcement *and* measure and reward performance accordingly. Put more succinctly, officers' attitudes and personality characteristics may bear a systematic but complex relationship to their use of force.

Research on these questions should be designed to capture these complexities. Previous observational studies have not been so designed. For both the Black-Reiss and PSS studies, the units of sample selection (within precincts and neighborhoods, respectively) were shifts. Active or busy shifts were oversampled in order to maximize the number of police-citizen encounters that observers could record. For the Black-Reiss study, 589 officers were observed for one or more shifts; the average period of observation per officer was two and a half shifts (Friedrich 1977). For the PSS, 522 officers were observed; more than half of the officers were observed for only one shift, only sixty officers were observed for as much as twenty-four hours (or about three shifts), and only twenty-four officers for as much as thirty-two hours.[31] But if the use of force is infrequent, and if the distribution of the incidence of force across officers is skewed, then officers should serve as the units for sample selection. Officers who use force most frequently could be oversampled; the sampling frame could be stratified according to the numbers of (sustained or unsustained) citizen complaints, arrests for resisting arrest, use-of-force reports, or other departmental indicators (including the reports of other officers—see Bayley and Garofalo 1989). The balance of the sample would be composed of other officers with similar assignments, and officers would be weighted for analysis. If observation were extended to include debriefing officers about individual encounters, to obtain data on the decision rules by which they choose courses of action (Mastrofski and Parks 1990; Worden and Brandl 1990), and if these observations were complemented by a well-conceived survey instrument, then one might conduct a relatively powerful test of psychological hypotheses.

Finally, this analysis provides modest support for an organizational explanation of police brutality. It suggests that elements of formal organizational structure affect the incidence with which force is used. It does not, however, suggest that this effect is a simple product of restrictive policies, in terms of which discussions of administrative controls are too frequently cast. The theory on which this analysis is based and the structural variables that were conceptualized and measured point toward more fundamental—and less easily altered—features of the organization. Future research should continue to explore the ways in which organizational forces affect the incidence of officers' use of force, but it should have a broad theoretical grounding that reaches beyond policy and procedure with respect to the use of force (and complaints about the use of force). Evidence on these propositions will accumulate slowly because comparable data on the use of force in multiple departments will be difficult to find or very expensive to collect (see chapter 3). But evidence will not accumulate at all unless research is guided by sound theory.

NOTES

I am grateful to Alissa Pollitz Worden, Gordon P. Whitaker, Hans Toch, and Dennis Blass for their thoughtful comments on an earlier draft of this paper.
    1. However, the converse—that every theory has implications for reform—is not true.
    2. See, for example, Sherman (1980b), whose discussion of violence by police focuses almost exclusively on the use of deadly force.
    3. Black holds that the quantity of law can be conceived as a continuous variable, but quantitative research on police has with few exceptions conceived and measured it as a dichotomy.
    4. I return to the issue of race below in a review of studies of the use of nonlethal force.
    5. See chapter 4 for a more thorough assessment both of the commission's analysis of problem officers and of violence-prone officers more generally.
    6. The other types are "professionals," "clean-beat crime-fighters," and "avoiders" (see Worden 1995): "Professionals . . . are . . . willing to use coercive means to achieve desirable ends, but they use it with a keen sense of when, and in what proportion, it is necessary. . . . They believe that . . . the application of the law should be tempered by a sensitive appreciation of its consequences, justifying the enforcement of the law in terms of helping people. . . . These officers are neither overly aggressive on the street nor resentful of legal restrictions on their authority." "Clean-beat crime-fighters . . . stress the law enforcement function of the police. . . . they justify uniform (non-selective) enforcement in terms of its deterrent effect." They are very energetic and aggressive on the street, although they lack the street sense of the tough cop. "Avoiders . . . [are] unable to cope with the characteristic exigencies of police work. . . . They prefer to do as little police work as possible, only that amount of work necessary to meet the minimum expectations of supervisors; otherwise, they adopt what has elsewhere been called a 'lay-low-and-don't-make-waves' approach to policing."

7. Brown (1981) makes the argument that one of the core themes of the police culture is individualism. Fielding (1988) maintains that some officers ostensibly go along with the dominant value system, but "once confident of their place and ability to use the necessary justifying rhetoric in relation to their own complex of values, officers begin to move in and through the culture to secure their own ends" (p. 185). However, many other (less convincing) accounts of the police culture tend to highlight the forces that have homogenizing effects, both on officers' outlooks and on their behavioral patterns; little attention is given to the differing interpretations of and conformity with the norms of the culture. For example, Hunt (1985) describes the effects of peers on individual officers' conceptions of proper force and their justifications for the use of force, and while she also observes that some "violence-prone" officers repeatedly "exceed working notions of normal force" and are "not effectively held in check by routine means of peer control" (336), her analysis does not allow for officers who use less than "normal" force.

8. Such a shift in expectations and incentives could perhaps be effected with the adoption of community policing, which the commission recommended. That such a model of policing—and of police administration—would reduce the incidence of improper force is itself a largely untested (albeit plausible) hypothesis. For a theoretically rich and illuminating study that offers some support for this proposition, as well as a sobering account of the likely obstacles to implementing this model, see Guyot (1991).

9. About half of all state and local police agencies employ fewer than ten full-time sworn officers (Reeves 1993: 9).

10. Reiss's (1968a) analysis of the same data reports that force was used improperly in thirty-seven cases. Friedrich's analysis rests on the characterizations of the coders, who "examined pertinent passages of the observation reports to determine if physical force had been used and if it was justified in terms of self-defense or the need to make an arrest," while Reiss "had an expert panel decide whether or not force on the order of an aggravated assault was used" (1980: n. 12; also see Reiss 1968a).

11. These expectations were based largely on Wilson's (1968) analysis of police styles and the organizational contexts with which they are associated. In the light of later research, especially Brown's (1981), it should be clear that these expectations are faulty. For many years, the LAPD was regarded as the epitome of police professionalism; elements of that professionalism, we now realize, may make the use of force *more* likely.

12. Croft's analysis also shows that when citizens in these incidents verbally abused or disobeyed officers, officers typically responded by issuing a command, whereupon citizens attacked the officers.

13. According to a PSS memorandum (coding update number 3, dated 29 May 1977), this category encompasses "instances where the officer is attempting to make a citizen come with him, or is attempting to separate citizens who are fighting, or similar acts. The sense here is that the officer is restraining or moving the citizen without the intent to beat the citizen."

14. The PSS coding memo cited in note 13 specifies that this code should be used "for instances where the officer is 'kicking ass.'" A gun was drawn by one or more officers in fifty-three encounters, and in one of those the gun was fired (albeit at a rattlesnake); another type of weapon was drawn in thirty-three encounters.

15. The coded data provide little information about the temporal sequences of events. For example, the data indicate whether the citizen fought with the officer and whether the officer(s) used improper force, but they do not indicate whether the force preceded the citizen's resistance, continued after the resistance ceased (unnecessary force), or was more than that required to subdue the citizen (excessive force).

16. Even so, most encounters in which force was used—whether reasonably or improperly—involved neither a violent offense nor an automobile pursuit. None of the encounters

in which force was used originated as a suspicion stop or police-initiated field interrogation; indeed, few of the encounters in which force was used were initiated by officers. If the use of force is a by-product of police aggressiveness, then it would seem not to be a direct outgrowth of an aggressive style of patrol that involves frequently stopping suspicious persons or vehicles (Wilson and Boland 1978; Whitaker, Phillips, and Worden 1984); it might nevertheless be a consequence of an overly assertive or confrontational posture vis-à-vis citizens in a variety of contexts.

17. Each citizen's demeanor was coded at the beginning, during, and at the end of the encounter. This analysis conservatively uses the citizen's demeanor at the beginning of the encounter, lest we confuse antagonistic behavior that prompts the use of force with antagonistic behavior prompted by the use of force. A small number of the citizens coded by observers were actually groups of citizens; if the group was not homogeneous with respect to race, gender, or age, it was coded as mixed.

18. As I have conceived the use of force as a nominal variable with three categories, I have estimated the parameters of a multinomial logit model, which is the "standard method" (Aldrich and Nelson 1984: 37–40) for analyzing a polytomous, unordered dependent variable. As an alternative, one could operationalize the use of force—reasonable and/or improper force—as a dichotomy and apply other multivariate techniques, including the widely used ordinary least squares regression, the analytic approach that Friedrich (1980) used. In the PSS data, when regression equations for reasonable force and improper force, respectively, are estimated using OLS, some but not all of the findings are congruent with the multinomial logit results. Binomial logit results are largely—but not entirely—consistent with the multinomial logit results. As OLS regression is not appropriate for dichotomous dependent variables (Hanushek and Jackson 1977: ch. 7; Aldrich and Nelson 1984: ch. 1; and, more generally, King 1989), there is good reason to prefer the logit results. Also see Brehm and Gates (1992) for a discussion of alternative techniques and applications to the Black-Reiss data.

19. Black (1980: ch. 5) comes to a similar conclusion based on his analysis of dispute resolution by police using the Black-Reiss data.

20. This is not the same as saying that for each of these variables the two coefficients are significantly different from one another; on the contrary, in each case the confidence intervals for the two coefficients overlap.

21. The OLS results indicate that race has a statistically significant effect on the use of reasonable force but not on the use of improper force. The discrepancy between the results of the logit analysis and those of Friedrich's analysis may be methodological artifacts.

22. In some encounters that involved use of force, the officer who was designated as the "primary" or observed officer, and for whom survey data could be connected to coded observations, did not use force. Thus these findings are based on only the primary officers who were observed to use force, and exclude other officers who used force in the observers' presence.

23. The two measures of officers' use of force differ very little, inasmuch as no officer was observed to use excessive force more than once, and only seven officers were observed to use reasonable force more than once (five used it twice and two used it on three occasions). Moreover, the estimation of model coefficients does not hinges on the measure or the statistical technique used. When the use of force is measured as an event count, both OLS and Poisson regressions (see Inn and Wheeler 1977; and, more generally, King 1989) yield comparable results; when the use of force is measured as a dichotomy, binomial logit yields results that are congruent with the OLS and Poisson regressions.

24. This variable is an index formed by summing officers' responses to the two questionnaire items. Neither item by itself achieves statistical significance in separate OLS analyses, although both are significant (one at .07 and the other at .03) in the Poisson regression.

25. This too is an index formed by summing officers' responses to the questionnaire items about the use of force in "tough" neighborhoods and about who (if anyone) in addition to police is qualified to judge allegations of improper force. In a separate analysis, the former item achieves this same marginal level of statistical significance, and the effect of the latter is insignificant.

26. This index is the sum of the standardized variables. Smith's (1984) analysis of the PSS data is based on an index of bureaucratization that was formed in a similar fashion (but using a somewhat different set of variables).

27. It is also nearer the mark of police "professionalism" than are indicators of officers' educational achievement (cf. Smith 1984).

28. Because the survey was intended to collect information relevant to the sixty study neighborhoods, selection procedures generally identified would-be respondents who had responsibilities in those areas—for patrol, supervision, or administration. In the six largest departments, samples of officers and supervisors assigned to those areas, in addition to command staff, were selected; in the smaller departments, all officers, supervisors, and command staff were selected. In two departments, samples of all officers were selected regardless of their assignments to study neighborhoods or to other areas. Overall, of the 1,435 officers selected, two refused to be interviewed, eight could not be contacted, and eight others were not interviewed for unidentified reasons. Aggregated responses in each department are based only on respondents with a rank below sergeant, i.e., those whose primary responsibility is patrol and who are most likely to have occasion to use force.

29. These results are based on a model that omits measures of the collective attitudes of patrol officers, none of whose effects achieve statistical significance; results are available from the author.

30. Black (1976: 7) points out that his theory of the behavior of law "predicts and explains . . . without regard to the individual as such. . . . It neither assumes nor implies that he is, for instance, rational, goal directed, pleasure seeking, or pain avoiding. . . . It has nothing to do with how an individual experiences reality."

31. In fairness to the PSS, it should be noted that it was not designed for the purpose of analyzing police brutality.

CHAPTER THREE

Measuring the Prevalence of Police Abuse of Force

KENNETH ADAMS

This chapter is organized into three parts. The first part deals with conceptual and analytical problems in studying the use of excessive force. It looks at the problems of defining "excessive force," computing rates, and the influence of risk factors. The second part reviews the findings of empirical studies that bear on the prevalence of excessive force to see what we already know about how frequently the police employ force. The third part compares different ways to research the extent of excessive force—official records, surveys of police and citizens, and field observation.

Conceptual and Analytical Issues

In attempting to define excessive force there are a number of difficulties. Foremost, labeling force as excessive renders a judgment that in a given set of circumstances police actions have overstepped the bounds of necessity.[1] Judgments, however, may be purely subjective assertions that cannot be scientifically verified. Research may be unable to prove that force was excessive in a given situation, just as it cannot prove that a painting by Monet is beautiful. When there is a widespread consensus on a judgment, it is tempting to think that we are dealing with facts, but the ephemeral nature of consensually validated "facts" is quickly revealed as definitions of what is excessive (or beautiful) change.

This is not to say that the prevalence of excessive force and other related questions cannot be researched or that science has nothing to contribute to the understanding of social problems. For example, a set of rules and procedures by which to make judgments of excessive force can be established. There are two problems in taking this approach, however. We must agree, first, on the relevant criteria for making judgments, and, second, on the application of these criteria to a given situation. The second problem tends to be the more difficult, especially when the information needed to make judgments is incomplete or ambiguous. This problem is exacerbated in the study of excessive force because fairness moves us to judge events from the perspective of the police officer involved (especially in relation to perceptions of threat, of available options, and likely outcomes of various courses of action), and placing oneself in another's shoes requires considerable speculation.

Courts and administrative bodies have had to wrestle with the definition of excessive force, and researchers can turn to them for help in formulating a definition.[2] The Supreme Court has ruled that the use of force at arrest must be "objectively reasonable" in view of all the "facts and circumstances of each particular case, including the severity of the crime at issue, whether the suspect poses an immediate threat to the safety of the officers or others, and whether he is actively resisting arrest or attempting to evade arrest by flight" (*Graham v. Connor*, 490 U.S. 386, 1989). But the Court has gone on to state that "the calculus of reasonableness must embody allowance for the fact that police officers are often forced to make split-second judgments—in circumstances that are tense, uncertain, and rapidly evolving—about the amount of force that is necessary in a particular situation."

Although researchers might find the objective reasonableness standard useful in studying the incidence of abusive force, the problem remains its application to situations in which "split-second judgments" are arrived at. Even when a situation appears unambiguous to most observers, their view may not be shared by others, as the Rodney King case has shown.

An influential early definition of excessive force was offered by Reiss (1968a) in an observational study of police activities conducted for the President's Commission on Law Enforcement and Administration of Justice (see chapter 2). Field researchers observed thirty-seven instances that, in their judgment, involved improper use of force. The research team made efforts to ensure that their judgments were consistent (reliable). The criteria they used ostensibly relate well to the concept of excessive or unreasonable force (face validity). However, when a panel of experts reviewed the incidents, only twenty of the thirty-seven were found to involve excessive or unnecessary force (President's Commission on Law Enforcement and Administration of Justice 1967b).

Who is right—the field researchers or the panel of experts—given that almost twice as many incidents were labeled as excessive force by one group as compared to the other? The question may be impossible to answer, however, because applications of definitions to incidents always will be open to challenge.

Dealing with Error

In attempting to measure the extent of excessive force, researchers must eventually confront the problems that derive from errors of measurement. Courts and administrative tribunals try to be scrupulously fair in making judgments, given the high stakes for police officers and citizens caught up in allegations of excessive force, and they employ numerous procedures designed to reduce the chances of factual errors and mistakes in judgment.

Social scientists may occasionally be more tolerant of inexactness. For example, if a researcher's primary interest is comparing groups or geographic regions, it may suffice to say that a city or a police department has more or fewer cases of excessive force than another, even if it cannot be said precisely how many more or fewer.

When researchers venture into the area of public policy analysis or when their findings may be used for making public policy changes, they need to proceed in a more precise manner because the implications of mistakes are broader and more significant. Thus, the scientist must consider what the real-world consequences might be if the findings are misinterpreted by scientists or nonscientists or turn out to be in error.

The real-world consequences of research error obligate researchers to discuss the strengths and weaknesses of their data, emphasize the proper interpretation of findings, and warn of possible misinterpretations, especially by those who may not appreciate fully how the scientist has approached a problem—even at the risk of having the public and practitioners conclude that the researcher's findings have no practical application.

Researchers also take a different view of error than do legal and administrative systems. Although scientists share an interest in minimizing error, they recognize that error will always be present in scientific investigations. For this reason, scientists do not try to eliminate error at any cost but instead decide how much and what types of error can be tolerated. They also have developed many techniques for dealing with the error that inevitably occurs, and many of these techniques can be of use in studying the extent of excessive force by police.

The simplest strategy is to identify the nature and source of error so that conclusions can be drawn as to its effects. If a measure is known to undercount events, we know that the observed count is a minimum estimate. Conversely, if a measure is known to overcount events, we know that the true number must be less than that observed. These rules can be used to advantage by the researcher. For example, if it is easier to count the use of force than the use of excessive force, we might use the more inclusive count to identify a maximum value for the more restricted count. Furthermore, if we can discern the degree of overcounting or of error, we are in an even better position to estimate the true count.

Another strategy for dealing with error is replication, in which other scientists investigate the problem in the same way to see if they get the same results. This strategy works best at catching human errors that are easily avoidable (errors in addition, subtraction, etc.), but it is only occasionally useful at revealing the inherent limitations of data sources or research methods.

Another, more complex, technique is that of multiple indicators. This technique is based on a strategy of triangulation and is particularly useful when the concept being studied is hard to define. Several measurement techniques are used, each with different strengths and weaknesses which often will bias the data in different ways. (The strategy is not unlike that used in economics, where multiple indicators are invoked to assess the economic condition of the country.) If all the measures agree, we can be more confident that measurement error has not unduly influenced the conclusions of the study. If the individual measures differ in their findings, then we need to be more cautious in presenting the conclusions of the research.

Hindelang (1974) used a strategy of multiple indicators to count crimes, a problem not unlike that of counting instances of excessive force. In the study, he compared crime statistics collected by the FBI to those collected through victimization surveys in order to avoid possible detection and reporting biases in official crime statistics. Hindelang's conclusion was that, although official statistics seriously underestimated the number of crimes relative to victim reports, the rank ordering of cities in terms of levels of criminal activity was the same for both arrest statistics and victimization statistics. Therefore, official statistics could be used to say that the crime rate was higher or lower in one place as compared to another, even though the number of crimes was not precise.

In another use of the multiple indicators strategy, Sherman and Langworthy (1979) compared two measures of the number of persons killed by police in thirteen jurisdictions—mortality statistics maintained by the National Center for Health Statistics and police department internal affairs records. Their analyses revealed that the two counts were substantially different for many cities. Given the magnitude of some discrepancies and the fact that neither measure could be described as consistently overcounting or undercounting, they further concluded that issues of relative incidence—the rank ordering of cities in terms of rates—could not be addressed reliably by either measure.

Use of Excessive Force Versus Excessive Use of Force

A partial solution to the problems of defining and identifying the *use of excessive force* is to expand our research efforts to include the *excessive use of force*. The suggestion involves more than a simple turn of a phrase; it calls for a redirection of focus, relinquishing exclusive concern with situations in which police use too much force and broadening our view to include circumstances in which force is applied frequently. Using this strategy, we can sidestep the problem of defining what is excessive force, at least for some research purposes, and, in the process, acquire knowledge that bears on excessive force issues.

Research that gauges police use of force, whether excessive or not, has practical applications in the same way that tracking the mortality rates of hospitals is useful. When the mortality rate of a hospital exceeds a specified threshold, it is placed on a watch list, and medical practices are scrutinized more closely. The watch list designation makes clear that a high mortality rate may be due to a variety of factors, such as a large caseload of high-risk patients, so that questions of substandard care or of malpractice are not always at issue. Yet the system is useful because drawing attention to potential problems may result in medical services being improved.

The strategy of examining officers who use force more frequently than the *average*—a distinctly lower standard than Klockars's (see chapter 1)—was used by the Christopher Commission report, which documented that a small group of Los Angeles police officers used force with above-average frequency (Independent Commission on the Los Angeles Police Department 1991).[3] As noted elsewhere in this volume (see chapters 2 and 4), the interpretation of these findings is not a straightforward matter because consideration needs to be given to such factors as the officer's work style and assignments. Some officers are more active in their crime control efforts, and self-initiated officer activities are more likely to arouse resentment and resistance among citizens (Reiss 1967); some officers are assigned regularly to high-risk areas, where the proportion of violence-prone offenders is higher. However, when its findings were corroborated by a variety of indicators, the commission concluded that officers who use force recurrently are a good place to start looking for officers who use excessive force. Toch also used this strategy to identify violence-prone police officers for an intervention program (Toch, Grant, and Galvin 1975).

Further support for an association between frequent use of force and use of excessive force can be found in the President's Commission's observational data in three cities as reported by Friedrich (1980). The data indicate that the rank order of cities with respect to police use of force is the same as that for excessive force. We should not make too much of this finding, however, given that observations in only three cities are involved. Still, it suggests a possible relation between the use of force generally and the use of excessive force.

From a methodological point of view, it is easier to count instances in which police use force than to count instances in which police use excessive force, especially if the counts are to be made on a regular basis. If we accurately identify all use-of-force events, all events that involve the excessive use of force necessarily have been included. If research could demonstrate that rates of force and rates of excessive force are reliably correlated, then a more convenient and readily available measure (frequent or excessive use of force) can be used as a surrogate for a less accessible measure (use of excessive force).

From a theoretical perspective, we can question whether productive explanations and significant insights can be derived from studies that focus exclusively on excessive force. Most leading police researchers emphasize the transactional nature of police-citizen encounters (Bayley 1986; Binder and Scharf 1980; Toch et al. 1975; Reiss 1967). Research in this tradition indicates that police and citizens may provoke violent reactions from one another on the basis of perceived insults and challenges. At each step of a police-citizen encounter, both parties may act in ways that contribute to a higher probability of violence. A focus on excessive force tends to emphasize the outcome of events, thereby obscuring the police officer's contribution to the transaction, especially in the initial stages of the encounter.[4] Furthermore, when an officer provokes a violent reaction from a suspect and then responds in kind, the police officer's use of force, even if not excessive, can be seen as unnecessary (see chapters 1 and 8).

Computing Rates Based on Events and Participants

The distinction between counting events and participants (and generating rates) matters because a single event may involve multiple individuals, just as a single individual may be involved in multiple events. For example, two police officers may pull over a car with five drunken teenagers and use force on three of them. The encounter can be viewed as a single use-of-force event, as three citizens subject to the use of force, or as two police officers using force. Similarly, a police officer may receive ten citizen complaints for excessive force, which could be counted as one problem police officer or as ten allegations.

In analyzing event and participant tallies, when the numerator refers to individuals we can estimate the probability that a person will experience (if counting citizens) or use (if counting police officers) excessive force within a given time period. In this form, the data permit comparisons with the rates at which other types of events are experienced by people. This information can be especially helpful in allocating resources when planning interventions. In contrast, when the numerator counts *events,* we can estimate how often excessive force events will occur. These data can be especially useful for viewing excessive force events in the context of other work activities of police (e.g., arrests).

In computing rates, the selection of a denominator also can provide information useful for different purposes. All other things being equal, as the population at risk grows larger, rates become smaller and vice versa. Rates of excessive force can be computed on the basis of the number of persons in the general population, the adult population, the arrest population, or the population of suspects against whom force of any kind is used. Rates might also be computed on the basis of the number of calls for service, police-citizen encounters, potentially violent police-citizen encounters, or arrests. In each case the population at risk is narrowed considerably, and rates become systematically higher, assuming that the number of victims or forcible events does not change dramatically.

As a general rule, the denominator should portray as accurately as possible the population of events or persons at risk. A common problem is that the most desirable measure of the at-risk population is not readily available. For example, it may be useful to compute rates on the basis of potentially violent police-citizen encounters (see chapter 8; Binder and Scharf 1980; and Scharf and Binder 1983), but police departments do not routinely collect the information needed to make this distinction accurately. In this situation, a proxy measure, such as calls for service or arrests, will be used instead. On the one hand, calls for service overcount the population at risk because some calls (e.g., assisting a sick or injured person, locating a missing person, false burglar alarms, escorting court witnesses, checking on abandoned vehicles) have a negligible potential for conflict between police and citizens. On the other hand, arrests will underestimate the population at risk given that police sometimes use force in situations where no arrest is made. In the former case (calls for service), the rate will be biased in a negative direction (low), while in the latter (arrests) the rate will be biased in a positive (high) direction.

Similar methodological difficulties can be encountered when the denominator is persons. Not all police officers have responsibilities that bring them into regular contact with citizens or with criminal suspects. Likewise, general population counts may include the very young and the very old as well as the institutionalized, groups that are at negligible risk for becoming the subjects of police violence. In such cases, it is possible to reduce counts of the at-risk population— by excluding police officers having only administrative responsibilities or by excluding certain types of calls for service, for example.

Ideally, the population of events or persons in the denominator should be narrowed to those that can be characterized as having a potential for violence. Sometimes the information can be obtained from published or unpublished sources, but in many cases the data needed to enumerate the at-risk population may not be recorded.

Several observational studies provide data that allow for a comparison of rates based on different definitions of the at-risk population (Bayley and Garofalo 1987; Reiss 1967; Fyfe 1988). The results of these studies indicate that differences in rates can be considerable. For example, Bayley and Garofalo (1989) report that a minority of police work tasks can be characterized as a "potentially violent mobilization," generously defined. According to their data, the incidence rate of police use of force based on potentially violent mobilizations is more than three times higher than a rate based on police calls for service.[5] In similar fashion, Reiss (1967) found that only a minority of citizens who have contact with the police can be described as criminal suspects. In terms of these data, an incidence rate of excessive force based on contacts with criminal suspects is almost eight times greater than a rate based on all citizens who come in contact with police.

On occasion, statistics are reported not as rates but as frequency counts. Some police department annual reports include tallies of events that bear on use-of-force issues, including citizen complaints. These frequency statistics are problematic in making between-group comparisons, between police departments or between geographic areas, as the size of the population at risk is likely to be different. The frequency counts themselves, however, may be useful in examining changes over time if the unit of observation remains the same. Thus, in comparing the number of complaints that a police department receives over time, in the short term the number of police officers, the number of potentially violent police-citizen contacts, and the number of citizens living in the area may remain constant. Over the long term, however, these assumptions become increasingly doubtful.

Comparing Prevalence Rates across Populations:
Varying Risks Associated with Subpopulations, Locations, and Time of Occurrence

Crude rates, or rates that examine the number of events in relation to a total population, can be misleading in making comparisons across police departments or groups of police officers. Such rates fail to account for important differences between the items being compared. For example, the rate at which police in St. Louis use force may be twice that of police in Salt Lake City, but the difference may be attributable to the proportion of violent offenders in the population. The general strategy for dealing with this problem is to analyze rates for specific subpopulations. This disaggregation strategy can be used to make more reasonable comparisons between cities or police departments or even individual officers. The procedure can also identify or confirm the influence of unknown or suspected risk factors.

In the computation of rates, populations often are disaggregated on the basis of such demographic characteristics as age, race, and gender. For example, studies indicate that most use-of-force events involve young suspects. Croft and Austin (1987) found that 64–72 percent of incidents in their study involved suspects between eighteen and twenty-eight years of age. Rates computed on the basis of general population totals can misrepresent the use-of-force picture, as persons in this age category typically make up less than 20 percent of the total population. The use of arrest population totals helps identify a more appropriate at-risk population, as discussed previously. However, the issue of whether the rate of conflict with police is higher for younger as compared to older *arrestees* can only be resolved by computing age-specific incidence rates based on the age distribution of the arrest population.

The available research on the question of whether the rate of excessive force is higher among minorities is far from determinative. Research conducted for the President's Commission in the 1960s indicated that white suspects experienced higher rates of excessive force (Reiss 1967). In contrast, a later Gallup (1991a) poll found that nonwhites were more likely to report that they had been physically

mistreated by police (see chapter 5). Given the ever-changing state of race relations and of police operations, one might be inclined to judge the later figures as
more representative. However, the Reiss data were based on direct observations,
whereas the Gallup data were based on unsubstantiated reports by victims, and
this difference in methodology may be a factor in the interpretation of findings. Yet
Worden's analysis (see chapter 2) of a different set of observational data than Reiss
employed lends some support to the perceptions identified in the Gallup poll.

In addition to race, the research literature suggests that low social class (Reiss
1967; Russell 1967), the presence of fellow officers (Reiss 1967; Croft and Austin
1987), alcohol use by suspect and officer (Reiss 1967; Fogel 1987), relative youth-
fulness of suspect and officer (Croft and Austin 1987; Bayley and Garofalo 1989),
and relative inexperience of police officers (Bayley and Garofalo 1987) may be risk
factors for excessive force. However, at this time the number of research studies
is so small that few conclusions can be drawn (among the efforts to derive such
conclusions is Worden's in chapter 2).

Geographic location is associated with rates of crime, and the issue is an important one, since excessive force may be extremely high in ghetto areas and extremely
low in suburban or business areas. Also, the fact that an officer has a relatively high
number of use-of-force reports may be related to the location or type of patrol assignments. Reiss (1967) found that many incidents of excessive force occurred in
patrol cars or police lock-ups, while another study for the President's Commission noted that in one police department the majority of excessive force complaints
were received from jailed suspects (President's Commission on Law Enforcement
and Administration of Justice 1967a). These observed locational differences may
be confounded, of course, by differences in population composition, and this possibility needs to be taken into account in the interpretation of such findings.

Finally, the geographic location of excessive force incidents may present measurement problems if many incidents take place in isolated or out-of-the-way
locations where use of excessive force is more likely to be unobserved or unrecorded. The problem may not be insurmountable, however, given that the use
of force surprisingly takes place in the presence of citizen observers (Bayley and
Garofalo 1989) and given that police often have an interest in documenting their
use of force when an arrest is made or an injury results. Fyfe observes (chapter 8)
that officers engaged in willful abuse of force may take steps to conceal their activity whereas officers whose abuse of force stems from ineptness may not.

Time also may operate as a risk factor for excessive force, according to crime
data showing that assaults are more likely to occur on weekends, from twilight to
early morning hours, and during the summer months (LeBeau et al. 1992). Similar
temporal patterns have been observed for use-of-force reports, and these patterns,
which can be reflected in shift assignments, may be critical in understanding individual differences among police officers in their use of force.

Observational research has been able to capitalize on ostensible risk factors for police use of force as a means of studying these relatively infrequent events more efficiently. Most observational researchers who have studied police use of force concentrate their efforts on night and weekend shifts in high-crime areas. Furthermore, observational researchers often carry out their activities during the summer months, mainly for convenience but also because the use of force is expected to be more frequent. The strategy addresses the difficulty of studying relatively infrequent events by biasing counts of excessive force upward. If these counts are used to compute event- and person-based rates, it must be recognized that the rates apply more appropriately to high-risk circumstances.

How Often Are Force and Excessive Force Used?

In this section, the empirical research on the prevalence of police use of force generally and of excessive force is reviewed. The appendix at the end of this chapter summarizes the findings of the research studies. Because the number of studies is not large, reflecting a general lack of research on police use of force, caution should be exercised in the interpretation of findings.

Use of Force

Several researchers have estimated the prevalence of police use of force without making a distinction between appropriate force and inappropriate force. These data can be used to identify upper limits for the prevalence of excessive force.

The data indicate that as many as 6 percent of arrests involve the use of force by police. The Christopher Commission estimated that 1 percent of arrests in Los Angeles involve force, a figure that is low in comparison with other research findings (Independent Commission on the Los Angeles Police Department 1991). Croft and Austin (1987) report that from 1984 to 1985 about 5 percent of arrests in Rochester and about 4 percent in Syracuse involved some use of force.[6] In terms of rates, these data indicate that there were between forty (Syracuse) and fifty (Rochester) use-of-force incidents for every thousand arrests. Observational research by Smith found that 6 percent of arrests involved the use of force (see Croft and Austin 1987: C-36). When use-of-force reports are viewed in relation to calls for service, the proportion becomes extremely small. For example, the Rochester data indicate that an officer will use force twice out of a thousand calls for service. As discussed previously, arrests represent a small portion of police activity, and officers and citizens are at higher risk for violence in arrest situations.

Observational studies typically focus on police-citizen contacts, especially on contacts that involve a potential for violence. These data suggest that as many as 10 percent of "potentially violent" police-citizen encounters involve police use of force. Friedrich (1966) found that about 5 percent of encounters with potential offenders involved force. On the basis of the same data, Reiss (1987) estimated that about 9 percent of offenders were handled with gross force. Bayley and Garofalo (1989) observed force used in about 8 percent of potentially violent citizen encounters; in another study, Fyfe (1988) observed force used in 10 percent of such encounters.

When the use of force is viewed in relation to the number of police officers, a different picture emerges. The research indicates that the rate of violent incidents for a group of officers is much higher than comparable rates based on arrests or police-citizen encounters. Early statistics suggested that more than one-quarter of police officers are involved in the use of force each year (Brooks 1965). Data by Croft and Austin (1987) indicate that force is used at a rate of between 111 and 312 incidents per 100 officers per year. These data also show that the amount of time an officer spends on the job and the number of arrests he or she makes are related to the number of times force is used.

The data confirm that an individual officer is at much greater risk for violent encounters than an individual arrestee or citizen. This occupational reality, which is recognized by officers, no doubt shapes their approach to their work. Relative comparisons, however, can obscure the fact that the average officer will use force only one to three times a year.

The observational research suggests that police use of force occurs at least twice as often as suggested by official use-of-force reports. A plausible reason for this that finds support in the research findings is that field observers count many more instances of low-level force than are recorded by police. For example, Bayley and Garofalo (1987: B-35) found that in 84 percent of forcible incidents the police officer grabbed, pushed, or restrained a citizen.[7] Furthermore, they observed only ten injuries to citizens, nine of which were caused not by police officers but by other citizens. On the basis of their observations, they concluded that "violence, more accurately, conflict during patrol encounters was very rare" and that "most of the conflict was verbal" (p. B-21).

These findings and conclusions contrast sharply with data presented by Croft and Austin (1987) showing that from one-third to one-half of police use-of-force reports involve citizen injury. The issue of definitional thresholds, then, is an important one to keep in mind. It is not just that police do not file reports when force is used, but that they fail to file reports when minor force is used. In the case of more serious violence, use-of-force reports offer a more convenient picture of prevalence than observational studies and, perhaps, a more accurate one, given that observational studies rarely compute rates by type of force or extent of injury.

In general, research indicates that the use of force by police is a relatively infrequent event. The infrequency of police force (involving about 10 percent of potentially violent encounters) raises methodological issues typically associated with the study of low-base-rate events. For such events, many observations need to be made in order to identify an adequate number of cases for analysis.

Excessive Force

Studies of excessive force have relied on three major data sources: citizen complaint records, observations of police behavior, and surveys of citizens. Data on citizen complaints are the most plentiful, probably owing to the fact that many police departments maintain records of complaints. In contrast, surveys and observational studies on the excessive use of force are few, probably due to expense and time limitations.

In a pioneering study of police misconduct, Chevigny (1969) found that citizen complaints of excessive force constituted a substantial proportion of all complaints filed. Research by Croft and Austin (1987) indicates that 5–10 percent of use-of-force incidents involve complaints about excessive use of force. These figures translate into rates of 50–100 complaints per 1,000 use-of-force incidents.

The first point to keep in mind is that not all experiences of excessive force lead to complaints, and not all complaints of excessive force are valid. There is good reason to believe that complaints undercount excessive force relative to the experiences of *citizens* or *suspects*, while there are good arguments to suggest that complaints overcount the use of excessive force relative to experiences of *complainants*. A statistic cited by Brooks (1965) indicates that approximately one citizen complaint, of any nature, is filed for every 1,000 arrests.

Some studies have expressed excessive force rates in terms of the number of officers employed by a department working specific types of assignments. A large-scale study found that, on average, ten complaints of excessive force are filed per 100 officers per year (New York City Police Department 1986). There is considerable variation in this rate, however. Croft and Austin (1987) report the annual rate of complaints for excessive force per 100 officers to be 21.3 in Rochester and 5.3 in Syracuse. As mentioned previously, legitimate factors having to do with exposure, such as number of arrests or days worked, can account in part for differences between groups. Yet, there is no doubting the fact that officers in some cities or departments are more besieged by citizen complaints relative to their peers elsewhere.

Looking at rates in terms of the experiences of citizens and all criminal suspects, observational data suggest that around 30 suspects out of 1,000 (or around 3 percent) experience excessive force, but if we were to narrow the scope to suspects against whom force is used, the rate would be considerably higher. A survey by Gallup (1991a) found that 5 percent of citizen respondents, and 9 percent of nonwhite respondents, said that they have been physically abused or mistreated by police. Winick (1987) also reported that 5 percent of respondents in a New York State survey said they had been mistreated by police in the preceding five years. However, 4 percent of his respondents said they had experienced verbal abuse, whereas only 1 percent reported physical abuse. The difference between the two studies may be attributable to the fact that Gallup's figures represent lifetime experiences and Winick's figures cover a five-year period. Or it may be that respondents in the Gallup poll did not interpret the question correctly and reported experiences that include verbal abuse.

Gallup (1991a) found that 20 percent of respondents, and 30 percent of non-white respondents, said that they knew someone who had been physically abused by police. Once again, although Winick (1987) observed a comparable figure (17 percent for all respondents), the data contained a large number of reports for verbal abuse. Both sets of findings confirm that knowledge of excessive force events or of police misconduct extends well beyond the participants. Furthermore, the fact that nearly one in three nonwhite respondents claim to know someone who has been abused by police helps explain why police often face serious public relations and collaboration problems when policing nonwhite communities.

A Comparison of Research Methodologies

In this section I compare the advantages and disadvantages of three types of research methodologies—official records, surveys and field observation—for studying issues of excessive force.

Official Records

In approaching the study of police use of force, the first research strategy to come to mind is apt to be one based on official records. An analysis of official records is relatively inexpensive and convenient in comparison with other research strategies. Furthermore, official records typically generate large numbers of observations that are particularly useful in the study of relatively infrequent events, such as uses of excessive force by police.

Although there is not yet any useful national reporting system for officers' use of force (Geller and Scott 1992),[8] it is not uncommon to find a number of agencies collecting the same or comparable information in their official records (such as data about their use of pepper spray or other nonlethal weapons). The widespread availability of these records can facilitate comparisons across police departments, cities, or regions of the country. These records can also be used to make comparisons within a given agency between police officers or patrol areas. Partly for these reasons, a 1992 U.S. Department of Justice investigation relied on federal court records in a nationwide study of excessive force (DeParle 1992), and the Christopher Commission used Los Angeles Police Department records to estimate the number of officers using excessive force.

Official records can be used for longitudinal analyses that examine changes over time within or between units of study (e.g., city, police department). These analyses can be particularly useful in studying the impact of policy changes or of larger scale social change. Finally, when several types of records are available on the same phenomenon, the records can be invoked as part of a multiple indicators research strategy.

Although there are many attractive reasons for using official records in research on excessive force, the strategy is not without limitations (see, generally, Geller and Scott 1992). Some concerns are based on practical issues of how the data are collected or on the availability or allocation of resources. Other difficulties can be addressed fully only by changing the types of information collected or by standardizing record keeping systems.

Researchers who attempt to use official records to study excessive force may sometimes find access difficult, given that the topic is a sensitive one which may embarrass the agency. However, it often is possible to work out satisfactory arrangements for access.[9] More significant, the quality of the data (e.g., accuracy, dependability, and coverage) hinges on how well the record-keeping system operates. A variety of reporting biases, as well as differences or changes in reporting methods, can influence counts dramatically. Even relatively simple errors like miscounting or misclassifying information can be a serious problem. For example, Fyfe (1988) and Geller and Scott (1992), studying tallies of civilians killed by police, have found large discrepancies between internal police agency counts and the tallies those same agencies forward to the FBI. Also, Croft and Austin (1987) report that the rate at which force was used in the Rochester police department doubled within a few years, an increase they attribute to better compliance by police in filing use-of-force reports. These problems are not necessarily catastrophic for researchers (the impact on police practitioners may be radically different, of course), provided that something can be learned about the nature and distribution of the errors.

A more significant problem is that of missing data or information that should be available in record-keeping systems but is not. Although there are various statistical techniques for dealing with problems of missing data, the procedures involve assumptions that can be questioned. At some point, however, the number of missing cases becomes so large and the number of valid cases so low that reliable statistical analyses are impossible. Problems of missing data are compounded in comparative studies because the nature and extent of missing data will vary from agency to agency.

Even when information in agency records is meticulously collected, the data may not be especially useful from a research point of view. Agencies maintain records for administrative and bureaucratic purposes and rarely have research in mind when establishing a record-keeping system. This may severely limit the conclusions that can be drawn from statistical analysis. For example, Croft and Austin (1987) found that in Rochester, where the police department maintains computerized records on the use of force, the type of force used was described in 80 percent of incidents simply as "physical restraint." For many research purposes, this classification will not be especially informative. When Croft and Austin (1987) themselves collected data on the type of force used by the Syracuse Police Department, they were able to classify incidents in more potentially useful terms based on specific acts, such as armlocking, using mace, wrestling, grabbing, striking, and choking. According to this classification scheme, only 17 percent of incidents in Syracuse involved "simple restraint" or an armlock.

Finally, researchers may encounter situations where the data that are most useful and relevant to the question at hand are simply not available in official records. The problem can be addressed by having the agency add new information items to its record-keeping systems, but in many cases this solution is not practical.

In an attempt to explore the potential uses of official records in studying police use of force, a brief survey form was mailed to thirteen police departments. The departments were not chosen randomly; rather, they were selected intentionally to include a cross-section of medium to large police departments across the country. The survey requested information on eleven areas: weapons use, use-of-force records, civil litigation, citizen complaints, citizen injuries, police injuries, resisting arrest charges, total arrests, total arrests for violent crimes, weapons charges, and number of full-time police field officers. Initially, the plan was to compute a variety of rates, using different information in the numerator and denominator, to examine whether consistent patterns emerge within and across police departments. However, when the data were received, problems of noncomparability and of missing and incomplete data were such that little meaningful analysis could be carried out on this small sample. The data confirm some of the findings of the 1993 survey on the police use of force carried out by the Police Foundation (Pate and Fridell 1993). That study also suffered from problems of noncomparability of data and other methodological difficulties (*Crime Control Digest* 1993).

Nearly all police departments can provide statistics on the use of firearms in terms of how many times and under what circumstances weapons were discharged. However, these data are limited in their research use because police rarely discharge their firearms, and in many departments accidental discharges and animal shootings account for almost all the reported firearms incidents. Likewise, nearly all police departments can furnish the number of citizen complaints, including those of excessive force, along with information on the disposition of the complaints. But there is tremendous variation in the number of excessive force complaints and, as I shall discuss later, a significant portion of this variation can be accounted for by the local operation of grievance procedures.

Perhaps the survey results are most informative in terms of the types of information that are not available. For example, only four departments, or less than one-third, could provide statistics on citizen injuries other than firearms-related injuries. More than half the departments were unable to provide any information on the number of citizen injuries. Similarly, almost half the departments could not furnish statistics on the number of times police used force, and the proportion of nonsuppliers was well over half for injuries that did not result from police use of a weapon. In contrast, nearly all departments could provide statistics on the number of times police officers were assaulted and injured. This is testament to several influences: general concern about officer safety, workers' compensation considerations, and the aggressive collection of such data by the FBI.

In view of this situation, dramatic improvements in the types of information police departments collect on the use of force are needed if we are to understand the nature and scope of the problem of police abuse of force. Many police departments are unable to describe the basic parameters of their problem, including the number of times citizens were injured by their officers. In the absence of such basic information, it is difficult to deal effectively with the problems surrounding police use of force.

I now turn to some methodological issues associated with various types of official records.

COURT RECORDS. Litigation over police use of excessive force may involve criminal charges or civil claims and can take place in state or federal forums. Researchers have relatively easy access to court records, which for the most part are maintained carefully. Detailed descriptions of events are available through transcripts, but this information tends not to be useful for research purposes because it is expensive and laborious to analyze. An advantage of court records is that the verdict provides a definite classification of police use of force as appropriate or inappropriate; however, when a case is settled out of court there may not be a specific admission of fault, confounding such classification.

The most serious limitation of court records for studying the prevalence of excessive force is that only a very small proportion of cases is litigated. Thus, the number of civil claims filed against police for excessive use of force vastly underestimates the incidence of police use or abuse of force.[10]

The Christopher Commission revealed the frequency with which claims (a prelude to filing lawsuits)[11] were filed concerning personal injury or property damage resulting from police use of force in Los Angeles: between 1986 and 1990 there were more than 2,500 such claims, an average of 500 per year. The Commission also reported that during the same period an average of almost seventeen claims per year resulted in settlements of more than $15,000 (Independent Commission on the Los Angeles Police Department 1991).

CITIZEN COMPLAINT RECORDS. Nearly all police departments have procedures by which citizens may lodge complaints against officers. In larger departments, specialized internal review units receive complaints and conduct investigations (West 1988; for discussion of different complaint systems, see chapter 11). In smaller departments, procedures tend to be more informal, with the chief or another high-ranking officer typically dealing with complaints on an ad hoc basis.

The complaint process has a major influence on the number of complaints received. To begin with, the process of filing complaints differs from that of filing court claims in important ways. Complaints are easier to file, and the screening process takes place after the charge is brought, rather than before, as in court claims. For these reasons, the number of citizen complaints is almost always greater than the number of court claims for a given police department.

Several studies in the 1960s found that the police may use various strategies to discourage citizen complaints (President's Commission on Law Enforcement and Administration of Justice 1967b). After hearings, the NAACP (1995) recorded that "many people reported that their attempts to file a complaint of misconduct are discouraged by the police departments. They may actively resist the complaint by denying it then and there, or by harassing the prospective complainant" (p. 55). One study found that 35 percent of complainants were charged with resisting arrest (Hudson 1970), while another study reports a figure of 25 percent (Wagner 1980). Police may negotiate with complainants, offering to drop the resisting arrest charges in exchange for not filing a complaint. Potential witnesses also may be charged with resisting arrest to challenge their credibility as impartial observers. Police also may warn complainants that criminal charges will be brought for filing a false report if the complaint is unsubstantiated, and they may follow through on this threat as regular practice. For example, in 1962 the Washington, D.C., Police Department brought criminal charges against 40 percent of those who complained of police misconduct (President's Commission on Law Enforcement and Administration of Justice 1967a). At times, police may require complainants to take a polygraph exam.

Some techniques that police use to discourage complaints are more subtle or less overt. Citizens may not know how to make complaints, and information on the complaint process may be difficult to come by. Moreover, citizens who file complaints may not be notified of the outcome.[12]

In view of this situation, we can expect the rate of complaints to vary considerably across cities or agencies as a function of how the complaint process operates. A recent study of the six largest police departments in the United States confirms that there is considerable variation in complaint rates. The data indicate that in 1986 the annual rate of complaints per 100 officers ranged from 5.6 in Philadelphia to 36.9 in Houston, nearly a sevenfold difference (Pate and Hamilton 1991: 144). A broader study, covering more police departments, reveals even greater variation (New York City Police Department 1986). Between 1983 and 1984, the rate of complaints for excessive force per 100 officers ranged from 0.3 in Nassau County

(Long Island), New York, to 21.3 in Chicago, more than a seventyfold difference.[13] Pate and Fridell (1993), in their recent national survey, found that complaint rates varied across types of agencies. For instance, municipal agencies collectively averaged 4.8 excessive force complaints for every 100 sworn officers, while state agencies collectively averaged 1.6 complaints per 100 officers (both, annual figures and both subject to methodological errors).

Changes in the rate of use-of-force complaints from one year to the next for the same city also showed considerable variation in the NYPD study (1986). The complaint rate increased about 40 percent in Houston and dropped about 80 percent in Gainesville, Florida, in one year. Given that the specific reasons for differences in complaint rates were not investigated, it remains to be determined how much variation can be attributed to the manner in which complaint processes operate.

It should not be surprising that when police departments make the complaint process more open and receptive to citizens, the number of complaints increases dramatically. For example, a study showed that the annual number of complaints of excessive force in New York City ranged from a low of 106 in 1956 to a high of 231 in 1962 (President's Commission on Law Enforcement and Administration of Justice 1967a; Brooks 1965). When the city's complaint reception unit moved to a more attractive building in 1965, the number of complaints doubled (Brooks 1965). Furthermore, when the complaint process was modified under threats of external review, 181 complaints were lodged in the first three months of 1966, making for an estimated annual total of more than 700 complaints (President's Commission on Law Enforcement and Administration of Justice 1967a). Ostensible improvements in complaint procedures, however, do not always increase the number of complaints. For example, when Great Britain instituted a Police Complaints Authority to oversee the disciplinary process, the rate of complaints for police excessive force dropped almost 25 percent in the first year of operation, from 2.6 to 1.9 per 100 officers.

The trend in the United States has been for police departments to make it easier for citizens to lodge administrative complaints. A survey of thirty-one large cities indicates that 77 percent of police departments receive complaints at police stations, 84 percent receive complaints by any method (e.g., phone, mail, in person), 90 percent will investigate anonymous complaints, 81 percent do not require notarized statements from complainants, and 77 percent do not prosecute for false complaints (New York City Police Department 1986). But another 1988 survey of police departments mainly in larger cities and counties revealed that only half of the departments distribute information on the complaint process and only half publish complaint statistics (West 1988). Furthermore, only two-fifths of respondents in a New York State poll were aware of the procedures for making allegations of excessive force against police (Winick 1987; see also chapter 5).

Two studies estimated the degree to which citizen complaints may undercount the prevalence of excessive force. Reiss (1967) observed thirty-seven instances of excessive force (as judged by researchers), only one of which resulted in a citizen complaint. While these numbers are far too small to serve as a foundation for generalizations, if the pattern held it would suggest that the degree of undercounting is very large—that 97 percent of excessive force incidents go unreported. Winick (1987) found that one out of three respondents who claimed to have been a victim of excessive force indicated that they filed a complaint over the incident—a 67 percent nonreporting rate.

A substantial difficulty in using complaint records to gauge the prevalence of excessive force is uncertainty concerning the proportion of claims that are legitimate. Some point out that only a small percentage of complaints are substantiated, thereby proving that instances of excessive force are rare. They suggest that offenders make complaints frivolously or with the purpose of securing an edge in the plea-bargaining process. On the other hand, it is argued that police agencies are reluctant to discipline officers and do not take seriously their responsibility for investigating citizen complaints. The NAACP (1995) reports that "the consensus of the citizens and representatives of community organizations . . . is that the internal review investigators overwhelmingly side with the police, generally concluding that the officers need proper force. Many felt the internal affairs complaint process was a waste of time" (p. 65).

An examination of the dispositions of citizen complaints provides evidence to support both arguments. The proportion of substantiated complaints is indeed low, generally not more than 10 percent, while the proportion of complaints not sustained is large, typically around 70 percent (Wagner 1980; Fogel 1987; Brooks 1965). The pattern has been observed both in the United States and abroad (Fogel 1987; chapter 14). As an extreme example, the 1967 President's Commission identified a police department where not a single allegation of excessive force had been sustained out of 121 such complaints made over five years (President's Commission on Law Enforcement and the Administration of Justice 1967a). The Pate and Fridell 1993 national survey found that of 1,911 complaints adjudicated, less than 13 percent were sustained.

Studies also show considerable variation across jurisdictions in the proportion of sustained complaints. A survey of thirty-six cities with populations of 250,000 or more reports that the percentage of substantiated complaints ranges from about 3 percent to about 67 percent, with a median of about 24 percent (Heaphy 1978). Another survey of cities in 1984 found that the percentage of substantiated complaints ranged from zero in San Antonio and Milwaukee to about 45 percent in Washington, D.C., and Kinston, North Carolina (New York City Police Department 1986). The proportion of unsubstantiated complaints (those adjudged to contain insufficient evidence for a definitive verdict) ranged from 100 percent in Milwaukee to zero in Memphis and Puerto Rico. The category "unsubstantiated" is in itself a problem. The NAACP (1995) points out that "the language suggests a rejection of the claim, not that a level of proof has not been met" (p. 61).

A difficulty in interpreting disposition statistics is that the difference between sustained and unsustained declarations often hinges on the availability of a third-party witness. Furthermore, many exonerated and unfounded rulings are based on the testimony of a fellow police officer. In situations where there is no third-party witness, it is often impossible to reach agreement on what actually transpired between the officer and citizen. It would be presumptuous to say that most of these complaints are invented by disgruntled offenders because they were apprehended by the police, nor that most of these complaints have a solid factual basis. Perhaps the best estimate of complaints that could be sustained with sufficient investigatory effort derives from a legal aid project by the New York Civil Liberties Union (Chevigny 1965). It was the experience of this project that 16 percent of all complaints, including complaints of excessive force, can be sustained, in the sense that corroborating evidence for the complaint could be found.

In Los Angeles, 38 percent of all complaints are declared "unfounded," meaning that noninvolved citizens or police witnesses contradict the story of the complainant (Independent Commission on the Los Angeles Police Department 1991). A national survey indicates that the proportion of unfounded complaints ranged from 57 percent in Nassau County, N.Y., to zero in Kinston, N.C., Puerto Rico, and Memphis. Similarly, in Great Britain almost half of the complaints against police are withdrawn by the complainant (Fogel 1987). It could be argued that "unfounded" decisions are influenced unduly by police officer witnesses who refuse to break the code of silence. The British figure may also reflect the influence of coercion by police. In any case, the data are sufficiently ambiguous that more research is needed on the operation of police complaint procedures in order to make an informed judgment on the proper interpretation of complaint statistics (see also chapter 11).

ARREST RECORDS. In studies of police excessive force, arrest records have an important use in identifying the population at risk for the computation of rates. In addition, through arrest records specific rates can be computed on the basis of offense and offender characteristics. In making comparisons across states, however, care must be taken to ensure that variations in local definitions of crimes or local arrest charging practices do not unduly influence research findings. In part, this problem can be addressed by using Uniform Crime Report data, which rely on a standardized format for the classification of arrests.

Use-of-force incidents do not necessarily involve an arrest, and not all arrest reports describe what force, if any, was used by the police; thus, arrest records tend to undercount use-of-force situations. The President's Crime Commission observational study reported that arrests were not made in about 20 percent of use-of-force situations and 40 percent of situations where the force used by police was judged by researchers as excessive (Reiss 1967; Friedrich 1980). The second finding, however, is compromised by the definition of excessive force, since the use of force without an arrest was always judged to be excessive. These findings suggest that arrest reports fail to capture a significant number of violent police-citizen conflicts.

A related issue is how arrest records can be used in combination with other official records that bear on the use of excessive force as part of a multiple indicators strategy. Croft and Austin (1987) found that 97 percent of officially recorded use-of-force incidents involved an arrest. Given a situation in which there is almost no reporting discrepancy between arrest reports and use-of-force reports, no independent information on the incidence of police-citizen violent encounters is gained by combining these two types of records, although as a practical matter one source of information might be preferred over the other when generating tallies.

Finally, charges of resisting arrest merit special attention as an indicator of police-citizen conflict. Having already noted that many citizens who file complaints against the police are charged with resisting arrest, we recall that resisting arrest charges are filed in roughly 60 to 70 percent of the incidents captured by use-of-force reports (Croft and Austin 1987). Chevigny (1969) explains such findings by arguing that resisting arrest charges are used by police to protect themselves in situations where questions may arise concerning illegitimate use of force. If Chevigny is correct, resisting arrest charges could be used as a gross indicator of excessive use of force,[14] and the overlap between resisting arrest charges and other gross indicators of excessive force, like citizen complaints and use-of-force records, could be exploited in a multiple indicators strategy.

USE-OF-FORCE REPORTS. At various junctures, use-of-force records have been discussed in relation to other official records. These records can be used to describe violent acts both by police against citizens and by citizens against police. Also, use-of-force data often provide information on the type of force used. Most police departments require a report any time deadly force is used (Geller and Scott 1992; Pate and Fridell 1993), and many large departments require a report on any incident involving the use of force. Records on assaults against police officers are maintained almost universally, and statistical summaries of this information are available from the FBI Uniform Crime Reports unit. These data should not be overlooked in pursuing a multiple indicators approach to the study of excessive force.

INJURY RECORDS. Police departments maintain records on injuries to citizens and police, even if use-of-force records are not kept. The injury records of interest are those that describe interactions between police and criminal suspects. Injury records capture a subset of use-of-force events, situations in which the amount of force used was great or in which the consequences of using force were serious. These data can be particularly useful if one is interested in studying more serious use-of-force events, or if one subscribes to the position that "not every push or shove, even if it may later seem unnecessary" should be at issue in examining the use of excessive force (*Johnson v. Glick,* 481 F.2d 1033).

Survey Methods

When investigating issues of excessive force, survey methods can be used to survey the police as well as the public, or to survey special at-risk populations, such as arrestees. Survey research holds considerable potential in studying excessive force because the collection of information is tailored to the research question and because some reporting biases of official records are avoided. As with official records, survey data can be used to estimate the rate of excessive force and to identify risk factors for police and citizens. Also, survey methods are much more convenient for generating lifetime prevalence rates.

Survey research methods typically involve the use of interviews (either face-to-face or by telephone) or questionnaires administered by mail or in person. The advantages and disadvantages of various survey methods have been discussed extensively in the research literature, so only a brief overview of issues will be presented here.

Among the problems encountered in survey research are the following: interpretation (words may have multiple meanings or be ambiguous), veracity (people may not tell the truth), noncooperation (people may refuse to answer), social desirability (people may give answers they expect others want), recall (forgetting events, forgetting details of events, or getting details confused across multiple situations), and telescoping (bringing past events forward in time into the reference period of the question).

Interview techniques that involve face-to-face contact between the interviewer and respondent can be expensive and time-consuming, but they allow for complex question formats (e.g., skip patterns). Also, the interviewer is available to clarify ambiguous questions and has an opportunity to gain the trust of the respondent by explaining the nature and purpose of the research project. However, interview effects, where the characteristics of the interviewer (e.g., age, race, gender, demeanor) bias the interviewee's response, become an issue.

Telephones offer quick and convenient access to households spread across large geographic areas. However, the homeless and many low-income households are excluded by this method. Since evidence suggests that persons of lower social standing as well as drunks and vagrants are more likely to be victims of police misbehavior, telephone survey methods will tend to undercount the incidence of excessive force. Questionnaires sent by mail probably are also not practical for studying excessive police force, given the likelihood of low response rates and the related problem of selection bias.

In using survey methods to study police excessive force, there may be a need to address the problem of a low base rate in the sampling procedures. The base rate problem is perhaps not as acute in sampling police officers (an easily defined and easily accessible population) as it is in sampling civilian populations. Various sampling strategies could be used to overcome the base rate problem, including limiting study to high-risk populations (e.g., arrestees), or stratifying the sample in order to oversample high-risk populations (e.g., certain geographic areas). There also is the possibility of using network sampling techniques in which respondents are asked to identify other subjects who fit the criteria for inclusion in the study (Czaja and Blair 1990).

SURVEYS OF POLICE. Two basic types of questionnaire or survey instruments can be used with police officers: self-report instruments and peer nomination or evaluation techniques.

Research using self-report instruments that ask respondents to describe their criminal and delinquent behavior have been used widely in criminology. The widespread use of these methods to study law-violating behavior suggests that they also might be used to study police use of excessive force.

Among the most obvious problems in using self-report methods to study deviant behavior are noncooperation, veracity, and social desirability. Though early criminologists who used self-report methods were surprised at the willingness of people to admit to criminal behavior, it could be argued that police officers will be more sensitive than offenders to the consequences of their admissions.

The wording of questions can be problematic in survey research and is likely to be a serious issue in self-report studies of police. It would be absurd to ask a police officer whether he or she ever beat up a criminal suspect for the fun of it. Self-report items will have to be worded more diplomatically. One possible strategy would be to inquire about observations made of other police officers. For example, one might ask a police officer whether he or she has ever seen another officer use force that he or she thought was unnecessary. Likewise, one could ask officers about the number of encounters in which a suspect or citizen voiced complaints over the unnecessary use of force. Depending on the nature of the question, it may be possible to check official records to validate the self-report information. Also, in view of the sensitive nature of the questions asked, it may be desirable to use randomized response techniques to encourage honest answers and to protect the identity of respondents.

In its ambitious statewide survey of 1,200 sworn police officers (mostly rank-and-file), the Illinois Criminal Justice Information Authority inquired about the respondents' career experience with excessive force. Illustrative questions included:

- Have you personally observed a police officer who used considerably more force than necessary to apprehend a suspect (a) in the past 12 months? (b) anytime during your career?
- Have you personally observed a police officer fail to report an incident of excessive force by a fellow officer (a) in the past 12 months? (b) anytime during your career?
- Have you personally observed a police officer cover up an incident of excessive force by a fellow officer (a) in the past 12 months? (b) anytime during your career? (Geller 1994)

Finally, rather than asking about behaviors, one might attempt to gauge attitudes, values, opinions, and judgments that may be related to the use of excessive force. The Christopher Commission did just this and was surprised to find that 30 percent of officers surveyed agreed that "the use of excessive force is a serious problem facing the Department" (Independent Commission on the Los Angeles Police Department 1991: 34). A much smaller, but not inconsequential, percentage agreed that "an officer is justified in administering physical punishment to a suspect who has committed a heinous crime" (4.9 percent) or "to a suspect with a bad or uncooperative attitude" (4.6 percent). Lester (chapter 9) observes that after behaviors have changed—such as in racial integration in housing, the workplace, or schools—attitudes are likely to change as well. By contrast, changing attitudes as a tactic for changing behavior is less likely to succeed. Lester suggests that studying shifts in officer attitudes toward use and abuse of force might serve as a barometer of changes in the prevalence of officer use-of-force behaviors.

If survey strategies, especially self-report strategies, are used to make multiple assessments over time and if the information is used in ways that bring negative repercussions, respondents may alter their reporting behavior, and a change in reporting behavior might be interpreted as a drop in prevalence. Perhaps the best use of these techniques would be in small-scale methodological studies aimed at clarifying reporting and other changes in more readily available official records.

Police officers use a variety of techniques to justify as "normal" force that the public (or some segments of the public) might consider excessive (Hunt 1985). However, most police officers recognize when their fellow officers exceed the bounds of occupationally defined propriety. These judgments are made with reference to peer-group norms, not legal or administrative norms; officers will be viewed as brutal if they consistently use force that exceeds what police define as "normal" (Hunt 1985). As Jessie Brewer, a retired assistant chief in the Los Angeles Police Department, told the Christopher Commission, "Reputations become well known. . . . We know the ones who are getting into trouble more than anyone else" (Independent Commission on the Los Angeles Police Department 1991: 32).

Research indicates that police officers are also relatively good judges of a fellow officer's quality performance. Bayley and Garofalo (1989) asked a group of officers to identify peers who are especially skilled at managing incidents involving conflict. They found that not only are officers willing to make such judgments, but that there are observable differences in the work-related behaviors of officers identified as particularly skilled. Bayley and Garofalo's data indicate that judgments were not made on the basis of age, street experience, race, or gender, and that evaluations made by officers were consistent with departmental evaluations by supervisors. They concluded that "police rank and file respect colleagues who exhibit behavior police departments want to encourage. . . . It respects qualities that the public respects and would intuitively associate with the ability to minimize violence " (p. 17; see also chapter 10). Another study by Love (1981: 147) used techniques of peer nomination, ranking, and rating in relation to nine performance dimensions of work. The researcher concluded that officers "provide accurate and consistent performance information" and that "friendship among officers does not bias the accuracy of evaluations."

The Oakland and Kansas City Police Departments experimented with a peer review panel as a method for dealing with officer misconduct (Broadaway 1974; Toch and Grant 1991: 286). The panel accepted self-referrals and referrals by other officers. It also reviewed the files of officers who accumulated a designated number of citizen complaints, arrests involving charges of interfering with an officer, firearms discharges, and assaults on an officer. Many referrals came from fellow officers, suggesting that under the right conditions police will identify fellow officers who are viewed as potential problems.

CITIZEN SURVEYS. Just as police can be surveyed, citizens may be asked about their experiences with police officers who use force. In surveys, the focus is on direct involvement and observations in order to gauge the prevalence of excessive force, as well as on opinions and attitudes in order to better understand the public's perception of the problem. Questions concerning police use of force could be incorporated into ongoing national victimization surveys at modest expense. More limited surveys, such as those covering specific cities, areas of cities, or even high-risk populations, could be conducted in response to local concerns over police violence. Victimization surveys concerning police abuse of force could be compared to actual reports, as is done with studies of the prevalence of crime generally, to determine the rate at which the public reports police mistreatment to authorities. Or, as in some public opinion polls, respondents could be asked about their reporting practices or inclinations. If a valid reporting or nonreporting rate for publicly observed or experienced police abuse of force could be determined, it might support cautious estimates of the prevalence of actual police abuse based on the number of reported abuses.

Potential problems of question wording and recall error should not be underrated in polls on police use of force. Winick (1987) found that 7 percent of those who claim to have witnessed or experienced excessive force state that deadly force was involved, a figure that is extremely high in relation to records of police shootings (Geller and Scott 1992). When these persons were re-interviewed and asked to provide more details, it was found that, while the display of firearms was involved, none of the incidents involved a shooting or police misuse of a weapon. Winick (1987) concluded that the highly charged nature of police-citizen conflict had led to recall distortion and telescoping of events. However, since the survey did not define deadly force, it may be that respondents provided their own commonsense definition of the term that included broad potential for fatal injury.

Finally, prevalence estimates can focus on recent or distant past events. The Illinois Criminal Justice Information Authority used a straightforward model for capturing both recent and lifetime experiences in its survey of police officers; the researchers asked about observations during the past twelve months and during the respondents' careers.

Field Research

Field research has a number of strengths. It provides detailed behavioral data that are not available through any other manner. It also is an excellent way to study sequences of events or interpersonal transactions. For example, Sykes and Brent (1980) were able to transcribe the verbal encounters between police officers and suspects and then analyze these data with sophisticated statistical techniques. In this regard, field research excels at capturing the nuances of behavior that often go unrecorded in other methods. While it may be possible to conduct similar analyses using interview techniques or official records, interviews often do not provide a sufficient number of cases for statistical analysis, and official records usually do not contain sufficiently detailed information.

In studying violence between police and citizens, official records may bias descriptions in favor of the police officer's viewpoint, while interviews or surveys of citizens may contain information biased toward the aggrieved citizen's point of view. Observational research incorporates the perspective of a third, hopefully impartial party—the researcher. Field observations, however, must be reliable and valid, requirements that present no small problem when deploying a research team throughout a city. Among others, the work by Reiss (1967) and by Bayley and Garofalo (1989) demonstrates that it is possible to systematize field observations in order to meet scientific standards for data collection. Worden (in chapter 2) presents newly analyzed data from the Police Services Study, another historically important field study.

A limitation of field research is that it is not an economical method for studying the excessive use of force because police spend a lot of time doing things that have negligible potential for the use of force. The President's Crime Commission study deployed thirty-six field observers for seven weeks to watch about 600 police officers. At the end of this effort, the researchers had observed a total of 5,360 police mobilizations, only thirty-seven of which involved the improper use of force. Similarly, Bayley and Garofalo (1989) used six field observers to follow sixty-two police officers for several weeks and identified only thirty-seven incidents in which police used force against a citizen. They concluded that "an enormous number of routine patrol shifts would have to be observed to accumulate a respectable number of use-of-force cases for thorough analysis" (Bayley and Garofalo 1989: 11).

In addition, observational studies tend to be restricted in both scope and scale and are not especially practical in making comparisons across geographic areas (compare chapter 2). Furthermore, observational methods are not especially practical if there is an interest in studying individual police officers. In the President's Crime Commission field study, only two police officers were observed to use improper force more than once (Reiss 1967). We have also mentioned that observational strategies tend to concentrate on high-risk precincts, high-risk times of day, and high-risk seasons of the year when studying police use of force. These selection strategies create an upward bias in the computation of general event- and person-based rates.

Another issue for field research is that the presence of researchers may change the behavior of the police officers being observed. However, field researchers report that, in fact, nearly all police officers go about their business in seemingly normal fashion, especially after they have had some time to become accustomed to the presence of the observer. Researchers who have used observational methods conclude, moreover, that it is very hard for an officer to change his or her behavior, especially if quick and decisive action must be taken and if habits are ingrained to the point of being reflexive.

The fact that police officers will violate rules or even break the law in front of field observers is often taken as proof that the presence of a researcher has no real effect on the officer's behavior. However, it is difficult to know how a researcher's presence influences a police officer's behavior in terms of actions *not* taken. Presumably, observational strategies exhibit a negative bias that leads to an undercounting of events. Such strategies as having the researcher remain as unobtrusive as possible and spend a fair amount of time in the presence of the subject can help to minimize the bias, but probably will not eliminate it entirely. The magnitude of the undercounting effect is an issue that future research may have to address.

Given the value of field observations, one could also consider modified uses, which could include:

- Combining tallies of use of force by observers with inventories of other police behavior, such as positive contacts with civilians or stops of suspects in public places; community problem-solving efforts that are likely to engage police with suspects; and other proactive enforcement and peacekeeping activities.[15]

- Using participants as observers. In police self-study, for example, officers could collect data as part of a project in which they are engaged.
- Targeting observations, so as to study the behavior of specific officers or specific situations.[16] One could also devise a study of police responses to individuals or groups of people who in the past have been—or believe they have been—overrepresented in police use-of-force encounters. Such an approach would build on the learning (from studies of crime patterns) that there are high-rate offenders, high-rate locations, and high-rate victims— what some have termed "ravenous wolves," "dens of iniquity," and "sitting ducks," respectively (Bieck et al. 1991: 78–79; Spelman and Eck 1989).

Field observation can also be combined with videotaping, which becomes cost-effective when a camera is controlled or invoked by the observer or the subject of observation (e.g., squad car-mounted audio-video recorders).

The National Reporting System

The Violent Crime Control and Law Enforcement Act of 1994 directs the Attorney General to "acquire data about the use of excessive force by law enforcement officers" and, further, to "publish an annual summary of the data" (Violent Crime Control and Law Enforcement Act of 1994, Title XXI, Subtitle D, Sec. 210402). This legislation stands as the most ambitious initiative by the federal government to gauge the extent of police abuse of force, given the limitations of previous efforts along this line—in particular, the 1992 national survey of federal civil rights complaints and the 1993 nationwide survey of police complaint systems.

How might the Attorney General best carry out the mandate to compile annual data on the excessive use of force by law enforcement officers? In keeping with themes developed in this chapter, data collection could focus on the more general issue of police-citizen violence and could use multiple indicators, each describing a different facet of the problem. It would seem prudent to approach the task in two stages. In the short run, statistics could be compiled on a limited number of police departments using existing data sources. In the longer term, serious consideration could be given to the collection of data that would provide a more complete picture by covering a greater number of police agencies and by providing information that is currently not available. A two-step approach of this sort could address the urgent need for information on police abuse of force while providing sufficient time for the planning, testing, and implementing of new data-collection strategies.

In the near term, it is a manageable task to compile, for example, annual statistics on the fifty largest police departments in the United States, making use of existing records. Citizen complaint records can be used to count alleged instances of excessive force. *Indirect* measures of abuse of force include tallies of charges filed for resisting arrest and assaulting a police officer. Such charges may also provide a general indication of the level of violent conflict between police and citizens. In assembling these statistics, however, all arrests involving such charges should be tallied—not just arrests in which these are the most serious charges, as is the common practice. Finally, some police departments keep use-of-force records, and these could also be included in the survey.

This short-run strategy would, of course, have its limitations. It would suffer from problems of interpretation and comprehensiveness similar to those of previous survey efforts, particularly to the extent that the same data sources and information items are used. Police complaint records, for example, suffer from a variety of shortcomings that are discussed in this chapter, although they enjoy the virtue of being a widely available indicator of excessive force.

Short-run efforts also could contribute to the development of an improved methodology for gauging prevalence by tapping records that have not yet been used in research. For example, when citizens in police custody are in need of medical attention, some record of treatment will be made, if only for the purpose of preventing lawsuits. Given that records on the delivery of medical treatment pursuant to an arrest exist in almost all police departments, the challenge is to gain access to and analyze this information in a way that will illuminate issues of the excessive use of force.

In many jurisdictions, records on serious injuries incurred during arrest are maintained by three or four organizations—the city police department, the central jail, the county hospital, and possibly the country comptroller's office—thereby providing different points at which statistics can be generated. This arrangement not only offers multiple opportunities for data collection but also allows for cross-checking the reliability of information from a given source. A potential problem with accessing these records is that they may not be computerized. It may be possible to tally the records manually, however, depending on their number. Some portions of police offense reports and hospital and jail records probably are in computerized systems, so that generating statistics on citizen injuries could be a matter of entering additional information into the automated systems. Regardless of the strategy for accessing these records, it is important to be able to identify instances in which injuries are inflicted on a citizen by a police officer as part of an *arrest*, as police officers become involved in—and generate records about—many situations in which a person's need for medical treatment is not the result of *police* use of force.

While a short-term data collection strategy is deployed to comply with the Attorney General's obligations under the 1994 statute, a long-range plan should be designed to improve the completeness and quality of existing data sources. Serious consideration should be given to a variety of new data collection efforts, which could be carried out by local police agencies and sheriff's departments, by federal agencies, and by independent researchers. In the long run, it should be possible to generate annual compilations on police use of excessive force that are at least as good as the reports on police officers killed and assaulted that are now generated as part of the Uniform Crime Reporting system. To improve on the quality represented by these yearly UCR reports, one would need to conduct multivariate analyses of officer use of force so as to place the data on prevalence in the context of relevant demographic characteristics and pertinent information about police and citizen activity.

Conclusions

A number of methodological issues are involved in studying the prevalence of police use of excessive force. The definition of excessive force is problematic, and it is important to ensure that researchers, research subjects, and consumers of research understand clearly what is being studied. The situation also requires researchers to be forthcoming about the limitations of their studies, and, in considering the implications of their findings, to explore conscientiously all plausible explanations. Problems of definition also hold consequences for the audiences at which research findings are directed. It is unlikely that in studying the prevalence of excessive force a single numerical count will emerge as beyond challenge. (For example, there was public disagreement between ostensible collaborators on the Police Foundation–International Association of Chiefs of Police study of police abuse of force, as reported in *Crime Control Digest* 1993). Consumers of research findings need to understand and scrutinize the process by which statistics are generated.

With regard to the actual prevalence of excessive force, two conclusions seem evident. First, assessments of the magnitude of the problem depend on the type of data collected (official records, surveys, field observations) and on how rates are computed. Second, regardless of how prevalence is measured, the use of force by police, whether excessive or not, is, from a statistician's point of view, an infrequent event. From a police department's or community's point of view, however, one cataclysmic abuse of force can preempt addressing other crucial problems.

Official records always involve the presence of gatekeepers or intermediaries who decide that a given event qualifies for recording, and official data consistently show the lowest prevalence figures for use of excessive force. When the reporting intermediary is bypassed, as in survey or field methods, the prevalence figures are higher. However, the results of survey research are influenced by the behavior of respondents: citizens, suspects, or police officers must interpret survey questions properly, recall events accurately, and answer candidly. By comparison, the results of field observations are influenced by the behavior and judgments of researchers, though the criteria for judgments are explicit and more consistently applied. One may not agree with a researcher's criteria and judgments, but at least one is more certain as to what one is disagreeing with.

The number of research studies on excessive force is few, although their findings about prevalence are consistent. When the average citizen calls the police with a problem, the chances that force will be used by the police are minuscule. Most calls for service involve situations that have only the remotest potential for violence. Furthermore, even among situations having more than a trivial potential for violence, the probability that police will resort to force is low. When the focus of concern shifts from police-citizen encounters to the police officers themselves, however, the probability that an officer will use force during his or her career is considerable, and some officers will accumulate a fair amount of experience with the use of force. Finally, once the decision to use force is made by an officer, there is an appreciable chance that the force will be viewed as excessive and that the citizen or suspect will file a complaint.

The fact that there are so few studies on police use of force, and even fewer on excessive force, argues for a concerted effort to describe and understand the problem. At minimum, this research will have to deal with low base-rate problems through sampling procedures. For example, surveys of high-risk populations, such as arrestees or persons living in certain geographic areas, should be carried out on a regular basis. This information would provide an estimate of the prevalence of police-citizen conflict and help us to understand the detection and reporting biases in official data. Also, modest field studies designed to illuminate how police-citizen conflicts become part of the official record could be carried out, again with the purpose of understanding how official records are generated.

In the long term, official records probably hold the most potential for studying problems of excessive force because researchers could get to a point (with sufficient support from within the ranks of police and from political leadership) where these records are widely compiled on a routine basis. At present, there are manifold difficulties in using records for research purposes, and a better understanding is needed of how various records relate to each other in both statistical and substantive ways. This line of research could be implemented relatively quickly. If official records, either singly or as a group, can be shown to be reliable and valid indicators of excessive force, the payoff would be considerable for both social science and public policy.

I have suggested that a multiple-indicators strategy in conjunction with a broadening of research perspective to include all violent events, not just excessive-force events, is the best way to proceed with research that seeks to tap the potential of official records. Even though a multiple-indicators strategy may not yield precise numerical measures of excessive force incidents, useful relative comparisons, such as between cities, police departments, or individuals, may be quite feasible. For example, it is possible to identify cities where all types of force are used regularly, where complaints by citizens about abuses of police power are many, where lawsuits alleging excessive use of force are commonplace, and where serious injuries to police and citizens are numerous. In such cities, the probability that a serious problem of excessive force exists is relatively high.

There are steps that police administrators can take in the short run that will help to improve our understanding of the extent to which police use and abuse force. Many police departments do not routinely collect statistics on citizen injuries or on the circumstances of police-citizen violence. Every police agency should be able to say how many citizens were hurt or injured in conflicts with police and how badly they were hurt,[17] and police officers should have to report to their supervisors each time they have used force against a citizen. Such reporting systems exist in most departments of corrections, where officers are required to detail both major and minor uses of force. The operation of these reporting systems has not proved unreasonably cumbersome, given the relative infrequency with which force is used, and significant advantages in defending lawsuits have resulted.

In the absence of local initiatives along these lines, the field will await the implementation of the national reporting system required under the Violent Crime Control and Law Enforcement Act of 1994. Compliance with the reporting obligations set by the new program could be ensured by linking the provision of needed data in some fashion to federal support (Geller and Scott 1992: 44–49). Another option, which could be pursued in parallel with a national, government-sponsored reporting program, is to include requirements for citizen injury and police use-of-force records among national accreditation criteria. To the extent that police are not required to report violent encounters with citizens or can successfully ignore such requirements, other counting strategies, including survey research, will have to be used on a regular basis if we are to understand the parameters of the police violence problem.

Finally, police administrators can improve complaint procedures to encourage more citizens who feel that they have been treated roughly or hurt unnecessarily to come forward with their stories. Although better complaint mechanisms may contribute in only minor ways to a fuller understanding of the use of force picture, basic notions of accountability in a democratic government require that citizens be given full access to grievance mechanisms. Then, after improvements have been made in the amount and types of information on the use of force, administrators will be in a position to use this information to take action. Our resolve to deal with police violence must start with a willingness to describe the problem in its various aspects, for it is difficult to change what is unknown.

Appendix: Summary of Research Findings on Police Use of Force (Chronological by Data Peric

Author	Year(s) Studied	Place	Method	Unit of Observation
Brooks	1964	Detroit	Official records	Police-citizen altercations
Brooks	1964	New York City	Official records	Citizen complaints
Friedrich	Summer 1966 (7 weeks)	Boston, Chicago, Washington, D.C.	Observation	Police contact with potential offenders
Reiss	1966	Boston, Chicago, Washington, D.C.	Observation	Police contact with potential offenders
				Police-citizen encounters
Chevigny	1966–1967 (16 mos.)	New York City	Official records	Citizen complaints
Cruse and Rubin	1976–1977 (6 mos.—summer)	Miami	Observation	Police-citizen encounters
				Violent police-citizen encounters

Total Number	Use of Force			Comments
	Number	Rate	Percentage	
			27% of police officers	
231 complaints		1.1 per 1,000 arrests		
1,600 encounters		31.6 per 1,000 suspects	5.1% encounters used force	26 observers watching 600 police officers
			1.8% encounters used excessive force	
1,394 suspects		41.9 per 1,000 white suspects	9% offenders handled with gross force	
		22.6 per 1,000 Black suspects		
3,826 encounters		9.7 per 1,000 encounters	42% offenders treated with firm handling	
10,564 citizens		4.2 excessive force incidents per 1,000		
		5.9 for whites 2.8 for blacks		
441 complaints	164 assaults			17 assaults authenticated by corroborating evidence
1,059 encounters			4% moderate or high threatening behavior	Observed 12 patrol officers
			13% any physical contact considered as aggressive (nonfriendly)	

Appendix (*continued*)

Author	Year(s) Studied	Place	Method	Unit of Observation
Smith (personal communication to Croft)	1977	24 cities	Observation	Arrests
New York City Police Department	1983, 1984	26 police agencies	Official records	Citizen complaints
Croft and Austin	1984–1985	Rochester, N.Y. (R) Syracuse, N.Y. (S)	Official records	Use-of-force reports

Total Number	Use of Force			Comments
	Number	Rate	Percentage	
			6% of arrests	
',507 use of force :omplaints (1983)		10.2 use-of-force complaints per 100 officers		
',621 use of force :omplaints (1984)		10.3 use-of-force complaints per 100 officers		
,248 incidents R)		40.3 incidents per 1,000 arrests (R)		4% of arrests (R)
i14 incidents (S)		50.6 incidents per 1,000 arrests (S)		5% of arrests (S)
!,516 officer nvolvements (R)		0.94 incidents per 1,000 calls for service (R)	0.19% of calls for service (R)	
!,156 officer nvolvements (S)		0.94 incidents per 1,000 calls for service (S)	0.19% of calls for service (S)	
		0.6 incidents per 1,000 officer patrol days (24 hr) worked per year (R)		
		0.5 incidents per 1,000 officer patrol days (24 hr) worked per year (S)		
		312 incidents per 100 officers per year (R)		
		111 incidents per 100 officers per year (S)		

Appendix (*continued*)

Author	Year(s) Studied	Place	Method	Unit of Observation
Croft and Austin (con't)				Citizen complaints
				Citizen complaints
Bayley and Garafolo	Summer 1986	New York City	Observation	Potentially violent encounters
Christopher Commission	January 1986 to December 1990	Los Angeles	Official records	Citizen complaints
Christopher Commission	January 1987 to March 1990	Los Angeles	Official records	Use of force reports

Total Number	Use of Force			Comments
	Number	Rate	Percentage	
121 complaints use of force (R)		48.5 per 1,000 use-of-force incidents per year (R)	9.7% of all use-of-force incidents (R)	
27 complaints use of force (S)		26.3 per 1,000 use-of-force incidents per year (S)	5.2% of all use-of-force incidents (S)	
		21.1 per 100 officers per year (R)		
		5.3 per 100 officers per year (S)		
		24.0 per 1,000 officer force involvements per year (R)	4.8% of all involvements (R)	
		18.0 per 1,000 officer force involvements per year (S)	3.8% of all involvements (S)	
467 encounters	37 use-of-force encounters		Force used by police in 7.9% of encounters	Force almost exclusively grabbing, restraining
8,274	2,167 (est.) excessive force	6.4 to 7.8 (est.) excessive force per 100 officers per year	24.7% excessive force	2% excessive force sustained; 4.8% improper practice sustained
	3,367 (est.) excessive force and improper tactics	10.2 to 12.1 (est.) excessive force and improper tactics per 100 officers per year	39.2% excessive force and improper tactics	
			1% of arrests (est.)	

Appendix (*continued*)

Author	Year(s) Studied	Place	Method	Unit of Observation
Winick	1987	New York State	Telephone survey	Households in 7 counties with major urban areas
Fyfe	1988	Dade County, Florida	Observation	Potentially violent encounters
Gallup	1991	United States	Telephone survey	Households

Total Number	Use of Force			Comments
	Number	Rate	Percentage	
1,000 households			5% of household members victims of police misuse of force in last 5 years	Sampling error is ± 3% 4% verbal 1% physical
			17% of household members witnessed police misuse of force in last 5 years	
1,383 encounters			Force used by police in 9.8% of encounters	Does not include display of weapon
			5% of respondents ever physically mistreated or abused	9% of nonwhites 5% of whites
			20% of respondents knew someone physically mistreated or abused	30% nonwhites 26% in big cities

1. Defining excessive force in a way that makes a contribution to understanding and controlling it is not a simple matter; see additional efforts to fashion useful definitions in chapters 1, 6, and 8.

2. Chapters 1, 8, and 13 discuss pertinent court cases.

3. These officers received a large number of citizen complaints that did not necessarily involve use of force issues, suggesting the possibility that officers who are physically aggressive are associated with a wide variety of problems.

4. A similar argument can be made for studying events in which force could have been used but was avoided. This facilitates studying officers' contribution to averting violence (see Geller 1985a).

5. Calls for service were defined in terms of self-initiated field encounters, radio dispatched calls, and citizen-initiated field encounters.

6. In an earlier study, Croft (1985) found that an average of 2 percent of arrests in Rochester involved force. The researcher attributes the increase in the later study to better compliance by officers with use-of-force reporting practices. Thus, the Rochester data do not indicate a doubling of violent incidents, and I discuss the more recent figures as they can be presumed to be more reliable and representative.

7. Missing cases were excluded from the computation of statistics.

8. The 1994 Federal Crime Bill contains a provision for the establishment of a national reporting system. It is discussed below in this chapter and in chapter 15.

9. It is worth considering, as more data are accumulated in the years ahead, whether the most open police departments (those which most readily furnish force- and abuse-of-force data to researchers) will appear to have more of a problem with force than agencies which are less willing to disclose data voluntarily. Such a phenomenon would present what Bayley (chapter 14) terms "the paradox of openness."

10. This does not mean that civil litigation goes unnoticed by police agencies, the lawyers who defend and advise them, or the elected officials who influence them. On civil litigation generally, see chapter 13.

11. A 1992 study by the Department of Justice illustrates some of the limitations of using lawsuits and related legal records to study police violence. The study examined "the number of police brutality complaints received by the Justice Department" over a six-year period (DeParle 1992: A1). These complaints may serve as preludes to lawsuits brought by the Justice Department for civil rights violations (see chapter 13). On releasing the results of the survey, the Justice Department said that it "was unable to draw any conclusions about when, where or why police officers engage in police misconduct" (DeParle 1992: A1). The shortcomings of this study are many: it did not include complaints brought to local prosecutors, police departments, or review boards; the results were reported as raw frequencies of complaints, which does not take into account differences in risk factors such as the size of the police department or the number of arrests; important information regarding police training and use of force policies, along with important characteristics of the complainants (such as their race and extent of alleged harm), were not included. The study found that the highest ranked city in the nation had an average of 35 complaints per year (that found their way to the U.S. Justice Department). In view of this low figure, a single aggressive lawyer could easily double the number of complaints sent to the Justice Department concerning any police department in the country.

More important, the study highlights our lack of knowledge regarding the prevalence of police violence, and it argues for increasing the accountability of police departments via better and more standardized information collection and reporting.

12. See chapter 12 on the contribution that keeping citizens informed can make to

achieving a sense of "procedural justice" for complainants. For additional discussion of the obstacles citizens face to complaining about police use of force, see Independent Commission on the LAPD (1991) and chapter 4.

13. Although the survey included thirty-six large cities or agencies, these comparisons are based on twenty-six cities for which complete data were available.

14. Reiss (1967) argues that resisting arrest is not used as a cover charge and can best be understood as occurring in situations where an officer's authority is threatened.

15. Observations can also be used to cross-validate arrest reports, to provide case material for training purposes, and to assess the effectiveness of training.

16. Sometimes for better and sometimes for worse, in many departments such officers are still in active operational assignments despite their record of frequently using force and being named in civilian complaints (Nelson 1995a-f; McElroy et al. 1993: 121–22; Independent Commission on the LAPD 1991; Kolts 1992).

17. Bayley (chapter 14) reports that police in Victoria, Australia, are experimenting with a twelve-point scale for documenting the degree of harm produced.

CHAPTER FOUR

The Violence-Prone Police Officer

HANS TOCH

T he focus of this chapter is the individual violence-prone police officer. I shall start by reviewing what the Christopher Commission (Independent Commission on the Los Angeles Police Department 1991) had to say about candidates for this designation. I shall then turn to other sources of information about individual officers who are disproportionately involved in conflicts with citizens.

The Christopher Commission's report contains a targeted study: data sources, including self-reported uses of force, citizen complaints that allege improper use of force, and litigation that charges misuse of force, are invoked to pinpoint a group of "problem" officers. The categorization rests on the fact that the officers had been overrepresented in statistics detailing their use of force (or citizen perceptions of their use of force) in the past.

The key fact is that of dramatic overrepresentation. For example, "the Commission staff identified from the LAPD database the 44 officers with six or more allegations of excessive use of force or improper tactics for the period 1986 through 1990" (p. 39). The typical number of allegations (lodged against two out of three Los Angeles officers) was zero. Combinations of such indices make inferences more reliable, in the same sense in which more smoke makes an observer more legitimately concerned about a fire. If more data are available one can also spread a greater net in nominating candidates.

The strongest case can presumably be made if we combine multiple index behaviors and find extreme overrepresentation. The forty-four officers referred to, for example, "received an average of 7.6 allegations of excessive force or improper tactics compared to 0.6 for all officers reported to be using force; the top 44 received an average of 6.5 personnel complaint allegations of all other types, compared to an average of 1.9 for all officers reported to be using force; and the top

44 were involved in an average of 13 uses of force compared to 4.2 for all officers reported to be using force" (p. 40).

It is important, of course, to exclude the possibility that the officers have done what they have done for reasons that are not related to a propensity to generate problems. The most obvious variable that could produce a spurious high-incidence-of-force officer (that is, one whose frequent use of force may not be problematic) is his or her assignment. Some officers may face a profusion of situations requiring the lawful exercise of force. These situations may result from locally high rates of crime, or from a proliferation of suspects who assault police officers or physically resist legitimate arrests. An officer may also be highly productive and may initiate a larger-than-usual amount of enforcement activity. He may disrupt the felonious plans of many disgruntled (and complaint-prone) offenders.

The authors of the Los Angeles report consider such exonerating arguments and note that there are data available to counter them. They write: "Misconduct is not established merely by the fact that an officer has many use of force reports, repeated personnel complaints, or even several shootings. It may be argued that active officers assigned to high-crime areas or specialized duties will appropriately use force more often, and may generate more complaints against them, than the 'average' officer. Yet, there are many 'productive' officers in high-crime areas who do not accumulate complaints, shootings, and use of force reports in relatively large numbers. The extreme concentration of these data cannot be explained solely by officer assignments or arrest rates" (p. 38).

One can try to exclude extraneous variables by showing that they are just as prominent in the lives of officers who do not have recurrent problems. This need not mean that inhospitable circumstances have nothing to do with problem chronicity or are irrelevant to the use of excessive force. Given the same volatile situation (say, recalcitrant suspects), the force deployed may be more substantial or more indefensible among officers who have a low boiling point or a penchant for engendering or escalating conflict than for officers who show greater equanimity or have better social skills. The situations may be catalytic for anyone, but more so for officers who respond to them with unseemly enthusiasm or lack of grace. High crime rates combined with promiscuous proactivity can lead to higher incident rates than those that would result from more judicious exercises of discretion, given high rates of crime.

The main assumption I make to start with is that officers who are involved in difficulties more frequently than one would expect, based on the involvements of other (equivalent) officers, contribute to the difference between expected and observed frequencies. Something in the officers' approach to their work would seem to make a difference. Such officers would be said to manifest a *propensity* to use force, and one could predict that they would continue to manifest this propensity, given invariant conditions.

As this sort of prediction may have serious consequences, one does not lodge it casually or lightly. The lines one draws through statistical distributions must be conservatively drawn to cement the certitude of predictions, and to protect officers from unfair and hasty prejudgments. However, drawing lines can also mislead observers who take numbers literally. As an example, Dan Rather, who narrated the CBS program *48 Hours,* informed a national television audience that "investigations of Los Angeles police after the Rodney King incident reveal that few officers cross that thin blue line, but that those who do, do so repeatedly" (Rather 1992).

Rather may not have realized that the number of problem officers varies with the way they are selected and nominated. He also may not have recognized that the designation of some officers as problem officers does not permit us to label other officers as nonproblem officers, even if (as in Los Angeles) problem officers account for a lion's share of the use of excessive force. Officers with low incident rates may have low-order problems, or few occasions to manifest problems. A continuum may extend from officers with a horrendous problem through officers with a less than horrendous problem to somewhat problematic officers, to clearly nonproblem officers. Lines between gradations may also be differently drawn, yielding varying sets of estimates.

Distributions of other deviant conduct that has been studied (such as criminal behavior) are often skewed by redoubtable individuals who account for disproportionate shares of a problem through disquieting frequency of offenses (Wolfgang et al. 1972; Greenwood 1982; Wolfgang et al. 1987). But the bulk of a deviance problem can still be accounted for by less stellar and reliable contributors who fall in the moderately habitual range (Chaiken and Chaiken 1984). These persons' propensities are less reliably or redundantly manifest than those of extreme chronics, but are still appreciable, making predictions and classifications difficult.

Whichever the case, chronic deviants are an element in the use-of-force picture and must be accommodated in explanations. But once chronic deviants have been isolated, we have only started to address issues of causation. We cannot say that the officers are the key to the problem nor that the origin of the officers' propensity necessarily is intrapsychic and personal. Some of the same officers in other settings might not be violence-prone, and their behavior may be reinforced by the organization for which they work. In turn, though, we must not concur with the lawyer of one of the officers involved in the Rodney King incident, that "what happened out there was what these guys are taught, trained and expected to do by the L.A.P.D." (Quindlen 1992). While individual-level variables may fall short of explaining an organization's excessive-use-of-force problem, contextual variables cannot fully explain an individual officer's actions, especially when the officer's behavior is unrepresentative, deviant, and extreme.

The Los Angeles Model of Violence-Related Propensities

After we have isolated problem officers by looking at statistics, we expect to find that the officers have problematic values, motives, or attitudes that express themselves in situations in which they react violently. We expect such values, motives, or attitudes to be held disproportionately by the problem officers or to manifest themselves to a greater (and less desirable) degree among aggressive officers than among others.

The literature often deals with such presuppositions without fleshing out the details. The Christopher Commission, for example, posited an across-the-board connection between prejudice and use of force but did not specifically say that problem officers are prejudiced, nor that their uses of force are discriminatory acts.[1] The commission asserted that "attitudes of prejudice and intolerance are translated into unacceptable behavior in the field" (p. xii). The report noted that the prevalence of bias can be extrapolated from informal communications between field units, testimony about the problem by Los Angeles officers (including minority officers), and questionnaire responses by the agency's rank and file.

The commission inferred that "the nexus between racial and ethnic bias and the use of excessive force is sharply illustrated by the results of (the) survey recently taken by the LAPD of the attitudes of its sworn officers" (p. 69). However, the survey data were in fact not conclusive. The key questionnaire item — "an officer's prejudice toward the suspect's race may lead to the use of excessive force" — yielded only 27.6 percent agreement, compared to 57 percent disagreement and 15 percent abstentions. In other words, the statement that posited only the *possibility* of a nexus between prejudice and behavior was still *rejected* by over half the respondents. A companion item — "racial bias (prejudice) on the part of officers toward minority citizens currently exists and contributes to a negative interaction between police and the community" — yielded almost identical results (p. 69). Such data at best make a case for the existence (and relevance) of prejudice, but they fall short of establishing the nexus to which the commission referred.

The commission linked the bias it thought could be documented to an enforcement-centered departmental philosophy and saw the two as exercising a compounded effect. The commission concluded: "If combined with racial and ethnic bias, the Department's active style of policing creates a potentially grave problem. Because of the concentration of . . . crime in Los Angeles' minority communities, the Department's aggressive style — its self-described 'war on crime' — in some cases seems to become an attack on those communities at large. The communities, and all within them, become painted with the brush of latent criminality" (p. 74).

The model implied in the above paragraph embodies the presumption that officers could be predisposed to overaggressive policing if the crime-fighting thrust of an agency helped them to express preexisting discriminatory feelings, or if they were zealous crime-fighters who in the course of crime fighting develop hostile sentiments toward denizens of high-crime-rate communities (who are disproportionately minority group members). The commission also pointed out: "Patrol officers are evaluated by statistical measures (for example, the number of calls handled and arrests made) and are rewarded for being 'hardnosed.' This style of policing produces results . . . but it does so at the risk of creating a siege ('we/they') mentality that alienates the officer from the community" (p. 98).

The propensity that is implied here does not require racial prejudice; it is that of an across-the-board aggressive, proactive, and peremptory approach to encounters with citizens that leads to escalations of conflict, and that can be motivated by the desire to garner as many crime-related contacts or arrests as possible. The commission noted: "LAPD officers are trained to command and to confront, not to communicate. Regardless of their training, officers who are expected to produce high citation and arrest statistics and low response times do not also have the time to explain their actions, to apologize when they make a mistake, or even to ask about problems in their neighborhood. They must write the citation or make the arrest and rush off to answer the next call as quickly as possible" (p. 104).

This hypothesized propensity to zealous activism makes it particularly unsurprising that—in the words of an assistant chief who testified before the commission—"the sergeants . . . know that some of these officers who do generate the most complaints are also the ones who make a lot of arrests and write a lot of tickets and so forth" (p. 32). It also explains the fact that the performance evaluation reports for problem officers were largely found to be "very positive, documenting every complimentary comment received and expressing optimism about the officer's progress in the Department" (p. x).

We can see that the Christopher Commission's model is not very explicit in what it says about personal motives. There are no statements that help one to distinguish between the dispositions of prejudiced officers and nonprejudiced officers, or the more extreme and lesser practitioners of violence, or among officers who are personally predisposed toward violence, those who are shaped by organizational pressures, and those who fall in between. The model as developed leaves room for violence-prone officers to arise as in-house products or to be recruited ready-made and then protected by departmental policies, or to be a result of a combination of predispositions and reinforcements. The commission provided some examples, to be sure, of more-or-less "pure" dispositions, featuring legendary officers who habitually lost their cool. The commission also emphasized the desirability of greater attention at intake to the recruits' involvement in strings of civilian conflicts. It is safe to assume that the commission saw some problem officers as personally predisposed to violence and felt that many other officers had preexisting personal motives fatefully reinforced by organizational rewards.

Police Socialization

The role of the person-organization relationship highlighted in the Los Angeles situation is obviously a complicated one. The motives of violence-prone officers tend to be compatible with hard-nosed ("let's go get 'em") organizational goals, which make the officers appear subservient to mandates from the organization. But legalistic agencies also have all sorts of non-hard-nosed mandates (such as "observe due process and earn community acceptance") that are ignored by aggressive officers. In other words, aggressive officers go out of their way to intersect with crime-fighting ends and may pursue these ends selectively.

An emphasis on crime-fighting productivity makes it possible for officers who do not initiate conflict-laden encounters to be held in lower esteem by an agency than aggressive officers, until (as in Los Angeles) the latter become an embarrassment. When this occurs, the agency can point to highly productive officers with low use-of-force records to disclaim responsibility for the predations of problem officers.

In the interim, crime-fighting goals can shape the self-image and reputation of violence-prone officers. Aggressive officers can define themselves by differentiating themselves from low-productivity officers (regarded as lazy bums who don't do police work) or by downgrading due-process concerns (those of administrators seen as playing politics to garner popularity). Given this set of norms, susceptible non-proactive officers can be seduced to aspire to be more enforcement-oriented without drawing fine distinctions between types of enforcement orientation.

Such an influence on susceptible recruits is most likely to take place through informal socialization, which occurs as an adjunct to the formal socialization that takes place during training. The academy can deliver double messages as well (see chapter 8), despite emphases in its curriculum on legality and human relations. A particularly insidious tendency is the practice among instructors in many training programs to regale recruits with unrepresentative war stories that feature the use of violence (van Maanen 1973, 1974).

The most substantial impact on recruits is exercised by field training officers, who have been singled out for emphasis by the Christopher Commission. The training officer's impact during early on-the-job experience is reinforced by doubts about the relevance of classroom education to the "realities" of policing. "It was a common feeling," writes McNamara (1967), "that academy personnel must have never worked in field units" (p. 248). McNamara described consensus in the ranks of police departments on the premise that "efficient police work would be impossible if an officer were to follow the Rules and Procedures to the letter" (p. 241). The observed consensus raises the question of how far outside the Rules and Procedures recruits are informally told they must work to accommodate the reality of street policing.

One stance officers who respond to subcultural norms can take is to assume that rule violations are inevitable. But this need not lead the officers to a career of no-holds-barred enforcement. Van Maanen (1974) has written that the average officer can evolve a "lay low and don't make waves" strategy, which postulates that "the best way in which he can stay out of trouble is to minimize the amount of work he pursues" (p. 108). Proactive policing in particular can come to be avoided because (among other things) there is the risk that one must use force that can be adjudged excessive. Van Maanen (1974) points out, "working hard increases the number of citizen contacts an officer may have. . . . Such encounters are strained interpersonally, troublesome legally, and almost always invite disrespect" (pp. 108–09). In the words of one officer quoted by van Maanen, "either some civic-minded creep is going to get outraged and you'll wind up with a complaint in your file or the high and mighty in the department will come down on you for breaking some rules or something" (p. 108).

But in many enforcement-oriented agencies this kind of risk-aversive behavior may be less than fashionable, because in these departments crime-fighting and proactivity are universally admired and heavily rewarded. A derivative problem can be engendered in such departments through deviance monitoring and control (chapter 11). If an agency is strongly proactive but also punishes overaggressiveness in officers, it creates (as the officers see it) a wrong-if-you-do, wrong-if-you-don't dilemma, which translates into discordant ("go get 'em," but "be careful out there") norms.

Rookies can be critiqued by their elders for demonstrating a gung-ho attitude or being a hotdogger. On the other hand, the acceptance of young officers by their peers can hinge on the recruits' demonstrated willingness and capacity to engage in physical combat. Van Maanen (1974) notes that "while hot calls are relatively rare on a day-to-day basis, their occurrence signals a behavior test for the recruit. To pass, he must be willing to use his body as a weapon, to fight if necessary. . . . Through such events, a newcomer quickly makes a departmental reputation that will follow him throughout his career" (p. 94).

The criteria used to ascertain that an officer can be depended upon transcend his or her swift responses to back-up calls and extend to risk-taking behavior in other situations, such as to his or her readiness to get involved in physical encounters. Hunt (1985) points out that "new officers . . . learn that they will earn the respect of their veteran coworkers not by observing legal niceties in using force, but by being 'aggressive' and using whatever force is necessary in a given situation" (p. 318). In Hunt's view, "for a street cop, it is often a graver error to use too little force and develop a 'shaky' reputation than it is to use too much force and be told to calm down" (p. 321). Officers who are anxious for approval can assume that being accepted hinges on their proficiency in combat.

Harris (1978), among others, points to an emphasis on an "ethic of masculinity" in police locker rooms. This ethic leads recruits to prize a man-of-action image, "with the emphasis both on the *man* of action and the man of *action*" (p. 288). Harris confirms Hunt's impression that "the recruit who did not manifest the man-of-action image was not as highly esteemed as his fellow-classmates, and he certainly was not accessible to the inner circles" (p. 289). This pressure is also experienced by female officers. For example, Hunt (1985) reports that "women [who] are believed to be physically weak, naturally passive and emotionally vulnerable" (p. 318), may feel that "it becomes crucial for [them] to create or exploit opportunities to display their physical abilities in order to overcome sexual bias and obtain full acceptance from coworkers. As a result, [these] women rookies [may be] encouraged informally to act more aggressively and to display more machismo than male rookies" (p. 310).

Social Norms and Personal Dynamics

Officers' needs for a positive reputation, high self-esteem, and organizational approval make it important to them that they encounter serious criminals on their beats. "To some degree," writes van Maanen (1974), for the officer "the anticipation of the 'hot call' allows for the crystallization of his personal identity as a policeman" (p. 94). Crime-related calls are deemed "real" (as opposed to required) work. Westley (1970), the dean of police experts, points out that such calls are rare but prized highlights of police work. He writes that "hours will go by with absolutely nothing happening, and then everything will break loose. They will start out with a shooting at such and such an address, a reported robbery at another, a family quarrel at a third. This is the action to which the men look forward throughout the monotonous hours of driving up and down the streets" (p. 35).

Self-esteem and organizational approval can be derived simultaneously in encounters with consequential suspects. Live, crime-related calls can yield arrests (pinches), which are consensually salient criteria of productivity and achievement. Arrests can lead to convictions, and, according to Westley (1970), "a conviction reassures [the officer] of his own competence and at the same time of the worth of his job. It makes him feel that he is actually achieving something. It thus gives meaning to his life and his work. It provides for him a reassurance as to the correctness of his judgments" (p. 81). But as Westley also notes, such calls can be psychological ends in themselves. They are high points in routines otherwise marked by monotony and lack of prestige-yielding tasks, particularly for officers who are action-oriented or who have strong crime-fighting orientations.

Danger is often cited in surveys as a source of stress for officers (Kroes 1985). Yet the prospect of danger and conflict (including a consequent need to exercise force) can acquire a positive—or at worst, mixed—connotation. Van Maanen (1974) points out that "without danger as an omnipresent quality of the work setting, patrolmen would have little of the visceral pleasures that contribute to their evaluation of performing difficult, important, and challenging (if unappreciated) tasks" (p. 102).

Fear also enters into use of excessive force. It sparks overreactions in some situations in which needless force is employed (Kirkham 1976; International Association of Chiefs of Police 1990). Fear also inspires compensatory conduct to "prove" its nonexistence. Danger is titillating to some officers because it assures them of worthy opponents and provides proving grounds for bravery. Dangerous situations are heavily overrepresented in war stories officers tell other officers (Toch 1993). Narratives of this kind can send the wrong message, particularly to officers who nurture self-doubt and a sense of inadequacy. Failure to exercise precautions—including such elementary safeguards as calling for backup when a situation requires it—can be motivated by the desire to demonstrate one's worth by charging into dangerous situations.

I have noted that the willingness and ability to handle physical conflict are requisites for peer acceptance for new officers, whose capabilities are untested. Officers with a strong need for peer approval can seek out encounters with potential for conflict whose resolution earns approval. In the absence of more legitimate opportunities, officers with strong need for approval may manufacture situations in which conflicts arise. Officers who feel inadequate can be hungry for challenges that furnish proof of adequacy to boost their level of self-esteem, and can assess their own responses to citizens in terms of group standards (or their perception of group standards) that yield measures of worth. As a result they may engage in destructive demonstrations of bravery and toughness at the expense of citizens (Toch 1969).

Some officers are especially prone to dispense street justice or to engage in punitive reactions against citizens who are designated "wise guys" or "assholes" (Westley 1951, 1970). Van Maanen (1978) points out that dispensing street justice can be a convenient rationale for brutal officers. He notes that "the specific situated behavior of a citizen that is taken as a sign which leads to isolating, ignoring, teaching or castigating a given individual is no doubt quite different across patrolmen. Here, the police game continues as it does because, in part, the asshole label swallows up and hides whatever differences exist across patrolmen" (p. 234).

Dispensing Street Justice

The norm of street justice has to do with countering disrespect or lack of deference from citizens. Westley was among the first to point out that "the officer thinks of himself not as an instrument of the government, but as a person in interaction with another person. He tends to feel that the derived power is in himself and that by withholding it he himself is doing the other person a favor. He therefore expects gratitude for his personal favor, gratitude and acknowledgment of his own competence. The man who typifies the antithesis of both these reactions is the 'wise guy,' again a recurrent character in the drama of the police versus the public" (Westley 1970: 59).

The reason a challenging attitude "justifies" the use of force for many officers is that disrespectful citizens are seen as defying the institutions the officer represents and as persisting in this defiance when the officer asserts his or her authority. In the words of van Maanen,

> In essence, the "asshole" is one who refuses to accept (or, at least, remain silent for) the officer's definition of the situation. Hence, the person complains loudly, attempts to fight or flee, disagrees with the officer, does not listen, and generally, in the officer's eyes, makes a nuisance of himself. . . . From the patrolman's view, the asshole is one who makes his job more difficult, and such actions are not looked upon kindly. In fact, if the asshole persists in his actions and pays no heed to an officer's repeated warnings to "shape-up," he may find himself charged with considerably more than he first thought. Or, in the extreme case, he may be severely "thumped" if the officer is so inclined. In the patrolman's world, such physical retaliation for the antics of an "asshole" is justified according to the doctrine of "street justice." This form of police action is designed to both punish the offender immediately and to reestablish the officer's control of the situation. (1974: 119)

One problem is that the officer's person and his or her role are apt to be confused with each other, as they are when an arbitrary deployment of power is seen (by the officer, not by the citizen) as an assertion of legitimate authority. A second problem arises when the officer reacts under color of law to back up illegitimate demands. The President's Commission (1967b) quotes O. W. Wilson to the effect that "The officer . . . must remember that there is no law against making a policeman angry and that he cannot charge a man with offending him" (p. 181). Violations of Wilson's injunction can lead to exercises of excessive (or, at least, avoidable) force where no crime has occurred. Conflicts with citizens often stem from field interrogations that are compounded by officer discourtesy or occur in the course of misdemeanor arrests that suspects view as capricious (President's Commission 1967b; Reiss 1971a; Margarita 1980a). In turn, arrests can be solely or primarily precipitated by the citizen's expressed resentment and failure to pass the officers' "attitude test" (Hindelang 1976).

Some arrests are relatively undiluted exercises of "street justice," in defiance of the President's Commission's (1967b) dictum, "if citizens show disrespect for an officer, such conduct alone, while reprehensible, does not justify making an arrest or taking other action" (p. 181). The most egregious transgressions against this rule occur where suspects are arrested for resisting an arrest that is based on feeble or unconvincing grounds. Charges of resisting arrest (or of assault on officers) may be frequently filed to "cover" or try to justify exercises of force (Chevigny 1969). This practice is prevalent across agencies, and repeated filing of charges of resisting arrest can be a reliable indicator of excessive use of force by individual officers (Toch, Grant, and Galvin 1975).[2]

This type of practice creates a somewhat symbiotic and paradoxical relationship between productivity and uses of force, in which "officers do not merely transgress to make 'good pinches,' but make 'good pinches' to conceal transgressions" (Bittner 1978: 46). Repeated use of cover arrests by an officer can simultaneously make uses of force by the officer implicitly legitimate, convert the officer's victims into suspects—thus, low-credibility complainants, and add to the officer's record of quantifiable productivity.

A department that is serious about controlling use of force by its officers may increase their propensity to make cover arrests. Egon Bittner (1978) observed:

> It has been reported that in the New York Police Department, known for its stringently punitive discipline, officers who violate some official rules of deportment while dealing with citizens simply arrest potential complainants, knowing the complaints of persons charged with crimes are given no credence. Incongruously, while in New York the Police Department is much more likely to discipline an officer for brutalizing a citizen than elsewhere, it in fact rarely gets a chance to do it. For whenever there is a situation in which it is possible that an officer could have an infraction entered in his record, an infraction against an explicit regulation, he will redefine it into an instance of police work that is not regulated. Thus, while citizens everywhere run the risk of receiving a beating when they anger a policeman, in New York they run the added risk of being charged with a crime they did not commit simply because its officers must keep their records clean. (p. 45)

Some officers can become dispensers of street justice because they have limited verbal or interpersonal skills, which they "back up" with demands or assertions of authority. Officers also can invite the resistance to which they react by habitually treating citizens discourteously, provoking their expressions of resentment. A third variable is the officer's level of sensitivity to being affronted. Officers may repeatedly tend to take disagreements by citizens personally or react to them angrily. Such oversensitivity to affronts can derive from an underlying sense of inadequacy or feelings of self-doubt (Toch 1969).[3]

Attitude Clusters

Some street justice has a frustration-aggression or retaliatory flavor, which may express a strong sense of alienation among disaffected officers. Van Maanen (1978) writes, "Whether the officer responds by placing the handcuffs on the person's wrists such that they cut off circulation (and not incidentally cause intense, almost excruciating pain) or pushes a destitute soul through a shop window, these actions release some of the pent-up energies stored up over a period in which small but cumulative indignities are suffered by the police at the hands of the community elites, the courts, the politicians, the uncaught crooks, the press, and numerous others. The asshole stands, then, as a ready ersatz for those whom the police will never—short of a miracle—be in a position to directly encounter and confront" (p. 235).

Niederhoffer (1967), among others, has pointed to the existence of attitude clusters, such as cynicism, which can become accentuated in the course of police work. While some such evolving attitudes may exist, the consensus is that these do not add up to a violence-related "working personality" in officers (Tifft 1974; Chandler and Jones 1979; Wilt and Bannon 1976; Rafky et al. 1976). Studies that have sought to isolate potentially compromising constellations of values (such as authoritarianism or closed-mindedness) among officers have yielded consistently negative findings. These findings do not negate the fact that *some* officers will score high on attitude scales or other measures that tap alienated conceptions or outlooks. But even high-scoring officers need not act on their philosophies in dealings with citizens across the board; at worst, they may on occasion let their feelings show in individual incidents.

A similar point holds for officers who are prejudiced along ethnic or other lines. Verbal expressions of prejudice can be prevalent among officers who do not enact their prejudices through discriminatory dealings with citizens (Reiss 1971a). But this in turn does not mean that prejudice plays no role in citizen encounters: prejudicial attitudes sometimes translate into action by contaminating diagnoses of "wise guy" behavior or inviting resistances (to contemptuous approaches by officers) from citizens who are singled out for attention. Prejudiced officers may not be invariably violence-prone, but when they are, may express their prejudice in early stages of degenerating encounters.

Violence-Related Dispositions

I started with the presumption that violence-prone officers can invite, or promote, conflicts with citizens. This means that the dispositions these officers bring to their work will contaminate their relationships with some suspects and exacerbate the potential for conflict of some of their arrests. Yet it is difficult to pinpoint the officers' characteristic violence-related dispositions and their manifestations. One-to-one correlations between personality traits and officer misbehavior have not been established. Instead, one infers that some traits contribute to some misbehavior of some officers in some situations. Equations that spell out such contributions may have to contain more than personality descriptions and characterizations of conduct. At minimum, a trait (such as emotional instability) may have to be evoked by a situation (such as one that irritates the officer) to produce a state (such as rage or panic) that leads to overreaction.

Such statements can also be made about efforts to find disproportionate representation of demographic subgroups among officers who are involved in misconduct. Though this approach is not psychological, sociologists (such as Sherman 1980) refer to it as "individual-level" research, because disproportions are attributed to special motives of subgroup members. Typically, the approach yields modest findings, such as (at best) low correlations, countered by no differences elsewhere, or even low correlations in opposite directions. This is the result one would expect if psychological dispositions are imperfectly related to demographics or differently distributed in several demographically homogeneous samples.

The research does not tell us that psychological dispositions do not exist, nor that demographic subgroups are irrelevant. To illustrate this fact, consider two excerpts from an article in *Psychology Today* (Meredith 1984: 26), which hypothesize demographically related psychological dispositions:

> Many police psychologists say that youth is a major contributing factor to violence on a police force . . . most view it as a developmental phase. . . . Then they move into the adolescent phase. That's when they are the most dangerous to themselves and to citizens. This is the stage when you see them wearing mirrored sunglasses and trying to carry a .44 magnum with a six-inch barrel. They spend time at home in front of the mirror, just practicing how to look like police officers. If they survive that phase, after three to five years, they become good police officers.

> The growing number of women on the force has also helped make alternative policing styles more acceptable. Once-hostile male partners have started noticing that women sometimes get results when they can't. Because of their limited physical strength, women often use words instead of force; they are usually better than male officers at offering sympathy to victims, male and female, an ability that makes questioning more productive; and their presence exerts a calming influence on violent people.

Such assertions seem at first glance hard to reconcile with the fact that studies portray younger officers as showing only a slight tendency to be more often involved in incidents (Croft 1985; Blumberg 1986, 1991; Shortreed 1989; Cohen and Chaiken 1972) or with research that shows weak or nonexistent gender effects on behavior (Greenwald 1976; Grennan 1987).[4] The answer is that statistically weak relationships can mask substantial subgroup differences. It is likely that there exist subgroups of young officers who manifest a "hot dog" syndrome that includes overaggressive or inappropriate proactivity. This disaggregated propensity would yield a low negative correlation between age and use of force if the officers are few, if the propensity comes hand-in-hand with other violence-related dispositions in seasoned officers (such as increased cynicism or alienation), or if it is tempered by supervision or other organizational restraints. A failure to find strong relationships can disguise conflicting dispositions within a particular group. It is possible that many female officers have conflict-reduction skills that are effectively exercised, while others become involved in violence to gain the esteem of male colleagues. Demographics offer clues to dispositions, but these are mere clues until relevant disaggregation is effected.

Various subpopulation mixes (for instance, larger proportions of females) may also change the behavior of officers. Different settings (featuring divergent philosophies or sets of constraints) may affect levels of behavior such as hot doggishness. Much research must be done before these sorts of interaction effects can be uncovered and explained. Strategies comparing some violence-involved officers with equivalent nonviolence-involved officers in comparable settings can help. Some disaggregating studies of this kind are already available in relation to use of lethal force (Geller 1985a; Binder 1983; Scharf and Binder 1983; Blumberg 1986), and similar research designs have been suggested for nonlethal force (Croft 1985; Renner and Gierach 1975).

Studying Police-Citizen Encounters

The literature that most directly faces the question of why violence-prone officers react violently is that which deals with incidents in which force is deployed. The "problem officer" by definition experiences degenerating incidents with frequency.[5] Incident-centered approaches become person-centered approaches when one compiles incidents over an officer's career and sees the officer as a composite of the incidents in which he or she has been involved. We can then not only ask why the officer reacted as he or she did on particular occasions, but why he or she repeatedly reacted in this way. Based on a sample of incidents, we can discuss consistencies of behavior that express the officer's violence-related dispositions (Toch 1969).

Incident descriptions are available in complaints and arrest reports and can be secured by observation or through interviews. Incident-centered research has been perfected in unrelated approaches, including decision theory, transactional analysis, and symbolic interactionism, which rest on the analytic dissection of citizen-officer contacts (Hudson 1970; Wiley and Hudik 1974; Sykes and Brent 1980; Sykes and Clark 1975). Beyond illuminating academic debates, incident-centered approaches yield two benefits. The first is that they can disclose *patterns* of encounters, which help explain the involvements of problem officers and make contingent statements about officer behavior. The second advantage is that a step-by-step dissection of incidents reveals junctures that matter in the genesis of violence and exposes the relative contribution of officer and citizen participants at each stage and the judgments by the officer that contribute to his or her involvement in incidents. Such analysis is particularly critical in the design of training and retraining programs for violence-involved officers (see chapter 8).

The fact that a violence-prone officer is repeatedly involved in violence not only is a requisite of definition (as is the fact that one person cannot walk in single file) but also is an attribute of individual prediction. When a person has never committed an act of violence, we cannot foretell whether he or she will commit one; if an individual has committed violence once, the probability that he or she will do so again is so low that the safest prediction is that he or she will not be violent again (Wenk et al. 1972; Pollock 1990). After the fourth (or fifth) violent act, the probability of recidivism becomes high. The safest prediction is then that the person will be violent again, unless he or she has appreciably aged or has been somehow immobilized (PROMIS 1977). Such facts enter into assessments of "dangerousness" (Shah 1981) and are considered in risk-management decisions.

But repeated violence also permits contingent predictions (Monahan 1981b; Toch 1986) if persons who are violent act out in comparable ways under similar circumstances. Some repeatedly violent persons explode "all over the place," but most favor certain types of targets, are provoked by a small range of stimuli, and find themselves in similar situations when they become violent. Such consistency may be descriptively ascertainable or superficial or "phenotypic" (such as if an officer always assaults handcuffed suspects after a high-speed chase), or it may be more subtle and "genotypic" (as with officers who react when they interpret some citizen behavior only *they* notice as an aspersion on their concept of self).

Given contingent consistencies, a useful prediction is that, given a specifiable set of circumstances, the person will be violent, or—*when* the person is violent—one expects certain conditions to obtain (Monahan 1981b; Toch 1986). Morris (1974) calls this kind of statement an "anamnestic prediction" and points out that one implication is that we can reduce the person's violence if we can keep him or her away from situations in which violence occurs. Where we cannot control the person's environment, however, other options can be exercised. One such option is that we can assist the person to gain insight into his or her pattern of violence and help the person discover or invent a different mode of response to situations in which he or she reacts violently. In a police context this approach has been used by peer review or action review panels in retraining violence-prone officers (Toch, Grant, and Galvin 1975; Toch and Grant 1991; also see chapter 10). The approach differs from retraining generally in that it capitalizes on contingent consistency; it also relies on police peer influence, which has long been recognized as a potent way of affecting officer behavior (National Advisory Commission 1973).

Dissecting incidents into moves, stages, or decision points makes reviews more systematic (Toch 1969; Bayley 1986; Bayley and Garofalo 1989; Reiss 1980; Binder and Scharf 1980; Scharf and Binder 1983) and offers advantages in both reactive and proactive approaches. It permits assessment of an officer's skills in the gathering and use of information at each stage of an incident and review of the effectiveness of decisions the officer makes at each stage. The premise in an incident-centered analysis is that violence evolves cumulatively, with mistakes at early junctures fatefully foreclosing subsequent options. "To manage sequential choices," writes Reiss (1980), "requires information about choices and their options and about opportunities to control the choices as they are made sequentially" (p. 128). Both violent incidents and avoided potentially violent incidents can be examined through dissection (Binder and Scharf 1980; Bayley and Garofalo 1989). The effectiveness of decisions can be ascertained irrespective of violent or nonviolent outcome (Scharf and Binder 1983).

Training approaches (see chapter 8) can center on the information used by the officer or the interaction with citizens at each stage of an incident, starting with entry into the situation. This is particularly critical with opening moves by officers which spark resentment in citizens, or with precategorizations of incidents by officers in which hasty conclusions are reached based on cursory reviews of selectively garnered data. This is important because violence-prone officers often get themselves out on limbs from which retreat has been effectively foreclosed at early stages of incidents, or they put citizens in positions in which the citizens' options are restricted (McNamara 1967). Such behavioral propensities of officers can be addressed in training through systematic review of degenerating encounters.

Targeting Interventions

Some approaches to police use of excessive force are broadly targeted and do not presuppose that the violence-involved officers have been identified or that one has ascertained why they become involved in violence. Lethal force, for example, can be curtailed by policies that sharply restrict the situations in which shooting is permissible (Uelman 1973; Fyfe 1978; Geller and Scott 1992). Recruit training can similarly affect violence levels by disseminating skills (such as communication or interpersonal skills) that enhance the competence of recruits (Geller 1982; Scharf and Binder 1983; Independent Commission 1991). Working with the field training officer (FTO) who picks up the recruit when he or she leaves the academy is also important. The FTO can be selected as a worthy role model, based on a record of invariably exemplary dealings with citizens such as might be attained by the "highly skilled officer" posited by Klockars (chapter 1). Broader organizational interventions can also help: for instance, changing an agency's philosophy and its reward system to emphasize positive involvements with citizens can decrease violence levels. A departmental reorientation toward community policing can expand the types of contacts that officers have with citizens, improve the attitude of citizens toward the police, and modify the attitudes of officers in a constructive way.

If we can identify violence-prone officers, however, we can try to address directly their propensities to behave violently. Retraining and counseling are in order when the first signs of problems have arisen. More serious options, like disciplinary dispositions and punishments, must target officers who use demonstrably excessive force. These strategies must be used without hesitancy, but they share a number of problems that are difficult to resolve. One problem is that it is hard to punish violence-involved officers without lowering morale among nonviolence-involved officers (Toch 1976). A prominent reason for this fact is the solidarity that officers manifest in the face of negative sanctions by superiors who are seen as "desk jockeys" (Reuss-Ianni 1983). Many officers also find the distinction between violence-involved and nonviolence-involved officers elusive. This happens despite the negative reputation that some violence-prone officers have in the locker room and despite most officers' remarkable accuracy in ranking the interpersonal skills and violence potential of their peers (Bayley and Garofalo 1989; Love 1981).

One argument resistant officers may use is that police encounters are invariably complex and ambiguous, making any officer's culpability in a given situation hard to ascertain. Uninvolved officers may feel threatened when a degenerating encounter is reviewed, because they suspect that the assignments of culpability are arbitrary. The officers may feel uncertain about the outcome of reviews of their involvements given the "judgment calls" they must make. Officers may also feel that adverse decisions insufficiently account for suspects' contributions to violence and discourage police from taking forceful measures when their lives are endangered.

Such concerns must be addressed by supervisors in implementing interventions to the extent that this is possible (see chapter 11). Specific details in charges and shared information about reviews of incidents are essential. And using nonpunitive interventions, such as retraining, is always preferable to using punitive interventions, to the degree that circumstances permit. Last, the involvement of rank-and-file officers in the decision-making process—and in the intervention itself—can do much to allay suspicion and resentment (Renner and Gierach 1975; Vaughn 1981; Broadaway 1974; National Advisory Commission 1973; Moran 1978; McFarlane and Crosby 1976).

Where officers can suffer adverse consequences from disciplinary decisions, due process observance is absolutely essential (National Advisory Committee 1973). Given the definition of "problem officers" as repeaters, one difficulty agencies face is that punitive actions based on the fact that officers have accumulated long strings of unsubstantiated charges (such as suggested by the Independent Commission 1991) may not meet this standard. Police departments must try to be consistent and uncompromising models of fairness in their dealings with both officers and citizens (see chapter 12). One could argue that this must be one aspect of a community-oriented philosophy conveyed to recruits and senior officers, to preclude a "zero-sum" view of the interests of police and community, that is, the assumption that for one party to "win," the other must "lose."

On the other hand, officers who engage in demonstrably unconscionable conduct must be reliably sanctioned under this philosophy on the grounds that they are a threat, both to the community and to their peers. A strong public response to such officers must be unequivocally supported within an agency, including by police unions (see chapter 10). Resistance to disciplining violent officers is misconceived: It wrongly implies an affinity between malefactors and the average officer; it suggests that offenders are offenders because they are officers, not despite the fact. And if the police want citizens to know that brutality is aberrant, they must treat officer-offenders as aberrants. This calls for solidarity *against*, not *on behalf of* the violent officer.

Consensus related to merited punishment is a corollary of community relations. The malefactor is an enemy of community. Defending a bully against discipline on the ground that "there, but by the grace of God, go I," or "who knows whom they'll get next?" shortchanges the impact of the bully and makes his victims feel doubly unprotected. Citizens feel vulnerable where police ranks close in defense of violence-involved officers.

Last, it is essential that interventions should have a forward-looking as well as reactive emphasis. Citizens are entitled to feedback, to reduce fear of *in camera* whitewashing, and to differentiate circumstances in which complaints are warranted from those in which they are not. Kerstetter (in chapter 12) argues that citizens' acceptance of adverse rulings on complaints assists agencies to cement procedures that show greater respect for citizen input. Officers in turn must learn from past incidents to help fellow officers with problems. They must learn from reviews of the involvements of violence-prone officers what approaches or actions to avoid in dealing with citizens. They must also learn what approaches and actions merit their own concern when they witness them. Protecting malefactors through silence does not express concern. Concern can instead be expressed through informal peer pressure or counseling, or—if need be—through consultation with supervisors. The earlier such interventions occur the better for everyone, because timely support can help violence-involved officers to interrupt their destructive or self-destructive patterns. And where violent careers are thus interrupted, this can not only reduce harm to citizens in the community but also redirect officers to make valued contributions in the future.

NOTES

1. The controversy about ethnic discrimination as a variable in the use of force by police (see chapters 2 and 6) is enduringly obdurate. A satisfactory resolution is unlikely because it is logistically difficult for police to pursue offenders without concentrating their

efforts in areas where statistical disproportions of offenders exist. James Q. Wilson (1978: 64-65) points out, "No doubt many officers are prejudiced (indeed, one study indicates that the vast majority are) and this prejudice may make matters worse. But the crucial point is that large numbers of innocent Negroes would still be treated in (to them) unjust ways even if all policemen were entirely free of race prejudice so long as a disproportionate number of Negroes are lower class . . . . Among the consequences of this generalization will be continued police suspicion of blacks and continued Negro antagonism toward the police."

2. Using types of arrests to locate problem officers presupposes that police agencies have arrest data included in databases that identify arresting officers, so that officers can be credited with arrests. The same point holds in studying the relationship between police productivity and use of force. Police information systems, unfortunately, rarely combine officer data with arrest data, because arrest data are viewed as measures of organizational productivity, whereas officer performance is assessed impressionistically.

3. Harris (1978) points out that overly sensitive male officers may equate disrespect with aspersions on their masculinity. He notes, "It would seem that an officer would be less likely to react to disrespect personally if he feels secure with himself. Concomitantly, it would be those officers least secure in their masculine image who are prone to react violently to perceived threats to their masculinity" (pp. 290-91).

4. Age differences and sex differences appear more robust as new studies are done. Data suggesting that younger officers are disproportionately involved in violence and that women are underrepresented are provided in a survey conducted by the Police Foundation and the International Association of Chiefs of Police with support from NIJ (Pate and Fridell 1993).

5. The same holds true of "problem suspects." Police-citizen conflicts can be assaults on officers by civilians who have a propensity to overreact, which is displayed though repeated assaultive behavior. A citizen who has a checkered dossier studded with pugilistic encounters must be suspected of being the prime initiator of any altercation with a problem-free officer. By the same token, "problem officers" in fateful encounters with "problem suspects" can produce messy escalations for which culpability may be shared. Where neither the citizen nor the officer has a past record of assaultiveness, hypotheses about the genesis of their incident must be advanced with caution.

CHAPTER FIVE

Public Opinion about Police Abuse of Force

TIMOTHY J. FLANAGAN and MICHAEL S. VAUGHN

The public view of law enforcement is an ambivalent one. Citizens perceive the police as friend and enemy, much like the police perception of the citizenry (van Maanen 1978; Wiley and Hudik 1974). Westley (1970: 90) says that police contacts in general "are friendly on the surface but contain an undercurrent of mutual distrust." Niederhoffer (1967) observes, "At one moment the police officer is a hero, the next a monster . . . to people in trouble he is a savior . . . to criminal suspects he is a demon" (p. 1). The police are loved and admired but, at the same time, hated and feared. This relationship places the police in a difficult situation because, "to the law-abiding citizen who needs him, the officer must be all-powerful and all-loving. To the law-abiding citizen who commits a violation, the officer is an unloving persecutor" (Bonifacio 1991: 29–30).

Police agencies have frequently aggravated the problem of public ambivalence by becoming more militaristic, reactive, and secretive (Reiss 1968a, 1971a). However, over the past two decades, police agencies have attempted to become proactive through community, neighborhood, and problem-oriented policing. Aware of the misunderstanding, alienation, and aloofness that reactive policing strategies fostered, many police agencies have begun to implement reforms designed to promote police-community cooperation and even collaboration (Skolnick and Bayley 1986; Goldstein 1990).

Although some ambiguity surrounds the concepts of problem-oriented, community, or neighborhood policing (Goldstein 1993), it is clear that the new policing strategy involves participation from the entire community (Strecher 1991; Williams and Wagoner 1992). It involves structural changes in police attitudes, organization, and subculture, as well as changes in the community (Toch and Grant 1991; Vaughn 1992). The hope is that citizens will see the police in a more positive light when community leaders provide input into police operations, community solutions, and community-police activities. As citizens understand that they have a direct role in policing, the traditional barriers in police-community relations are expected to break down. Moreover, this new approach to policing encompasses the understanding that the circumstances under which police-citizen encounters occur influence the police view of the public and the public view of the police (Smith and Hawkins 1973). The approach is designed to defuse hostility before it erupts into civil unrest through police understanding of the cultural, ethnic, and racial traditions of the community. In turn, the approach assumes that the image in the public eye of police brutality and excessive use of force may be partially determined by the extent of citizen contacts and the level of citizen-police cooperation in the community (Meredith 1984).

The Context of Attitudes toward Police Use of Force

Public attitudes toward the criminal justice system and law enforcement are diverse and multidimensional. Public opinion regarding the excessive use of force by police exists within a broader set of attitudes toward the police (McIntyre 1967; O'Brien 1978). These attitudes have been studied extensively over the past quarter century, so it is possible to discern *trends* in attitudes toward the police. In addition, some of the *correlates* of attitudes toward the police are well-established in the opinion research literature. Knowledge of trends and patterns in attitudes toward the police puts opinions about police abuse of force in perspective.

A great deal of research on attitudes toward the police was conducted during the latter half of the 1960s and the early 1970s (Scaglion and Condon 1980; Thornton 1975; White and Menke 1978). This activity was encouraged by such groups as the President's Commission on Law Enforcement and Administration of Justice (1967b and 1967c) and the National Advisory Commission on Civil Disorders (1968). The latter group, known as the Kerner Commission, inferred a direct link between police-citizen discord and the urban riots of the late 1960s. The Crime Commission, appointed by President Lyndon Johnson, highlighted the critical role of police-citizen cooperation in determining the effectiveness of the police in fighting crime (see, e.g., Reiss 1967). This view of the collaborative relationship between the police and the public was stressed throughout the Crime Commission's *Task Force Report: The Police* and is the philosophical foundation for today's community policing efforts (Trojanowicz and Bucqueroux 1990).

A number of useful summaries of research on attitudes toward the police exist (see, for example, Decker 1981; Garofalo 1977; the reviews cited in Sullivan et al. 1987; Thomas and Hyman 1977). Research on the topic has used a wide variety of measurement techniques. The earliest conceptualizations of attitudes toward the police were measures of "support" for the police and "satisfaction" with police services. Survey researchers asked respondents to report the extent to which they "supported" or "approved" of the work of their local police department, state police, or federal law enforcement agencies.[1] Support for the police department was frequently tapped by questions about the chief of police. Satisfaction with police services was measured by questions on topics ranging from response time for calls for service to the courtesy with which police dispatchers handled telephone calls.

Researchers have subsequently expanded the focus of attitudes toward the police to include measures of "confidence" in the police (Flanagan 1988). Confidence has been measured in many different ways, but the most common approach has been to ask citizens about their confidence in the capacity of the local police to prevent crimes, to solve crimes, to protect citizens from crime, and to bring suspects to justice (Huang and Vaughn 1996). Alternatively, surveys have asked whether the police agency should be "doing more to fight crime."

In addition to these measures of the efficacy of police efforts, studies of public confidence in the police have examined citizens' views as to the integrity of the police. This dimension of community attitudes includes such subjects as police corruption, fairness, and evenhandedness in the enforcement of the law; political influence on police decision making; and civility toward community residents. Public perceptions about excessive use of force by the police are best understood as an element of police "integrity," a critical component of public confidence in the police.

In addition to recognizing that public opinion on police use of force is part of a larger set of attitudes toward the police, it is important to realize that the term *excessive use of force* denotes a continuum of activities and interactions rather than some specific behavior on the part of a police officer. Reiss observed that "what citizens mean by police brutality covers the full range of police practices" (1968a: 11). In addition to physical brutality toward suspects and others, this continuum includes general incivility toward community residents, denigrating speech, harassment and threats, "roughing up" arrestees and others, and other forms of misuse of authority and inappropriate use of force.

Correlates of Public Attitudes toward Police

Nearly all of the substantive research on public attitudes toward the police has found that the majority of the general public are supportive of (i.e., satisfied with, favorably disposed toward) their local police. Twenty-five years ago, Reiss reported that in the United States, "dissatisfaction with the policing of everyday life is far from widespread in our population and the police can count more on citizen support than opposition" (1971a: 218). Today, the public opinion polls essentially conclude the same, but we have learned that attitudes toward the police vary with the characteristics of citizens (Murty et al. 1990; Peek and Lowe 1981), the characteristics of neighborhoods (Mirande 1980; Primeau et al. 1975), and the frequency and type of citizen-police contacts (Huang and Vaughn 1996; Zamble and Annesley 1987; Zevitz and Rettammel 1990).

For example, attitudes toward the police consistently vary by race and age of respondents (Boggs and Galliher 1975; Bouma 1973; Jefferson 1988): members of minority groups and young people generally report less favorable views of local police than do older persons and persons in the racial majority (generally, whites). Decker (1981) suggests that the effect of race and age on attitudes toward the police may be mediated by other variables. He suggests that socioeconomic status, frequency of contact with the police, the nature of those contacts, "neighborhood culture," and other factors are important in fashioning attitudes toward the police. Thomas and Hyman summarized these relationships as follows: "Those citizens . . . whom the police are statistically more likely to encounter in the performance of their duties (blacks, younger citizens, those who are less affluent, and residents of inner-city areas) are significantly less favorable in their evaluations than are other categories of the population" (1977: 316).

In addition to these attributes of persons and places, such crime-related variables as fear of crime, perceived risk of criminal victimization, and actual victimization have also been found to affect attitudes toward local police (see Block 1971; Garofalo 1977; Maxfield 1988). These latter relationships are not well understood, however, as some researchers have concluded that these "experiential" variables are unrelated to evaluations of the police (Thomas and Hyman 1977).

Studies of Attitudes toward Police Violence

As noted above, a substantial body of research exists on Americans' attitudes toward the police; however, far less is known about Americans' views about police use and abuse of force. Williams et al. (1983) thus observed, "Surprisingly . . . there has been very little empirical research directed specifically at the public perception of specific situations in which the use of force is viewed positively or negatively" (p. 38).

In an early study on police violence, Westley (1970) asked lawyers, black citizens, unionists, and social workers the question: "What do you think of X police department?" While Westley's sampling techniques were crude and his sample nonrepresentative, his work represents an early attempt to gauge public opinion on police use of force. Nine of twenty lawyers said the police were "brutal and inefficient" (p. 21). Two of fourteen social workers said the police were "aggressive and brutal" (p. 52). Eight of thirty-five blacks indicated that the police "use too much brutality" (p. 54), and one of eight union stewards said the police were brutal. Westley's early review of public perception of police use of force identified a diverse citizenry, although small in number, who believed the police were "ineffectual, brutal, corrupt, and ignorant" (p. 105).

A series of studies by Blumenthal et al. (1972) investigated attitudes toward violence in a national sample of American men. Their work was an effort to understand the violence of the 1960s, manifested in assassinations, urban riots, and campus unrest. Blumenthal and his colleagues studied attitudes toward police behavior as an indicator of "support for violence for social control." They found that men's backgrounds and corollary attitudes influence opinions about the use of force for social control. Support for violence as a means of social control was related to age (older men were more supportive) and race (black men were less supportive). Beliefs about the role of poverty, discrimination, and lack of jobs as contributory to violence were also related to support for police violence as a means of social control. Finally, Blumenthal found that (self-reported) *involvement* in violence was related to *support* for violence for social control.

Gamson and McEvoy (1972) studied responses from a national survey conducted for the National Commission on the Causes and Prevention of Violence. They created a three-item "support for police violence" index and found that race, education, age, and political party affiliation differentiated Americans who supported violence by the police from those who opposed it. They argued that some Americans "trust" the police as agents of lawful authority more than other Americans. As a result, "Extra-legal police actions directed against unpopular targets are unlikely to draw censure or even disapproval from those substantial segments of the American public for whom the police are the 'good guys'" (p. 342).[2]

Williams and his colleagues (1983) analyzed data from the General Social Survey conducted in 1980 by the National Opinion Research Center. They constructed a scale of "support for police use of force" from several questions concerning approval of a police officer striking an adult male citizen. Their analysis showed that the following composite individuals are most likely to support the use of police force in a variety of situations; "older white males, who approve of force by 'others,' are intolerant of 'deviants,' and are politically conservative" (p. 46).

Research on public opinion and the police waned during the mid- to late 1980s as other issues concerning the administration of criminal justice gained prominence (Sullivan et al. 1987). This trend was unfortunate, because in many American cities racial and ethnic demographics changed dramatically during this period. Racial and ethnic groups that were minorities in some American urban centers had developed into majorities. The ranks of the police also had become much more diverse, especially along racial, ethnic, and gender lines.

The work of Sullivan and his colleagues (1987) illustrates the consequences of these developments. In a survey of adult and student residents of the greater Miami area, they examined patterns of attitudes toward the police among samples of Anglos, Cuban Americans, and African Americans. Their analyses confirmed that attitudes toward the police were not uniform across these groups. Rather, Sullivan found that the underlying cognitive structure of attitudes toward the police differed markedly between youths and adults in Miami and between age-homogeneous ethnic groups. In short, it became obvious that these elements of the community do not share a common set of cultural definitions or expectations about the police, and, as a result, they have different attitudes toward the police.

Waddington and Braddock's (1991) research in southern England underscores the point that it is "an error to regard 'ethnic minorities' as sharing a common attitude" (p. 32; among young men in particular, "the central issue around which perceptions of the police are organized . . . is that of police power and how it is used" (p. 40). Waddington and Braddock argue that young males perceive the police either as "guardians" or as "bullies," depending on the legitimacy they grant to police authority. Their data suggested that "racial groups differ in their perception of the police: that young blacks (unlike their white and Asian counterparts) have virtually *no* conception of the police as 'guardians'" (p. 42).[3]

A 1988 study of university students in Portugal suggests that young peoples' political ideology may be important in understanding their perception of police use of force. Vala et al. (1988) found that radical students perceived aggressive behavior by suspects or the police differently than did conservative students. Remarking on the futility of searching for "a consensual meaning of aggression in a social vacuum," they concluded, "When judging aggressive persons belonging to different social groups, conservative and radical subjects not only differed in their judgments of the severity of punishment, they perceived the violence of the act differently, they varied in the degree of perceived responsibility of the actor, and they also used different types of explanation" (p. 236).

Limitations of Public Opinion Data on Attitudes toward Police Violence

If public opinion, perceptions, beliefs, and attitudes about the police affect citizens' behavior on such matters as reporting crimes to the police and serving as witnesses and jurors, it is essential that public sentiment be ascertained. The exact role that these data can and should play in the ensuing policy debate on police use of force is, however, less certain.

Several cautions should be kept in mind in considering public opinion on sensitive issues like police use of excessive force (see Moore 1992). In fact, a statement first published in *Public Opinion Quarterly* more than fifty years ago summarizes critical aspects of public opinion data: "Since public opinion is demonstrably sensitive to events and organized pressures, each survey should be taken as a photograph of opinion *taken at a particular point of time*. All interpretations of these measurements of opinion must take this time factor into account" (Rae 1940: 75). Polls about public attitudes toward police use of force are usually conducted in reaction to a highly publicized incident; there are very few periodic time series data on this topic and on related subjects. Rae also pointed out that "poll results can be interpreted only in the light of the specific question asked and, consequently, that differences in the wording, phrasing or manner of presentation of the question to the respondent cannot be ignored" (1940: 75–76).

As noted in chapter 3, it is important to remember that even national surveys fail to assay the opinion of "the public," as they usually exclude significant segments of the population. For example, national polls often include only noninstitutionalized persons over the age of eighteen, while polls conducted via telephone exclude the 5 to 7 percent of the population who do not have telephone service. In addition, polls require substantial training of interviewers to avoid biasing "interviewer effects" and usually produce shorter, less detailed answers than face-to-face interviews (Bradburn and Sudman 1988). Finally, the highly summarized accounts of public opinion surveys that are published in the media create the false impression that public opinion is monolithic. When substantial majorities of the public agree about an issue it is tempting to speak about the "public outcry" or a "mandate for reform." This conclusion assumes that people agree for common reasons, that they hold their views with uniform certainty and tenacity, and that significant pockets of minority opinion can be ignored.

Public Experience with Police Use of Force

A 1984 Roper Poll asked a national sample of respondents whether they thought that "police brutality is a very serious threat these days to citizens like yourself" (cited in Komarnicki and Doble 1985).[4] Fewer than one in five respondents felt that police brutality was a "very serious" threat, one-quarter responded "moderately serious," and one-half said police brutality was either "not much of a threat" or "not a threat at all." The 44 percent of respondents who felt that police brutality was either a "very serious" or "moderately serious" threat was very high in relation to the proportion of Americans who report having been actual brutality victims or knowing actual victims of police abuse of force (presuming, of course, that we can guess what definitions of police brutality the respondents brought to bear on this survey). If the perceived personal threat of police brutality is considered as a form of victimization, the 44 percent figure must be regarded as a serious concern, even if the experienced threat is much smaller.

Winick (1987) surveyed New York State residents regarding their experience with excessive use of police force. When asked, "Have you or any member of your household been the victim of any police misuse of force in the past five years?" 95 percent of his sample said "that neither they nor members of their household had *experienced* police misuse of force in the last five years," but nearly 17 percent of the sample reported that they or members of their households had witnessed police misuse of force during the period (p. A21). According to Winick, "The persons who witnessed or were victims of misuse of force (N=166) had been exposed to four kinds of activities: verbal abuse (49 percent), physical abuse (46 percent), nightsticks or twisters (24 percent), and deadly force (7 percent)" (1987: A21). The high rate of reported experience with deadly force led Winick to reinterview households who reported it. These in-depth interviews concluded that, "what happens in a situation where police display a gun, in an emotionally charged context where there is a perception of crisis or danger, may be subject to considerable distortion when it is recalled by participants and/or spectators. The reinterviews even suggested that some of the initially reported 'deadly force' incidents probably had not involved any officer misconduct at all" (1987: A21).

A national survey on experience with police use of excessive force was conducted by the Gallup Poll in March 1991, following the highly publicized beating of motorist Rodney King by members of the Los Angeles Police Department (LAPD) (Gallup 1991a).[5] In the Gallup Poll, 5 percent of respondents answered yes to the question, "Have you ever been physically mistreated or abused by the police?" Among nonwhite respondents, 9 percent said they had personal experience with police abuse. In addition, 8 percent of Americans claimed that someone in their own household had been physically mistreated or abused, and 20 percent of respondents said they knew someone who had experienced physical mistreatment or abuse at the hands of the police. This vicarious experience with police brutality was reported by 26 percent of big-city residents and by 30 percent of nonwhite respondents (Gallup 1991a, reprinted in Maguire et al. 1993: 173).

In summary, in both the New York State and national polls, only about 5 percent of respondents reported personal victimization by police. However, the surveys indicate that knowledge of others' victimization is much higher than personal victimization experiences, and that both types of victimization are probably not uniformly distributed throughout the population.

Public Attitudes toward Police Use of Force

Pollsters have been gauging public sentiment about police use of force for many years. These questions seek information about respondents' perceptions of the incidence of police misuse of force, whether the problem is serious in the area in which they live, whether certain groups are singled out for mistreatment, and what measures can be adopted to control the excessive use of force by police.

Perhaps the longest-running series of data on this issue is a set of five questions that have been presented to random samples of Americans between 1973 and 1991 by the National Opinion Research Center's General Social Survey (GSS) (see Flanagan and Maguire 1992; Maguire et al. 1993: 174-77). In this series of questions, respondents are first asked, "Are there any situations you can imagine in which you would approve of a policeman striking an adult male citizen?"

Responses to this item have been fairly stable from 1973 to 1991, ranging from 78 percent of respondents answering in the affirmative in 1983 to 66 percent in 1991. The percentage of Americans who said they can imagine a situation in which they would approve of a policeman striking an adult male citizen has hovered at about 70 percent for the past two decades.

This generic item is followed in the GSS by four specific examples of police use of force. These scenarios include "a policeman striking a citizen who . . . (a) was attacking the policeman with his fists, (b) was attempting to escape from custody, (c) had said vulgar and obscene things to the officer, and (d) was being questioned in a murder case." Data reveal important differences in support for police use of force in these different situations. They also indicate variation in support for police use of force among different groups.

First, these items show that Americans clearly distinguish between serious situations (a physical attack on the police officer or an attempted escape from police custody) and less serious situations (e.g., verbal abuse of the officer) in assessing the appropriateness of police use of force. These situational differences in support of police use of force characterize the GSS data throughout the 1973–1991 period. Second, there is less consistency in respondents' reactions to police use of force in the less serious scenarios than in the more serious circumstances. For example, approval of a police officer striking a citizen who was attacking the officer ranged from 90 to 98 percent across demographic groups. In contrast, support for an officer striking a citizen who was attempting to escape from custody varied substantially according to the sex, race, education, income, and religion of respondents. Women, nonwhites, persons with grade school education, persons in the $5,000 to $6,999 annual income category, and people eighteen to twenty years old were less likely to approve of physical violence toward a person attempting to escape than were members of other groups. Year-to-year variation in the approval of police striking a citizen in these specific situations has been relatively small; differences in approval ratings across situations have always been greater than differences within situations across years.

Pollsters have measured public attitudes toward excessive use of force by the police in many different ways. A May 1980 Gallup survey of black Americans asked: "Do you think there is any police brutality in the area in which you live?" Twenty-six percent of respondents said there was "a great deal" or "a fair amount" of police brutality in their area (Komarnicki and Doble 1985: 78). A poll by Research and Forecasts, Incorporated, during the same time period asked: "Do the police use too much force?" When the question was asked in that manner, 12 percent of a national random sample of Americans responded yes (Komarnicki and Doble 1985: 78). In yet another variation of wording, a 1982 survey asked residents of Louisville and Jefferson County, Kentucky, if they agreed with the statement, "Police officers in this neighborhood use more force than is absolutely necessary." In that survey, 14 percent of citizens responded "strongly agree" or "agree," 70 percent said either "disagree" or "strongly disagree," and 17 percent said "don't know" or did not respond (Urban Studies Center 1982). Interestingly, a smaller percentage of Louisville and Jefferson County residents agreed that police officers verbally harass people than agreed that police use excessive force.

A series of New York City polls examined residents' views on police use of force. A February 1985 poll by the *New York Daily News* found that while only 7 percent of white New Yorkers agreed that police "often use too much force" in making an arrest, 26 percent of black and Hispanic residents agreed with the statement. Similarly, while 18 percent of whites agreed that it was "common practice for New York City police to rough up suspects illegally after they have them in custody," 56 percent of blacks and 44 percent of Hispanics thought that this was common practice (Begans 1985). A *Daily News* poll taken in April 1985, following the highly publicized case of Queens police officers charged with torturing a suspect, found that the percentage of respondents who perceived such mistreatment to be "common practice" increased to 23 percent among whites and to 46 percent among Hispanic New Yorkers.

Racial differences in perceptions of police use of excessive force in New York City also were highlighted in a March 1987 *New York Times* poll. Respondents were asked, "Do you think that New York City police often engage in brutality against blacks, or don't they?" "Yes" was the response of 36 percent of whites, 70 percent of blacks, and 46 percent of Hispanics. When asked the same question about brutality against *whites*, 19 percent of whites, 24 percent of blacks, and 23 percent of Hispanics responded "yes."[6]

A Gallup Poll conducted in 1988 for *New York Newsday* dealt with criticisms of the New York Police Department following several accidental shootings and police-citizen confrontations (Gallup 1988). In that poll, 45 percent of city residents thought that the facts that "the police are too quick to use their guns" and "the police use too much force" were "important" reasons why police get involved in such situations. In contrast, 65 percent of respondents considered the fact that "the police force is understaffed," and 70 percent that "the police are under too much pressure," to be important reasons for the confrontations. The point that such public perceptions change over time is illustrated by a follow-up Gallup Poll conducted for *Newsday* one year later (Gallup 1989). In 1989, only 29 percent of New Yorkers agreed that "the police use too much force" (and only 9 percent "strongly agreed"), but 67 percent felt still that "the police are under too much pressure."

A perspective on trends in public attitudes toward excessive use of force by the police is provided by data from the Greater Cincinnati Survey, a poll that has been conducted each fall since 1979. The question that has been repeated is "In your opinion, would you say that Cincinnati police generally use too much force in making arrests, about the right amount of force, or too little?" Responses have been fairly stable from 1979 to 1992, ranging from a high of 27 percent who said "too much force" in 1982 to a low of 16 percent in 1984 and 1985. In the 1992 poll, 23 percent of Cincinnati residents felt that too much force was used in making arrests (Bishop 1992).

Winick, in his New York State survey, asked residents for their perception of the trend in police use of force. One-quarter of New Yorkers thought that police misuse of force had increased between about 1981 and 1986, whereas a majority thought it had remained the same (Winick 1987). One-third of New Yorkers thought that misuse of force had increased between 1966 to 1986.

The Impact of the Rodney King Incident

As mentioned above, public opinion polling data are highly volatile and susceptible to the influence of major events. The televised videotaped beating of motorist Rodney King on March 3, 1991, in Los Angeles is a classic example of a media event that can provoke discussion of topics previously ignored by the media, sensitize the public to an issue, and change public opinion. As an illustration of the last point, consider the nationwide Gallup Poll conducted during the period March 14–17, 1991. Fully 92 percent of respondents had "seen or read [something] recently about the videotaped incident in Los Angeles in which policemen were seen beating a motorist" (Gallup 1991a: 53). More than two-thirds said such incidents occur "very frequently" or "somewhat frequently" in "police departments across the country," and 20 percent testified that such incidents occur "very or somewhat frequently" in their "local police department in their area." In response to the question, "Do you think there is any police brutality in your area, or not?" 35 percent responded "yes" (Maguire et al. 1993: 173), nearly four times the number of affirmative responses received in a 1965 survey on the same question. How much of the fourfold increase in perception of police brutality is directly attributable to the King videotape cannot be determined, but knowledge of the incident was widespread, and its likely impact on the poll responses is, therefore, substantial.

The data show that in 1991 the following subgroups of Americans were more likely than others to believe that police brutality existed in their area: males, persons younger than fifty years, residents of Western states (the King incident occurred in California), residents of large cities, nonwhites, college-educated persons, political moderates, and persons who claim no religious affiliation. With few exceptions, these attributes are similar to well-known correlates of general attitudes toward the police and toward police use of force.

Another poll conducted by *Time* magazine and CNN accentuates the differences between African Americans and Anglos in interpreting the actions of the police shown in the King videotape. After the officers who beat King were acquitted in the first (state court) trial, the poll found that 72 percent of whites and 92 percent of blacks believed that the amount of force shown on the videotape was excessive. Moreover, 82 percent of black respondents believed the verdict would have been different if both the police officers and the man they had beaten had been white, whereas only 44 percent of white respondents believed this. In addition, 89 percent of blacks (compared to 52 percent of whites) said the verdict would have been different if the police had been black and the man beaten had been white (Lacayo 1992; see also chapter 6).

Lasley (1994) conducted a time-series of Los Angeles citizens' attitudes toward police use of force before, shortly after, and several months after the Rodney King incident. He found that during the pre-King phase, all respondents reported increases in positive attitudes toward the police. However, after the videotaped beating, attitudes toward the police declined, most among blacks. Several months after the beating, positive attitudes toward the police among Hispanics and whites began to rise, but among blacks they continued to decline significantly. Minority disapproval of the Los Angeles police later in 1995 manifested itself in widespread endorsement of the acquittal of O. J. Simpson.

Referring to the impact of the police use of force on public opinion in the minority community, Los Angeles Police Chief Daryl Gates (1992: 2) commented that "any visual depiction of force can appear worse than it is." According to Gates, the Rodney King "incident would automatically evoke a greater response than if the man had been white or Hispanic. Race is often interjected and can become a significant factor when really it shouldn't be" (1992: 3). Studies on police use of force taken in their totality indicate that some portion of the high level of perceived police brutality is probably due to the extraordinary media attention given to the King incident, and later to the tape of police detective Mark Fuhrman's remarks. At the same time, patterns of variation in attitudes toward the excessive use of force by the police, measured after 1991, are consistent with previous research.

Role of the Media

Individual and social factors play a part in the formation of personal beliefs, making it difficult to associate a specific attitude with a specific event or a particular source (Surette 1992). Similarly, attitudes toward the police and opinions on police excessive use of force originate in a complex interaction of many forces, including the media. The extent to which the media affect citizens' attitudes toward the police is a topic of considerable debate (as is the controversy concerning media influences—especially movies and television—on rates of violent crime committed by American youngsters).

Police officers believe television shows lionizing the police lead the public to expect too much from law enforcement personnel (Arcuri 1977). Unrealistic expectations and the tendency to simplify and trivialize portrayals of police agents characterize the media (Haney and Manzolati 1981; Goldstein 1993). Some police officers have been portrayed as supercops, capable of solving any crime (Warr 1980). Other police officers are portrayed as incapable of the basic requirements of police work, as incompetent or sadistic (Culver 1978; Rarick et al. 1973). Media portrayals of illegal or questionable methods of enforcing the law, including excessive use of force, lead many to believe that police agencies are staffed by brutal and corrupt individuals. These perceptions, whether justified or not, have contributed to the idea of the police as superhuman yet flawed crime fighters (see also Skolnick and McCoy 1985).

The power of television to bring visual messages into our homes has greatly changed the ability of the media to influence public opinion (Garofalo 1981; Graber 1980). This influence is heightened by the fact that for many people, the sole source of information about the police is television and film portrayals of police activity (Dominick 1973, 1978). Establishing and measuring these effects are difficult tasks owing to the vast number of media outlets and their varying degrees of influence (McLeod and Reeves 1980). Among the effects deserving further analysis is the possible influence of film and television depictions of police work on police self-images (see Geller and Scott 1992: 95, 331).

There is "some doubt about the ability of the mass media to affect attitudes through the unorganized, unplanned content of news" (Surette 1992: 86), but a highly "organized" media campaign may greatly enhance the media's ability to sway public opinion. According to Gates, for example, the Rodney King incident sent "the entire LAPD hurtling into a bottomless pit of distrust and public disfavor" (1992: 4). In public opinion polls immediately after the King incident conducted by the Los Angeles Times, 50 percent of respondents said the King beating made them lose confidence in the police.

According to Fishman (1978) and Surette (1992: 62), "once a news organization adopts a crime theme, others will likely pick it up as well. If the focus becomes industry-wide, a media crime wave results."[7] Sabato (1991) called the intense media scrutiny of the King incident a "feeding frenzy." According to Gates, "the Los Angeles Daily News alone ran 500 stories on the LAPD in 125 days," indicting the LAPD on "racism, brutality, and gross mismanagement" (Gates 1992: 352). Gates would probably argue that he, too, was the subject of a feeding frenzy: "The media continued to berate us, continued to spotlight every blemish, every failure, every little chink in LAPD armor, anything that could take the shine off the department" (1992: 352).

The effects of the media on attitudes toward the police "differ depending on the subjects, the medium, and the content communicated" (Surette 1992: 80). Surette says that "newspapers tend to affect beliefs about crime, whereas television more affects attitudes" (1992: 80). Although anecdotal evidence suggests that news programs may attempt to boost ratings by emphasizing the sensational aspects of crime stories, Dominick (1978) reports that no studies have correlated crime wave reporting with attempts to increase ratings.

Surette (1990) has identified two areas in which research is needed to determine more scientifically the media influence on public perception of police use of force. First, what are the possible *long-term* effects of a feeding frenzy, such as stories about the Rodney King videotape or the Mark Fuhrman tape played during the trial of O. J. Simpson, on public attitudes toward use of force? Longitudinal studies could explore the type and kind of medium that has the most effects, whether it be news programming, dramas, or documentaries. The differences between print and electronic media influences might also be explored in the context of public perceptions of the police abuse of force. For example, although the Rodney King incident would probably not have made as big an impact if the incident had been recorded in the print media instead of on videotape, research is still needed to determine how big the difference might have been. In addition, the cumulative effects on public opinion of repeated exposure to police use of excessive force episodes, such as those involving Rodney King and Mark Fuhrman, remain to be explored. Second, what demographic groups are most susceptible to media influence? Public relations efforts could be aimed at these groups to rectify the damage caused by overexposure to police abuse of force.

Observations and Recommendations

There is some evidence that Americans' faith in a broad range of social institutions has weakened since the 1980s. Lipset and Schneider (1983) have referred to this phenomenon as a "confidence gap." Mistrust of governmental entities and ambivalence toward the police are exacerbated by the fact that police officers—along with correctional officers and, arguably, certain mental health workers—are the only people in civilian society with the authority to use discretionary force. Westley's (1970) observations of a quarter century ago remain true today, namely that the public's perception of police brutality is based on little knowledge of the routine demands of police work. A public educational campaign could address this problem and could be enhanced by coverage of community policing strategies. Perhaps the media as well as the public need greater exposure to the routine aspects of police work, especially in relation to the activities involving a low incidence of police use and abuse of force.

Public opinion may also act as a vehicle of social control, restraining police use of force. In the aftermath of the state court acquittal in 1992 of the officers who beat Rodney King in Los Angeles, the police department did not respond to violence in the streets for several hours, presumably because of the fear of what the public would say about the hasty use of force. Between the beating of King in March 1991 and the postverdict April 1992 riots in Los Angeles, officers in the LAPD were labeled by some as inept cowards. Daily media stories on alleged police brutality led to a cumulative diminution of public confidence in the Los Angeles police and an increase in frustration, cynicism, and uncertainty among officers. Before the riots, dispirited, indecisive, and tentative officers were making fewer arrests and having fewer contacts with citizens (Eagan 1992). After the riots, public confidence in the police dropped even further. A poll conducted by the *Los Angeles Times* indicated that 80 percent of Angelenos believed that the police responded too slowly to the riots (Clifford and Ferrell 1992). No doubt the negative public perception of the LAPD's use of force, owing to the King beating and subsequent investigations, contributed to the inappropriate police response in the early stages of the riots and to the public's subsequent condemnation.

Different segments of society and incongruous community groups want different kinds of police practices. Individuals who have never had an unsatisfactory encounter with the police are generally supportive of the police or at least ambivalent (Cashmore and McLaughlin 1991). As Locke points out in chapter 6, ethnic and racial minorities historically have viewed the police as oppressors of individual rights and freedoms. The NAACP (1995) has concluded that "perhaps the most serious problem facing the minority community is police use of excessive and deadly force in the name of law enforcement" (pp. 29–30). White residents in the suburbs have a different idea of police use of force than inner-city blacks. Both the 1967 Presidential Commission and the 1991 Christopher Commission recommended that police agencies become more involved in neighborhood policing to improve community relations and to address the public's crime and disorder problems. The NAACP (1995) points out that "In the final analysis, the police know that if they are serious about reducing crime in the 'inner city,' they cannot do it without the help of the community. . . . It is incumbent on law enforcement to win back the trust of the citizens they serve" (p. 106).

In addition to better recruitment, selection, and training of police officers, we consider it essential to develop retraining programs aimed at reducing violence among current police officers. This is crucial because the Christopher Commission (as well as earlier researchers) found that LAPD officers with a high number of brutality complaints were also the most productive officers in enforcing the criminal law (Independent Commission on the LAPD 1991).[8] Future researchers also need to examine the impact of the police subculture on legitimizing violence among police officers, even minority officers.

This chapter's review of public opinion data on attitudes toward police abuse of force leads to an intriguing but unresolved dilemma. If we believe that public perceptions that excessive use of force is common are inaccurate, then efforts are needed to educate the public about the realities of police work and the relative infrequency of abuse of force. If we believe that these public perceptions are accurate—that they reveal police brutality in the United States as a serious problem—then perhaps organizational and structural changes in the way police agencies conduct their operations are needed. The most likely situation is that both conclusions are valid, that police abuse of force is indeed a problem in this country and that the perception of the problem is exaggerated, especially among certain groups. If both conclusions are accurate, then the most sensible long-term strategy is to educate the public and change the police. This dual objective seeks to improve the nature and quality of police-citizen relationships in America, for the benefit of both.

NOTES

1. See chapter 10 on the popularity among John Birch groups of the "Support Your Local Police" campaigns around the United States.

2. Gamson and McEvoy's general conclusions were supported by polling data after the 1992 Los Angeles riots. For example, Church (1992) found that the law-abiding public may allow the police to use more force in times of high crime than when society is peaceful and tranquil: "White fear of black crime is so high as to lead some to excuse almost any behavior on the part of the police who are supposedly protecting them against it" (p. 25). Thus, there is some evidence to suggest that citizens' fears about crime legitimize police use of force.

3. For example, after the state court acquittal of the police officers in Los Angeles shown in the videotaped beating of Rodney King, a *Time/CNN* poll showed that more African Americans than Caucasians believed they received unfair treatment from the police. Twenty-three percent of whites believed that in an encounter with police they run the risk of being treated unfairly, an opinion held by 48 percent of blacks (Lacayo 1992).

4. Much of the polling data cited below derives from *American Public Opinion Index (1980–1990)* (Gallup 1991b).

5. A Louis Harris poll on public ratings of local police reputations for using excessive force was conducted in 1992 (see Maguire et al. 1993: 172).

6. Similar racial differences were shown in a *Los Angeles Times* poll conducted in February 1990. Respondents were asked for their impression of law enforcement in their neighborhood "when it comes to pushing people around." Sixty percent of Anglos, 50 percent of Latinos, and 33 percent of blacks reported "favorable" impressions. On another item, 19 percent of Anglos, 33 percent of Latinos, and 48 percent of blacks said there was a "great deal" or "fair amount" of police brutality in their area.

7. Also see Leff et al. (1986) for a discussion of "crusading journalism" and public policy formulation. See also Skolnick and McCoy (1985) for a discussion of the types of police problems that do *not* lend themselves to broadcast (especially television) news coverage.

8. Productivity as appraised by these studies may or may not resemble productivity according to community policing and problem-oriented policing standards.

CHAPTER SIX

The Color of Law and the Issue of Color: Race and the Abuse of Police Power

HUBERT G. LOCKE

Every public officer who under color of authority, without necessity, assaults or beats any person is guilty of a violation of [law].—Judge Stanley Weisberg's instructions to the jury in the state trial of the four officers accused of using excessive force against Rodney G. King

This chapter addresses a feature of the issue of police use of excessive force in which the problems of discussion are as much definitional and political as they are empirical and analytical. The definitional and political problems are intertwined; a number of persons might prefer—perhaps insist—that the issue be stated as one of racism and police brutality, while others would bridle at these words. Both terms point to a volatile problem in American society today: race is a factor in the way some persons behave toward others, and, on occasion, police officers do use more physical force than is lawfully necessary in interacting with citizens. It is the interconnection between these two realities—whether race is a factor in circumstances in which police use excessive force—which has long been subject to fierce debate, one that has been raised to unprecedented visibility, if not volatility, by the events surrounding the videotaped assault on Rodney G. King by Los Angeles police officers on March 3, 1991.

To defuse the discussion of an issue raised to intense national prominence by the King assault, state trial of the accused police officers, verdict, violent aftermath, and subsequent federal trial of the accused officers, this chapter has a less politicized title. The acknowledged risk of losing the attention of those who believe that the problem of police excessive force toward persons of color persists, in part, because of an inability of analysts to "tell it like it is" is assumed precisely because of the persistence and volatility of the problem. Its control and, it is to be hoped, eventual eradication depend in large measure on the degree to which the issue can be stripped of its emotional content and consequences and instead viewed as a problem of gross lawlessness by those sworn to uphold the law.

Viewing the problem from the perspective of law—what is licit or illicit behavior—provides a relatively precise definition of what is at issue. In some quar-

ters, any unwarranted or unwelcome police conduct may constitute brutality—
including the use of a racial slur or profane or abusive language. As crude and
inappropriate as such language may be, it does not aid the examination of the issue
to lump it together with excessive physical force under the rubric "brutality." Any
definition or category that designates too much ultimately describes nothing usefully. Moreover, and by extension, a legal perspective on excessive force offers a
reasonably clear and concrete set of examples of the events and circumstances in
which specific and, on occasion, documented behavior is at issue.

Ironically, while some might wish to broaden its application, it is the narrow,
legal definition of police use of excessive force—acting "under color of authority,
without lawful necessity"—that most persons of color would agree is at the core
of their complaints about police misconduct.[1] One of the reasons that the Rodney
King beating engendered so widespread and uniform a reaction from nonwhite
Americans is the perception that police officers frequently act toward "minorities" in ways that are demeaning, if not physically abusive, because they enjoy the
protective color and authority of their office.

Violence is an experience far too common in the cultures of poverty. What may
appear to be officially sanctioned violence—excessive force "under color of authority"—therefore becomes especially odious to a person of color, who through
diligence may escape other circumstances of violence only to be subject to violence
at the hands of the police. What a single incident in Los Angeles in March 1991
made an issue of intense public attention has long been a problem that aroused
passion in urban ghettos across the United States.

The Legacy of the 1960s

In December 1964, just after the first in what would be a four-year wave of summer civil disorders, the Practicing Law Institute (New York), with the assistance
of the Rockefeller Fund, convened a three-day forum on "The Community and
Racial Crises." The meetings were attended by municipal, state and federal officials, police chiefs, prosecutors, law professors, and representatives of civil rights
and community relations agencies. Both the agenda and the discussions were re-
flective of the national mood of the time and, among the agency representatives
present, of the relative levels of awareness and sensitivity to issues of race in their
various fields. One of the topics of discussion, "Racial Tensions and the Police,"
touched off a fierce exchange between representatives of the police and civil rights
agencies on the issue of police brutality (Stahl et al. 1966).

Two articles from *The Police Chief* among the background materials presented
to conferees encapsulate attitudes toward police brutality by police administrators in the 1960s. The thrust of the first article, by the International Association of
Chiefs of Police's executive director, was evident in its opening sentence: "I know
of no period in recent history when the police have been the subject of so many

unjustified charges of brutality, harassment and ineptness." With references to an editorial in the same journal, the author went on to decry "baseless charges of police brutality" made to cover "excesses and illegal conduct on the part of some demonstrators involved in the current racial tensions," as well as the excesses of "hoodlums" who "falsely [fly] the banner of civil rights" (Stahl et al. 1966: 120).

The same theme was echoed by the second IACP official, who described police brutality as "a commonplace and almost automatic accusation attached to any physical action taken by an official to control disorder" and as "a battle-cry . . . used by supposedly responsible Negro leaders to whip up support among their followers" (ibid.: 126). Police positions on the issue at the time tended to be reinforced by elements of the media; a *U.S. News and World Report* article listed Supreme Court rulings, civil rights pressures, and cries of police brutality "as signs of an impending breakdown in law and order throughout the nation" (Locke 1967: 625).

In less strident tones, the community side of the controversy was stated by an official of the NAACP:

> Concerning the basic facts, there can hardly be any dispute. Police brutality does occur, and the only question is how much of it there is, and where. . . . Unnecessary force is sometimes used in making arrests, although the determination of what is and is not "unnecessary force" is often extremely difficult.
>
> Neither can it be denied that, at present, large numbers (majorities in some instances) of Negroes have come to regard policemen as oppressors rather than protectors. . . . Finally, it is clear that no police force, operating under conditions short of a police state, can hope to function effectively for very long in a situation of crisis deriving from resentment or resistance on the part of massive proportions of the community in which it works.[2] (Stahl et al. 1966: 169)

During the 1960s the issue of police use of excessive force polarized police officials and large segments of the nation's Black populace and civil rights community (on the role of the civil rights community in forcing reform on American policing, see Williams and Murphy 1990). Three decades later, the assertions by the NAACP representative remain at the core of current discussions regarding the police and their behavior in communities of color across the nation: How widespread are incidents of the use of excessive force, where and under what circumstances do they occur, and does the excessive force problem cause the police to be viewed in nonwhite communities as oppressors rather than as protectors?

The Literature

What may be one of the earliest research inquiries concerning the police and "minority community relations" was also a subject of discussion at the 1964 conference. A collaborative study by the IACP and the U.S. Conference of Mayors had been designed to "gather information on police policies, practices and problems with respect to community relations and racial demonstrations in U.S. cities of over 30,000 population." The study serves as a benchmark on the police and their relationships with communities of color on the eve of what would become an era of immense change in American policing (Stahl et al. 1966: 143–58).

Much of the survey, which covered 165 cities, was calculated to discover the extent to which the cities were prepared for handling large-scale racial demonstrations; several questions, however, elicited findings on more basic race-related concerns. For example:

- One-half (N=83) of the cities reported difficulties in recruiting Black officers because "applicants fail exams and standards."[3]
- Six departments, in their personnel assignments, restricted the arrest powers of nonwhite officers; thirty-four assigned nonwhite officers to predominantly nonwhite sectors of the city (see also Williams and Murphy 1990: 8); forty departments paired white and nonwhite officers only on special details.[4]
- Forty-eight departments reported they were under charges of brutality; forty-six were charged with "differential treatment" (of white and nonwhite citizens). Only two departments processed citizen complaints through a police review board.

The IACP-U.S. Conference of Mayors' early 1960s survey appeared just as academic interest in American policing was taking off. By 1970, the first of a torrent of research on police behavior began to appear in scholarly and professional journals (Sherman 1980a: 69). A quarter-century later, that research has produced an avalanche of publications. On the critical issue of the police use of excessive force, however, the research tells us far less than we would like to know about a problem that has been at the center of a long-standing debate between police and communities of color.

The questions that concern persons of color and researchers alike are fairly easy to specify. Are white police officers inclined to be racially and ethnically prejudiced? Do they discriminate against nonwhite citizens? Are incidents of excessive force the consequence of a few "rotten apples" in the ranks of policing, or does the police system encourage and support such behavior? To what extent is the disproportionately high number of Black (and, increasingly, Latino) victims of excessive force due to internal police practices (e.g., police are more inclined to use excessive force against nonwhite citizens) or to external circumstances (e.g., a greater involvement by persons of color in criminal activity)? Are "minority" police officers disproportionately represented among those who use excessive force? Is there an organizational or occupational climate (i.e., a police culture) or a rank-and-file climate (a police subculture) that actively encourages or tacitly condones the use of excessive force?

Problems of Inquiry

The search for answers to these questions has encountered innumerable problems that aggrieved citizens would consider insignificant, if not trivial, but which are of fundamental importance to scholars and legal system officials. One has to do with collecting the facts. As late as 1978, the Federal Bureau of Investigation would not release data on the police use of force (Takagi 1978); much has changed in this regard at both the federal and local levels, although there is still a need for more standardization and goal-oriented compilation and reporting of data (Geller and Scott 1992).[5] In 1992, there was a pitched dispute between the chair of the House Government Operations Committee and the U.S. Department of Justice over the release of a review of 15,000 complaints against police (some, but not all, concerning excessive force) received by the Department's Civil Rights Division, its Federal Bureau of Investigation, and United States Attorneys over the previous six years (*Seattle Times*, March 4, 1992: A9; DeParle 1992).

A similar controversy surrounded a Chicago Police Department internal study of fifty persons allegedly abused by police; its release had to be ordered by a federal judge (*Chicago Sun-Times*, February 8, 1992: 4). By contrast, however, Chicago's and many other big-city police departments have for several years been releasing data on shootings in which police were involved, albeit shootings the vast majority of which are considered justifiable by police administrators (Geller and Scott 1992).

Next to the importance of adequate data are the methods of analysis. Griswold reviewed most of the research literature up to 1978 to see whether the police discriminate against "minority group members." For nearly every finding presented, criticism of the measures used or the failure to control for other possible influences, or counterevidence could be offered that pointed to other possible explanations. Griswold (1978: 65) states: "What conclusions, if any, can be made about differential treatment of blacks by the police? The conflicting evidence paints a rather fuzzy picture, with no clear evidence which can be presented to resolve the issue."

Two years later, Sherman (1980a: 69) noted that the preponderance of police research tended to examine two-factor assumptions about the causes or associational features of police behavior. "The present state of the field," he wrote, "is best characterized as a series of bivariate assertions about the impact of certain variables on police behavior about which a moderate amount of empirical evidence has accumulated." A decade later, the evidence is much more extensive; the findings, however, continue to show what Sherman termed "weak relationships between a wide range of the hypothesized causes and police behavior" (see also Sherman 1980b). In lay terms, this simply means that researchers do not know or cannot assert much, with empirical reliability, about whether there are racial reasons for police behavior because other possible explanations cannot be ruled out.[6]

After data have been collected and analyzed, there is the problem of the generalizability of findings. Most studies, for reasons of accessibility, manageability, and funding, are of local police agencies or samples of police documents, officer attitudes, court cases, or other data sources in one or several police jurisdictions. Occasionally, as with the studies by Fyfe on the police use of deadly force, the insights or conclusions gathered from a single department or several-department study are sufficient to prompt significant policy initiatives (Fyfe 1982). Often, however, the findings from a single department have—or are treated as having —significance only for that department. The cumulative evidence from single-department inquiries may confound rather than clarify an issue, reducing the likelihood that any general conclusions can be drawn.

I do not mean to imply, however, that it is impossible for generalizable, single-agency studies to be devised to answer questions about whether race is a contributing factor in police use of improper force. If the evidence from a series of such studies seems impossibly inconsistent—as it often does—then perhaps researchers are asking the wrong questions. Perhaps one of the questions to ask would be under what *conditions* race is a factor in abuses of force. It may be that the effect of race is contingent on the social context, as some studies of sentencing have revealed. Or it may be, as Fyfe has found in the context of police use of *deadly* force, that the effect of race is contingent on organizational context (e.g., the values expressed by the police chief). Much remains to be learned, given the primitive nature of the research data to date.

Finally, there is the awkward, seldom discussed, but not infrequent problem of research bias. Research is generally viewed as important for, among other reasons, its capacity to set aside political or other assumptions in order to examine an issue dispassionately and without preconceived notions.[7] Since the monumental study of Gunnar Myrdal on race in America (1962), we have known this general proposition is considerably weaker when questions of race are at stake (pp. 1035–64). Scholars are seldom comfortable with the reminder that their work might be affected by other than scientific dictates; the comparative inattention to the issue of police use of excessive force against persons of color, for example, when placed against the unending examination of correlates between race and crime, suggests that research and the setting of research priorities may not be value-free.

This is not a sweeping indictment of the entire research community. To be sure, virtually every study of police behavior in general, and of the use of force in particular, has attempted to address the effects of race, and many of these studies have been motivated by the issue of differential treatment by race. Some of the scholarly inattention to the use of nonlethal force and the effects of race may be due to the paucity of existing data and the difficulty of primary data collection. Still, as the will to learn about a problem rises, the funds to enable the learning may increase (depending largely, of course, on the power of those who wish the learning to occur).

What Do We Know?

The evidence is indisputable that, compared to general population distributions, persons of color are disproportionately represented among those subjected to police use of force where the discharge of a firearm is involved (Binder and Scharf 1982; Mendez 1983; Trujillo 1981; Geller and Karales 1981b; Fyfe 1981a, 1981b; Geller and Scott 1992). Beyond this finding, researchers can assert little empirically about the police use of appropriate and excessive force that is not in dispute.

For reasons related to the protocols of research, many inquiries regarding excessive force have focused on police shootings, because shooting incidents tend to be unambiguous as to whether force is involved (although whether the force is excessive remains an open question), and since the early 1980s the data (police shooting review reports, autopsy and coroners' inquest reports, newspaper accounts, etc.) have been relatively abundant and accessible. A large number of police shooting studies (summarized in Geller and Scott 1992) find that nonwhites constitute a disproportionately high number—compared to their percentages in the general populace—of victims of such incidents.

If we pursue the matter further, however, we find many individual, situational, organizational, or legal circumstances that have a potential impact on this general finding. Friedrich, in the same year in which Sherman summarized the state-of-research knowledge regarding four aspects of police behavior (service, detection, arrest, and violence—Sherman 1980a), offered a summary analysis of research on police use of force. Friedrich reviewed the three primary explanations advanced for variations in the use-of-force phenomenon: individual characteristics of police officers, situational characteristics of encounters between police and citizens, and the organizational culture of police work. He concluded, a decade after extensive research inquiries had been undertaken on the topic, that "many factors commonly thought to affect the use of force have little effect" (1980).

As noted above, what every study of police use of fatal force has found is that persons of color (principally Black males) are a disproportionately high percentage of the persons shot by police compared to their representation in the general population (Goldkamp 1970; Kobler 1975; Peirson 1978; Takagi 1978; Fyfe 1978, 1981a, 1981b, 1982; Geller and Karales 1981b; Binder and Scharf 1982; Binder and Fridell 1984; Horvath 1987; Sulton and Cooper, n.d.; Geller and Scott 1992). Where the studies diverge are the reasons for such disproportionality. Fyfe found uses of force to depend in part on real and immediate police hazard in specific incidents in one police jurisdiction (1981c) and in part on internal police practices in another (1982). Takagi (1978) questioned both the assumption-of-danger thesis as well as the culture-of-violence explanation, pointing to a number of compounding problems in the data which make for poor inquiries on the issue. Geller and Karales (1981b) found that Blacks and whites were equally likely to be shot by police, given their exposure to forcible felony arrests. In a related Chicago study, Geller (1981) found most variances in shooting participation by officers of different races to be explainable by the residency and deployment patterns of the officers involved. Binder and Scharf (1982) attribute the disproportionality of Blacks who are shot by police to community characteristics (e.g., the high rates of violence in inner cities); Goldkamp (1970) tentatively advanced a corresponding explanation based on arrest rates for violent crime.

Mendez (1983), after analyzing deadly force rates and population in relation to violent crime arrests, property crime arrests, reported crime, and the length of public service, found only two offense rates related to the use of deadly force: robbery and larceny (the first, positively related; the second, negatively related). Binder and Fridell (1984), in a review of police shooting studies, found any conclusion about a pattern of racial discrimination in police shootings to be confounded by variables that support alternative explanations. Horvath (1987), reanalyzing the data used by Fyfe (1980a), disputed Fyfe's conclusion that there might be a geographic relationship between the rates of police shootings and the incidence of criminal homicides; Horvath found the relationship "spurious" and suggested the correlation is probably due to a third, unknown factor. Significantly, none of these studies, with the exception of Takagi (1978) and Fyfe's 1982 study of Memphis, suggest a racial motivation behind the high number of deaths of persons of color at the hands of the police or find any evidence to support the allegation that racial bias operates *systematically* as a factor in police shooting (see generally, Geller and Scott 1992). Worden, in chapter 2, departs from most prior findings by suggesting that race may play a contributing role in police use and misuse of *non*lethal force (see also Black 1980).[8]

The notoriety surrounding the Los Angeles Police Department, highlighted by the Rodney King affair, prompts special attention to a study of firearms discharges by Los Angeles police officers (Meyer 1980). Based on information supplied by the department, the study found that of 584 suspects shot at during a five-year period (1974–78), in cases where the race of the suspect was known, 321 (55 percent) were Black, 126 (22 percent) were Hispanic, 131 (22 percent) were white, and 6 (1 percent) were of other nonwhite origin. The race of 21 suspects was unascertainable (they were excluded from the total in calculating percentages). In 1979, 46 (45 percent) of the 102 suspects shot at were Black, 32 (31 percent) were Hispanic, and 23 (23 percent) were white.

Meyer's Los Angeles study also found that a higher proportion of shootings at

Black suspects were reported as caused by suspects disobeying the order of officers to halt and by suspects appearing to reach for weapons. A greater proportion of Black (28 percent) than Hispanic (22 percent) or white (20 percent) persons shot at by police were ultimately determined to have been unarmed, although a somewhat greater percentage of Black (54 percent) than Hispanic (48 percent) or white (49 percent) victims were carrying guns. There was no significant difference in the number of shots fired at suspects by race when other circumstances surrounding the shootings were controlled statistically.

Looking at the Los Angeles Police Department about a decade later than Meyer, the Christopher Commission (Independent Commission on the LAPD 1991) implied a pervasive relationship between officer prejudice and mistreatment by the department of minority citizens. Polling of officers in the LAPD even disclosed some belief among the rank and file that prejudice contributed to such abuses of force. The Christopher Commission stated: "If combined with racial and ethnic bias, the Department's active style of policing creates a potentially grave problem. Because of the concentration of . . . crime in Los Angeles' minority communities, the Department's aggressive style—its self-described 'war on crime'—in some cases seems to become an attack on those communities at large. The communities, and all within them, become painted with the brush of latent criminality" (p. 74).

Perhaps the most important policy contribution of two decades of research on the issue comes from a line of studies on the control of police use of deadly force. Fyfe (1978, 1980a, 1981a, 1981b, 1981c) discovered a significant impact on the nature and frequency of police-citizen violence in New York City from stringent departmental guidelines and shooting review procedures. This finding was reinforced by Fyfe's study in Memphis (1982), where he found that police officers frequently engaged in "elective" shootings (i.e., where the officer's life or that of a citizen other than the person confronted is not in danger). Geller and Karales (1981b), Geller and Scott (1992), Binder and Fridell (1984), and Wilson (1980) have all commented on restrictive shooting policies as control strategies for reducing police shooting incidents (particularly when such policies are coupled with other training and officer safety initiatives).

Perceptions

Although the role of race in police use of excessive force may remain empirically uncertain to researchers, it is far from problematic for countless citizens of color in America. Murty et al. (1990) found that most citizens are satisfied most of the time with the police, except for Black Americans (see also chapter 5). Lasley (1994) found that the attitudes of poor Hispanics and poor whites were more favorable toward Los Angeles police than were the attitudes of poor

African Americans. Lasley (1994: 249) also reports that "numerous studies . . . have found attitudes toward police to be most favorable among Caucasians and lowest among African-Americans, even while controlling for community context and demographic differences (Bayley and Mendelsohn 1969; Hahn 1971; Benson 1981)." Wagner (1980), reporting on a city in which Black residents were 41 percent of the populace, found that they filed twice as many complaints against the police as white residents (compare the findings of the Police Foundation's NIJ-funded study of excessive force—Pate and Fridell 1993). Davis (1990) found the urban poor and minorities to have the least favorable attitudes toward the police in New York City; Murty et al. (1990) found the same to be the case in Atlanta; and Lasley (1994) reached a similar conclusion in a study of inner-city Los Angeles residents. The finding transcends social status, as Boggs and Galliher (1975) found persons of higher socioeconomic status among Black citizens to hold more negative attitudes toward the police than whites of similar status.

The recency of several of the articles mentioned suggests that these perceptions persist even though policing has made significant progress in overcoming the conventions of law enforcement of the 1960s. In many communities a new generation of police leaders presides over a new generation of officers who come to police service with higher educational backgrounds and far better professional training than that of three decades ago. The ranks of policing are relatively more diverse today, with respect to both race/ethnicity and gender (see Williams and Murphy 1990: 12). The fact, however, that resentment in communities of color is not directed only toward white police officers and that studies show that non-white as well as white officers are likely to be high-rate users (but not necessarily abusers) of force (Fyfe 1978; Geller and Karales 1982; Geller and Scott 1992) suggest the problem is more complex than white/nonwhite equations. One study (Brandl et al. 1994) suggests that citizens' *attitudes* toward the police shape their perceptions and evaluations of their *contacts* with the police as much as, or more than, their *contacts* with the police affect their *attitudes* toward the police. The implication seems to be that changing citizens' attitudes may require more than changing the nature of their direct experiences.

Issues

If the bulk of the social science evidence remains unclear as to the salience of race in excessive force situations, the issues surrounding color and the police abuse of power are far less so. To some extent, the sifting of the evidence has contributed to a sharpening of the issues which, in turn, have become specific foci of attention for analysts, activists, and police administrators alike.

It had been commonplace in law enforcement for decades to blame the failures of police work—from corruption scandals to brutality charges—on a few "bad cops." By focusing too much on rotten apples, one can miss the possibility that the barrel is rotten and is spoiling the contents. These are perspectives on *causation*—officer predisposition versus socialization to a brutal work group. No matter which is the case, it is important to know whether officers accused of using excessive force are likely to be multiple offenders. Conventional wisdom and healthy suspicion combine, in this instance, to underscore a belief that the disproportionately high number of citizens of color involved in excessive force incidents are victims of a relatively small proportion of officers, who commit these offenses several times (see chapter 4).

An early clue to the repeat-offender phenomenon came from a source that, while it would not rank high on the scale of academic research, proved to be an important source of data. In February 1983, an investigative report on WMAQ-TV in Chicago was announced as the exposure of "a police system which fails to deal with the cops who are beating justice." The five-part telecast was based on a review of all lawsuits brought in federal court over a five-year period (1978–82) in which police brutality was alleged (see chapter 13 for additional discussion of such litigation). In all, 435 Chicago police officers were identified in the suits, 107 of whom subsequently were found to have been charged in two or more official complaints during the previous ten years, either in court or at the police department. Further investigation found that 13 of 68 officers in a single police district had been the subject of complaints three or more times over a two-year period.

The investigative report was not research in any academic sense, nor did it claim to be. Ironically, it did not set out to deal with police brutality nor, after shifting to the excessive force issue, with repeat offenders. Both were accidental discoveries that led to a report which set the agenda for Chicago mayoral politics during the winter of 1983 (Leff et al. 1986) and made a contribution to knowledge about excessive force complaints.

Academic research provides some evidence to support the Chicago discovery about repeat offenders. In a study of police shootings in Philadelphia between 1970 and 1978, Waegel (1984a) discovered that 0.2 percent of the sworn force (13 of 8,000 officers) accounted for 10 percent of all shooting incidents. Sixty-seven officers in Philadelphia—0.8 percent of the force—were involved in more than one shooting incident and accounted for 34 percent of all shootings.

A more recent study of the Los Angeles Police Department finds the same basic pattern. From 1986 through 1990, allegations of excessive force or improper tactics were filed against approximately 1,800 officers, more than 1,400 of whom had only one or two complaints. But 183 officers had 4 or more allegations, 44 had 6 or more, 16 had 8 or more, and one officer had 16 complaints. The 10 percent of officers with the highest number of excessive force or improper tactics allegations accounted for 27.5 percent of all such complaints (Independent Commission on the LAPD 1991; also see chapter 4).

The data involve only two urban police forces. Moreover, they do not control for the areas in which the officers were assigned, the race of the involved officers or civilians, the level of violence or the rates of arrest in the assigned areas, whether the officers were on or off duty when the alleged abuses of force occurred, whether the persons against whom force was used were found to be armed or unarmed, or any of a number of other variables (see also Renner and Gierach 1975).

The raw complaint data, however, even without measuring possible influences, are sufficiently striking that police administrators and others in a position to influence law enforcement policy are not apt to await regression analyses to screen out relevant from irrelevant factors, important as they are. Assuming a sizable organization, a department is at its peril if less than 1 percent of its officers are involved in over one-third of its shooting or other use-of-force incidents. In all but very small organizations, for so minuscule a portion of personnel to account for a potentially sizable performance problem would be a red flag alerting administrators to the need for immediate analysis and possible personnel action. Absent clear evidence that an officer's assignment to unusually dangerous tasks has occasioned his or her string of violent encounters, police managers would do well to err on the side of caution and, at least for an evaluative period, change the officer's assignment. And, in the interest of the officer's career longevity and the department's preservation of good public relations, empathetic police commanders might well want to reassign the officer in question even if they conclude that it was the *assignment* rather than a *predisposition* to violent tactics that accounted for the pattern of violent encounters. To simply ignore the reasons for a growing string of shootings or other serious uses of force by a small number of officers (even if each episode has been determined to be within departmental policy) would pose important questions about how concerned a police commander is about officers who use (or possibly abuse) force frequently.

The issue of how seriously the excessive force problem is taken by police also is illumined by the research literature reviewed by Lester (see chapter 9). In a survey of police officer attitudes in a small Southern city, Barker (1978) examined the extent to which officers tolerated "deviant" behavior, i.e., behavior contrary to accepted standards among other officers in the department. "Deviant" behavior in the survey was measured by attitudes toward police perjury, drinking, sleeping or having sex on duty, and police brutality.

The study found that, first, the more officers perceived a given "deviant" behavior to occur, the more tolerant they were of it, and, second, the less deviant the officers considered a given behavior, the more common they perceived its occurrence to be. Third, and most striking, police brutality was perceived to be one of the least deviant behaviors, equal in seriousness to sleeping on duty and, simultaneously, one of the most prevalent behaviors; 40 percent of the force were perceived to have committed acts of brutality at some point in their careers. As brutality was considered a less serious form of deviance, officers indicated they would report a fellow officer for brutality less often than for any other of the stated "deviances."

A corresponding study of officers in a medium-sized department (Lester and Ten Brink 1985) found that officers most likely to report fellow officers for acts of excessive force were also most likely to report them for other offenses, like drinking on duty or accepting a bribe. Taken together, the two studies suggest that brutality or the excessive use of force is part of a range of deviant behaviors that are not considered by some officers to be any more serious than other offenses—perhaps, among some, less serious—and that those officers who have the professional integrity to report excessive force offenses would be just as likely to report other violations of professional norms. A federally funded study under way in Ohio and Illinois should provide additional findings of interest concerning the prevalence of police abuse of force and officers' willingness to report their colleagues' misconduct to supervisors.

Perhaps more important, Carter (1976) learned that 62 percent of his officer respondents (in a single police agency) believed officers were entitled to use excessive force in retaliation for assaults against officers. If people of color are disproportionately engaged in what police see as resisting arrest, an officer's propensity to respond with avowedly excessive force could well produce patterns of abuse with racial dimensions. Sykes and Clark (1975) offered a theoretical framework, which they termed a theory of "deference exchange," for thinking about such problems. They argue that police expect acknowledgment by the citizen that police-citizen interactions are governed by an asymmetrical status norm—the police are the boss. If people of color disproportionately reject this norm, then police encounters with people of color are correspondingly more likely to give rise to behavior by citizens that officers interpret as disrespect.[9]

Given the extent to which the excessive force issue involves persons of color, the relative seriousness that officers attach to the excessive use of force is of considerable importance. If some police officers are inclined to consider the excessive use of force as less serious than drinking, or no more serious than sleeping on duty, some officers of the law and many citizens of color are assessing police behavior by fundamentally different norms. The state court acquittal of the officers who assaulted Rodney King and its bloody aftermath suggest just how dangerous such differences can be. The beating and the verdict essentially reflected the norms of those who do not attach great seriousness to excessive force. The subsequent disorder in Los Angeles depicted just how much those norms of four police officers and eight of twelve state court jurors were at odds with people of color in the nation's second largest city.

Some encouragement may be derived from the Lester and Ten Brink study (1985), which suggests that there is a cadre of police officers who do attach significance to the excessive use of force and who are willing to report offenders. It is about such officers that we wish to know much more than we do: their representation among police officers, their values and other possible motivations, their backgrounds, their views of their work and of the communities they serve, especially if they serve in communities of color.

"Police culture" has long been a topic of interest and inquiry among researchers and observers of the law enforcement scene (see chapter 10). The best literature on the police culture has been the writing of police officers themselves, sometimes as reflections on their own careers (Niederhoffer 1967; Niederhoffer and Blumberg 1970) or as the observations of "insiders" (Rubenstein 1973), and occasionally as popular fiction (e.g., Joseph Wambaugh's work). The writings of police tell of an occupational world characterized by immense solidarity among those who enter its ranks, one which comes to divide society between "us" and "them," and one whose protocols dictate a strict code of silence if misconduct on the part of another officer is at issue. With respect to excessive force and persons of color, officer attitudes, values, and behavior may be shaped as much by peer group pressure or the unwritten codes of conduct as by the administrative directives or the professional norms of policing.

The finding in many studies (Fyfe 1978; Geller and Karales 1982; Geller 1981; and others) that nonwhite officers in some locales use force in more incidents than might be expected given their representation on police forces is, on occasion, reported as if it were evidence in support of the proposition that the police are not racially discriminatory, i.e., if nonwhite officers use force (albeit not necessarily *excessive* force) frequently, the problem of police misuse of force cannot be one of racial attitudes or bias. An alternative conclusion might be that the overaggressive peer culture of policing in some agencies is so strong that it pressures Black officers, who might know better, into abusing minority-race citizens.

In point of fact, most of the studies showing disproportionate use of *deadly* force by minority-race officers do not attribute these patterns to punitive or other inappropriate motives. Instead, the studies suggest that residential and deployment patterns in many jurisdictions place officers of color in exceptionally dangerous places—where they are, more than fellow white officers, likely to have to use deadly force *legitimately,* both on and off duty. But the careful presentation of such findings by most researchers cannot prevent others from consciously or unconsciously twisting the conclusions to meet a preconceived text exonerating white officers of abuses solely because their nonwhite colleagues use violence just as or more often. If empirical evidence were to suggest disproportionate use of *excessive* force by officers of color, then it might indeed be valuable to research whether organizational climate and peer pressure—the culture and subculture of policing—are so influential as to override even racial background in shaping officer behavior.

Several studies also found that the demeanor of the citizen may have much to do with the behavior of the police officer. In common parlance, this problem is known as "flunking the attitude test" or "contempt of cop"; in the research literature, it first appeared as an almost incidental discovery or was reported inadvertently as a rationale for police conduct (Ferdinand and Luchterhand 1970). Piliavin and Briar (1964) were the first to note that demeanor was an important factor in police contacts with juveniles; Friedrich (1980) found demeanor to be one of two significant factors in the police use of force.

The demeanor of offenders is itself a complex issue, quite apart from questions of race. In innumerable instances an officer must deal with someone who is inebriated, under the influence of drugs, or, especially following the era of deinstitutionalization of mental health patients, mentally ill. Force used in these circumstances, if it is reasonably applied, is likely to be less problematic or, at the least, to be viewed with greater sympathy in doubtful situations.

Problems arise more often when force is used in circumstances where initial police conduct (e.g., the reason for a pedestrian or vehicle stop) is doubtful and where the resulting legal uncertainty of the situation triggers a verbal and then physical confrontation. When such problems repeatedly or disproportionately occur in encounters between police officers and persons of color, a serious problem in police-citizen relations as well as in police administrative responsibility occurs. This is best described by an assistant chief of the Los Angeles Police Department: "We expect people to go out and aggressively identify people, and then investigate them, and that puts these police officers in the middle between what we evaluate them on and what they are able to do legally. And so it results in police officers bluffing their way into situations and, when they stop people on the street, frequently the guy knows, you don't have any reason, and he knows that very well. And he knows they're bluffing. And that gets us in, time after time, into these conflict situations that end up, frequently, with use of force, frequently with manufacturing or at least puffing of the probable cause" (Independent Commission on the LAPD 1991; see also Muir 1977).

Two other interesting clues are to be found in the research literature. Friedrich (1980) was among the first to note the visibility of a police-citizen encounter to other officers and to the public as a significant factor in the police use of force. Wagner (1980) found that officers in two-person patrols were more likely to be targets of excessive force complaints than one-person patrols, supporting observations in an earlier monograph by the Police Foundation (Milton et al. 1977; see also Heaphy 1978). Finally, in the few studies to assert that the police may discriminate for racial reasons (e.g., Powell 1981, 1990), the bias was found to be prevalent primarily in "nonfelony mid-level types of offenses" (such as domestic disturbances, speeding, driving while intoxicated), perhaps because officers have the greatest discretion in such cases (see also Fyfe 1982; chapter 2; Tonry 1995).

The methodology of such studies typically limits their generalizability, as is often true also with studies of single jurisdictions.[10] Accordingly, it is prudent to consider these studies primarily as offering clues and informed speculations about the circumstances that surround certain police behavior. These clues are sufficient, however, to permit a hypothetical typology or profile of the circumstances under which the use of excessive force is most likely to occur.

Police use of excessive force is most likely to occur in a proactive encounter (initiated by the officer and not a citizen) when more than one officer is present. The officers will be from a department in which abuse of physical force is considered a minor to mid-level offense. Perhaps most important, the suspect will not act with complete deference toward the officer and probably will be disrespectful.

This hypothesized typology also describes with accuracy the Rodney King incident. The episode began with a police chase of King's vehicle by two California Highway Patrol officers; when King's vehicle was finally halted, ten minutes after pursuit began, twenty-one police officers were at the scene. All but two were officers of the Los Angeles Police Department. Testimony to the Christopher Commission by a retired thirty-eight-year veteran of the LAPD who served as assistant chief indicates the extent to which excessive force was, at the time (1991), considered a relatively minor problem:

I don't see anyone bringing these people up and saying, "Look, you are not . . . measuring up. . . ." I don't see that occurring.

The sergeants . . . are not held accountable so why should they be that much concerned . . . ? I have a feeling that they don't think that much is going to happen . . . if they try to take action and perhaps [they think they won't] even be supported by the lieutenant or the captain . . . when they do take action against some individual. (Report of the Independent Commission 1991: 32)

A second assistant chief of the department testified: "And so, that's an area that I believe we have failed miserably in, is holding people accountable for the actions of these people" (ibid.: 33).

Finally, there are the computer and radio messages transmitted between officers immediately following the beating of King. The comments of the officers ("he pissed us off, so I guess he needs an ambulance now"; "we had to chase him. . . . I think that kind of irritated us a little") reflect their perception that King had not acted toward them with the proper deference.

Future Directions for Research

While police chiefs and commanders continue to grapple with the volatile problem of excessive force and with its particularly explosive racial and ethnic features, scholars and researchers will continue to probe the multiple aspects of this phenomenon. What new lines of inquiry might be explored that could produce insights helpful to police administrators and policymakers?

In addition to those suggested earlier (e.g., learning more about officers who will stand up against peer pressure and criticize colleagues' abuses of force), the most promising pursuits may be avenues of professionalism and community policing. While community policing in some respects is a catch-phrase for a host of new (and often untested) police strategies and tactics (Goldstein 1993; Mastrofski 1993; compare Sparrow et al. 1993), it has the primary virtue of focusing attention on the relationship between those who deliver police services and the public. Professionalism, on the other hand, is a matter of continuing interest in policing. Taken together, community policing and professionalism constitute major elements in a research agenda that, politically, police officers can view positively rather than as adverse to their interests (Kelling and Kliesmet also advance this point in chapter 10). Substantively, such a research agenda would be based on the premise that police professionalism is measured, in part, by the way in which police services are delivered to various communities. The interests of both the police and the public may be served by research efforts that examine the quality of policing through the eyes of different segments of the service population.[11]

Inquiries on the police and "minority" problems in the past seldom have been undertaken by asking what the interests and priorities of minorities might be. For example, it will be instructive to learn how communities of color assess "effective" policing. What priorities would citizens of color set for the police in their communities? By what criteria would such citizens measure police performance? How do citizens of color assess police professional conduct? How significant is the race or ethnicity of a police officer in measures of police effectiveness by citizens of color?

Quite possibly, one would find little divergence between the views of citizens of color (or within communities of color[12]) and the views of professional-minded police officers on these questions (see chapters 5 and 9). It is also possible that some unexpected, helpful insights might emerge concerning differences between police and public opinions.

When the community policing and problem-oriented policing notions were first advanced, some scholars were surprised to discover the priority that residents placed on the removal of abandoned cars in their neighborhoods—symbols of community decay and public neglect that did not rank high on the priorities of the police; in all likelihood, few researchers would have attached much importance to them (see, generally, Goldstein 1990; Wilson and Kelling 1982). Similar discoveries might come from research inquiries that begin with identifying the concerns of people of color about policing (see Williams and Murphy 1990).

Conclusion

Research often proves frustrating or disappointing to those who do not engage in it (and not infrequently to those who do). What may appear as obvious or self-evident can, on careful analysis, turn out to be neither. Social science research is important to the extent that it forces those who are not content with unproven answers or unprovable propositions to continue probing the hard questions that confront societies.

In the wake of the state court trial of the LAPD officers who beat Rodney King and the subsequent riot, reporting on almost three decades of research most (but not all) of which fails to document a systematic relationship between race and the police use of excessive force risks being dismissed, if not scorned, in some quarters as of the same piece as the acquittal of King's assailants. To reject this body of research findings — or the present summary of it — because it seems to fly in the face of common knowledge would be a serious error, for at least two reasons.

In the absence of being able to confirm that racist acts — behaviors that are racially motivated — are pervasive in policing, we nevertheless have to deal with racially linked outcomes in law enforcement. The disproportionately high number of complaints filed by citizens of color which allege police misconduct (documented by Pate and Fridell 1993), the disproportionately high number of persons of color who are shot at, injured, or killed by police, the significant number of civil damage suits involving excessive force claims in which plaintiffs of color receive significant monetary awards all point to a police-minority community problem of considerable proportions. The problem of disproportionate harm to persons of color at the hands of police is much greater in some communities than in others; police and community leaders have worked at its resolution more urgently in some cities than in others.

In the final analysis, it may be more important to know that police abuse of force can be curbed or controlled (without impeding good, necessary police work) than it would be to establish whether it is race-neutral or race-biased (Tonry 1995). In terms of the concerns of communities of color, this is probably the most significant finding of the research literature on police use of force. Stringent guidelines on the use of force, accompanied by administrative directives that make clear to the rank-and-file that the guidelines will be enforced and followed by a review mechanism that assesses use-of-force situations and apportions the appropriate remedial or punitive action, succeeded in sharply curtailing police shootings (justified or otherwise) in many locales. As others in this volume have observed, it is important to realize that these positive results were obtained with the relatively visible police decisions to use deadly force; as yet we have little or no social science evidence that similar results can be obtained with nonlethal force.

Perhaps we will discover if such control mechanisms are effective against nonlethal abuses of force only when more police leaders take bold initiatives to shift police culture specifically on use-of-force issues and, more generally, on matters of police protection of the diverse communities they are sworn to serve. The at best dubious testimony of Los Angeles police detective Mark Fuhrman during the trial of *People of the State of California v. Orenthal James Simpson*, while not an abuse-of-force issue in physical terms, reflects an equally critical dimension of the problem of race and abuse of power in policing. Like periodic revelations of corruption in police ranks, Fuhrman's statements are powerful indicators that, in spite of the gains in policing over the past three decades, race remains the litmus test of progress or its lack in efforts to professionalize modern law enforcement. If techniques can be found to reduce police abuse of force against persons of *all* backgrounds, significant headway might be made in reducing a major problem in local policing, municipal governance, and American race relations.

NOTES

I am grateful to my graduate research assistants, Catherine Cornwall and Steven Klusman, for their stellar contributions to this essay. The typology of excessive force situations in the "Issues" section of this chapter is the work of Steven Klusman.

1. Obviously, there is not unanimity of opinion among communities of color on any topic, although there may be more agreement concerning issues of police service quality than on many other topics (see chapter 5; Murty et al. 1990; Boggs and Galliher 1975). But Lasley (1994: 250–51) found differences between poor Black and poor Hispanic residents of South Central Los Angeles in attitudes toward Los Angeles police officers. Before the Rodney King beating, Hispanics' attitudes were not as favorable as those of whites but not as negative as those of Blacks; and during the four months following the beating, African Americans' negative attitudes toward the LAPD "were much more profound and 'longer-term'" than were the critical perceptions held by whites and Hispanics.

2. Historically, there can be little doubt that for generations after the involuntary arrival of Black people in this country, the formal, officially approved role of police, both in the South and often in the Northern "free" states, was that of oppressor of these people of color—keeping slaves in their place and capturing and returning runaways to their owners and, later, enforcing Jim Crow segregation laws (Williams and Murphy 1990: 3–5; Richardson 1970: 19). Important for the purposes of this chapter, the early role of many Southern police in the "slave patrols" formally included inflicting corporal punishment on offenders (runaway or disobedient slaves) without prior judicial process (Williams and Murphy 1990: 4; Wood 1984: 123–24; Foner 1975: 206). While corporal punishment of Blacks—by today's standards grossly excessive force—may have been a formal police function in the slave states, history has recorded the attitudinal climate that prevailed toward Blacks in many Northern communities. When Alexis de Tocqueville studied American prisons during his travels in 1830, he not only discovered many Northern police capturing and holding

runaway slaves, as applicable laws required them to do, but also "was surprised to discover that there was more overt hostility and hatred toward blacks in the North, where slavery did not exist, than in the South, where it did" (Williams and Murphy 1990: 4).

3. Williams and Murphy (1990: 2, 9-10) observe that "several of the hiring and promotional standards, although influential as antidotes to the rampant nepotism and political favoritism that had characterized policing [for generations], proved to be detrimental to blacks—just at a time when, to a limited extent, because of their increasing political power, they were beginning to acquire the credential that would have allowed them to qualify by the old standards." By contrast, the first Blacks appointed to Northern police forces in the two or three decades after the Civil War were substantially *over*qualified compared to their white cohorts (Williams and Murphy 1990: 8; Lane 1986: 64-65).

4. Such practices had a long and sordid history. When Blacks were first appointed to some Southern police departments after the Civil War, whites often protested—and occasionally rioted over—the efforts of Black officers to use their lawful authority over whites (Williams and Murphy 1990: 8; Wharton 1965: 167). Williams and Murphy (1990: 8) report that a 1961 study "found that 31 percent of the departments surveyed restricted the right of blacks to make felony arrests; the power of black officers to make misdemeanor arrests was even more limited." This study was reported initially by the President's Commission on Law Enforcement and Administration of Justice (1967: 170). When a number of the current leading Black police chiefs in America began their careers as rookie officers in the 1960s, they were restricted to working in Black communities and could routinely neither partner with white colleagues nor arrest white lawbreakers. Some of their supervisors and fellow officers called them "niggers," and some departments would take a squad car out of service before allowing an officer of color to drive it. The outlaw subculture of some police departments was also a whites-only enterprise, excluding Black officers from any—or at least from their proportionate—share of payoffs. Black officers on patrol not infrequently were reported as "suspicious men" in citizens' calls to police emergency numbers. One former police chief who exemplifies this poignant career odyssey is attorney Gerald Cooper, who headed the Evanston (Illinois) Police Department and formerly served with the Chicago Police Department. He candidly discussed these "bad old days" with his officers at an organizational retreat (Cooper 1994).

5. While the FBI is now more willing to release data, the data available for release remain superficial and incomplete concerning police use of *deadly* force (Geller and Scott 1992) and so sporadic and ambiguous concerning police use of *nonlethal* force as to be worthless (see chapter 3).

6. Tonry (1995) reports in detail on a line of research that examined racism as a possible explanation of *arrest* decisions and found very little evidence of its *systematic* influence. With the important exception of arrests for less serious offenses (a category in which Powell [1981, 1990] suggests that police are more likely to abuse force for racial reasons), the studies generally reveal that police arrest persons of color in proportion to their participation in committing crimes. Crime participation rates are identified through victimization surveys—Census Bureau surveys in which victims report the nature of their victimization and, among other characteristics, the race/ethnicity of their alleged offender.

7. Compare Cordner (1985), on the limited power of research findings to shift organizational priorities except in directions the organization was leaning anyway.

8. Friedrich (1980), studying police use of *nonlethal* force, found that only the behavior of the offender and the visibility of the encounter to police peers and the public were significant influences on police use of force; race was not.

9. Theoretical frameworks are useful to the extent they serve as possible explanations—not necessarily justifications—for certain activities or behavior. Disrespectful citizens have long been triggers to police violence, and disrespectful officers have lit many a

fuse on a hot-tempered citizen. Today, "dissing" seems also to be an increasing cause of interpersonal violence for urban street gangs.

10. As noted above, the methodology of single-city studies can be improved to strengthen their generalizability, such as by making the central research questions ones like: Under *what organizational and social conditions* is race a factor in use- and abuse-of-force episodes?

11. Crawford (1973), in an officer and public opinion survey, discovered that officer prejudice stands as an impediment to police-community rapport of the sort required to make community policing work. Crawford found that "prejudiced" officers overestimate the resentment that the public actually feels toward the police.

12. But compare Waddington and Braddock (1991: 32).

CHAPTER SEVEN

Officer Selection and the Prevention of Abuse of Force

J. DOUGLAS GRANT and JOAN GRANT

The President's Commission on Law Enforcement and Administration of Justice (1967b) pointed out the potentially high cost to a police department of even a few high-risk officers. The commission wrote, "One incompetent officer can trigger a riot, permanently damage the reputation of a citizen, or alienate a community against a police department" (p. 125).

The report recommended psychiatric and psychological screening of aspiring employees and advocated grant support for research to develop valid tests and procedures for such screening. It suggested that "psychological tests, such as the MMPI [Minnesota Multiphasic Personality Inventory], and interviews to determine emotional stability should be conducted by all departments. Federal and State funds should be made available in the form of research grants for the purpose of devising reliable tests or other means of evaluating the characteristics of applicants which may be detrimental to successful police work" (p. 129).

This approach—clearing out the bad apples—has informed most of the efforts to use recruit selection to improve police performance. Yet more than a quarter of a century later, we have demonstrated that selection of effective police officers has to consider a much more complicated set of determinants than poor mental health and undesirable personality traits.

The Poor Track Record of Screening-Out Tests

Periodic reviews of police selection efforts and research studies over the more than twenty-five years since the President's Commission report uniformly point out the inadequacy of psychological screening in general and the use of the MMPI in particular.[1] A 1972 review (Kent and Eisenberg) of twenty-nine articles on police selection concluded that, with few exceptions, the quality of the research was poor and that many of the statements made supporting the value of psychological screening methods bordered on "charlatanism."

Five years later, Poland (1978) indicated that the studies he had reviewed did not provide a set of recommendations as to the best procedure for selecting police officers. The following year, Crosby (1979: 226), after surveying the use of both tests and clinical interviews, reported: "The foundations of clinical appraisal (psychological and psychiatric theory, and measurement technology) are not as secure and developed as we would like." He quoted Buros's (1970) discussion of the MMPI, which stated: "We are still at a stage where every test, regardless of its merits and deficiencies, is considered useful by some and useless by others" (Crosby 1979: 226–27).

In 1982, Mills and Stratton summarized an effort to demonstrate the validity of the MMPI in predicting successful policing in the Los Angeles County Sheriff's Department. They found no evidence to support the utility of the MMPI as a predictor of police performance. Like Kent and Eisenberg ten years earlier, they concluded: "To date there has been no systematic correlation of tests or interviews with an individual's subsequent behavior and success or nonsuccess in law enforcement. However, psychologists and agencies continue to reject candidates on the basis of unvalidated strategies whether they be tests, clinical interviews, or both" (Mills and Stratton 1982: 13–14). Another investigator (Daley 1982) said: "Neither psychiatric examination nor psychological screening has proven to accurately or systematically predict police performance" (p. 53). In 1987, White, in his introduction to a selected bibliography on police recruit screening, stated: "Only time will tell whether this care being taken at the front end of a police officer's career will make any difference."

One would thus be led to conclude that tests (and interviews) to determine undesirable personality traits have not been successful in predicting which recruits will make poor police officers. But what about predicting which recruits will be prone to the use of abusive force? We cannot assume that these two groups are the same. In Los Angeles, officers with more than their share of citizen complaints (the "bad apples" that are the focus of much police and community concern) were rated higher than average in overall performance by their superiors (Independent Commission on the Los Angeles Police Department 1991). If those supervisory ratings can be credited, then a proclivity toward violent behavior on the job is not simply a matter of poor job performance in general. And if we cannot predict poor job performance well, can we do any better in predicting a tendency to use abusive force?

Apparently not. Cunningham (1986) argued that although there are several tests that purport to measure an individual's potential to commit violent acts, few people actually commit them, making it extremely difficult to predict violence with precision. In consequence, "no test for violence potential has been created that has any demonstrated scientific validity" (ibid.: 24) Two studies of police misconduct, in Cunningham's view, demonstrate the difficulty of predicting violent behavior:

> Within shooting incidents, there are no easily apparent psychological or background differences between officers who fire their weapons and those who refrain from shooting. (Inn and Wheeler 1977, quoted in Cunningham 1986: 26) In an investigation of police officers using the "Personnel Selection Inventory Violence Scale" by London House, only a modest correlation was found between the number of times that officers said they *felt* like physically assaulting a suspect and their test scores on the "Violence Scale." Scores on the "Violence Scale" were *not* significantly correlated with the number of times that the police officers actually shouted at, pushed or shoved a suspect, nor were they significantly correlated with the number of times the officers actually used their weapons on suspects. (Jones 1982, quoted in Cunningham 1986: 26)

It has also been difficult to predict violent behavior using measures other than those tapping personality characteristics or a predisposition to violence. Talbert (1974) found that the height of police officers in Atlanta, Georgia, was not related to reports of police brutality or to the number of injuries incurred while on duty. Willoughby and Blount (1985), working with the Florida Marine Patrol, confirmed that both shorter and taller officers made the same number of arrests. Though the shorter officers were adjudged to have greater potential for aggression, they issued more warnings than did taller officers. Talbert speculated that shorter officers consciously or unconsciously held their aggression within acceptable limits.

Problems with a Screening-Out Strategy

The Christopher Commission report (1991) concluded that the initial psychological evaluation is an inexact predictor of an applicant's proclivity to use violence. Further, it raised questions about the utility of front end screening as the only approach to weeding out officers prone to the abuse of force. The commission argued that emotional and psychological problems may develop *after* selection, during an officer's tenure on the force, and cannot be detected by preemployment screening. But the commission recommended regular retesting of officers for psychological, emotional, and physical problems, thus tacitly endorsing mental health screening as an approach to handling the problem of abuse of force.

As we have seen, the evidence suggests that such screening has limited value, and the utility of psychological screening for reducing the use of abusive force is still a subject for debate (Barnhill 1992). And while the search for a test that will do a better job of predicting violent behavior continues, even optimistic researchers admit that "it's unrealistic to say we are going to have any one test that will eradicate this problem—though we have to try" (Inwald, quoted in Barnhill 1992).

The effort to predict violence from a knowledge of the individual's mental health is not only complicated by the fact that violence is a rare act, and that violence-prone people do not behave violently in all situations. Only a minority of people with mental health problems are prone to violence, and even those individuals with a tendency to behave violently may do so only during periods of acute disturbance. Thus, any relationship found between mental health and violent behavior is bound to be limited (Monahan 1992).

The effort to predict violent behavior is also complicated by the generally low validity of selection procedures (Cohen and Chaiken 1973; Cunningham 1986; Dunnette and Motowidlo 1976; National Advisory Commission on Criminal Justice Standards and Goals 1973; Poland 1978; Wollack et al. 1973).

Another general reason for the difficulty in predicting which recruits will make good police officers is that police departments have rarely been clear on what they were selecting for. Poland (1978) argued that we cannot deal usefully with the problem of police selection until we have developed good measures of police job performance.

And it is not easy to develop measures of effective policing. One problem is the diversity of tasks and performances that have always been required of the police (Cohen and Chaiken 1973). Different competencies, attitudes, and personality characteristics may be needed for the performance of different tasks. The duties of police officers have long been viewed as much more diverse than the dichotomy of "report writers," who arrive on the scene following an incident, or "wrestlers," who engage in physical conflict with offenders.

Selection procedures need to take into account not only the diversity of current police performance requirements, but also the changing demands on the police and the consequent changing nature of policing—for example, the growing development of community policing and problem-oriented policing (Greene and Mastrofski 1988; Skolnick and Bayley 1986; Trojanowicz and Bucqueroux 1990; Goldstein 1990). Both the perception and the reality of what is a good police officer change over time. The Christopher Commission (1991) found that prior violent behavior seemed not to have been a negative factor in officer selection in the Los Angeles Police Department, suggesting that a propensity to be "rough and ready" had been perceived as an asset to police performance rather than as a danger signal for potential violence. Such judgments may have to be revised over time as the nature of policing or the perception of what is a good officer evolves.

In an effort to deal with the problem of defining effective performance, Daley (1982: 53) proposed using measures of good judgment under stress. By screening out applicants who show the rigidity and stereotypical reactions of people suffering from psychological disorders, one could select applicants who might be better able to adapt successfully to difficult situations. Daley wrote, "It was, and continues to be my opinion, that the greatest possibility for successful police work lies in the selection of individuals with the greatest chance of withstanding the rigors of this line of work without becoming psychologically symptomatic." Daley reported that such a stress-resistant screening effort was being used in the New York City Police Department.

In addition to the problem of developing good outcome (performance) measures, we are faced with problems inherent in the measures we use to make predictions. Buros argued that we cannot be sure that tests measure what they are purported to measure, even when they are widely used. He wrote:

> The [MMPI] inventory is probably just as controversial, if not more so, than it was ten or twenty years ago. Nevertheless, the use of the MMPI has been growing at a phenomenal rate. Moreover, it is probable that its use will continue to grow at an ever increasing pace, especially now that computerized interpretive printouts . . . are available at a nominal cost. . . . The sterility of the research and experiential writing on the Rorschach and the MMPI is also applicable to other personality tests which have generated fewer publications. In no case, however, has the accumulated research produced an enduring body of generally accepted knowledge concerning the validity of the test under study. (Buros, quoted in Crosby 1979: 226)

Thus the tests used to describe mental health may not in fact provide an accurate picture of the individual's psychological condition. A further problem is that responses to test items may change over time. We cannot answer questions such as: How permanent are the "personality" responses of the officer following recruitment? (Anderson 1991; Pugh 1985a, 1985b). How much do these measures reflect permanent personality traits and how much do they reflect changing situations and attitudes?

Situational Factors

Responses to a personality test may be affected by not only the individual's traits and values but also by his or her class background and by socialization into an occupational subculture (Poland 1978). Mills and Stratton (1982) supported this conclusion, arguing that situational factors should be considered when we try to predict good or bad performance. Abusive behavior may thus be a manifestation of aggression gone out of control, but may also occur because the climate of a police department tolerates or encourages some kinds of abusive force.

An investigation in the Houston Police Department revealed the importance of situational factors in determining officer behavior (Perry 1987). Several problems were discovered, each contributing to a climate that encouraged poor police performance: investigations of reported incidents of police misconduct took so long that officers found guilty could not be disciplined; the investigations were often biased in favor of the officers; if officers were found guilty, county prosecutors were often not informed; records relevant to the incidents were frequently missing; and officers with mental health or alcohol or drug problems were hired or retained on the force against the recommendations of police psychologists.

The Christopher Commission (1991) has raised another issue we have already alluded to pertaining to efforts to improve police selection. Officers not only affect police operations but are affected by their participation in police operations, as well as by other events in their lives. Officers may thus change over time and may develop problems related to their performance long after their probationary period.

A final consideration in undertaking a procedure to screen out undesirable applicants is the problem of selection "misses." How many false positives (applicants wrongly judged desirable) are screened in by the approach used, and how many false negatives (applicants wrongly judged undesirable) are screened out? How important is each kind of selection "miss" to the effective operation of the department and to the community that the department serves?

It would seem that, twenty-five years after the President's Commission recommendation for the use of psychological screening by all police departments, it is time for such questions to be posed. Other theoretical approaches and strategies should also be applied to the problem of officer use of abusive force as well as to the problem of obtaining good officer performance in general.

Screening In

An alternative approach to screening out undesirable applicants for police work is the screening in of those who are desirable. It seems reasonable to expect that hiring only the "best and brightest" would provide superior personnel who would not make the sort of mistakes that result in the abuse of force.

The idea of screening in gained impetus and concern with the passage of the Civil Rights Act of 1964. A report of the U.S. Commission on Civil Rights (Margolis 1970: 32) dealing with the question of equal employment opportunity argued against screening practices used at the time because they resulted in too many false negatives (applicants wrongly judged undesirable): "The traditional process of screening, testing, and training police applicants and recruits needs to be thoroughly overhauled—first because it presently places a heavy burden upon blacks and Spanish-speaking Americans; and second, because there seems to be no demonstrable evidence that the system either brings in the best men for the job or teaches them the right combination of skills. . . . These [basic written] tests are clearly culturally biased. . . . No one knows precisely what they test or how well they predict a recruit's future performance on the job."

The initial rationale for screening in women and minorities was that of providing equal employment opportunities. An argument was also developing that such screening in will lead to increased operational effectiveness, including a reduction in the abusive use of police power. Women officers, it is thus said, are better at negotiating and averting violence than male officers (Greenwald 1976). Further, integrating police forces is said to reduce prejudice toward and the abuse and mistreatment of citizens (e.g., Hennessey 1992).

One approach to the problem of tests that may unfairly screen out people who are otherwise qualified for police work is to use differential validity measures, providing different selection equations and norms for different race/gender groups. These equations need to be updated constantly to account for changes in policing and police requirements over time.

Talley and Hinz (1990) used this type of approach with public safety officers at Duke University. They developed different MMPI predictors of good officer performance, with different norms for white, black, male, and female officers. Their study used a relatively small number of subjects (the subgroups ranged in size from 7 to 121) and a large number of predictor variables.

Using a .05 criterion of statistical significance, as Talley and Hinz do, unfortunately means that relationships between predictor and outcome measures (in this case, between MMPI measures and good officer performance) will be found twenty times out of one hundred by chance. The smaller the number of subjects and the larger the number of predictor measures, the higher the likelihood that some predictor measures for some samples will show a statistically significant relationship to outcome when no relationship in fact exists. The use of a differential validity procedure, as in Talley and Hinz's study, demands the division of subjects into small subsamples, which makes it likely that some statistically significant relationships will be found between predictor measures and performance that are due only to chance.

Talley and Hinz recommended that the differential validity concept be incorporated into the hiring practices of all police departments. This approach addresses some of the police and community concerns about screening in, but it is probably not feasible. It requires separate validity studies for each subgroup of interest. As there are a large number of conceivable populations from which a police department could hire and since for each of these it would be necessary to update validity measures over time, the necessary research would be prolonged, expensive, and beyond the reach of most departments. A further complication is that the use of separate norms for different groups may not be permitted under the Civil Rights Act of 1991 (Adler 1993).

Shifting the Role of the Mental Health Worker

Should police departments abandon their efforts to look at the psychological health of their applicants and employees? Not necessarily. Police officers are not immune to mental health problems, whether owing to preexisting personality traits or to situational stresses in their private or work life. Such problems can occur not only during selection and training but also throughout the officer's career.

Psychological testing can be helpful in determining the nature of an emotional disturbance when tests allow the individual to describe his or her problem. However, the context in which a test is taken can influence the way that test items are answered. Crosby (1979: 223), in discussing the use of psychological examinations in police selection, pointed out that "The applicants . . . are hoping to 'pass the test' so they can get a job they want; they are *not* seeking help in finding out more about their emotional health and adjustment to their life experience." It is one thing for a client seeking counsel to answer test items that will help a mental health worker understand the client's problems; in this case, the client's answers are confidential, or should be. It is another thing for an applicant to answer test items knowing that the answers will influence whether he or she will be hired.

T. G. Harris (quoted in Barnhill 1992) argued that psychological tests are best used to help people understand themselves. He said that "A lot of the traditional tests grew out of a cloak-and-dagger concept of psychology based on the notion that the psychologist as an expert could figure out things about people that they didn't know about themselves, or that they were trying to cover up. . . . What psychological tests are really good at is self-knowledge. With self-evaluation tests we get a chance to see ourselves as others see us, or to relate ourselves to our neighbors who responded to the same situation or question. The results give us a way of describing ourselves accurately, based on rigorous scientific research."

To the extent that employees and potential employees can be helped with problems (either personal problems or those arising from occupational stress), it should be possible to make them better able to function or, alternatively, to self-select themselves out of police work. In both cases, the result should be a more effective department and one less prone to using excessive force.

Employee Assistance

An innovative extension of the mental health professional's service is provided by the Los Angeles Police Department's peer counseling program (Klyver 1986). Specially trained line officers and civilian employees counsel officers who voluntarily seek help. The program, begun in 1981, is based on the premise that peers can be as effective as (or perhaps more effective than) professionals in helping police officers work through personal and work-related crises.

Mental health personnel thus have potential roles other than recruit screening: for example, engaging in counseling officers and training peer counselors. Another role is suggested by More and Unsinger (1987)—using psychologists to provide special training to facilitate the adjustment and retention of (in this case, female) police recruits.

The Christopher Commission implicitly supported such efforts when it argued that extended screening should be used on a regular basis. The commission report pointed out that "Many emotional and psychological problems develop during an officer's tenure on the force and cannot be detected by preemployment screening" (1991: 110). Ongoing diagnostic screening could also help to create a climate for self-referral as needed during an officer's career.

Using psychologists to assist recruits and other officers, directly or indirectly, with immediate problems rather than to screen out undesirable individuals has an advantage beyond the probable greater effectiveness. This approach helps protect an employee's right to privacy, an issue frequently raised in connection with the use of psychological tests (Inwald 1985).

In a recent national survey, however, 71 percent of responding police psychologists reported that one of their core functions is conducting preemployment screening of candidates (Scrivner 1994a: 8; Scrivner 1994b). Many psychologists do so despite the fact that they have reservations about screening methods that are currently in use. Scrivner (1994a) reports that "psychologists are generally respectful of how the complexity of human behavior, and all its contingencies, limits the accuracy of scientific prediction" (p. 17).

Among the innovations in preemployment psychological screening that Scrivner feels may prove more effective than current paper-and-pencil tests and psychological interviews are "automated assessment systems, interactive video testing, assessment centers, job simulations, and role playing exercises" (Scrivner 1994a: 18; Scrivner 1994b; see also Hogue et al. 1994; Booth 1989; Kolpack 1991). It is felt that such methods may strengthen screeners' ability to consider a candidate's capabilities on dimensions such as the following: how the person makes decisions; how he or she processes information under stressful conditions; how he or she solves problems consistent with community policing; how he or she interacts with people; and how he or she controls situations (Scrivner 1994a: 18; Scrivner 1994b: 1; see also Pugh 1985a; Baltzley 1991).

An example of innovative strategies that could be used are group exercises in which police applicants, under the watchful eyes of people with police and psychological expertise, role-play in scenarios designed to surface hostilities or prejudices that might not normally be apparent using other assessment methods. "Situational tests" of this sort have been deployed for a number of years (Booth

1989; Chenoweth 1961; England and Miller 1989; Hogue et al. 1994; Johnson 1983; Knowles and Peterson 1973; Pugh 1985a). However, rating systems for behavior during such exercises will still need to be well conceived and validated. Scrivner cautions: "Before new instrumentation can be used [to predict policing capabilities], there must be support for the extensive research needed to develop a job-related data base to show how well new assessment techniques can predict performance. Moreover, continued evaluation will be required so that a longitudinal validation of the testing process can take place" (1994a: 18).

Scrivner is not optimistic about the future of traditional preemployment psychological screening. She writes: "Since the commitment of time and money for important test validation research has not materialized in the past, it may be unrealistic to assume that departments will now be able to devote scarce resources to more extensive validation efforts. Consequently, police policymakers could be faced with the choice of either reliably *predicting* use of excessive force for a *limited* number of officers or *managing* use of excessive force for *all* officers"[2] (1994a: 20–21).

One of the fundamental ways in which psychologists and peer counselors can help officers is in better understanding their own contributions to undesirable incident outcomes and their capacities to help alter these outcomes. In her national survey of police psychologists, Scrivner (1994a: 19; 1994b) discovered that these clinicians placed higher importance on their involvement in training than on traditional methods to help officers reduce their problems with force. Further, psychologist-assisted training and counseling, along with supervisory monitoring of officer behavior, were seen by the respondents as potentially better control mechanisms than was periodic psychological testing of incumbent officers, a practice that prompts opposition from many rank-and-file groups.

Police psychologists, if they have sufficient opportunity to get to know a given police force, may be able to help police departments collect "human resource information that is relevant to policy" (Scrivner 1994a: 21). By profiling officers who tend to become involved too often in using too much force, psychologists can help police administrators and others to understand better the complex interaction of personal and systemic factors that contribute to abuse of force problems.

Obtaining Knowledge and Understanding

As pointed out in chapters 2 and 4, the failure to predict police performance using personality measures is not solely a matter of inadequate research; it is evidence that situations (organization, peer group, and community) are also determinants of behavior. There is probably an interaction between situation and personality (Bandura 1986), so that concentrating on the individual personality—the "bad apple" or the "best and brightest"—does not get us very far.

Three conclusions that have been documented have implications for police selection in general and reducing the use of excessive force in particular.

1. *A theoretical approach focusing on personality or mental health is too limited.* A 1985 review of the officer selection literature (Burbeck and Furnham) revealed no agreed-upon distinct police personality. Moreover, there are questions about the utility of psychological testing in distinguishing between police officers and members of the public or between successful and unsuccessful police officers.

There are three major limitations in the studies that attempt to link officer characteristics to their behavior on the street. The first is the distance of the data from the behavior of concern. The predictor variables (attitude and personality measures) are abstractions ostensibly related to street behavior. The outcome criterion is most likely to be a rating by supervisors, another abstraction also assumed to be related to behavior. (The distance between rating of performance and actual behavior is shortened when the evaluations of peers, working with the subjects, are used. These evaluations are reported to improve predictability [Bayley and Garofalo 1989].) The second limitation is the time between the measurement and the behavior of concern (Anderson 1991). Pugh (1985a, 1985b) has shown that measurements made at the time of recruitment are related to different kinds of police performance depending upon the length of time after recruitment that the performance measure is obtained. The third limitation is the characteristics of the samples used in the selection studies. These studies frequently report inconsistent findings. For example, officers rated high in effectiveness may show high sociability scores in one study and low sociability scores in another. Such inconsistency is due not only to chance variations in the samples but also to variations in the size of the samples, the magnitude of the differences in sociability scores between officers rated high and low in effectiveness, and the range of sociability scores obtained.

The likelihood of inconsistent findings is compounded by efforts to develop separate prediction norms for groups defined by gender, race, and location. This approach may be logically consistent with civil rights concerns, but when coupled with the changing nature of police work over time, it collapses from the demand for continual subsampling. In addition to the tenuousness of any findings obtained through making predictions by smaller and smaller subgroups, the findings could well be made obsolete by the length of time needed to obtain them.

2. *Multiple performances are required for effective policing.* Efforts to predict recruit success or failure raise the question, Success or failure at what? An exemplary effort to answer this question is Dunnette and Motowidlo's (1976) use of critical incidents to determine the dimensions of police performance. There have been many other studies using screening and selection process data to determine characteristics of officers associated with kinds of performances or kinds of police functions (Cohen and Chaiken 1973; Wollack et al. 1973). One of these functions

is the use of force or power, and such analyses could help define the dynamics and determinants of excessive force.

3. *Policing and its performance requirements are changing rapidly.* Predictions of performance today are probably not relevant for even the near future. Brengelman (1982) pointed out that recruit selection procedures no longer reflect current social conditions or the abilities required in contemporary policing.

Johnson (1983) recommended using the police selection process to screen in not only positive attributes but training potential. Hancock (1984) wrote of creativity and abstract mental attitudes as qualities to be identified and advised that those possessing them be assigned to investigative careers. In the 1990s there is growing recognition of the value of problem-oriented policing and the need for patrol officers who have problem-solving skills.

In addition to the changing nature of police functions, there is evidence that the relationship between officer characteristics and police behavior changes over time. Pugh (1985a, 1985b) found that recruits judged to be good police officers two years after selection were those who had been rated high at the time of selection on efforts to fit in, gain trust, and become part of the police department. After four and a half years, however, the recruits judged to be good police officers were those who had been rated high on maturity, responsibility, and social skills. Such findings would appear to have implications for the study of motivational need patterns, which apparently vary over different periods in an officer's career (Chusmir 1984).

Improving Community Relations

Selection procedures and the abuse of force are problems for both the police department and the community. They are frequently perceived as problems *between* the police and the community (Kansas Advisory Committee to the U.S. Commission on Civil Rights 1980).

Several studies suggest that community input into the police selection process could improve both the process and relations with the community. O'Hara and Love (1987) reported a police-community approach to two selection concerns: the validity of traditional selection procedures and the feasibility of instituting more accurate procedures within the city's budgetary constraints. Community input, involvement, and acceptance of an innovative assessment center were gained through interviews and a mail survey and by training selected community residents to help assess police candidates. Costs were cut, and a follow-up survey showed that residents saw the project and its candidate selection as successful.

Selection interviews by a panel with community representation were unbiased vis-à-vis minority candidates, according to a study by Hazlett (1985). Ellison et al. (1985) described the development of an officer selection procedure incorporating community members for an urban-suburban community of 40,000. The procedure included developing appropriate selection criteria, compensating for the advantage of candidates who were sophisticated about testing, creating a structured interview, and selecting members of the interviewing panel.

Ellison (1985a) described an experiment giving recruits previews of their job in a group session with officers from their department. The officers discussed their experiences and perceptions of police work and answered the recruits' questions. Such a procedure could easily be expanded by having citizens present their experiences with the police as part of the discussion. Ellison (1985b) reported that the involvement of a variety of community members in developing the recruit selection process provided a basis for making decisions based on qualitative judgments.

These selection innovations and developments suggest ways in which police-community relations—a foundation for police-community collaboration—could be improved by having officers and citizens share in recruit selection and training and in the study and solution of other police problems of concern to both groups.

Officer and Organization Development

New officers come into a department with a set of preexisting attitudes and values, which are in turn shaped by a socialization process that begins the moment they are selected as recruits. This socialization affects the new officers' behavior directly, but it also affects it indirectly by contributing to the organizational climate of the department as a whole. In both ways, socialization can affect the department's proclivity for the abuse of force.

There have been several studies of the police socialization process. Van Maanen (1974), as a participant-observer, documented the power of friendship networks in officer development during preentry recruit training and probation. This socialization process, which can take as long as two years, affects the attitudes of the individual officer and the norms of the police organization.

Mills and Stratton (1982) argued that selection procedures should pay more attention to situational pressures on the officers, pointing to the work of Zimbardo et al. (1975), who produced aggressive and dehumanizing behavior toward "prisoners" in a sample of college students in a role-play prison study, and of Kirkham (1976), who joined a police force and documented radical shifts in his own attitudes and behavior.

Gavin and Hamilton (1975) documented the socializing power of preentry procedures, which often take a year or longer, as well as the impact of recruit and field training during probation. This is a significant period of experience before severe civil service limitations are imposed on attempts to reject a candidate, and still allow judgments based on observed behavior and performance. Gavin and Hamilton described an assessment center selection method which used, among other procedures, role-playing and leaderless discussion groups to assess dimensions of effective police performance. The groups identified and assessed these dimensions by examining "critical incidents" of police performance. Such discussions can be an integral part of the socialization process, creating a climate for the study both of oneself and of the organization as a whole. This performance aspect of the assessment center method suggests a way to merge selection with socialization. Rather than leaving to chance the socialization that occurs during the selection process, one can increase the chances that socialization becomes a recognized force for both officer and organization development.

Field training is one way of introducing positive socializing experiences, particularly when recruits are paired with officers who are skilled in resolving problems on their beat. Such experiences can include systematic discussion of situations encountered on patrol (as in the Friday Crab Club, discussed in chapter 10). Dissecting incidents and responses to them can build skills for the recruits' later participation in problem study. This process has the further advantage of increasing the problem-study skills of the field training officers through teaching others.

Selection, training, community relations, and organization development can all be addressed if there is department-wide concern with developing new officers as problem solvers (Toch and Grant, 1991) from recruiting through the entire probation period. This focus could mobilize support to help prepare and socialize the recruit for community and problem-oriented policing. It could also help bring to light organizational problems and enhance the problem-solving competence of the department as a whole.

Problems that could be studied during a recruit's training period include not only street incidents but also the recruit's relations with the community and interaction with the locker-room culture, and his or her own socialization. One problem suggested by Geller (1985a) is that of an officer's use of restraint in the face of situations that could escalate into violence. Actual incidents, preferably tape-recorded, but at least fully reported, could be analyzed with recruits, line officers, and community representatives. There could be discussion of both the incident and the situation that led up to it, leading to a better understanding of cause-and-effect dynamics and approaches to defusing street situations that might otherwise lead to the use of force.

Both community and staff resources (officers experienced in problem-oriented policing) could be available to recruits for study projects. The recruits could also have available the resources of the department's mental health staff during and after the training and probation period (Scrivner 1994a). Such staff could provide support for those recruits who select out of a police career and those who need greater personal strength to stay in.

Recommendations

• Use the entire recruit training and probation period for retention or rejection decisions, based on intensive observation of performance.

• Use the expanded selection period not only for officer training and development but also for improving police operations, creating an effective organization climate, and promoting good community relations. These are all needed functions, and both time and money can be saved by merging them as part of an extended selection procedure.

• Divert mental health resources from selection decisions to support services for recruits in particular and police employees in general.

• Develop ways to promote officer participation in devising police operations and an organizational climate to support it.

• Extend community policing and problem-oriented policing by building community participation into selection and into officer and organization development.

• Expand active outreach to the community, creating genuine participation in addressing police problems. This should counteract the impression (and sometimes the reality) of police-community relations as "us against them."

• While keeping current with developments in personnel selection research (Goldberg 1993), direct the thrust of prevention efforts toward the situational organization climate and socialization determinants of the problem of use of force (Lore and Schultz 1993).

NOTES

1. A 1994 national survey revealed that police administrators do not generally place much confidence in psychological screening tests. They rated background investigations as the most effective screening tool, followed by polygraph exams and then psychological written tests or interviews (Horvath 1994: 79–80).

2. Some of the requirements of the Americans with Disabilities Act, not yet fully clarified by the federal Equal Employment Opportunity Commission, may give impetus to innovations in preemployment screening techniques, particularly as it appears that such widely used written screening tools as the MMPI will no longer be usable to screen candidates before they are offered police employment (Scrivner 1994a: 17; Scrivner 1994b).

CHAPTER EIGHT

Training to Reduce Police-Civilian Violence

JAMES J. FYFE

Discussions of strategies and techniques to prevent and reduce police use of force should be informed by the distinction between two types of excessive force. Extralegal violence—*brutality*—is "the willful and wrongful use of force by officers who knowingly exceed the bounds of their office." *Unnecessary force*, by contrast, is the result of ineptitude or carelessness and "occurs when well-meaning officers prove incapable of dealing with the situations they encounter without needless or too hasty resort to force" (Fyfe 1986: 207; see also Skolnick and Fyfe 1993: 37–42). I contend that the varying causes of both forms of excessive force can be reduced by training.

Brutality

Because police brutality is a conscious act rather than the result of an unintended mistake, the connection between it and police training may seem indirect. It is not. The major purpose of professional training is to prepare trainees to handle work-related problems better than the layperson. Brutal police do not pass muster: any group of physically fit laypeople with no regard for the injuries they may inflict can subdue a badly outnumbered individual. Police who handle tough situations brutally do so because of uncontrolled rage and/or because they are calculatedly oppressive (see, for example, Klockars 1980; Skolnick and Fyfe 1993; Van Maanen 1978; chapters 2 and 4).

The development of successful boxers, diplomats, combat soldiers, and trial lawyers demonstrates that maintaining one's temper under stressful and confrontational conditions is a skill that can be taught. At the broadest level, police training designed to do so may involve providing students with what Muir (1977) calls *understanding*, which he defines as a nonjudgmental sense that peoples' behavior, no matter how bizarre or provocative, may usually be explained by factors that go beyond the dichotomy of good and evil. For police trainers, this translates into convincing officers that they should not take personally the insults and attacks they may experience at work. This training often includes a heavy cross-cultural component designed to acquaint officers with their jurisdictions' subpopulations and their norms and ways of dealing with authority figures like the police.

Even if genuine understanding, as defined by Muir, cannot be imparted to individuals who bring extremely narrow views to policing, officers can be told in training that they simply will not be permitted to act out their prejudices through violent or even discourteous conduct. Where such officers are concerned—and there is no reason to believe that prejudice is any rarer among police than among the general population—the more modest goal of training must be to teach the skill of suppressing hostile impulses rather than to replace them with the more kindly instincts that Muir would prefer that officers possessed (Toch, Grant, and Galvin 1975; Toch and Grant 1991).

The goals of training, however, go beyond the transmission of skills and techniques and the suppression of a few officers' hostile impulses. Police training also has an attitudinal component: it socializes officers into their departments and teaches them their employers' philosophies, values, and expectations. As Wilson (1968) suggests, there are significant differences among police departments' self-conceptions. There also is considerable evidence that these differences among departments have great effects on police officers' behavior on the street. Gerald Uelmen (1973), for example, studied police shootings among fifty-one Los Angeles County police departments and found that the major determinants of their shooting rates were not their communities' levels of crime and violence but the personal philosophies and policies, written or otherwise, of their chiefs. Similarly, Fyfe (1988a) reported that the rate of police shootings in Philadelphia had more to do with whether "law and order" politician Frank Rizzo was mayor than with any quantifiable measures of the threats to police officers' lives or safety. In short, police departments vary in their tolerance of the use of force by officers, and, to the extent that formal training reflects these variations it affects officers' decisions to engage in force.

Just as training involves more than transmission of specific skills, it takes place in settings beyond the classroom. Everything that supervisors do or tolerate, every interpretation of broad departmental philosophy, every application of specific rules and policies is a training lesson that has at least as much impact on officers' performance as what they may have learned in their rookie days (see, e.g., Bennett and Greenstein 1975). When sergeants or older officers give young cops those fabled instructions to "forget what they told you in the police academy, kid, you'll learn how to do it on the street," formal training is instantly and irreparably devalued. Worse, when officers see firsthand that the behavioral strictures in which they were schooled are routinely ignored in practice, formal training is neutralized and the definitions of appropriate behavior are instead made in the secrecy of officers' locker rooms.

On occasion, this disjuncture has been carefully crafted by administrators, who leave a paper trail of apparently stringent policy and training that belies their unstated philosophy of encouraging officers to exact crude forms of street justice. More often, supervisors tolerate—or even encourage—police violence because they themselves lack the skills to take appropriate preventive or corrective action. It is not easy under any circumstances to be a successful police sergeant, lieutenant, or captain; it is virtually impossible to flourish in these positions without being prepared for them by training in leadership and specific supervisory strategies and techniques (see, e.g., St. Clair et al. 1992).

In their day-to-day routine, successful police supervisors and commanders must lead tightly knit societies of people who do dangerous and unpredictable work, usually in places where it cannot be monitored firsthand. Further, police bosses must get their officers to "produce" within rule-bound bureaucracies that typically place great limits on supervisors' ability to reward good work or to correct substandard performance. Thus, even during ordinary police operations, supervisors are greatly challenged by their responsibility to see that their officers do their jobs with a minimal degree of force. These managerial problems multiply—and change—dramatically when officers are pushed into direct contact with groups engaged in behavior that, through intent or indifference, may provoke the police by publicly challenging their authority and legitimacy. Day to day, police supervisors oversee at a distance the performance of officers who work in low-visibility settings essentially as individual free agents. At demonstrations or mass confrontations, by contrast, police supervisors must adopt a role more akin to that of military commander or football quarterback, directing and coordinating large numbers of officers performing in very public settings. In such situations, collective brutality or needless violence is virtually inevitable unless commanders and supervisors change roles and become direct overseers of officers' actions. When not trained to do so, commanders and supervisors default on their leadership responsibilities, and events are instead shaped by the most volatile elements among the officers present. The most notable results of this sort of mismanagement include the police riot at the 1968 Chicago Democratic convention (Walker 1968) and the 1988 police assault on demonstrators in New York City's Tompkins Square Park (Johnston 1988).

Unnecessary Force

All reasonable police administrators recognize that unnecessary force can be directly affected by training. Unnecessary force occurs when police officers who know no better cause bloodshed in situations that might have been resolved peaceably and bloodlessly by more capable officers. The impact of unnecessary force should not be underestimated. Ironically—despite events in Los Angeles in 1992—unnecessary force is far more likely than brutality to generate widespread resentment of the police or civil liability for the police. However heinous police brutality can be, it rarely causes open police-community friction because, barring the serendipitous presence of a person trying out a new video camera, it typically takes place out of the public's sight. Like ordinary criminals who carefully plan their crimes, brutal police officers usually take precautions to assure that their misdeeds escape detection.

Unnecessary force, by contrast, is unplanned and, quite often, public. Frequently, it begins with police intervention into relatively minor conditions that escalate into violence because of police haste and/or inability to establish communication with the people involved. Sometimes this occurs because officers are unfamiliar with the folkways of racial or ethnic minority groups. Many brawls and much bloodshed have followed when officers have inadvertently challenged the manhood and pride of Hispanic young men during interventions in disputes and in disorderly street-corner groups, for example. At the most spectacular and large-scale level, it has occurred in incidents like the 1971 Attica, New York, prison uprising (McKay et al. 1972) and the 1985 Philadelphia police siege and bombing of the headquarters of the MOVE cult (*Philadelphia Inquirer*, May 14, A1). In both cases, notwithstanding possible acts of unsanctioned illegal violence by individual officers involved, those in charge pushed the police into precipitous actions that had unnecessarily bloody outcomes.

More recently and more routinely, officers have ineptly put themselves in harm's way during encounters with the emotionally and mentally disturbed people who have appeared on the streets in increasing numbers over the past few decades (see, e.g., Murphy 1986). Consequently, the police have had to forcibly extract themselves or colleagues from danger. An excellent model for avoiding this "split-second syndrome" (Fyfe 1986) is provided by the great success of the police in developing policy and training designed to avert violence in hostage and barricade situations (see, e.g., Bolz and Hershey 1979). This early application of problem-solving techniques to policing involved diagnosis of crises that identified recurrent patterns and themes (e.g., that hostage takers generally fall into one of three types); careful analyses of the causes of these crises (e.g., identification of the motives of each of the three types of hostage taker); and careful development of means to assure that police did everything possible to resolve them with minimal bloodshed (e.g., identification of police strategies and tactics dependent on the type of hostage taker involved). As a consequence of this effort and the subsequent demonstration of its success in thousands of hostage situations, these encounters are no longer handled on an ad hoc basis. Instead, a set of principles and protocols developed which are widely known among well-trained police throughout the

United States and abroad. There is no reason that a similar methodology cannot be applied to such other recurrent police crises as encounters with emotionally disturbed persons, apprehensions at the end of vehicle pursuits, responses to robberies and other violent crimes, and off-duty interventions into suspected crimes. Such efforts will give officers better—and more experientially grounded—guidelines in dealing with them, as well.

Training to Prevent and Reduce Police-Citizen Violence

Thus far, this chapter has offered plenty of theory, abstraction, and criticism. I now turn to concrete recommendations.

Effective Training in Violence Prevention and Reduction Must Be Realistic

Training for any endeavor should simulate as closely as possible the actual working conditions for which trainees are being prepared. This is a difficult task, especially when training must prepare individuals to make decisions under volatile and life-threatening circumstances. No matter how hard police tactical trainers strive for realism, trainees know in advance that they and everybody else will remain physically unscathed when their lessons are over. There obviously is no such guarantee when doing actual police work, where danger and uncertainty grab participants' attention and affect performance in ways impossible to duplicate in training. Good evidence of the difference between training and the real thing, police firearms instructors know, is the deterioration in shooting accuracy by many officers when, instead of shooting at paper targets, they confront people who are shooting back.

Although it cannot be eliminated, the artificiality of police training can be minimized. Perhaps the best way to do this is in role-play scenarios in facilities that duplicate as closely as possible the conditions officers encounter in the field, both indoors and outdoors. In the scenarios, experienced instructors or even fellow trainees play citizens or adversaries. The dangers of the streets cannot be simulated, but role-play trainees become extremely involved in these scenarios. Role-plays frequently take place in front of other trainees, and those acting opposite trainees can quickly alter their actions based on officers' behavior. Under this psychological pressure, participants—especially experienced officers—take great pride in demonstrating their skills by, for example, not "losing" violent encounters or behaving inappropriately in less dangerous situations. Consequently, unlike participants in many other police training formats, role-play trainees pay extremely close attention to the lectures or other training that accompanies the role-plays, as well as to the performances of their classmates.

Role-play training is, of course, a very labor-intensive activity. Role-play scenarios based on common police-citizen encounters (e.g., traffic stops or police encounters with mentally disturbed persons) typically are one-on-one or two-on-two situations that require as many training staff members as trainees. This should not be a bar to this training format, however, since role-plays typically are quick—how long do police spend at domestic disputes, for example?—and may be analyzed in detail afterward. In addition, it is not always necessary that all members of a large training class actually take part in role-plays. Instead, a few may participate in scenarios that are presented before a group and later analyzed by the group. Where available, videotaping for detailed "instant-replay" discussions and analyses by class members is a very useful technique in getting the entire group involved.

The realism of one-on-one encounters with flesh-and-blood human beings is a benefit of role-play training absent in the many interactive film and computer video training programs that have become available over the past several years. These typically consist of electronically presented scenarios that must be resolved by officers armed with blank pistols or laser guns. However technologically advanced, this electronic training is seen by many officers as little more than a video game: "It's fun and it really impressed the press and the community council when we put them through it," said an officer whose opinion reflects that of many other police trainers, "but I don't know what it has to do with life on the road."

In addition to the loss of real human contact, interactive film and video role plays introduce to training several sources of artificiality that seriously limit their effectiveness. Even when the scenarios presented are set in outdoor locations, interactive electronic training invariably takes place in classrooms or auditoriums that do not reflect the terrain or other conditions. In one scenario, for example, trainees—typically standing in a darkened room—are asked to assume that sheets of plywood and other items strewn about are objects of cover that they should employ during their encounters with the screen's jerky images of armed suspects beneath an elevated highway at midday. Furthermore, as they might—and probably should—during the real thing, trainees cannot observe these subjects from a distance while they use their radios to direct other officers to the scene from different angles of approach. Unlike real life and well-executed role-plays, video training is two-dimensional and allows officers to confront bad guys from only one angle: that of the camera.

The most important source of artificiality in this training is that it generally drops officers into the middle of situations that, in real life, begin far earlier (see Binder and Scharf 1980; Scharf and Binder 1983). In the field, patrol officers typically become aware of potentially violent situations at a distance, as when their radio dispatchers advise them of conditions requiring their presence or when they decide to stop suspicious pedestrians. In these circumstances, officers have opportunities to structure a confrontation in ways that diminish the likelihood that it will escalate into violence. When patrol officers learn of a robbery in progress, for example, they may use their radios to plan and coordinate their approaches with other officers to minimize risk to innocent people and themselves. In doing so, they also reduce the chances that suspects will be hurt by, for example, defensive reactions by officers who have put themselves in vulnerable situations. In addition, well-coordinated approaches to confrontations can also cut off escape routes and make successful flight nearly impossible.[1]

As this discussion suggests, successful resolution of potentially violent situations depends heavily on the skills with which officers coordinate and structure their confrontations with possible adversaries. Although the skills police need when actually confronting violent suspects are critical, what officers do in the moments immediately before that point is far more important than whether they can find cover, draw quickly, and shoot straight once they find themselves at risk (see Fyfe 1988b, 1989a). Carefully planned approaches to volatile situations by officers can *prevent* violence by creating circumstances in which potential adversaries instantly recognize that both resistance and flight are impossible and that surrender is their best option. Once officers' hasty approaches have put them in harm's way, however, their combat skills can only help to determine who prevails when violence erupts. It is certainly desirable that officers come out on top in violent encounters, but it is far better to prevent violence in the first place.

The skills required to structure confrontations in the safest possible manner have been neglected by police administrators and trainers. Instead, and perhaps influenced by the legal test of justification for the use of force—was the officer in danger *at the instant* he or she employed force?—police historically have focused on what Binder and Scharf (1980) call the "final frame" of incidents that actually begin when officers become aware that they may confront potentially violent people or situations (Geller 1985a; Geller and Karales 1981a; Geller and Scott 1992; Reiss 1980; Toch 1980). This tendency has changed somewhat since the days not so long ago when police firearms training consisted almost exclusively of shooting at bull's-eye targets, but it still exists. Where it does, as suggested above, it obscures the important question of whether officers' actions contributed to danger from which they subsequently had to forcibly extract themselves.

Regardless of its sophistication and its novelty, interactive video training has a "final frame" focus that cannot impart the tactical skills that officers should use to assure that they come face-to-face with adversaries in circumstances that make violence unlikely. These skills—how to plan and coordinate approaches to potential violence—are more complex and tougher to teach than the skills of ducking, drawing, and shooting. They can, however, be presented in lectures and seminars, or by simple explanatory films or videos, and they may be tested in role-plays. They cannot be taught or measured by two-dimensional interactive presentations that begin only after trainees have been placed virtually face-to-face with armed people under circumstances that good street officers would have tried hard to avoid in the first place.

Police administrators who seek to develop training programs designed to minimize police-citizen violence should keep in mind Herman Goldstein's admonition that "the gadgetry of technological improvements holds a certain fascination and dramatic appeal for large segments of the public; it feeds the 'Dick Tracy' concept of what policing is all about. Investment in technological improvements has been used by some police agencies and by state planning agencies as a way of avoiding more difficult problems" (Goldstein 1977: 325).

The "more difficult problem" here is to get officers to deal with routine, potentially violent incidents as skillfully as police have learned to handle hostage situations. This can be best done through training that causes officers to interact and match wits with other people rather than with electronic figures on a screen. While interactive electronic training may be a useful supplement to more traditional forms of training, it is no substitute for it.

Violence Reduction Training Must Be Tailored to the Officers' and Community's Experiences and Needs

Some tactical concepts are universal. Regardless of where they are, police should approach potential violence carefully: officers should never get too close to people with knives; officers should follow generally the same procedures whenever they make traffic stops; officers should stand to the side whenever they knock on doors; and so on. But every community also possesses unique characteristics that create specific challenges for officers, and these must be taken into account in training.

The most important such characteristic is the nature of the population which, in many jurisdictions, changes constantly. Unless police carefully monitor these changes and use training to let officers know about them and their implications for police work, officers are likely to deal insensitively with members of groups that, seemingly out of nowhere, have grown to significant size and have come to perceive themselves as mistreated. To complicate matters, such population changes may also cause bitterness and resentment among existing racial or ethnic communities who feel that their places on the local social ladder are threatened by the newcomers.

The potential costs of ignoring or inadequately responding to these changes are high, especially in places with previously well-established social orders (no matter how inequitable). In 1980, in the midst of the great social change caused by long-term Cuban immigration and by the massive Mariel boatlift, Miami suffered its Liberty City riot after several white and Hispanic police officers were acquitted in the beating death of a black man. During the late 1980s, Washington, D.C.'s Mount Pleasant district became home to large numbers of Hispanic immigrants. In 1990, a riot broke out there when a black female police officer shot a man during a Hispanic street festival. Afterward, Hispanic leaders complained that the city and its police department had been treating Hispanics as invisible. As if to confirm this claim, many long-time Washingtonians expressed surprise that there were enough Latin Americans in Washington to hold a festival. In 1992, while Los Angeles was in the midst of massive population shifts,[2] the acquittal of the officers accused of beating Rodney King caused long-standing tensions to explode into a riot. Also in 1992, witnesses' accounts of a police shooting—subsequently determined to have been inaccurate—sparked a riot in New York City's Washington Heights, an area which had rapidly become a community of Dominican immigrants during the late 1980s and early 1990s.

It is easy for police administrators to ignore the need to monitor and respond to large-scale changes in the population they serve. The people, after all, are the field officers' clientele, so that changes in the population and, hence, the need for modifications in police operating styles might appear to be most readily visible to street cops. This reasoning is flawed. First, even a startling change in a community may be so gradual that it goes unnoticed by those closest to it. Like a mother who doesn't see how much her child has grown until someone else notices, officers who regularly patrol a neighborhood may not even realize that changes over time have meant, in essence, that they are working in a different place.

Second, even when field officers do see the forest for the trees, they generally are not sufficiently familiar with the norms and sentiments—or even the language—of the newcomers to be able to respond to them in appropriate ways. How, one might ask, does a white ethnic male police officer adjust to the replacement of Washington Heights' long-time Irish-American population by poor, Spanish-speaking, Dominican immigrants? How does the black female Washington, D.C., cop, herself a member of two historically marginalized groups, learn how to deal with the rural Hispanics who have suddenly become the largest single group in the formerly African-American neighborhood she patrols? How does the veteran white Los Angeles officer thread his or her way through the conflicts among the Hispanics and Asians who have moved in among the blacks in his or her district? The answer is that all of these officers can do this only with difficulty, unless administrators take pain to monitor communities, to carefully consider the implications for police work of any changes in communities, and to see that street officers' training reflects these changes and their implications.

This may be most easily accomplished when police personnel closely reflect the community's diversity. Police hiring, however, often lags far behind changes in the community at large. Consequently, as a blue-ribbon Milwaukee commission pointed out, it is imperative that formal training reflect an appreciation of community diversity and dynamics, no matter who wears a police uniform (Milwaukee Mayor's Commission 1991: 4).

The need to fit training to the needs of individual communities is yet another reason why police agencies should regard commercial or other out-of-house training as a complement to their own training effort, rather than as a substitute for it. No commercial vendor who directs training at a wide market can possibly anticipate or address the characteristics of individual jurisdictions. And despite their greater proximity to the departments they serve, it is extremely difficult for state or regional academies to do so. Assuring that training is congruent with community demographics requires hands-on efforts by local police departments.

One of the best ways to assure that training closely fits the needs of the community and the police is to base it on the real experience of the community and the police. Noteworthy police encounters with citizens—both those that have come to unhappy endings and those in which potential disaster was averted—should be documented and reviewed thoroughly for their training implications.

This was the model followed in the Metro-Dade Police-Citizen Violence Reduction Project (Fyfe 1988b, 1989a), and it appears to have had some success. During this project, a task force of experienced police officers—street officers and supervisors, investigators, tactical specialists, and trainers—was asked to review a random sample of reports detailing citizens' complaints of police abuse, officers' use of force, and injuries to officers during contacts with citizens. Each member of the task force was asked to take at face value the description provided in each report and to identify individually every decision made by the officer involved, to describe its effects on the outcome of the situation, and to prescribe alternative actions that might have produced happier endings.[3]

The task force members read and discussed each other's analyses and provided project staff with their conclusions. This work, and consultation with a citizens' advisory board comprising community leaders and activists, identified four broad types of incident (routine traffic stops, disputes, responses to reports of crimes in progress and stops of suspicious pedestrians, and high-risk vehicle stops) as the most common potentially violent situations. It also produced a list of do's and don'ts for these situations based on the thinking of these officers and citizens. These do's and don'ts were incorporated into a role-play training program and tested under social science experimental conditions. The results of the experiment suggested refinements that led to a five-day role-play training program. Preliminary examination of data indicates that this training has been followed by substantial (30 to 50 percent) reductions in injuries to officers, officers' use of force, and citizens' complaints of abuse (Skolnick and Fyfe 1993; Fyfe and Klinger forthcoming).

*Violence-Reduction Training Must Not Make Matters Worse by
Creating a Sense of Paranoia among Officers*

When new officers enter police departments, they have very little appreciation
for what their jobs will be like. Fed on movies and television shows such as *Dirty
Harry, Lethal Weapon,* and *Hill Street Blues* and made more anxious by their
families' concerns for their safety, new police officers, teenagers in many jurisdictions,[4] are likely to believe that they are entering a world where death lurks
around every corner, where every contact with a citizen may prove fatal. One of
the major challenges for police recruit trainers is to bring many trainees' fears in
line with reality and to convince new officers that while policing has dangers, life
in a patrol car has little in common with duty in a military combat zone.

Instead of treating the dangers of police work as real but generally manageable, much commercially available training material exacerbates officers' fears. As
a consequence, some officers have come to believe that their work is one continuous tactical exercise and have overreacted with needless violence to minor provocations or to no provocations at all.

A widely used police training text is illustrative. It begins with this quote from
an officer billed as a "survivor of an armed confrontation with a mentally deranged
suspect who had slashed a man's chest open with a razor":

> I like the edge, the challenge. I get a high off it. You're out there in the con-
> crete jungle or the cornfield jungle. You know the guy you're up against has
> no regard for authority or society. He doesn't care about you. But he knows
> he's got to go, and you've got to get him.
>
> I like the element of danger. It makes me feel *alive*. But I don't expose my-
> self to danger blatantly. I'm not going to give anybody the opportunity to get
> even just a little bit of me if I can help it. Going up against danger and coming
> out whole because I'm prepared tactically, that's what the rush comes from.
>
> My dad used to say there are no new frontiers . . . they've all been explored.
> But in our society, there's still one: the street. It's the only place you can be that
> has any edge to it. (Remsberg 1986: inside front cover; emphasis in original)

Similarly, electronic interactive programs, especially the earliest ones, often appear to be based on incidents that, if they occurred at all, must be virtually unique
in police history. It may be valuable for police to know about such incidents, but
it may be dangerous for young officers to be encouraged to generalize to their
experience events such as the following, all of which appear in commercially available police training films:

- A police officer stops a group of unkempt bikers. Unknown to him, one of
  the bikers has modified his vehicle's handlebars so that twisting the throttle
  will produce a shotgun blast from the end of the bar.

- A police officer calls to a prepubescent boy on a bicycle. The boy stops his bike, draws a gun from his waistband and begins shooting at the officer.
- A police officer goes to a suburban home, apparently to respond to a report of some sort of disturbance. As he approaches the front door, it is opened by an old woman in curlers and a robe. She produces a handgun and begins shooting at the officer.
- Police officers in search of an armed and dangerous suspect see a young man and call to him. He walks toward them, and both officers loudly and repeatedly command him to stop. They draw their guns and point them, but he continues to walk toward them. He reaches into his back pocket as he walks. When he finally gets close enough so that they can read it, he produces a wallet containing a card explaining that he is deaf. The film clip does not explain how the subject could have mistaken the intent of two officers who, with guns directed at him, had obviously been signaling frantically for him to stop.

Worst-case scenarios like these, the Los Angeles Sheriff's Department recently acknowledged in response to the criticisms of a blue-ribbon commission, may have a place in training but "must be balanced with a consistently strong message that such incidents are usually the exception in law enforcement" (Los Angeles County Sheriff's Department 1992: 153).

Violence-Reduction Training Must Be Continuous

In addition to preparing veteran officers to deal with changes in law, departmental rules, and the dynamics of their communities, there are two major reasons for training to be ongoing. First, some of the most critical police violence prevention and reduction skills are needed so rarely that they are likely to atrophy into uselessness unless officers receive frequent refresher training. This may be especially so in suburban and rural jurisdictions. Despite the blood-and-guts tenor of much commercial police training material, for example, officers in most places are not likely ever to run into hostage takers; but if they do, lives will depend on their ability to recall and apply their training. Thus, as in medicine and other emergency professions, constant in-service training is necessary to keep officers' most critical, but rarely employed, skills at a useful level.

The second reason to require constant refresher training in violence prevention skills reflects a perversity of police work: most often, it does not matter whether officers' actions conform with their tactical training. Police officers who receive careful recruit training in the tactics of vehicle stops, for example, graduate to duty where they discover that virtually every traffic violator they stop is nothing more than an otherwise law-abiding taxpayer. Instead of the escaped murderers they have been trained to understand they may find behind the wheels of cars that have run red lights, new officers instead find, to the disappointment of some, that most traffic violators are apologetic, subservient, ingratiating, and anxious only to escape fines and increased insurance premiums.[5] Similarly, officers who respond to reports of burglaries typically find that the tactics they were taught are moot, because the vast majority turn out to be false alarms.[6] Under these circumstances, it is very easy for officers to regard their training for both car stops and responses to burglaries as something akin to preparing to avoid lightning strikes and to place it in the category of useless things learned in the police academy. Without scaring such officers into paranoia, periodic training reminds them that there are real dangers out there.

Violence-Reduction Training Must Address the Role of Police Officers during Their Nonworking Hours

There are 168 hours in the week, of which police officers generally spend only 40 in uniform. During the rest of their time, they do what other citizens do, with one exception: the law generally authorizes them to take enforcement action while they are off duty, and citizens expect that officers' decisions to take appropriate police action will not be bounded by their official working hours.

Answers to the question of what is *appropriate* police action, however, vary dramatically depending on whether an officer is on duty. It is relatively easy to prescribe appropriate police action for officers who are in uniform, in easily identifiable police vehicles, in radio contact with their colleagues, and not a party to the situations that give rise to the need for police intervention. But these prescriptions may be singularly inappropriate for an officer who enjoys none of these conditions and who may find that his or her actions may simply make bad situations worse.

Administrators must be careful to define what they expect off-duty officers to do (and to refrain from doing) and how they expect them to do it and to train officers in these expectations. When this does not occur, some off-duty officers invariably will use their police powers to resolve personal disputes, and the good-faith attempts of some officers to intervene in relatively routine crimes will turn into tragedies (see Fyfe 1980b).

Appraise the Effects of Violence-Reduction Training by Concentrating on Officers' Conduct Rather Than Incident Outcomes

The stringent requirements of social science experimentation need not be followed in developing such training, but one important rule should be observed assiduously: until there has accumulated enough experience to allow statistical analysis, assessment of the appropriateness of police officers' conduct in crisis situations—and the adequacy of related training—should focus on conduct, not the outcomes of these situations. Too often we forget that interactions between police and citizens are two-way streets. On occasion police officers may act in the most inappropriate or, even, openly provocative manners during encounters with citizens, and no violence or other immediate negative consequence ensues. This is so because the citizens involved do not take advantage of officers' ineptness or do not respond to their provocations. On other occasions, serious violence between police and citizens is unavoidable, even though officers may do everything reasonably possible to avert and minimize it. In such situations, to paraphrase an old medical saw, the operation was a success even though the suspect wound up in the hospital.

The implication of this reality for police administrators is that, like assessments of surgeons' efforts, judgments about the propriety of officers' conduct and the adequacy of training should be based on what officers *did*, rather than on the outcome of what they did. To do otherwise is to overlook inappropriate conduct until it results in disaster and to discourage officers whose best and most appropriate efforts were unable to prevent violence because of decisions made by their adversaries.

Conclusions

There is much more that can be said about training to reduce violence between police and citizens. In the main, however, police administrators are well-advised to follow the wisdom of the courts as articulated in the *Monell* case and decisions derived from it. As I interpret this case and others that have followed it (my interpretive lens is that of a police manager and social scientist rather than that of a lawyer), it appears that the courts generally demand that the police:

- identify the predictable police crises characteristic of their communities;
- develop policies and tactics to help officers resolve these crises with as little bloodshed as possible;
- carefully train officers to implement these policies under crisis situations;
- carefully review officers' actions in these situations to determine whether they have behaved in accord with policy and training and, equally important, whether policy and training are appropriate; and
- take corrective action where indicated: discipline officers who have unreasonably deviated from policy and training, nonpunitively guide and retrain officers whose deviations from best practices were not wilful, and modify policy and training where it has proven inadequate or inappropriate.

These are reasonable expectations. Meeting them will not guarantee that unnecessary bloodshed will be eliminated. But experience and research indicate that attending to them will help reduce such problems to an absolute minimum.

NOTES

1. The preceding critique of interactive video training applies to technologies employed widely in police training. If, as some technologists believe, virtual reality technologies can overcome the sequencing, dimensionality, and other artificiality problems noted above—and if police departments can afford to adopt such training tools widely—then it is possible that *some* of the human interactive training this chapter advocates could be supplanted by electronic devices.

2. Over the long term, the change in the composition of Los Angeles' population has been no less massive than the change in its size. In 1950, 11 percent of Angelenos were nonwhite; by 1990, the city was 63 percent nonwhite (U.S. Bureau of the Census 1952: 5–51; Independent Commission on the LAPD 1991: viii).

3. This task force approach also brought to bear on this problem the considerable expertise of experienced street officers who were regarded as outstanding by their supervisors and colleagues (see chapter 1, in which Klockars extols such use of highly skilled officers as role models). Often, despite their unequaled qualifications for doing so, such officers have little input into the formulation of training related to problems that most directly affect them and their colleagues (see, e.g., Toch 1980; Bayley and Garofalo 1989; Goldstein 1990). In addition, the task force approach enhanced other field officers' receptivity to the training that resulted; as one trainee told me, "It's nice to see that the brass don't think that they have a monopoly on what it takes to develop training for road officers."

4. Strawbridge and Strawbridge (1990: 17–22) asked 80 U.S. municipal and county police departments with 500 or more officers for information about minimum age at appointment as a police officer. Seven of the 45 responding departments allow appointment at age 18 or 19, as (I know from personal contacts) do several of the nonrespondents.

5. In only 27 (2.4 percent) of the 1,051 routine traffic stops recorded by in-car observers during the Metro-Dade experiment, for example, did officers encounter motorists who were annoyed, demeaning, hostile, or disrespectful. The others were classified by observers as "nervous and apologetic" or "respectful and deferential" (Fyfe 1988b: K-52).

6. Officers in one of the patrol districts observed during the Metro-Dade project responded to 230 electronic burglar alarms; 220 were defective, 9 were accidentally tripped by homeowners or merchants, and one signaled an actual burglary (Fyfe 1989a).

CHAPTER NINE

Officer Attitudes Toward Police Use of Force

DAVID LESTER

P olice officer attitudes toward the use of force and excessive force are an important area of study. Not only do these attitudes play a role in determining the use of force by police, but the attitudes held by police officers can also function as a barometer of changes in police use of force.

Explanations of Police Behavior

The two major theories of why police behave in the way that they do have been labeled *situational* theories and *attitudinal* theories (Worden 1989). Situational theories examine factors in the structure of the situation confronting police officers which shape their response, such as the characteristics and behavior of the suspects. Attitudinal theories focus on the style of policing of the officers, which in turn is affected by the officers' personalities, attitudes, and socialization in the police force. Both theories, of course, accept that police do not mechanically enforce the law but have a great deal of discretion in deciding what to do in each situation they encounter. Attitudinal theories extend beyond attitudes and examine any kind of psychological trait, including motives for becoming police officers and personality traits. Worden (1989) noted that research on these theories has been less extensive and less rigorous than research on situational theories. However, research does indicate that police officers have a great deal of variation in their attitudes (and their behavior), and this variation allows attitudinal theories to propose causal elements in police behavior.

A complete theory of police behavior would combine both situational factors and attitudinal factors so that, for example, we might propose that one type of officer would behave one way in a specific situation while another officer would behave in a quite different way (Toch, in chapter 4, extends this analysis). In this chapter, though, the focus is on attitudes.

The attitudes of police officers toward the use of force and excessive force have not been studied extensively. There are several possible reasons. First, given the choice of studying the attitudes of police officers toward excessive force or studying their actual behavior, researchers may have chosen to focus more on the behavior. Second, the definition of excessive force is imprecise and open to debate, and so researchers may have preferred to study actual killings of civilians by police officers (for example, Lester 1982; see chapters 1 and 3 on definitional problems). Third, many studies of police officers' use of excessive force have used participant observation and resulted in descriptive rather than quantitative reports (for example, Hunt 1985), which have not stimulated further research (compare chapter 2 and the studies discussed).

Research into police use of excessive force has also had a limited focus. In discussing the causes and reduction of police abuse of force, Geller (1985a) suggested that useful information could be acquired from the study of officer *restraint*. Some police officers are adept at escalating police-suspect encounters into fights, while others are equally adept at avoiding the use of force. Even in this general area, Geller noted that we know almost nothing about the personal characteristics and methods used by these two extreme types of officers. Part of the problem is that researchers do not study "nonevents"—the many situations in which police officers do not use excessive force. Since "nothing" happened, the situation is not marked for special study. An exception is that in some observational studies (which are quite expensive), data can be deployed to explore the motivations and behavior of officers who did and did not resolve potentially violent encounters violently (see chapter 2; Bayley and Garofalo 1989).

Despite these problems, research into police attitudes in general remains a core area for police studies, and research into police attitudes toward force in particular would greatly advance our understanding of police use of force. This chapter will review the research that has been conducted and propose a research program for the future.

Police Attitudes

General Attitudes Toward Police Misconduct

Barker (1978, 1983) questioned police officers with an average of ten months on the job and found that they reported widespread use of excessive force by fellow officers. Corruption of authority was the most common deviant behavior noted, followed by sleeping on duty and then the use of excessive force. (Queries were made about fifteen deviant behaviors.) Although police brutality was considered to be as common as sleeping on duty, it was seen as less deviant. In fact, police brutality was seen as less deviant than four other deviant behaviors (drinking on duty, perjury, sleeping on duty, and sex on duty). The likelihood of an officer reporting a fellow officer for these deviant acts matched the perceived deviancy of the act.

Macfarlane and Crosby (1976) asked police officers to rank various rules of conduct for police for their fairness as written and for the fairness with which they were enforced. Rules on the use of physical force were ranked fifth on both scales out of fourteen areas. Rules on courtesy by police and gratuities were ranked as the most fair and rules on grooming as the least fair.

Attitudes Toward Police Use of Force

Corbett et al. (1979) surveyed police officers about a variety of issues, including use of force. Of those surveyed, 22 percent agreed with the statement, "There are times when it would be better for a police officer to take the law into his own hands rather than turn a suspect over to the courts," while 67 percent disagreed, and the remainder were unsure. Forty-two percent agreed that police officers are too restricted in the amount of force they can use in dealing with suspects; 39 percent disagreed.[1] Scores on these items (and on one other item on constraints on the police) were added to provide a measure of favoring a "strong police role." Scores on this scale were lower for officers who felt that the public supported the police, for those who were less racist, for those who trusted the political system and people in general, for those who did not regret becoming police officers, for those who were relatively older, and for those less willing to strike for a pay increase. Scores on the scale were not related to rank, division, years of experience, father's or mother's occupation, spouse's occupation, party identification, ideology (liberal or conservative), religiosity, personal self-confidence, or other attitude items (such as job satisfaction and a perception that police work is dangerous).

Instead, the attitude of police officers toward the use of excessive force seems likely to be related to other attitudes, such as general attitudes toward police misconduct and violence. For example, in a study of the police officers in one small-town department, Ten Brink and Lester (1984; see also Lester and Ten Brink 1985) found that police officers who were more likely to report fellow officers for brutality (verbal abuse, physical abuse, or the murder of suspects) were also more likely to report fellow officers for other misbehaviors, including drinking on duty, smoking marijuana off duty, accepting free cups of coffee, and accepting bribes. They were also more willing to serve in an internal affairs unit to investigate fellow officers. Police officers who socialized mainly with fellow officers while off duty were less likely to report the misconduct of their colleagues.[2] Just over half of the officers responded that they would participate in the street execution of a suspect known to have killed a police officer; officers who socialized mainly with fellow officers were more likely to admit this.

Brodsky and Williamson (1985) presented police officers with written scenarios in which an officer had used excessive force (such as beating a suspect). Police trainees and experienced officers had lower approval scores than a comparison group of firefighters. However, Brodsky and Williamson did not compare the attitudes of police officers and firefighters toward other forms of violence.

Carter (1976) surveyed the police officers in one department and reported that 89 percent asserted that few officers use excessive physical force. Some 23 percent believed that excessive force is sometimes necessary to show an officer's authority, while 62 percent felt that officers have the right to use excessive force in retaliation for physical attacks by suspects. Only 16 percent felt that excessive force, when used, was a result of ethnic or racial discrimination.

When asked about verbal abuse, 59 percent felt that it was permissible for officers to talk roughly with citizens, and 53 percent felt that rough talk was the only way to make some people listen. Carter explored correlates of the officers' opinions about the use of excessive force and reported that their toleration or acceptance of physical and verbal abuse was stronger if they expressed less satisfaction with their job.

The Independent Commission on the Los Angeles Police Department—the Christopher Commission—reported that in a survey of 960 officers in the department, about 5 percent approved of the use of physical force on suspects who had committed heinous crimes or showed a bad and uncooperative attitude; 11 percent reported having "no opinion," leaving 84 percent who disagreed with these propositions (1991).

Justifying the Use of Excessive Force

Waegel (1984b) explored how police officers justify the use of deadly force. His comments also apply to the use of excessive force. He noted that tales of past shootings are prominent in police folklore and are frequently recounted to rookies. Waegel noted three major themes which police officers use to justify shooting suspects.

First, they acknowledge that sometimes mistakes are made and that officers shoot when there is no legitimate cause to do so. However, they focus on the risk that they might have been killed if they were to underestimate the danger in a situation. A favorite phrase is, "I'd rather be judged by twelve than carried out by six." They give examples of officers getting shot when they did not fire first. Second, police officers also share the beliefs of the general public that some offenders are despicable people. The presumed moral inferiority and the race of suspects lead the police to see them as less than human, thereby justifying brutality. The same practice is common in war; the enemy is denigrated by derogatory terms (such as "Hun" or "gook"). Pogrebin and Poole (1988) have documented how humor is used by police officers to denigrate individuals or groups.[3] Third, Waegel noted also that police officers are often cynical about the operation of the criminal justice system which, from their viewpoint, lets offenders off too lightly. They are often tempted to dispense justice themselves, and in this they are often supported by the attitudes of the general public. Waegel saw these rationalizations as consistent with the strategies used for neutralization of guilt by criminals (Sykes and Matza 1957), strategies that release the actor from conventional rules and prohibitions.

Opinions about the Use of Deadly Force

In a study on police officers' opinions about the use of *deadly* force, Brown (1983) asked officers in two departments to rank, in order of preference, four possible department policies on the use of deadly force. The policies and rankings were:

1. A police officer should be allowed to use a firearm only to apprehend a suspect who has committed a violent felony and if the officer believes that death or serious bodily harm will result if the suspect is not apprehended immediately; or an officer may also use a firearm in defense of himself or another against death or serious bodily injury. [ranked first by 42 percent of the officers]
2. A police officer should be allowed to use a firearm to apprehend a suspect who has committed a felony, or in defense of himself or another against death or serious bodily harm. [ranked first by 32 percent of the officers]
3. A police officer should be allowed to use a firearm only to apprehend a suspect who has committed a specified violent felony (aggravated assault, armed robbery, rape, murder) or in defense of himself or another against death or serious bodily harm. [ranked first by 20 percent of the officers]
4. A police officer should be allowed to use a firearm only to defend himself or another against death or serious bodily harm. [ranked first by 5 percent of the officers]

Thus, the officers did not support the most restrictive policy (4). However, Brown noted that although both departments permitted the use of deadly force to apprehend a fleeing felony suspect, many officers declared that they would not use deadly force in that situation. Thus, police officers may use more restraint than they are given credit for or than their agencies require.[4] Brown noted that legal repercussions, possible civil suits, and departmental punishments may deter officers from using deadly force even when they may legitimately do so.

Brown (1984) presented patrol officers with hypothetical situations and asked them to rate the appropriateness of shooting in each. There were great differences in the ratings depending on the situation, but the officers' responses were also affected by their level of education, length of experience on patrol, percentage of time working alone, experience of assault by civilians/suspects, race, age, and sex.

Dwyer et al. (1990) presented sheriff's deputies with sixty scenarios and asked them whether they would draw their weapon, aim, or shoot. They found that the deputies were more likely to shoot if the suspect had a weapon, if the suspect seemed to have an intent to harm, if the suspect was committing a felony, and if the suspect was leaving a building. The setting of the incident (such as daylight, rain, or public location) and characteristics of the suspect (such as race, age, or sex) did not predict a shooting decision. Dwyer et al. concluded that these results supported the notion of the police officer as a professional, making the decision to shoot based on the suspect's actions and intentions. However, as with other studies of attitudes and hypothetical responses, it would be interesting to explore the extent to which these responses parallel actual behavior.

What Determines Police Attitudes Toward Excessive Force?

There are several possible theories of what might shape a police officer's attitudes toward the definition and use of excessive force.

Occupational Environment

The work of being a police officer may in itself change and shape the attitudes of officers toward the use of excessive force. For example, police officers, by some measures run a high risk of being injured or murdered on the job. The risk of being murdered for an American police officer in the 1970s was about 22 per 100,000 annually as compared to 1.4 for police in England and Wales (Zunno and Lester 1982). Lester (1982) found that the states in which police officers were murdered at a higher rate were also those states where civilians murdered one another at a higher rate and where police officers killed civilians at a higher rate. In other words, police officers in violent areas tend to behave more violently. Lester (1984) suggested that the police may reflect the values of the communities from which they come or that working in a violent community may increase the likelihood that a police officer will use deadly force (see Friedrich 1980 for a rigorous appraisal of the geographic and other correlates of police use of deadly force). Working in a community where murder is common would probably also affect police attitudes toward the use of deadly force.

The expectation of danger on the job can have an impact on police officers. Lester et al. (1980) found that state police recruits who had a greater expectation of facing danger were less inclined to see their job as primarily helping citizens in the community. Corrigan et al. (1980) found that municipal police officers who had a greater fear of injury on the job were more willing to use their authority to control the behavior of citizens and felt more socially isolated from the nonpolice community. Thus, police officers' expectation of harm may lie behind their use of excessive force.

Teahan (1975) gathered some data on this by testing police officers on entrance into the police academy, on graduation, and eighteen months later. Some of his questions tapped officers' attitudes toward complaints about police brutality.[5] White police officers became less willing over time to admit that police officers are guilty of abusing citizens, while black officers agreed more with the proposition over time. In general, Teahan found shifts in various attitudes during both academy training and the period of working, but he does not document well the responses to the questions on police brutality.

Crawford (1973) found evidence that police officers may feel that the community is more hostile to them than is the case. For example, he found that, while 32 percent of the residents of one town felt that there was police brutality in their city, the officers on average expected that 49 percent of the residents would say so. The more prejudiced and less educated officers were especially prone to overestimate the hostility toward police in the city (see also chapter 6).

Peer-Group Socialization and Predisposition

Attitudes toward the use of excessive force by one's fellow officers may also shape an officer's view. In line with this hypothesis, Hunt (1985) noted that rookies soon learn that what is taught in the police academy is somewhat irrelevant to their work on the street. Department-issued equipment marks them as new recruits, and they quickly upgrade to the plastic nightsticks and flat-headed slapjacks that experienced officers carry ("slappers" are prohibited in many police departments today—Geller and Scott 1992). They learn to hit suspects in order to incapacitate them quickly, rather than to hit them on the "safer" areas of the body taught at the academy. They also learn that their colleagues reward them for aggressive and forceful action and punish them for caution. Cautious police officers are seen as unreliable and as risky partners. Hunt noted that female police officers were more quickly accepted in the department she studied when they participated in brutal actions. Thus, the rookie revised his or her definition of normal and excessive force and behaved more aggressively than taught. However, Hunt noted that there are limits to the use of force and violence, and that these limits, too, are taught. Excessively brutal police officers are chastised by partners, assigned to more mature officers who, it is hoped, will calm them down, and eventually transferred to duties without public contact.

Hunt noted that officers also developed ways of accounting for the use of what was excessive force even by their standards. Excuses deny full responsibility for the act but acknowledge its inappropriateness. For example, physiological or emotional stress often triggers excessive force in police officers, and they admit this. Thus, suspects are often abused after a high-speed car chase or when an officer comes close to killing an unarmed person.

Officers who justify their use of excessive force accept responsibility for the behavior but deny that it was blameworthy. Rationalizations usually refer to the situation that was thought to require force or to the fact that police authority was threatened. Thus, a suspect who physically threatens or attacks an officer or who symbolically assaults an officer (such as vandalizing the officer's car) is more likely to be the victim of excessive force. Excessive force is also felt to be justified against morally reprehensible persons, such as child molesters.

Hunt's descriptions of situations involving excessive force mix behaviors and attitudes, and it is difficult to disentangle the two. There may be police officers whose attitudes make them violent individuals (see chapter 4). They are violent on the job because it was their preemployment style. Walker (1982) found that police officers who were more approving of violence in general were more likely to have been physically punished as children and to have participated in contact sports. Younger officers were also more accepting of violence. Walker noted two possibilities: people who are more accepting of violence may be attracted to police work, or a career in policing may result in a greater tolerance of violence. Carter (1976), whose research was discussed above, found that police officers who were less satisfied with their job showed a greater acceptance of physical and verbal abuse of suspects.

Opportunity

In studies of criminal behavior, opportunity theory focuses on the possibility that behaviors may occur when there are opportunities for them. Decreasing opportunities sometimes lessen the occurrence of the behavior. If a casino opens, there is an increase in the incidence of compulsive gamblers. Installing automated banking machines leads to an increase in robberies at such venues. Conversely, reducing the opportunities for criminal acts often decreases their frequency without displacement to other criminal acts (Cornish and Clarke 1987).

An opportunity theory of excessive force by police focuses on their opportunities to engage in such force (especially since supervision is typically absent). For example, officers now occasionally videotape encounters with suspects for use in court (typically from cameras mounted in their cars and with wireless body microphones). Such videotaping would be expected to decrease the use of excessive force on suspects since the officers would know that the tapes would be reviewed later—that is, the officers' opportunity to interact with a suspect *unwitnessed* has been reduced.

A Research Program

As there has been so little research on this issue, this section will suggest avenues for future research into police attitudes toward excessive force. A research program first requires one or more satisfactory scales to measure the attitudes of police officers toward excessive force. For example, research into police attitudes in general was greatly stimulated by the development of a cynicism scale by Niederhoffer (1967). Publication of the scale led to a great deal of research using it, as well as critiques of the scale itself, which led to the development of alternative scales.

After a scale has been developed, research into police attitudes toward the use of excessive force would benefit from an exploration of the simple correlates of such attitudes. What other attitudes are associated with officers' attitudes toward the use of force, which personality traits, and which antecedent experiences (which might suggest hypotheses for the factors affecting the development of the attitudes)? What serendipitous experiences and typical occupational hazards change an officer's attitudes toward the use of force? What kinds of training programs and techniques best change officer attitudes?

It would also be worthwhile to examine the attitudes of police officers toward the different forms of police deviance (malfeasance, misfeasance, and nonfeasance) and toward the different behaviors included in each of the categories. Are all the behaviors viewed similarly?

In social psychology it has long been recognized that attitudes are often not strongly related to behavior. Indeed, changing attitudes by forcing people to change their behaviors is more effective than the reverse strategy. An important question is whether the attitudes of police officers toward the use of excessive force bear any relationship to their actual behavior in this area. A working hypothesis that would support methodological work on estimating the prevalence of abuse of force would be that officers who abuse force more often than their colleagues would express the opinion that officers frequently have no choice but to use rough tactics to satisfy the pressures on them to fight crime and disorder. Worden (1987) found that the attitudes of police officers accounted for very little of the variation in their actual behavior in traffic enforcement, preventive patrol, or dispute resolution and his research should be extended to the use of excessive force.

Another important approach to systematizing this research is use of typologies. Scharf and Binder (1983) proposed that research be conducted on a typology of officers involved in high-risk encounters. Geller (1985a) suggested surveying officers about such issues as: (1) the types of incidents in which they consider shooting; (2) the situations in which they feel that they could lawfully shoot but do not; (3) the situations in which they could lawfully shoot and probably would; and (4) the closeness of their individual and personal values on these matters to the informal organizational norms expressed through supervisory statements and actions and peer pressure. These suggestions are relevant to the concerns of the present chapter, and the research design could easily be extended to the study of excessive force.

In an example of this kind of inquiry, Lester and Arcuri (1994) studied the attitudes of a group of municipal and state police officers toward the Rodney King beating in Los Angeles at the time of the first (state) trial in 1992. The questionnaire was administered before the not-guilty verdicts, which led to riots in Los Angeles. The percentage of officers agreeing with the ten items are as follows:

1. The Rodney King incident has given police a bad name. 97%
2. When police hit a suspect, it's national news; when a suspect hits a police officer, no one cares. 95%
3. For every alleged Rodney King incident there are dozens and dozens of incidents where police are assaulted. 92%
4. The police officers who beat King were actually threatened before the video recorder began filming. 79%
5. The Rodney King incident represents a few bad cops. 77%
6. If the LA police officers who beat King are found guilty, they should go to prison. 59%
7. I have never witnessed any beating of a suspect. 37%
8. If I witnessed police beating a suspect, I would report him/her. 33%
9. The Rodney King incident happens only once in a lifetime. 27%
10. Rodney King got what he deserved. 21%

Although almost all of the police thought that police officers are more often abused by suspects than vice versa, they realized that the Rodney King incident had tarnished the image of police officers. A factor-analysis identified one major cluster of items in which the responses to the items were associated (items 3, 4, and 7 positively and 5 and 8 negatively). The total score on these items was not related to the age or years of experience of the officers, their level of education, or whether they were state or municipal police officers.

Those officers expressing more approval of the police behavior in the Rodney King incident were more in favor of the death penalty for murder and more likely to agree that they would hit a suspect who resisted arrest or verbally abused them; they also more often felt in danger on the job, admitted that they had hit suspects to subdue them, and said that they had been assaulted on the job. With respect to their reasons for becoming police officers (using a questionnaire developed by Lester 1983), these officers were less likely to give "helping people in the community" as a reason for becoming police officers and more likely to give "early retirement with good pay," "the excitement of the work," and the job's "power and authority."

Thus, it was possible to identify a cluster of items that assessed attitudes toward the Rodney King beating and to find meaningful correlates. Those supporting the police in the incident felt more in danger at work, liked the power and excitement of police work, felt that they had been assaulted more often, and would use physical force on suspects more often than would officers supporting King.

An attempt has been made in this chapter to show that the study of attitudes in general and police officer attitudes in particular is important for advancing understanding of police behavior. At present, the study of police attitudes toward the use of excessive force is in only an embryonic stage. There is a need for rival investigators to devise alternative scales to measure police attitudes toward force, so that the better ones can be identified. Correlates and antecedents of these attitudes must be sought, and research conducted to explore the relationship between attitudes and the actual use of force. This area is an exciting one and, it is to be hoped, one that will attract researchers in the future.

NOTES

1. Among many possible areas for useful new research is whether officer attitudes in this regard have changed after the pervasive adoption by departments of pepper spray as a nonlethal weapon.

2. On the other hand, a corruption scandal in the Miami Police Department in the 1980s, in which evidence suggested a wave of new recruits had not been socialized into the police culture and had, to an unusual extent, continued spending off-duty time with civilian friends of questionable character, illustrates the problem of bad influences in the neighborhoods increasing the likelihood of police misconduct.

3. Further explorations are warranted of the potentially positive role of gallows humor as a coping mechanism to mitigate the considerable stresses of police work (e.g., encountering human misery and inhumanity on a recurring basis). For such humor to be of psychological benefits (providing a release valve) does not mean that the content of the humor must be racist, sexist, or in other ways objectionable. The timing is all-important; after seeing a particularly bloody crime scene, the officers would not want to find a humorous way to release their own horror in the presence of loved ones of the victim or others likely to misinterpret the humor as callousness to human suffering.

4. The highest ranked deadly force policy in Brown's 1983 study was probably the prevailing policy—written or unwritten—in most police agencies at the time; and it was a policy bolstered in 1985 by the Supreme Court in *Tennessee v. Garner* (see Geller and Scott 1992; Walker and Fridell 1989).

5. Perez and Muir (see chapter 11) discuss the results of officer surveys concerning complaints and complaint review systems in Berkeley and Oakland, California. Note especially their finding that officers tend to prefer a complaint review system in which citizens have a role.

CHAPTER TEN

Police Unions, Police Culture, and Police Abuse of Force

GEORGE L. KELLING and ROBERT B. KLIESMET

A lthough serious police research is now in its fifth decade in the United States (if one starts with the 1950s American Bar Foundation's *Survey of Criminal Justice*), and experimentation in its third decade (if one starts with the *Kansas City Preventive Patrol Experiment* in 1975), research about the structure, function, and role of police unions has been at a practical standstill since the work of Juris and Feuille (1973). Moreover, major scholarly books about policing largely ignore police unions; if they discuss them it is only in a cursorily descriptive fashion, often presenting such generic union issues as collective bargaining and defining such terms as mediation and arbitration, adding a few comments about the lessons learned from the Boston strike in 1919.[1] Scholarly work about police unionism has just begun.

The reasons for this disregard of unionism are not immediately apparent. The argument that police unions are uncooperative with researchers is hard to take seriously; during the 1960s and 1970s, police departments were hardly enthusiastic about opening themselves for research, but their sheer number and fragmentation gave early researchers opportunities to penetrate at least a few departments and, once these were opened and the professional value of research was understood, police barriers to research collapsed across the country. We have no reason to doubt that the same situation holds in police unions: we could name a dozen unions that would gladly participate in meaningful research, about their most basic functioning in some cases. Lack of funds has been a problem for those who might want to become involved in research about unions; such research has not been on the agendas of foundations or national funding agencies, although the National Institute of Justice (NIJ) funded one research project on unions during the early 1980s. Still, "lone wolf" researchers have studied many issues in policing with little, if any, funding, and nothing keeps them from studying police unions as well.

As much as anything, most academics share a general unease about the legitimacy of police unions. Everyone understands their importance, but it is not clear what role they should play in policing. Most researchers enter police departments through management, collaborate with management in some research or evaluation project, and develop an ongoing relationship with chiefs. Rarely are unions involved in such research. Occasionally, local unions may oppose some innovations that they believe are threatening to their interests or grumpily raise questions about use of some research methodology, but serious opposition to research in police departments has been exceedingly rare.[2] On a national level, the International Union of Police Associations, AFL-CIO, has applied for research funds from several sources, with no success. For the most part, therefore, a research agenda in policing has developed independently of unions, with little union opposition, and with some token participation on panels reviewing proposals for research grants.

The Dominant View of Police Unions

A fairly predictable point of view is put forward when scholars give attention to unions. Walker's *Police in America: An Introduction* (1992), is a good example.[3] Walker concludes a brief and relatively balanced section on police unions (the last section of the final chapter) with a discussion of the police "professionalization" movement and unions—an issue at the core of this chapter. "When unions first appeared, many reformers were alarmed that they would destroy the professionalization movement. First, unions reduced the power of police chiefs. Historically, powerful reform-minded chiefs have been the major force for professionalization. Second, unions frequently opposed many specific reforms associated with professionalism. Some unions, for example, opposed incentive pay for officers with college educations. Unions in several cities opposed the creation of a fourth patrol shift. And many unions fought programs designed to improve police-community relations" (Walker 1992: 379).[4] The book ends on a discouraging note: "The possibilities for changing police organizations are limited by structural features such as civil service and police unions" (p. 380).

The view that unions retard professionalization of police is widely shared by police executives. Minneapolis Chief Tony Bouza (now retired) is perhaps one of the most outspoken chiefs on the issue: "The movement to unionize in the 1960s had to buck the by then commonly accepted objective of gaining the status of a profession—a dream that would never come close to being realized but that captured the police imagination for two-thirds of a century. The absence of altruism in union goals also ran counter to the concept of selfless service that at least theoretically guided soldiers, doctors, priests, lawyers, nurses, and cops" (Bouza 1985: 253).

This point of view—unions oppose the professionalization of police (not to mention their "absence of altruism")—is troublesome. Both Walker and Bouza claim that chiefs historically have supported police, in Bouza's words, "gaining the status of a profession." This is *not* in fact the case. Historically, chiefs have supported moves that *they* have christened as professional; however, some of these moves have been antithetical to the basic concepts of professionalization, as those concepts are commonly understood both popularly and in the literature on occupations. These moves, described below, were not only antithetical to the professionalization of line police officers but also incompatible with the recognition of line police as *craftspersons*. It is hard to exaggerate the extent to which labeling the reform agenda of early and mid-twentieth century police leaders as "professional" was a misnomer—indeed, it was an oxymoron (see Walker 1992: 13; see also Kelling and Moore 1987).

The moves that police reformers dubbed professional were, instead, *bureaucratic*—strong lines of administrative control and oversight, extensive rules and regulations, pre- and in-service training provided by police departments,[5] elimination of discretion, and simplification of work tasks. For good or ill, these moves not only shaped police departments; they were directly responsible for the shape and functions of police unions as well. To understand the values such reform efforts served and their impact on line police officers, further background is required.

The Reform Strategy of Policing

As Bittner (1990: 9) has put it, reformers "reinvented" policing during the early twentieth century. Their primary goals were to free policing from the excesses of political influence, end police corruption, and improve the efficiency of police. To achieve these ends, reformers had to resolve three basic issues: defining the function of police; developing the tactics or technologies that police would use to achieve their goals; and instituting the organizational structure and the managerial and administrative systems required to carry out the police mission. Function and tactics are not central to this paper, and we will only briefly note reformers' answers to these issues. The official definition of the police function in the reform model was law enforcement. That is, police would be focused on reacting to serious crime and would move away from crime prevention (except as an outcome of arrest), peacekeeping, order maintenance, and the provision of social and emergency services. Those functions would be given to other agencies; police would be "crime fighters," the front end of a criminal justice "system." Second, the tactics police developed would concentrate on serious "crimes in progress," with police patrolling in cars, intercepting crimes in progress, responding rapidly to calls for service, or investigating criminal events on a post hoc basis.

Police Organization and Management: Rank-and-File Response

While the managerial and administrative systems police reformers put in place were ostensibly military or quasi-military in form, they were primarily influenced by and patterned after the "scientific" management theories of Frederick Taylor developed during the early decades of the twentieth century. Briefly, Taylor's factory model urged centralization of authority, use of middle management to rationalize work, standardization and routinization of tasks, layers of control, span of control, and unity of command. In this view, labor was a commodity. Because work was standardized and routinized, labor was easily replaced. Workers were motivated solely by their vested interests—money and working conditions—and had little or no interest in the substance of their work. Left to their own devices, workers would avoid work and screw up. Managers would think, structure work, and command; workers would do.

August Vollmer, the founder of American police reform and the mentor of O. W. Wilson, advocated the view during his early efforts at reform while chief in Berkeley, California (1909–32), that the police officer should be a college-trained professional providing a broad array of police services. This view was later abandoned by reformers in favor of a view of the police officer as a tightly controlled and inherently limited functionary whose primary, if not sole, role was nondiscretionary law enforcement (see Kelling and Stewart 1991). As Walker put it, "The rank-and-file police officer was the 'forgotten person' of reform. Most reformers had *contempt* for ordinary officers" (1992: 14; emphasis added). Bittner, by no means sharing reformers' contempt for line police officers, notes reformers' views of both the capacity of urban police departments and the kind of persons needed to staff them.

> Other law enforcement agencies divided the tasks of dealing with crime taking place in banks, offices, boardrooms, government agencies, and so forth, which is almost entirely nonviolent and demands sophistication on the part of both the perpetrator and law enforcement. The preponderant majority of what is left for the police is what is sometimes referred to as "street crime." The salience of so-called street crime, which frequently involves acts of violence, in the perceived police mandate dictated the definition of the person suitable to wage the struggle against it. The strengths sought in recruits were the "manly virtues" of honesty, loyalty, aggressiveness, and visceral courage. It was also understood that police recruits should be able and willing to follow uncritically all received commands and regulations. Of course, they had to be literate enough to read instructions and to write short reports. But it was taken for granted that police work was not for people whose intellectual aspirations reached far beyond this level. (Bittner 1990: 6–7)

And Bouza gives us a modern rendition of the reformers' theme of how to control such persons: "Police agencies are *mainly controlled through terror*, and this terror is most aimed at the one or two percent who, if left to their own devices, would set a negative tone" (1990: 133; emphasis added).

And so, all of policing's control mechanisms were put into place: extensive rules and regulations, span of control, unity of command, specialization of work, overseers (sergeants), patrol in cars, reduction—or denial—of discretion, among others.

This preoccupation with control of officers pervaded all police reforms (see Kelling and Stewart 1991). Bruce Smith made this clear in 1929: "Without exceptions, all proposals for improvement of organization and control have necessarily been aimed at the weakening or the elimination of political influences" (p. 27). Thus, regardless of other values reform innovations in policing may have had,

> the UCR [Uniform Crime Reports] enabled police departments to be evaluated independently of political judgments. . . . Use of automobiles for patrol not only increased the range of patrol officers but also improved the ability of police executives to monitor and control them. . . . Communications systems further augmented administrative surveillance and control of officers. Data-based beat allocation systems, by facilitating equitable distribution of police services, gave police the high moral ground in the public mind if anyone, particularly politicians, attempted to force the police to allocate services on the basis of favoritism. . . . Civil service and the use of objective examinations to select and promote personnel limited the influence of politicians over personnel matters. Centralization of command and the replacement of geographical by functional organization . . . lessened significantly the influence of ward politicians. . . . Creation of centralized special units reduced the power of precinct commanders relative to the central command staff. (Kelling and Stewart 1991: 6–7)

Reformers' emphasis on control of line personnel extended to the private lives of officers as well. Police authorities "also imposed all kinds of conditions on officers' private lives, conditions designed to minimize exposure to temptation and corrupt influence. These included restricting officers from living in the areas they policed, from incurring debts, or from being involved in businesses in their areas, as well as requiring them to declare the business interests of their families" (Sparrow et al. 1990: 36–37). Moreover, officers had to live within a certain distance of police stations, had to carry weapons while off duty, had their financial and sexual lives monitored and regulated, and, in some cities, had to take their police cars home with them.

Arguably, the reformers' strategies paid off. Political influences over police, especially corrupt political influences, were reduced; police financial and political corruption was also reduced, as was inequitable and unjust policing; and police organizations were modernized. Simultaneously, and not surprisingly, the police union movement developed.

Scientific Police Management and Police Unionism

While the history of police unionism in the United States cannot be detailed in a chapter of this length, it should be noted that the move to unionize police was characterized by unusual virulence, even in a field well-known for its bitterness. Opponents of police unionism were so successful in forestalling it—primarily by firing anyone who attempted to organize until well into the 1950s and early 1960s—that police unionism, in contrast to other public sector unionism, remains inchoate, fragmented, and immature. For many of today's union leaders, this virulence is a matter of personal experience. One of the authors of this chapter (Kliesmet), for example, was harassed, arrested, and eventually fired for his union activities while a member of the Milwaukee Police Department. (Both the arrest and firing were later overturned.) Parallels between private sector unions and public sector unions, especially police, are important, however, and must be understood in some detail.

Late nineteenth- and early twentieth-century industry moved from production systems that relied on artisans who were organized into craft unions into alternate systems that relied on unskilled workers and scientific management. The need for skill, for artisanship, was eliminated by standardized and routinized production processes.

As artisans were eliminated from industry, their unions were largely eliminated as well. (Trade unions still exist in some occupational areas, however, like carpentry and plumbing.) Industrial workers eventually adopted industrial unions—the United Auto Workers, for example, represent a wide variety of job categories, from maintenance personnel to assembly line workers. In this model, workers, stripped of skills as the basis of their value, moved to define their value in other terms. John Hoerr describes this process:

> In order to defend workers against the abuses of scientific management, the new industrial unions accepted, even embraced, all that went with it—in particular, the rigid separation of thinking from doing, "managing" from "working." Cut off from decision-making responsibilities, unions focused on protecting workers from exploitation by using Taylorism as a base of shopfloor power. They negotiated multiple job classifications, linked wage rates to the job instead of a worker's skills, and established seniority as the basis for promotion. This "job control unionism" gave unions a negative power to hamstring management but not a positive power to influence operations. Rules bred more rules, eventually straitjacketing the production system and creating

unproductive hierarchies in companies and unions. (Hoerr 1991: 36; see also Rankin 1990)

This model of industry unionism, with its emphasis on seniority, rules and regulations, and jobs rather than skills is, of course, the model of unionism that has been transposed into policing.

Departments developed extensive rules and regulations to control police. Police unions, as they gained hold during the late 1960s and early 1970s, responded by negotiating extensive rules and regulations to protect street officers from excessive arbitrariness by supervisors and managers in applying not only the rules that defined the work of police but also the rules that impinged on their personal lives.

The view of using rules as a means of countercontrol in police organizations is not merely theoretical. Leibig (1993: 2), a labor lawyer, is quite explicit about this: "It is nearly impossible to have a situation in which a creative police organizer cannot find a rule, regulation, guideline, budget provision, benefit program rule, or personnel procedure which cannot be exploited to significantly increase the rights and benefits of working officers. . . . Management is bound by those rules. Read them. . . . Think of them as helping the working officer and binding management. Make management follow the rules. There may be more than a dozen levels of management controls and restrictions." Leibig lists at least ten sources of union countercontrol: the Constitution; federal statutes; state statutes and regulations; city ordinances; internal budget and personnel regulations and directives; Equal Employment Opportunity rules and affirmative action plans and court decrees; public disclosure, privacy, and administrative law rules; general orders; squad or division rules, directives, and guidelines; and personnel records.

Although the following description pertains to the private sector, it reads much like the police world. Industrial unions

> bargained for elaborate seniority procedures to ensure fairness in the distribution of jobs within the system. However, these procedures not only bred an intense loyalty to and a vested interest in scientific management, they also formed the basis for the widespread acceptance of the position that uniformity was a necessary condition for developing worker solidarity. Workers accepted the dull, deadening jobs in their earlier years with the understanding that later on in their work life they would be entitled to the "good" jobs. "Good" meant not necessarily more challenge or autonomy, but work usually free of heavy labor, on days, or in a warm, dry setting. As a consequence individual worker interests and the interests of scientific management were merged. (Rankin 1990: 27)

The views of "good" jobs in policing paralleled those in industry. Good police jobs were in quiet neighborhoods during the day with as many weekends off as possible. The "dog watch" (11 P.M. to 7 A.M.) in difficult neighborhoods was tolerated during the early days of one's career; as one persisted on the job, seniority ensured cushier assignments, not increased challenge, independence, or responsibility. Consequently, the core concerns of police unionism became: wages and benefits; job security; hiring, retention, promotion, and disciplinary processes; access to "good" jobs, shifts, assignments, overtime, etc.; and, regulation of work practices by rules.

And, just as rank-and-file industrial workers developed "an intense loyalty to and a vested interest" in scientific management, so police developed an intense loyalty to the reform strategy. The unions that grew in the context of Taylorism in policing ultimately embraced management beliefs that the issues of definition, tactics, and organization in policing had been solved.

The Union Agenda

As did their brethren in factories, police unions, once in place, focused their attention on rectifying the abuses that often typified reform management: arbitrary dismissals, scheduling, and work assignments; informal discipline (e.g., standing on a corner for three hours); citation and arrest quotas; cronyism in promotions; incursions into officers' personal lives; and others. They did this by getting the rules and regulations into the bargaining arena and then negotiating, politicking, mediating, arbitrating, and pressuring. After new rules and regulations that were more to their liking—seniority in bidding for shifts and assignments, for example—were in place, unionists had a profound commitment to continuation of scientific management.

Thus, by the late 1960s and early 1970s, police management and unions basically agreed on reform definitions of the police purpose supported by powerful images and metaphors; appropriate police tactics; correct administrative and managerial processes for police departments; and the respective domains of each. Having conceded these issues to management, police unions have little stake in organizational effectiveness or in the production of quality goods or services. As Weiler points out when discussing industrial unions: "The natural assumption on both sides was that management would continue to run the enterprise and would have the prerogative of initiating changes in the firm's operation and work organization" (Weiler 1990: 197). Thus, if management wants to change its product line, that is its prerogative. Likewise, management is free to change production processes (tactics) as well. However, as Weiler continues: "The role of the union was to react to these decisions, to challenge them in grievance arbitration, and eventually to regulate by contract the exercise of management authority where it significantly affected employees" (ibid.). Thus this model clearly defines roles: unions are interested in members' salaries and working conditions, while issues like the quality of goods and services, or their prices, are ceded to management. All of this, of course, is congruent with the basic assumptions of scientific management: workers are concerned about wages and working conditions, and management is concerned with the product or service line, quality, and profits.

This understanding of the historical concerns of police unions explains their current abrogation of any substantive interest in the quality or substance of policing, including concern for use of force, the primary focus of this chapter. "Thinking," management, and quality control are the prerogatives of top and mid-management. The most extreme version of this is in Boston, where unions managed to forestall efforts to develop field training programs. The union position is firm: no officer will evaluate any other officer; that is management's responsibility. Officers do "police work."

A Survey of Unions

Testing the idea that unions maintain a narrow range of interests, we informally surveyed eighteen police unions—most from southern, midwestern, or western states—about use of force and union policies. The survey was conducted during the spring of 1992, a year after the March 1991 Rodney King beating in Los Angeles. All locals were International Union of Police Associations (IUPA) AFL-CIO affiliates, and they ranged in size from 21 to 2,500 members, with the majority having several hundred members. Twelve were designated bargaining units; six were from states that did not formally recognize unions. The person interviewed most often was the president of the local. All the unions had policies of defending officers against use-of-force complaints, although the unit with twenty-one members had never been called on to defend any of its members.

We asked six basic questions:

1. Has your union published anything about the Rodney King incident?
2. Have you or anyone else in your union been quoted in the press regarding the Rodney King incident?
3. Has your union advised officers in any way regarding use of force?
4. Do unions have any role in developing use-of-force policy in police departments?
5. Should unions have any role in developing use-of-force policy in police departments?
6. Do you have any comments about the impact of the Rodney King incident on police and police unions?

Regarding the first three questions: no unions had published anything about the use of force; representatives from three unions had been quoted in the press regarding the Rodney King incident; and seven unions had advised officers about use of force. None of the three unions whose representatives had been quoted in the press had kept the articles, with one saying to our interviewer: "We don't save that kind of crap."

Of the seven unions that reported advising their members on use of force, the comments of the representative of a large western union were typical: "Yes, whenever we have delegate meetings we advise them to strictly follow the guidelines set down by the department because we don't want them to get into trouble. We emphasize that nothing is more important than your job and safety. Also we state that by following the rules they will also help the union save money because the high cost of representation will not be a factor. This may sound self-serving, but it only helps them and helps the union."

A representative from one mid-sized southern department who said the union had not offered advice on use of force added ruefully: "We have gotten together with the department on several deals to come up with seminars to explain abusive behavior, but as of yet, nothing has happened. The department does have a general order about excessive force."

As for whether unions have a role in use-of-force policy development and should have such a role (questions 4 and 5), twelve of the eighteen unions indicated they had no role in determining policy. However, seventeen unions indicated they believe they should have some role. Some of their explanations for why they should have a role follow:

- We have an obligation to the members and department to inform the hierarchy of policy problems and improvements.
- Officers need to receive instruction on use of force, meaning that officers are given weapons to apply force—nightstick, gun, mace—and are told how to use these weapons but are not instructed on *when* to use them.
- Because it [use-of-force policy] is going to be something that the union will be getting involved in once the complaint comes down.
- Because [sometimes departments have] civilians . . . manag[ing] law enforcement officers who don't have to deal with the force issue one-on-one and never will.
- The union should have a say, especially regarding use-of-force policy development, because this issue involves equipment and safety.
- People out here working the street know when and how to use force and should be brought into that decision-making process.
- Sometimes the department's policy is questionable and too arbitrary. . . . A lot of good officers are not sure how much force they can use anymore.
- We should have a voice in what it is that we are ordered to do or not to do.
- The union can give a different point of view than the administration. Management looks at the issue of excessive force from a possible risk of lawsuit point of view. Cops look at the issue from the point of view of a person who must make a split-second decision when confronted.

- It would be a better respected policy [if unions had input].
- The managers use pencils; we use force. Since we use the policy, it is only right that we should have a say so in its development, since we are the ones who apply it.
- Unions should be asking for use-of-force policies. The worst situation is not knowing what to do. At least with a policy you would have guidelines. It used to be that cops who discontinued a car chase were called wimps. But now since there are pursuit policies, a cop's integrity is no longer called into question if he chooses not to pursue or stops pursuit.

The one representative who opposed involvement in policymaking had an interesting point of view. "On the whole, as a general rule, unions should stay out of making the policy, because they will be defending officers against a policy they created." In their final comments about the impact of the Rodney King affair (made after the first trial and subsequent riots), union representatives expressed the belief that the incident had worsened the relationship between police and citizens, especially minorities; that worried them (see also chapters 5 and 6). They believed that the incident represented the actions of only a few in policing but that the consequences would fall on all officers, regardless of their values and performance. The repercussions they feared were both lack of community support and lack of departmental backing in use-of-force situations. However, some respondents were philosophical about the issue:

Basically, the incident focused a very bright light on police work. Now, every action we take is scrutinized. My only hope is that this attention brought to police work will benefit it in the long run.

The Rodney King incident has brought to the surface any and all problems existing in police departments. . . . Departments have now been placed under a microscope. As such, other problems, above and beyond use-of-force issues, have come to the light. Departments are now being looked at more closely in their handling of sexual harassment, alternative lifestyles (gay/lesbian), asked to be more culturally aware of their area—causing a tremendous amount of change in all departments. Because no matter your job, anytime an organization is subject to such scrutiny, change is bound to occur and it will affect everyone. Along with this change will come resentment, uncertainty, and fear. If departments and unions take the initiative on this, they could come out better than we were. We have to change. Society, with its changing demographics and cultural makeup, demands these changes. The problem is that some people think the change is too fast and others that the change is too slow.

In general, although union representatives believed that they ought to be involved in use of force policymaking, development of community policing, and other substantive issues, it was not for them a "mat," or negotiating issue. They may fuss because management ignores their capacity for input on these issues, but management's "prerogatives" in such issues are ceded. To the extent that unions encourage adherence to rules or the development of policies, regulations, and rules, they do so for protection of workers ("nothing is more important than your [union members'] job and safety") or for the protection of the union ("following the rules they will also help the union save money because of the high cost of representation"). Virtually no concern is voiced for improved police services.

It would be easy to be cynical about this and see police representatives as motivated purely by self-service and as evidence of Bouza's "absence of altruism in union goals." But this is a self-fulfilling prophecy. If management treats line personnel as only interested in wages, benefits, and salaries, refuses to involve them significantly in substantive issues in policing, and structures union-management relations on the factory model, unions will reflexively move into their own domain when queried.

The Need for Greater Organizational and Strategic Flexibility

In industry, scientific management flourished for management and workers before the emergence of the global economy. Quality of products might have suffered, but a broad marketplace existed nonetheless. When corporations were confronted with global competition and new demands for quality in products and services, however, they found their ability to adapt shackled by unwieldy rules and unwieldy processes to modify those rules. Moreover, given the preoccupation with rules and regulations by both management and unions in the past, no mechanisms existed to obtain workers' views—an untapped resource—of how to improve either productivity or quality.

Change affected the world of policing as well. The particulars that drove police organizations to develop a new strategy and the shape of this new strategy are beyond the scope of this chapter.[6] But just as earlier reformers redefined the police function, devised tactics to carry out these functions, and developed organizational structures and management practices to support these tactics, so contemporary police leaders have been required to make similar changes. These shifts have been labeled team policing, community and/or problem-oriented policing, and quality management.

In attempting to shift strategy, police leaders, like their corporate counterparts, are confronted both with unwieldy rules and regulations (to which police unions now have a deep commitment) and with few mechanisms for getting line input into methods of improving police services. Police leaders, however, are also confronted with a powerful, pervasive, and entrenched police culture, elements of which over time have gained broad popular and political support. Like all cultures, police culture is unlikely to change quickly.

Police Culture

The idea of a corporate, or organizational, "culture" gained popularity in organizational and business circles during the 1970s (Morgan 1986: 111). Morgan defines organizational culture as follows: "Shared meaning, shared understanding, and shared sense making are all different ways of describing culture. In talking about culture we are really talking about a process of reality construction that allows people to see and understand particular events, actions, objects, utterances, or situations in distinctive ways" (p. 128).

The idea of police culture developed early in police research and writing. Authors including Wilson (1968), Skolnick (1966), Manning (1977), and van Maanen (1973) have documented the power of a police culture to shape police behavior. Herman Goldstein has described how police culture overwhelms rules, regulations, guidelines, and instructions, as well as the authority of chiefs and mayors, in shaping how police officers use their discretion (Goldstein 1977, 1990). Reuss-Ianni (1983) and Reiner (1985), moreover, posit distinct police subcultures, particularly the subculture of "street cops." Bittner (1984) has summarized the schism between street and "management cops":

1. There is widespread belief among street cops in a past, golden age of policing during which the department was one happy family, united in a common cause, permeated by unquestioned trust and unbreakable loyalty, from top to bottom.
2. As seen by street cops, any indication of outside influence is evidence that management cops have sold out.
3. In the view of street cops, management has not just caved in to pressure; management cops found that in yielding to outside influence they could advance their own careers.
4. What is cooked up in headquarters is not only a departure from all established principles of policing, it also looks strange and often is incomprehensible. (Bittner 1984)

Other authors see additional ingredients in police culture: police solidarity, the hostile world in which police operate, officers' focus on "getting the job done," civilians never commanding police, and policing as a craft learned from other officers on the job, not from education or training (see, for example, Goldsmith 1990).

That unions often embody such belief systems will come as no surprise to most chiefs or unionists: in many cities such ideologies were the platforms on which police unions first developed and on which candidates still run. It must be recalled, however, that many, if not most, of the elements of police culture have their origins in management practices. Isolating officers from citizens and equating citizen involvement with corruption contributed to officer alienation from the

citizens they serve and to the "blue curtain." Creating military metaphors to describe policing—police as crime fighters and the "thin blue line"—led to narrow
definitions of the police function and a warrior mentality.

This warrior mentality has had a powerful impact on police unionism. It affects collective bargaining, the political stance of many unions, and even the process of union formation. For an example of political implications, Kelling, who
has often testified on behalf of line personnel in wage disputes, usually meets with
the union board the evening prior to his testimony. Almost inevitably a conflict
ensues. Board members urge Kelling to argue for higher salaries on the basis of
their "manly virtues": their role as crime-fighters, the danger of their work, their
heroics, and the costs of their work to their family lives. Many become incensed
that Kelling intends to emphasize not those issues but the complexity (see Goldstein 1993) and nuances of their work: their discretion; their autonomy, given the
inability of overseers to be present when officers make their most important decisions; the infinite variety of their work, including services police officers have
learned to despise as social work; and the lack of formal recognition for their
work. During testimony, however, when a complete line of thought about the
substance of police work is soberly and uninterruptedly developed, unionists become more and more attentive—nodding and shushing others so they can hear
more clearly. Afterward, even many doubters and skeptics come forward to say
that they had never thought about such things before. "Why wasn't all this better
known?" They come to understand that complexity and discretion were more important than heroics when it really mattered. To be understood as skilled analysts
confronted with complex problems is far better than being perceived as dumb,
but maybe heroic, cops who fight "scumbags." Still, getting this to "stick" in the
minds of unionists is extraordinarily difficult.

Commitment to the crime-fighting ideology reached such levels during the
1960s that many police, including unionists, began to flirt with the political
imagery of the far right's law-and-order rhetoric, especially that of the John Birch
Society. While most police unions have now moved into the middle of the political spectrum—having learned since the 1960s how to play political games with
considerable skill—their early flirtation with far-right politics is another example
of the extent to which unions became the ideological and organizational mirror
images of police reformers.[7]

Commitment to ideology has not only affected collective bargaining, it has
affected the pace at which police unions have developed. In Milwaukee, for example, Harold Brier, who was chief from 1961 to 1984, was deeply admired and
respected by line police officers. Brier, who was tenured for life, outspoken against
lawbreakers, and intolerant of outsider or civilian influence in policing, opposed
community relations programs, rejected any suggestion that any of his officers
were disrespectful or abusive toward minorities ("law-abiding citizens have noth-

ing to fear from police, only troublemakers need worry"), and had a reputation as a "tough cop."

Attempts to organize Milwaukee police into a union continually foundered on officers' unwillingness to appear to oppose Brier's ideology or to appear disloyal to his "vision." It was only his opposition to establishing a grievance procedure to protect officers from his tyrannical disciplinary system that finally resulted in line support for a union. But so loyal were the officers and so fragile were the attempts to unionize the Milwaukee Police Department that Brier could have aborted the union movement by reaching out to officers in any meaningful way. Brier so clearly articulated basic cultural beliefs of police that organization of the Milwaukee Police Association around bread-and-butter issues—wages and benefits—could easily have been forestalled with a modicum of administrative restraint in the area of discipline.

All of this testifies to the power and efficacy of the reform model of policing. A coherent, consistent, and emotionally powerful vision of policing, arguably, it may not have served communities very well, but that is another matter. It shaped the occupation and unions for generations of police officers.

Another View of Professional Policing: The Friday Crab Club

August Vollmer is generally acknowledged to be the originator of the professional (or reform) police model. This is not surprising. Two of his patrol officers, V. A. Leonard and O. W. Wilson, became prolific police writers and major architects of the model. Viewing Vollmer as the founder of this model is, on the one hand, seemly. His protégés, through writing, consultations, and practice shaped police practice through most of the twentieth century.

On the other hand, to see Vollmer as the initiator of the professional model as it has been practiced in American policing obscures his own police practice and innovations in Berkeley, California. For example, Leonard and Wilson were two of Vollmer's "college cops," a dozen or so college students or graduates in a department of twenty-five to thirty officers (Carte and Carte 1975: 43). This was a far cry from the reform model's "dumb cops"—and the year was 1921! Gene and Elaine Carte wrote in 1975, during an era dominated by reform policing and before community or problem-oriented policing began to take shape, of Vollmer's philosophy of policing. His officers were problem solvers. "He expected each man to be the 'chief' of his beat, to bear responsibility for dealing with problems of any nature that came up within the area he patrolled. . . . He was to work closely with merchants to establish preventive measures and to know the families on his beat well enough to detect delinquency problems or unusual needs" (p. 45). Officers were generalists. Specialists might have a function, but they were not imposed on patrol. "Although Berkeley had specialists in criminal investigations, they were not brought into a case unless the patrolman requested their assistance or unless they were led there as a consequence of other investigations in progress" (p. 45). Officers shared points of view with each other and Vollmer.

Collegial control was one means of guiding police methods. Outsiders were brought in to share their knowledge. "Every Friday, all officers not on duty attended a group meeting to discuss department matters. . . . The Friday meetings, informally called the Crab Club, were a combination of gripe and learning session. 'For instance, if you had anything against any man in the department, you said it right there in front of him, and after it was over it was forgotten,' remembered one officer. During the summer, guest lecturers were brought in, primarily psychiatrists and articulate criminals who shared their expertise with the group" (p. 47). On the agenda of the Friday Crab Club were such matters as controlling the use of deadly force. "One officer recalled: 'If you fired your gun, you would have to get up before the whole group on the Friday Crab Club hour and give the factors on what happened, and there was a decision made by the men from the standpoint of this way or this way; right or wrong'" (pp. 46–47). Note again *collegial* control, even in the use of force (on peer control of officers' use of force see Toch and Grant 1991).

In other words, Vollmer was experimenting with the development of a genuinely professional model of policing before the management theories of Frederick Taylor became integral to the reform model. Vollmer's model included higher education, collegial control, a generalist police practitioner, specialties at the service of generalists, devolution of authority to practitioners, and collaboration with other professions. The Cartes comment: "The Berkeley success came from Vollmer's ability to find good men to be police officers and to use their talents well. Professional policing began when Vollmer decided, rightly or wrongly, that the police officer required significantly special skills to do his job, skills that could not be learned on the beat by a recruit who was indifferent to the 'higher purposes' of policing. *That is why it is inconceivable to him that a policeman should become identified with workingmen whose sense of occupational purpose extended only so far as a decent wage and adequate conditions on the job*" (Carte and Carte 1975: 42; emphasis added).

Policing went in a different direction. What was inconceivable to Vollmer during his tenure in Berkeley became a set of operating assumptions for most of contemporary policing. Despite this view, we know from research that police continued to provide a rich panoply of services, especially social and emergency assistance, to neighborhoods and communities; officers identified with communities; they solved problems; they consulted with each other; and they sought authority from and collaboration with citizens. Unfortunately, most of these activities have gone unrecognized, unrecorded, and unrewarded. Fortunately, however, the ability of line personnel to contribute successfully to policing has been documented, albeit too rarely. We will briefly discuss efforts in four cities.

Collegial Control in Oakland

During the 1960s and 1970s, the Oakland, California, police department was considered to be a model of a legalistic, arrest-driven police department (Wilson 1968; see also comments about Oakland during the 1980s in chapter 11). The department emphasized high personnel standards, national recruitment, and quality training.[8] Despite emphasis in training on human relations, it was also struggling with the level of violent encounters between police and citizens; much of the police violence was considered unnecessary and abusive. Officer behavior was routinely monitored, and a planning unit analyzed police-citizen encounters.

Chief Charles Gain, aware of research by Hans Toch into police violence, requested Toch's assistance in dealing with violence-prone officers. The approach that developed under Toch's guidance, the Violence Prevention Unit, was based on at least two assumptions: patrol officers themselves could control other officers, and officers who had been violence-prone in the past could best assist officers who were having difficulties in the present. Hence the creation of a peer review panel staffed by patrol officers who formerly had been violence-prone. The project was a success in two respects. First, the *process* was successful: officers participated with considerable enthusiasm and caring. Second, the peer review panel reduced the number of violent confrontations between police and citizens.[9]

Problem Solving in Kansas City

During the early 1970s, the Kansas City, Missouri, police department, like many other police departments at that time, received funds to add a large number of new officers. Chief Clarence Kelley wanted to allocate new officers in the most intelligent way possible. Assisted by Police Foundation staff and consultants, especially Robert Wasserman, Kelley conducted a series of conversations with his top command staff to determine how to allocate these new officers. Frustrated by their prosaic suggestions, he created four task forces—one in each division and one in the special operations unit—consisting primarily of patrol officers and asked them to develop allocation plans.

The South Patrol Division, with Wasserman as its coordinator, first identified the primary problems in the district and then decided that the most serious problem was youth behavior around schools. Some of the officers wanted to use the new officers to deal with this problem. Other officers firmly believed in the deterrent value of preventive patrol and, while they agreed that something should be done about the youth problem, nonetheless wanted all the new officers to be assigned to routine preventive patrol. A vigorous debate resulted, with some officers arguing the value of preventive patrol and others arguing that it had little impact. Finally, the officers decided to *experiment* with levels of patrol to determine the efficacy of patrol before they decided how to proceed with the youth problem. Kelling was invited by the task force to help them develop a research design.

Kelley approved the ultimate recommendation of the officers that an experiment should be conducted—over the objections of many commanders. Patrol officers participated in every facet of the experiment, from monitoring the experiment, to data analysis, to write-up (Kelling et al. 1974). The Kansas City study, of course, found that variations in levels of preventive patrol had no impact on levels of crime, citizens' fear of crime, or citizens satisfaction with police.

Community Relations in Milwaukee

Regardless of one's current perspective on community relations programs, many police, academics, and those advocating change in policing during the 1960s and 1970s believed that community relations programs would help to resolve the antagonism between police and minorities. Community relations programs were one of the key recommendations of President Johnson's Commission on Law Enforcement and Administration of Justice.

In Milwaukee, Harold Brier was having nothing to do with community relations programs, despite strong demands for such initiatives from parts of the community. Many in Milwaukee at that time believed that Brier was unwilling to make any moves that would be seen as conciliatory toward the black community. Brier himself would not meet with representatives of black neighborhoods. Woe be it to any of his commanders who were tempted to. His stated point of view was that people should simply obey the law and they would have no trouble with Milwaukee's police.

Milwaukee's police union saw this issue differently. From the point of view of Kliesmet and the rest of the leadership of the Milwaukee Police Association, it wasn't Brier who had to be on the street and face the antagonism of black citizens; it was line police. As a consequence, unionists began meeting with citizen groups using community relations techniques. Attempts to formalize the program never succeeded, however. Funds to reimburse officers for time spent with citizen groups were not forthcoming. While government agencies like the Law Enforcement Administration Assistance (LEAA) would fund police departments to develop community relations programs, they would not fund unions; LEAA has been replaced by several funding bureaus within the Justice Department, but the failure to fund union projects persists to this day.

Broken Windows in New Jersey

Foot patrol in New Jersey cities during the 1970s was funded by the state in a unique Safe and Clean Neighborhood program: To receive state funding for foot patrol, New Jersey police departments essentially had to submit a map indicating when and where foot officers would walk. While there was some evidence that foot patrol was popular with citizens and politicians (this was before the Newark and Flint foot patrol experiments, which established empirically the value of foot patrol, were published in the early 1980s), chiefs in New Jersey almost universally opposed the program (Police Foundation 1981; Trojanowicz 1982). They wanted the funds to continue but wanted to use them to increase the number of officers in cars. For New Jersey chiefs at the time, foot patrol was largely a waste of time—a personnel pool if one lacked enough cars or discipline for intransigent officers at best, a sop to politicians or citizens at worst.

As a consequence, foot patrol in New Jersey cities was largely an undirected activity for which there was little training or integration with other patrol or special units. In some cities, rookies were assigned to foot patrol; in others, it was a disciplinary assignment; in yet others, it was voluntary, often selected because of the better hours. Evidence of supervision was rare. In one city, officers still used call boxes on a regular basis to inform the "desk" of their presence on their beats.

For the most part, especially in larger cities, foot officers patrolled in downtown, shopping, or high-crime areas. Most foot officers were white and, especially in high-crime areas, patrolled areas populated by minorities, primarily blacks. But officers were known to residents, business persons, and transients, often by name. Likewise, officers knew many citizens' names. For the most part, regardless of area, officers concentrated on maintaining order: regulating panhandling, managing youth in the area, enforcing informal rules of street conduct, checking businesses, monitoring public spaces, and so forth.

With the exception of the union effort in Milwaukee, all of these efforts are well-known in police literature. Yet the central role that line personnel played in each has been overlooked. Oakland is an example of collegial control of use of force; Kansas City, of officers' professional concern about dealing with problems and the quality of police services; New Jersey, an example of police collaboration with citizens, based on the initiatives of undirected officers when they are placed in close working relationships with neighborhoods; and Milwaukee, of union concern for police-citizen relationships, partially out of self-interest—officer safety—but also out of concern for citizens as well. These examples are congruent with the conclusions of Bayley and Garofalo: "Police rank and file respect colleagues who exhibit behavior police departments want to encourage. . . . It respects qualities that the public respects and would intuitively associate with the ability to minimize violence." The conclusion to be drawn from these examples, and many others, is that line personnel are a powerful and important resource when we think of ways to improve policing or improve the relationship between police and citizens — both at the core of managing use of force.

Another View of Police Unions

Now policing is again shifting its strategy — in a sense, retracing its steps and picking up where Vollmer left off. But what about unions? After all, with the exception of the Milwaukee experience, although *officers* were major players in the efforts noted above, the contribution of unions was marginal. Toch is silent about any union response in Oakland. In Kansas City, police unionism was not much of an issue during the 1970s. In New Jersey, unions supported research into foot patrol because they were trying to protect the state program — from their point of view a source of police jobs (some New Jersey cities were already in dire economic straits during the 1970s). Even worse, some critics (see Walker 1992, discussed above) view unions as active opponents of change.

The question facing police unions is whether, as management philosophy and practices change, unions can change as well. At least three specific and similar questions emerge:

- Can unions improve the relationship between police and citizens and help ensure that force is used wisely and prudently in policing?
- Can unions become intermediaries through which the substantive concerns of line personnel can serve to improve policing?
- Will unions move beyond their traditional concerns and develop enthusiasm for improving the quality of American policing?

If we look at our own data, limited though they are, our first responses to these questions are somewhat hopeful. First, we know that the vast majority of line personnel, given a chance to participate meaningfully in change and innovation, do so with enthusiasm and skill. One of the surprises for many — and it is unfortunate that it has come as such news — has been the level of enthusiasm and care that officers demonstrate when they become involved in problem solving. So we know that the readiness is there to be tapped.

Unions have unique access to the potential of police officers if they move to develop, as it were, a new union strategy in tandem with, if not in collaboration with, police management. As in Milwaukee during the 1960s and 1970s, unions understand that they have a vested self-interest in improving the relationship between police and citizens and, as an integral part of that, managing use of force. Unionists did not rally around the flag of solidarity after the Rodney King episode. Most wanted involvement in developing use-of-force policy, even if out of self-interest.

Second, there is tentative movement in the union movement to adapt to the move to community and problem-oriented policing. Again, although our sample is limited, union leaders appear to support community policing.[10] We found that their biggest complaint is the failure of management to include unions formally in planning—or informally when local regulations or political traditions prohibit union activities (Kelling and Kliesmet 1991).

The most interesting question is whether or not police unions, like craft unions in the past, can move to reclaim some legitimate responsibility for the recruitment and socialization of recruits and legitimate responsibility for maintaining the quality of policing in America. We believe that for unionism to be credible and viable, it will have to shift its concern as more enlightened management moves away from administration by rules and regulations to administration by values and mission (see, e.g., Sparrow et al. 1990). As Bittner, Goldstein, and others have pointed out for decades, rules and regulations, training, supervision, and administration in policing have been more concerned with managing the internal relations among ranks than with the content of police work. The shift to focusing on the content of police work—problems—is new and tenuous in many cities; traditionally the focus has been on where police are and how fast they get there rather than on what problems police face and what they can do about them.

Finally, it is now widely known that superior recruitment, training, and administration cannot adequately control use of force unless the culture of police work supports those changes. We learned this in Oakland during the 1960s and 1970s, and we have rediscovered it in Los Angeles during the 1990s. Left on its own, or at times encouraged by "thin blue line" rhetoric of chiefs, police culture has drifted in many departments into a besieged warrior mentality. Police who are genuine leaders can help shape this culture. But the shaping has to start by engaging them in the substance of their work regularly and systematically and regaining the service vision of policing a democratic society. A good way to begin would be the establishment—in a fitting memorial to August Vollmer's real genius—of Friday Crab Clubs in all departments. It would pick up a forgotten link in the move toward genuinely professional police.

NOTES

The authors gratefully acknowledge the valuable contributions of Lynne J. Scott, research director, International Union of Police Associations, AFL-CIO.

1. Two contemporary examples of important works that completely ignore police unions are Geller (1991) and Sparrow et al. (1990). By contrast, see Geller (1985b).

2. At times, unions are wary of surveys of their members, fearing that the normal diversity that opinion surveys inevitably demonstrate will be used to undermine union solidarity in collective bargaining. A planned multistate survey of rank-and-file officers concerning, among other things, their use and abuse of force, was narrowed in 1993 to two

states—Ohio and Illinois—when some police departments in Pennsylvania refused to participate. The funding agency is the Justice Department's Bureau of Justice Statistics.

3. Walker's book was selected for convenience; Kelling uses it as a text in one of his undergraduate police courses at Northeastern University. Other texts could be cited to illustrate our point.

4. It is hard to take opposition to a fourth platoon, which Walker uses as an example, as resistance to professionalization. It is an administrative means to allocate police over time—a scheduling issue in which line personnel and unions have considerable vested interest. But identifying it as a professional matter is typical of the confusion that results when the word *professional* gets bandied about as it does.

5. Professions rely on graduate schools for pre- and much in-service training, not on employing organizations. For instance, lawyers receive their basic legal training in law schools, not in law firms, prosecutors' offices, or other organizations for which they work.

6. For detailed discussion of these broad issues, see Kelling and Stewart (1991) and Kelling and Moore (1988).

7. This does not imply that police reformers were necessarily ultra-right wing. Police rhetoric developed, however, from police leaders like Los Angeles Chief William Parker and FBI Director J. Edgar Hoover, who linked lawlessness, communism, and anti-Americanism in strident terms that demonized criminals and communists (see Kelling and Stewart 1985). This rhetoric was picked up by the far right during the 1950s and 1960s in law-and-order campaigns; the John Birch Society's "Support Your Local Police" campaign in the 1960s was the best known. Feeling isolated for a variety of reasons, not the least being the successful resistance to their unionization, line personnel found this rhetoric attractive. Later, police unions found more natural political alliances, but the strident law-and-order rhetoric continues to have powerful appeal among line personnel. Also, although space does not permit discussion of the argument here, unionists discovered that collective bargaining in the public sector was considerably different than in the private arena, where bargaining is primarily a market process, partially shaped by laws and regulations. In the public domain, it is primarily a political process, again shaped by laws and regulations. We make this argument in some detail in Kelling and Kliesmet (1991).

8. Toch and Grant (1991: 79). This entire section is based on this source.

9. These findings were not replicated in Kansas City. See Pate et al. (1976). A variety of explanations are available. Kelling, who was the director of the Kansas City project, believes that in Kansas City an unusually broad interpretation of confidentiality for officers referred to the panel made it unaccountable. Shorn of the guidance Hans Toch provided to the Oakland panel, Kansas City's panel got out of control.

10. We mean at least what they *understand* as community policing. This is no slight to union leadership; the concept of community policing is so riddled with ambiguity and so many departments call any minor innovation community policing that, for many, community policing can mean nothing more than overtime foot patrol or rewarmed community relations programs (Goldstein 1993).

CHAPTER ELEVEN

Administrative Review of Alleged Police Brutality

DOUGLAS W. PEREZ and WILLIAM KER MUIR

In the past, most police departments dealt with civilian complaints of excessive force in an informal manner. The local precinct captain or lieutenant would attempt to pacify indignant citizens and investigate misconduct as his time permitted. Citizens were influenced, cajoled, and even threatened out of making complaints against the police (see also Independent Commission on the LAPD 1991). Such practices, while commonplace, were not the subject of controversy until the 1960s. Urban unrest, mass demonstrations, and what were later described as "police riots" illustrated for many previously unconcerned citizens the problems of police misconduct. Scholars and politicians alike traced unrest among black citizens and middle-class white students to such police abuses as the excessive use of force, verbal abuse, and discrimination in law enforcement.

Citizen complaint processes within police organizations received scrutiny from several of the commissions assembled in the 1960s. The McCone Commission, looking into the causes of the Watts riot in Los Angeles, called for internal review systems to be set up within police organizations (McCone 1965: 31). Scholars such as Edwin Schur echoed this appeal for "strong internal investigative units to insure . . . fair and effective means of handling citizen complaints" (Schur 1969: 142). In 1967, the Task Force on the Police of the President's Commission on Law Enforcement and Administration of Justice (1967b) declared, "without question the best means for ensuring that police personnel are complying with departmental policies and general notions of fairness is through effective internal police procedures." Supported by social scientists including George Berkley (1969) and Herman Goldstein (1967), this logic has been employed by police administrators to defend their internal systems.

Calls for civilian review also abounded during the 1960s and early 1970s (e.g., Platte 1971: 181; Skolnick 1969: 280). People of color in particular did not (and do not now) trust internal review (U.S. Civil Rights Commission 1966: 305, 455, 514;

Lohman and Misner 1966: 92). Former United States Attorney General Ramsey Clark (1971: 143) is illustrative on the subject: "Police review boards in which citizen panels finally determine allegations of police misconduct and appropriate penalties are desirable to most cities. Some civilian review of police conduct, whatever the form, is always essential. Ultimately, the police are responsible to the public, not to the Chief of Police."

The political potential of civilian review ideas was not lost on police administrators. The formation of rigorous, tenacious, and at times even tyrannical internal investigative units was seen as one method of forestalling the formation of such external review bodies. As put by O. W. Wilson (1963: 208), the highly respected Chicago police chief: "It is clearly apparent that if the police do not take a vigorous stand on the matter of internal investigation, outside groups—such as review boards consisting of laymen and other persons outside the police service—will step into the void."

The polarization created by this debate has retarded the development of civilian review. Skolnick (1969: 280) remarked in his study of the politics of protest: "At the outset, it was the distrust by minority group members of internal police review procedures which caused the demands for civilian review boards; the militant opposition of the police has only brightened this distrust. Thus, as might be anticipated, a cycle of greater and greater polarization has been set in motion."

In part due to the polarization of advocates for internal and civilian review, and in part because of practical reasons, a third, hybrid type of system has emerged: the civilian monitor oversight system. Because of its potential for mediating between aggrieved citizens and governmental officials, because it leaves the direct investigation of complaints to police professionals, and because it acts as an advocate for the citizen, this system holds great promise (Kerstetter 1985).[1]

It makes sense to study administrative police review systems in terms of these three models: internal review, civilian review, and civilian monitor. While interesting variations on these themes are operating in other jurisdictions, we shall focus on Oakland, California, to consider internal review, Berkeley, California to examine civilian review, and Kansas City, Missouri, for our study of civilian monitor. These systems are chosen because they offer pure models for analysis and in many ways are the best examples of each type of review procedure.

Internal Review

As noted by numerous authors, Oakland's "internal affairs" is respected throughout the country (Douglas and Johnson 1977: 265; Guyot 1991: 181; Potts 1983: 71; Skolnick and Bayley 1986: 156). No internal process is more thorough in its investigations. None is populated by more concerned investigators, genuinely honoring objectivity in the pursuit of their task.

The Internal Affairs (IA) Section of the Oakland Police Department works closely with the chief of police, who sets the tone for its rigorous investigations, and is housed within his office complex. The chief's no-nonsense approach to citizens' complaints directly influences the working style of IA investigators and of the officers on the street. Aside from the chief's preoccupation with its integrity, the beat cops of Oakland learn that assignment to IA is one way to enter the fast track to promotion. Also, officers rotate frequently (two-year assignments) through IA. Thus there are a number of officers within the patrol ranks who have worked at IA. They help to pass on its knowledge about citizens' complaints and educate the everyday cop about how IA works. Ideally these dynamics combine to make IA respected, understood, and feared by the cops it polices.

Internal affairs in Oakland, as in most jurisdictions, is operated by a staff of sworn police personnel. They conduct investigations in a fashion similar to criminal investigations. They interview witnesses, prepare statements, collect booking slips, review arrest reports, collect physical evidence, and so forth. Officers charged with misconduct and witness officers are required to give truthful statements to the IA section. Under the U.S. Supreme Court's decision in *Garrity v. New Jersey* (1967), officers who refuse to so cooperate can be disciplined or even fired. Officer statements are given to investigators in the presence of a representative of the police officer's association or an attorney. Complainants are not allowed to cross-examine police officers (compare Kerstetter's advocacy, in chapter 12, of a larger role for complainants in review procedures).

Anonymous complaints of force are usually investigated. Latitude does exist in all review systems to disregard, at the discretion of the supervisor, anonymous complaints that appear to be hoaxes, patently false, or impossible to investigate (Texas Law Enforcement Management 1994: 2). This latitude can be abused, of course. It allows the supervisor, who in most IA systems is a police officer, to avoid handling a complaint without having that decision reviewed.

A completed IA investigation is submitted to the chief and routinely forwarded for comment to the immediate supervisors of the employee concerned. If the investigation indicates that the officer was not in error, the matter is filed and closed. If the investigation indicates misconduct, the supervisor recommends a disciplinary finding. This convention follows the dictates of the classic police administration text by Wilson and McLaren (1963: 211) that "the first recommendation for action should come from the lowest command level, so that . . . the . . . officer . . . will not feel that he has been given a summary sentence." Aside from protecting the officer's feelings, this practice is meant to ensure that line supervisors take responsibility for the actions of their officers.

The case is then referred up the chain of command for review by each supervisor above the officer involved. Thus, patrol officers accused of misconduct will have their cases read and commented on by the sergeant, lieutenant, captain, and deputy chief of police. The report and all attending comments are then forwarded to the chief of police for final review. The chief decides if the charges are to be sustained. He also decides on a course of action in terms of discipline. Oakland finds its officers guilty of misconduct in approximately 11 percent of its cases—very close to the national average of 13 percent discovered by Pate and Fridell (1993) in their survey. The Oakland IA's workload consists of approximately 350 cases per year, and it spends slightly less than $1,000 for each complaint investigation it undertakes.

An additional review process may occur in Oakland. When an officer is penalized with more than one day's suspension, the officer has the automatic right to a hearing before the Civil Service Commission. These formalized hearings are rare.

While no avenue of appeal is available to the complainant within Oakland's internal review system, Oakland does possess a civilian review process outside of the police department. This system, while neither as independent nor as strongly institutionalized as is Berkeley's (Skolnick and Bayley 1986: 155), will take an internal investigation on appeal and review it for a complaining citizen. The Oakland civilian board's hearing process finds police guilty of misconduct in less than 1 percent of its cases. It has little authority as it is advisory to the city manager, who invariably accepts the chief's (and IA's) recommendations for discipline.

Civilian Review

Organizations that have labeled themselves civilian review boards have been set up in almost forty jurisdictions over the course of the past thirty years. There were thirty in operation in 1990 (Walker 1991). While each of these civilianized review systems is different in form, almost all of them are advisory to the chief of police. In contrast, the Berkeley board reports directly to the city manager with its recommendations. It has its own civilian investigatory staff and intake location. The Berkeley Police Review Commission is thus the most "independent" and long-standing (nineteen years) civilian review operation in existence in the country.

California law requires all police departments to accept and investigate citizens' complaints. Thus, parallel to the PRC, Berkeley operates an internal affairs section similar to that in Oakland. (Its case load, staff—two persons—and budget are smaller than Oakland's.) The Berkeley internal review system handles all citizen complaints that are filed with the PRC or with the police system itself. The PRC handles only those complaints that citizens wish to make public. Thus, the PRC handles fewer cases than the internal system. The PRC's caseload is approximately 100 cases per year and the internal system's about 145. And as a group the PRC's cases may also be more ambiguous or notorious than the pool handled by internal affairs. This is because citizens have chosen to make them public.

The commissioners of the PRC are appointed individually by Berkeley City Council members. Thus, the political heat that might be generated by concentrating such appointments in one set of hands is avoided to some extent. A mayor or city manager might be accused of slanting such a board in one direction or another. (This has been the case in Oakland, for example.) By dividing the responsibility for appointments within the council, Berkeley has avoided problems that might have developed from a process containing no "advise and consent" procedure.

The PRC conducts interviews and investigations along similar lines to those of Oakland's internal affairs unit. It gathers the same types of evidence and constructs cases that are remarkably similar to investigations developed by police officers. With respect to officer statements in Berkeley, an administrative procedure has been agreed on between the city manager, the police chief, and the PRC. The accused officer must appear for an interview when the PRC's investigators wish to talk with him or her. The officer who refuses is subject to disciplinary action, including termination, for refusing a direct order of the chief.

Originally, accused officers did not have to give statements to the PRC as a due-process protection that the PRC's creators believed was important in order to be fair to officers. However, it became clear immediately that such a procedural safeguard would severely limit investigations. The Berkeley Police Officers' Association's attorney advised officers to take no part in the PRC's processes if they were not required to. They did not, and for its first ten years the PRC put together cases without statements by accused officers. This procedure did not help the PRC gain acceptance among Berkeley officers. The cops saw the organization as a "kangaroo court" that put together one-sided investigations and held one-sided hearings. While Berkeley has dropped this protection, a number of civilian systems continue to allow it.

After investigations are completed by the PRC's civilian employees they are reviewed by the organization's director. Then the Berkeley process becomes much more formal and judicial than the one in Oakland. All investigations result in public hearings—"boards of inquiry"—before three of the nine commissioners of the PRC.

Boards of inquiry are semijudicial hearings. The standard of proof is one of "clear, convincing evidence." Evidentiary standards are rather lax from a judicial perspective. Much evidence, usually in the form of testimony, that is accepted at hearings would be considered hearsay and excluded by a court. An overall standard of fairness to the citizen is used. This is done so that citizens will have a great deal of latitude within which to attempt to prove allegations. This fact, of course, is not lost on Berkeley police officers. They are accustomed to courtroom procedures and know when hearsay is being admitted. They tend to resent this rather open-ended approach.

Accompanied by counsel or union representative, all Berkeley officers must testify before the PRC. Citizens may also be represented but usually do not obtain counsel. Officers usually do. Both sides are allowed to cross-examine all witnesses.

After testimony and an open discussion, the commissioners vote on suggested outcomes for each allegation. Formal notice of decisions is then sent from the commission to the accused police officer and to the citizen complainant. A copy of the findings and of the investigative report are sent to the city manager.

Only on rare occasions do the outcomes of the IA and PRC differ substantially. When the outcome is different, the city manager invariably sides with the chief of police. No official statistics are kept on these infrequent disagreements between the two review bodies, but according to the city manager they occur only a few times a year.

PRC investigations take longer to complete than do those of IA, causing a delay usually lasting more than a month. As a result, hearings can be convened to hear cases in which the internal system has already disciplined the officer(s) involved. This is rather awkward, given that the city manager usually goes along with the discipline handed out by the chief. Thus, PRC hearings sometimes become moot.

The commission has a dual role; it also discusses police policy questions in public hearings. Policy hearings are separate from boards of inquiry, but their substance may relate to specific cases or sets of cases that boards have heard. The PRC's second role involves giving community input to the chief and to the department about police policies of all sorts (in this dual role, the PRC is comparable to the Chicago Police Board and others around the nation).

The city manager believes the police department to be slightly *more* prone to find cops guilty of misconduct than the Police Review Commission. An early study found that "the Berkeley Police Review Commission has assigned blame in a far lower percentage of citizen charges against the police than has the Berkeley Police Department's internal complaint mechanisms" (*California POA News* 1974: 25). This dispositional pattern has not held up over time. Today, the PRC finds officers guilty of misconduct in 17 percent of its cases while the internal system finds fault 15.7 percent of the time (both are higher than the national average for excessive force case dispositions found by Pate and Fridell 1993). But Berkeley is the only civilian review board in history to have this pattern for attributing blame. Everywhere else that parallel outcomes have been tracked for civilian and internal review, *the internal system has been more prone to find police misconduct.*[2]

Finally, we must note that the Berkeley system is expensive. The PRC spends an average of nearly $4,000 for each case it receives. This must be added to the costs of the police department's internal system. That internal process spends an average of $970 per case, or almost exactly the same as the Oakland internal operation. Together, these costs raise the taxpayer expense for police review in the city of Berkeley to almost $5,000 per citizen complaint—an annual total of about $600,000 for a city of 104,000 people (see also Perez 1994: 246).

Civilian Monitor

The civilian monitor systems tend to operate along the lines of the Scandinavian ombudsman. Internal investigations by police professionals are monitored by nonpolice personnel for their completeness and objectivity (see Bayley, in chapter 14, discussing the ombudsman approach in Australia and other nations).

The Office of Citizen Complaints (OCC) is a civilian monitor operation in Kansas City. Civilian personnel take initial statements from complainants and then forward cases to the police department's internal affairs division for investigation. This civilian-run input structure operates along lines similar to Berkeley's PRC. The investigations done by internal affairs are similar to those done by Oakland's police-operated system.

Kansas City's Internal Affairs office spends a tremendous amount of time in creating investigative files that are complete and thorough. Every witness statement taken by an IA investigator in Kansas City is typed verbatim. Thus, Kansas City's investigative files are normally more voluminous and in some sense more complete than those of other IA organizations. They are even more detailed than those of the PRC.

Kansas City's Internal Affairs sends the completed case back to the Office of Citizen Complaints. An analyst and then the director review the case. The OCC can send a case back to internal affairs or to the chief, if such action seems appropriate, for further investigation.

Internal Affairs in Kansas City does not recommend possible investigation outcomes or disciplinary action. Only evidence, statements, and investigation summaries are included in IA files. After the OCC staff approves a complaint investigation, it formulates a recommendation regarding the case. The OCC process is then complete, and the investigation is referred to the chief of police.

Office of Citizen Complaints policy allows any complainant and/or his or her attorney access to the investigative file. There are some circumstances under which the chief of police has the right to withhold specific statements or pieces of evidence when a file is being reviewed. Generally, however, complainants are allowed to view the entire investigative file. This is not true in Oakland or at other police organizations. Such access generally is allowed by civilian review systems.

After a complaint has been forwarded to the chief of police, he or she makes the final complaint finding. On the rare occasion when the chief disagrees with OCC recommendations, the chief and the director of OCC meet. Agreement is normally reached after brief discussion.

As in Oakland, the Kansas City chief of police requests that line supervisors make recommendations as to disciplinary actions when a complaint results in a sustained finding. If a sustained complaint results in an officer being suspended for fourteen days or more, state statutes allow an automatic right of appeal, again similar to procedures in Oakland. The officer takes the appeal to the Board of Police Commissioners, which is appointed by the governor. The board holds open public hearings in a semijudicial manner similar to that of civil service in Oakland. These hearings are extremely rare, partly because the board invariably sustains the findings of the chief and OCC.

The right of appeal creates access to hearing processes that are more formal in their evidentiary rules but nevertheless similar to those held by the Berkeley PRC. In other words, hearings are a part of each of the systems studied. (And because of case law and statutes in virtually all jurisdictions, such hearings are a part of all police internal review systems.)

The officials who hear appeals tend to be quite conservative in their decision making. They either rubber-stamp the decisions of the chief, as they do in Kansas City, or they lessen penalties imposed by the chief, as they often do in Oakland. Nowhere does administrative review through police commissions or civil service boards tend to be "harder" on the subject officer than is the administrative review system (Bouza 1990: 266; Guyot 1991: 183).

This observation is of critical importance because these bodies are, to some extent, civilian review boards. They are composed of civilians, not police officers or administrators, who review police conduct and the operations of in-house review mechanisms. In observing that civil service boards never operate in a fashion that is more demanding than internal review, we see the same dynamic that statistics on civilian review boards indicate. When institutions put citizens in a position to review police behavior, they invariably act liberally toward the individual police officer (McLaughlin and Bing 1989). Civilian review is neither oppressive of police officer rights nor does it favor (in a "winner" and "loser" sense) the complainant.

Thus, experience shows that those in policing who expected that civilian review would be unfair and counterproductive due to overaggressiveness were incorrect. Those outside of policing who believed that civilian review would be a panacea for police abuses, finding more officers guilty of malpractice, were also wrong.

The Office of Citizen Complaints in Kansas City sustains misconduct at a rate of 17.9 percent, similar to that of internal systems and greater than that of all civilian systems. The cost per case of OCC operations is approximately $1,000—much lower than that of civilian review for several reasons. First, no functions are duplicated under the system. Second, the OCC rarely holds open hearings, which are very costly for any system.[3] Third, while the Kansas City system operates at a separate location, which may be less cost-efficient than having just IA in the police building, the civilians at OCC are paid less than police investigators. Thus, the extra site costs of OCC are to some extent absorbed by the lower wages of non-sworn personnel.

Comparing the Three Types of Review Systems

Three separate indexes of evaluation—integrity, legitimacy, and learning—will be used to compare the three model systems outlined above.

Integrity

An analysis of police review systems must first concern itself with the integrity of a given system. Is the complaint system unintimidating to the aggrieved citizen? Are its investigations thorough and competent? Is the adjudication of the complaint fair and objective? How likely is the decision of the factfinder to result in appropriate disciplinary action?

At the intake level, there is not much to debate with respect to different types of review systems. Put simply, other-than-police locations are always preferable. Citizens bringing complaints are more at ease in a nonpolice setting, and there are no offsetting disadvantages.

Many have suggested that reported abuse defines only the "tip of the iceberg" of real police excessive force (Black 1968: 94; Goldsmith 1991a: 21; Potts 1983: 85) (see also chapter 3). It is hard to know how many citizens do not complain out of intimidation, having been frightened by the police in the first place. A recent attitudinal survey we conducted found that 44 percent of those who brought complaints against the police would prefer to file a complaint at some kind of community center, 27 percent preferred a building other than the police department, 16 percent wanted someone to come to their home, and only 11 percent would feel comfortable filing a complaint at the police building.

While law enforcement personnel tend to question the assumption that the aura of police buildings is intimidating, the right to petition the government may very well be chilled by requiring that complainants come face-to-face with their "oppressors." The uniforms, badges, weapons, and paramilitary carriage of everyone at a police station may be too much to face for more passive complainants. A system that receives complaints should not be available only to those citizens who have the audacity to confront government agents personally.

Furthermore, complainants feel more comfortable with civilians at intake by a wide margin according to our surveys: 64 percent of complainants prefer to talk to civilians about their complaints, whereas only 19 percent wish to speak to police officers directly (to 17 percent it does not matter).

Most systems appear to do a thorough job of investigating alleged police misconduct—although we readily acknowledge that many citizens may believe otherwise (see chapters 5 and 6). In the case of Oakland, the high quality of investigations reflects the personal style of a chief of police who is determined to pursue abusive behavior tenaciously. In Kansas City, the civilian review of cases may translate into investigative thoroughness (although the recently retired chief, Steven Bishop, gained a well-deserved national reputation for his determination to prevent and redress police misconduct).[4] In Berkeley, the professional competence of the civilian investigatory process may be at least partially related to the size of the organization. With a staff of five and about 100 cases per year, their relative workload is far less than that of the other systems. (Berkeley's parallel internal review office handles 50 percent more cases with a staff of only two.)

Some internal systems allow informal handling of force complaints, which can open the system to criticism. Departmental personnel are allowed to decide summarily that a complaint is "minor." They may also unilaterally decide that a complainant is "satisfied" before an alleged incident is even written up.

There is a rather infamous example of the abuse of such discretion. In 1991 an audit was done of five years of complaints processed by the Los Angeles Police Department. The review indicated that hundreds of complaints, perhaps thousands, had been written off of LAPD's books without good reason (Independent Commission on the Los Angeles Police Department 1991: chap. 9). As reported by the Christopher Commission (ibid.), the police in Los Angeles would require citizens to wait for hours, alone, if they wished to file a complaint. The police would characterize force complaints as "minor" in nature, thus avoiding the review process altogether. They would thus use the atmosphere of the police station to quash complaints at the intake level (ibid.). Because of such practices, most review systems—internal, external, and monitor—have done away with untrammeled latitude where complaints allege excessive force. This is not to say, however, that excessive formality always produces a satisfactory process (consider Kerstetter's argument, in chapter 12).

In all the types of review systems, the decisions in use-of-force reviews are "objective" in a legalistic sense. That is, a removed observer would almost always determine that the facts of the case rather than the personal biases of any of the actors or reviewers have shaped the findings. Some corroboration for this assertion comes from the consistent agreement as to outcome reached between civilian and police reviewers in locations where we have been able to make comparisons. If one believes that, generally, civilian reviewers quickly become co-opted by— or for other reasons identify excessively with—police interests, thus failing to reflect the views of civilians in the community, then the consistency of conclusions between police and civilian reviewers would be less reassuring.

Even if one believes that civilian reviewers maintain their independence of view when working constantly on police misconduct investigations, this formal objectivity is of limited significance. Police review systems generally have standards of proof similar to civil courts—misconduct must be shown with "clear and convincing evidence." Often no abuse can be proven, even when misconduct has actually occurred, because the system cannot develop evidence independent of the statements of officers and citizens, who are often caught alone, perhaps late at night, in situations not witnessed by anyone else. With only statements on both sides, the "swearing contest" ends in findings of "misconduct not-sustained." Such findings make up a large portion of the outcomes of all types of review systems.[5] Such outcomes, which neither vindicate the complainant nor absolve the officer of wrongdoing, leave everyone involved dissatisfied (compare chapter 12 concerning the key ingredients of participant satisfaction *other than* case outcomes).

Civilianized operations tend to develop even higher numbers of unsustained findings than do police-operated systems. If we put this fact together with the tendency for police systems to find sustained outcomes more often than civilian ones, we reach a disconcerting conclusion for proponents of civilian review: civilian mechanisms are *less* likely to produce statistics that indicate they are "tough" on the police than are police-operated systems.

Finally, with respect to integrity, sustained outcomes typically require discipline (rather than nonpunitive corrective steps) to be handed out to errant officers. At the Oakland police department there is a difference between the disciplinary actions recommended by the accused officer's commanders and the chief. The IA commander estimates that such a disparity exists 50 percent of the time. The immediate supervisor tends to identify with and protect the accused employee. He or she is almost always a sergeant of patrol and at times is subject to the types of psychological pressures that lead to misconduct.

Supervisors above sergeants are more removed from the accused officer but also tend to go along with the recommendations of their subordinates. These command officers feel that the line supervisor knows what is best for the officer involved.

Because of these dynamics, the chief must often increase the gravity of punishment recommended. Removed from the street experience and possessing an organization-wide perspective, the chief is responsible to local political elites for the performance of the department and for the image of its disciplinary mechanism. In Oakland, since the 1960s chiefs have never failed to "harden up" disciplinary recommendations. As a result, Oakland's chief is often seen from below as abusive of officers.

An obvious question is whether this pattern in Oakland typifies departments nationwide. It may not. In other jurisdictions, chiefs tend to follow the same path of supporting the lower level chain of command's recommendations that middle managers do. In San Francisco, for example, the chiefs have tended to accept the recommendation that flows up from the line supervisor. In fact, the chief has tended to lessen discipline. Between 1984 and 1990, of the 129 complaints that were sent to the chief as "sustained" with requests for disciplinary actions, only 47 resulted in any discipline whatsoever being handed out (*San Francisco Chronicle*, May 29, 1990). Disciplinary decisions consequently appear lax to those outside of the police organization.

Central to this entire discussion is the question of how to balance the expertise of the professional against the objectivity—and potentially greater external credibility—of the external observer. "Police administrators, believing that they understand the subtleties of their profession better than those who are not a regular part of it, prefer to direct their behavior in a way which their special understanding warrants, a view which is shared, let us remind ourselves, by lawyers, judges, senators, teachers, and doctors, to name a few of the more obvious ones" (Hanewicz 1985: 46). Professionals generally hold that they possess a monopoly over theory, skill, education, and research in their particular fields, an expertise that should not be questioned by the layperson (ABA 1970; Delattre 1989: 93; McDowell 1991: 143).[6] While this dynamic is not unique to police work, what the police do is. Police work is unsettling to people in a liberal society. Police monopoly over the use of coercive force threatens citizens in very tangible ways. The fact that officers in internal review systems so seldom find their own peers guilty of misconduct seems to confirm the need for external scrutiny.

Yet other professions are equally guilty of self-serving, defensive tactics where alleged misbehavior is concerned. Lawyers are particularly important in this regard as they are at the forefront of efforts to change police review systems. It is not irrelevant to the police that the legal profession's own internal disciplinary mechanism seldom finds fault with attorneys accused of misconduct. Early research revealed that in only slightly more than 1 percent of the cases which it investigates did the bar's own grievance handling committee find fault with its peers (ABA 1970: Section II; Carlin 1966: 150).

There is no answer to the professional expertise versus external objectivity dilemma. One argument in favor of the civilian monitor system is that it accepts and defers to police investigative expertise while bringing to bear external perspectives in an advisory capacity, thus trying to capture the strengths of both approaches.

Legitimacy

It is critical to analyze how legitimate police review mechanisms are considered to be by groups vitally interested in their docket of cases. Apart from assessing the actual integrity of a system, it is important to know what people think about that system. Is the process seen as fair by the members of the police department? Is it seen as fair by the public (including the media, political officials, and the bar) so that they will stand up and defend it when it is under attack? Is it seen as fair by neighborhood leaders, especially of those communities in which allegations of police brutality more often arise? Does the system get the benefit of the doubt from the public? Does it allay the need for violent public protest?

Internally operated mechanisms fare well with respect to integrity. Their externally perceived legitimacy, however, is perhaps their major shortcoming. The completely in-house, police-operated system develops the least amount of acceptance in the community. In areas where police-community relations are tense, often with race as an issue, community acceptance is especially low.

As a way of lending specificity to perceptions of legitimacy, our surveys asked cops and complainants to reflect on the system's *integrity*. The police everywhere tended to support the local review system, no matter what form it took. The familiar seems to be preferable to the unfamiliar from the perspective of those being regulated.[7] Even cops subject to civilian review seem to have normalized it as simply a part of the rules of the game. As approximately 80 percent of complaint investigations handled by police review systems do not find the police guilty of misbehavior, it is understandable that police officer evaluations tend to find satisfaction with existing systems.

Citizen complainants, on the other hand, find almost all systems lacking in integrity (thus, the systems also lack legitimacy for citizen complainants). Most hold negative perceptions of the thoroughness, fairness, and objectivity of the various systems to which they complain. Even among those whose cases were treated by civilians at Berkeley, where satisfaction levels were somewhat higher, the system was still found lacking. Since complainants "lose" 80 percent of the time, this is equally understandable. If complainants "won" more often, they might feel more positive toward police review mechanisms of whatever form. In fact, 86 percent of those who lose their cases find review systems (of all types) to be unfair.

While most review systems seem objective and thorough, two problems limit the acceptance of all systems by complainants. First, legalistic proof requirements are imposed on review systems through codified law, administrative case law, and convention. These make some outcomes substantively unfair from the complainant's perspective and make many others seem arbitrary. Second, complainants do not seem to be able to differentiate between a satisfactory outcome and integrity. As review systems employ adversarial processes, the overwhelming majority of complainants will be disappointed with their treatment by *any* review system.

Most internal review mechanisms keep all information secret for several reasons. First, secrecy protects the police organization from the financial risk of civil suits (Schmidt 1985: 228). Police administrators and municipal governments may protect complaint investigation information so that it is not used against them in court. Second, secrecy can help officers develop positive behavior patterns (see section below on learning).

Third, because discipline and quality control are the province of management, any organization or professional group's leadership will seek to defend itself from external attack by creating secretive mechanisms of review. As Carlin (1968: 62, 65) notes in his study of the disciplinary systems of bar associations, "the organized bar through the operation of its formal disciplinary measures seems to be less concerned with scrutinizing the moral integrity of the profession than with forestalling public criticism and control." While this approach may still result in rigorous review, its legitimacy outside the organized bar will be limited. Defensiveness and secrecy are perceived as proof of corruption by those who expect the worst.

Some observers of civilian monitor systems believe that such experiments have been shams, fooling the public into trusting internal mechanisms (Meyers 1991; Terrill 1990: 82). But these critics miss an important point. Despite the intuitive assertions of some to the contrary, in the vast majority of incidents brought to the attention of any police review systems, police officers probably have acted legally and properly. This means that any case-by-case approach to complaints that is fair and honest will most often find the police exonerated of wrongdoing. But our studies tell us that the integrity of an internal system will not be understood or believed by outsiders *no matter how fair it is* (compare Kerstetter's argument in chapter 12).

Efforts to generate acceptance by "marketing" the system's integrity and by including civilians, even if they do not make a substantive difference in case outcomes, can be important for all interest groups inside police agencies, in the community at large, and in government. We should not, therefore, be too hasty in labeling efforts to bolster the image of police review as Machiavellian. To be concerned with the symbolic meaning of systems is not to be patronizing of the public. It is a rational exercise of importance to the police, to local political elites, and to the community.

Some police review organizations publish information on their findings and procedures. This policy costs the organization little and can be an important tool in developing external support for any kind of process. Only one-third of America's police internal review systems publish information about complaint procedures or investigative data (West, no date: 8; practices in other nations vary, as discussed in chapter 13). All civilian systems in the United States do so. Openness to the public gives civilian systems an advantage.

Community faith in internal systems, then, seems to be a problem for police-operated systems. The openness that civilian involvement in review can generate may develop faith in police accountability mechanisms. If only as symbols, civilians may be of considerable usefulness to police review systems and to police-community relations in general.

But this argument must be tempered with two realities. First, civilianization may *not* develop increased legitimacy. In Chicago, New York, and San Francisco, for example, civilianization has been extremely limited in its ability to generate external acceptance of review mechanisms because, as noted, these systems find few police officers guilty of misconduct (Brown 1991; Meyers 1991; New York Civil Liberties Union 1991; *San Francisco Chronicle*, May 29, 1990).

Second, civilianization is not *necessary* to develop legitimacy. Oakland presents a prime example. There, several high-profile examples of the rigorousness of internal review have been brought to the attention of the public in recent years. In a rather infamous incident, several officers were fired for harassing members of the Hell's Angels motorcycle gang. The chief's quick and decisive action drew praise from some local politicians and from the local press. The chief also drew criticism from "law and order" advocates, who felt he was unreasonably tough on the officers involved.

This and other events have won a legitimacy for internal review in Oakland that has not developed elsewhere. It may be one reason why Oakland has not experienced the civil disorders which have occurred in other cities as a reaction to incidents of police brutality.

Learning

Analysis must also focus on the propensity of review systems to affect police behavior. Does the system deter police from acting brutally? Does it teach errant officers to change their ways? Does it pinpoint the truly abusive cops and rid the department of them? Is it sufficiently inexpensive to operate without significant harm to other training mechanisms within the department?

The Berkeley Police Review Commission's role in policy formulation can help the police department learn from citizens' complaints. This civilian review mechanism is the only system studied that undertakes a systematic analysis of complaints and policy. Other systems focus almost exclusively on individual complaint adjudication. Thus, the organizational learning of almost all U.S. police review systems is very limited because "rarely do individual incidents produce a serious analysis of aggregate performance" (Moore and Stephens 1991a: 36). The systematic analysis of trends in complaints is one step forward in the direction of teaching the organization and individual officers.

On balance, internal review systems are the most effective mechanisms for influencing the behavior of police officers on the street.[8] The existence of police departmental review mechanisms is often on the minds of police officers on the street when they make discretionary judgments. One reason is that internal systems influence careers. By developing a reputation as a troublemaker—in the eyes of the chief, one's peers, or with internal affairs—the beat cop can limit his or her ability to operate effectively within the organization. The errant cop can find this sort of reputation a handicap in terms of promotion, a coveted transfer, or specific beat, shift, or partner assignments. More important, the officer prone to misbehave can find that the approval of his or her peers is withheld. Police subcultural solidarity being what it is, such support is essential to the individual officer. As one Oakland cop confided, "You gotta learn who the real cowboys are. Then you stay away from them. Just bein' around the real clowns will get you in the

shit with 'em." The review of peer professionals in internal affairs is taken seriously by street cops. The expertise of professional investigators generally produces
thorough investigations and reports. When motivated by a chief executive genuinely concerned with developing accountability, internal systems offer the most
effective potential for positive behavioral influence.

External systems are less effective in influencing police behavior in several
ways. First, due-process rights granted to officers by many external mechanisms
impose limitations. The price paid for procedural fairness is often a lessening of
substantive thoroughness. Second, the police investigator is motivated to clean
out the bad cops in part because of a personal, professional concern for the department's image. This concern does not often drive the civilian investigator to
the same lengths. The consequent lack of rigor in the civilian investigator has been
noted, for example, in the civilianized Office of Professional Standards in Chicago
(Brown 1991: 37). Third, when police review becomes formalized, involving judicial hearings, attorneys, and protracted procedures, police officers naturally tend
to become defensive. And when they have "lost a case" and have been disciplined,
they tend to become embittered and diffident. Sanctioning errant officers may be
considered an important part of review in that it punishes improper behavior and
presumably deters misbehavior in other officers. But the long-term effect of formality and punitive discipline on future behavior of an errant individual is almost
universally negative.

Civilian review mechanisms operate completely outside the cop's subcultural
peer group. They tend to be bureaucratic and formal, less open than internal systems to the informal handling of complaints. Use-of-force complaints are not
always "major." On some occasions, force complaints can be handled informally—
"handcuffs too tight," for example.[9] A system that has as its focus the modification of errant behavior patterns is best served by handling such complaints with
counseling and training or retraining. The informal comment from a peer or sergeant or a class in advanced handcuffing techniques may very well move an officer
to think twice the next time about applying excessive force in such a case.

But we have asserted that informal complaint handling can be problematic, as
in the Los Angeles example documented by the Christopher Commission. How
can these two dynamics be reconciled? The answer lies with the civilian monitor
system. In such a system, informal mechanisms use peer expertise and subcultural
strengths yet are monitored by the civilian participants to ensure that abuses do
not occur (see Kerstetter 1985). This assures optimum learning in the long run.

For the same reasons that they are most effective at deterring abuse, internal systems are the most likely to be counterproductive in various ways. Some
officers surveyed believe that on the street they feel handcuffed and prohibited
from doing their jobs effectively by overzealous internal review. But paradoxically
for opponents of civilian review, officers feel neither intimidated nor abused by
civilian review. Most (62 percent) feel it has little or no effect whatsoever on their

behavior. Several other studies confirm that civilian review does not tend to develop counterproductive tendencies inhibiting officers from the performance of
their charge (Sparrow et al. 1990: 159; Terrill 1982: 400).

Finally, a discussion of learning must consider the costs of each system. For
all of their theoretical utility, civilian review systems have proven to be expensive.
The Berkeley Police Review Commission spends a great deal of time and money
duplicating procedures carried out by the police department's internal mechanism.

As long as the police are required to investigate complaints, chiefs want to
have direct control over their officers, and as long as municipalities feel threatened
by the potential of civil litigation, internal review systems will exist. Duplication
of tasks is theoretically tantalizing because it responds to so many concerns. But
it is so costly as to be prohibitive in most jurisdictions.[10]

This is important to learning because of how police department budgets are
prepared. Police review is a part of any law enforcement budget that legally and
politically must be considered "essential." When police review becomes extremely
expensive, expenditures considered nonessential are cut back or eliminated. The
costs of training in particular are vulnerable. When more money is spent on review
expenditures, less is spent on interpersonal relations training, sensitivity training,
sergeants' training, field training officer programs, academy classes in ethnic relations, and so on. All of these programs are considered less critical. The sort of
double billing that Berkeley does by operating parallel systems can thus limit expenditures for proactive training programs that could alter officer behavior and
obviate some expenditures for review of misconduct allegations (consider, for example, the valuable investment made by the Metro-Dade Police Department in
officer violence-reduction training, discussed in chapter 8). The duplication of expenses in Kansas City's civilian monitor system, on the other hand, is limited.
Complaint intake expenditures for the city are borne by the Office of Citizen
Complaints, investigative budgets are found in internal affairs, and outcome expenses are borne back in the OCC. The city of Kansas City is billed only once for
each part of its system. Its cost per investigation is almost exactly that of internal
review in Oakland or Berkeley.

A Question of Trade-Offs

The multiple systems of Berkeley offer an open hearing process, a civilian perspective, and the right to confront and cross-examine the officer and any possible
witnesses. An internal review system is also available for those who wish the police
department to handle its own processes. In answer to what are prohibitive costs,
however, the usefulness of the Kansas City civilian monitor system is tantalizing.
The Office of Citizen Complaints allows the police to oversee themselves to a
certain extent, playing on the advantages of internal investigative systems and informal peer review. The system amalgamates the strengths of internal and external

review in a commonsense manner; it neither sanctifies nor vilifies police-operated internal review mechanisms.

What is more, in terms of police officer acceptance, the civilian monitor system speaks to our concern that the population policed must accept (at least tacitly) any review mechanism in order for it to be effective. On one hand, police officers surveyed indicate that they believe in the competence of internal affairs investigators. Seventy-three percent from cities with civilian review felt that civilians were less competent than police officers to investigate complaints. Not one officer of 150 believed civilians to be superior to sworn investigators (8 percent thought that both sorts were competent and 18 percent had no opinion). These numbers support the idea that the police feel that only they can effectively police their operations.

On the other hand, when asked to reflect on the ideal system, an unexpected 35 percent opted for a "combination" of police and civilian investigators. Even more surprising were officers' responses when we asked who they thought should sit on a hearing board to adjudicate important cases. Sixty-two percent of the officers thought a formal hearing board should be made up of a combination of cops and civilians.

This finding seems to fly in the face of conventional wisdom about police acceptance of civilian review. The officers studied are working in jurisdictions where they experience civilian review every day. Their limited acceptance of the idea of combined investigations and overwhelming agreement with the concept of civilianized hearing processes is testimony to the fact that civilian review neither abuses police officers nor interferes with police organizational interests.

Gellhorn (1966: 193) sums up many of the strengths of a civilian monitor (ombudsman) approach. He writes that the discharge of disciplinary responsibility in "all instances must be subject to an outsider's examination . . . with the object of publicly disclosing slipshod administration or adoption of wrong attitudes. That course should be acceptable to the police as well as to the public. . . . It does not remove from police hands the power to direct, judge, and discipline the staff members whose actions have been challenged, but, as in the case of other departments, leaves to the professionals the job of appraising fellow professionals."

The civilian monitor approach thus leaves intact the learning strengths and investigatory expertise of the internal system. It also can generate the external legitimacy and removed perspective of the civilian review board. Thus the civilian monitor system's strengths, together with its fiscal responsibility, make it come closest to answering all of the concerns of police review interest groups.

Future Study

After sixty years of speculation, we now know something about civilianized police review systems in operation. They are neither abusive of police officers nor abusive of police organizations. The most important drawback to civilian review in practice is that it is too easy on the police due to its distance from the individual police experience (see also chapters 1 and 12). In addition, the due-process protections afforded accused police officers by civilian review mechanisms are quite expansive. They may contribute to the reason why systems find legal guilt less often than events suggest is appropriate.

The civilian monitor system presents a balance between internal and civilian review that is intriguing. But to take full advantage of its potential, several areas of investigation must be pursued:

1. It is important to study how civilian investigators can be trained to accomplish their dual tasks of bringing an external perspective to police review and developing an understanding of police occupational standards. If civilians identify too much with the police, as has been observed in Chicago, civilianization loses its impact. Yet if they fail to understand standard police practices, they will be unable to evaluate police conduct fairly.

2. The several jurisdictions where civilian and police investigators work side by side need study. The organizational dynamics of using such a mixed group must be explored to see if the idea is manageable—and at what cost. Among the questions meriting study is whether greater cooperation is indeed obtained from both citizens and officers interviewed by a mixed group.

3. Hearings systems should be studied in Toronto and wherever mixed groups of citizens and police officers are charged with reviewing complaints (Lewis 1991). Do the long-term operations of such systems develop better police-community relations through a cross-pollination of perspectives?

If we are to take changing police behavior seriously, we must emphasize proactive training, peer review, counseling instead of negative discipline, and informal, nonthreatening review mechanisms; we also need to determine the standards by which officers should be judged (as Klockars argues in chapter 1). Observations and notes that should be considered in future research include:

4. Most complainants reject the legitimacy of *any* sort of police review system, no matter how "fair" it may appear to be, because they usually lose their cases. It is important, therefore, to experiment with mediation and conciliation processes that seek to satisfy complainants in more direct and personal ways than do bureaucratic adjudicatory systems (see chapter 12).

5. Police officers operating within an adversarial system, pushed to prove their "innocence" and to defend themselves at all costs, will rarely see the citizen's complaint and its investigation as grounds for changing their behavior. Thus, officers do not tend to learn from a formal review. For this reason, we need to know a great deal more about police review systems that attempt to teach officers from their mistakes in positive ways. We need to explore systems that seek to promote learning through counseling and training instead of through punitive sanctions (see chapters 1, 4, 8, and 10).

6. Police organizations rarely use their review systems to learn about systematic problems that lead to abuse. It is critical that we learn more about systems that develop policy—and recommend other changes—based on analysis of complaint patterns. Civilian boards such as Berkeley's PRC can help to illustrate the strengths of this approach.

7. Police organizations that seek to influence police officer behavior in a proactive manner should be encouraged. Training in interpersonal relations and other violence-reduction tactics is important, and early warning systems that attempt to predict misbehavior are critical. Peer review is another interesting alternative that should be encouraged and studied.

These ideas should be pursued in the interests of furthering police professionalism as well as protecting citizens from police excessive use of force. Every effort should be made to find ways to teach appropriate behavior to young cops, to reduce overly aggressive tendencies, and to treat police misconduct in a positive atmosphere where officers learn from their mistakes.

Simultaneously, the civilianization of review systems should be continued in order to help those citizens who believe they have been victimized by excessive force to feel that they are treated fairly and objectively. Community perceptions of legitimacy must be fostered in an era where increased violence and criminal behavior will require more, not less, cooperation between police and citizens.

NOTES

The research of which this chapter is a part has been partially funded by the Comprehensive Employment and Training Act (CETA) and by Skyline College, San Bruno, California. Additional discussion of this research is contained in Perez (1994).

1. Many systems that call themselves civilian review boards are, in fact, closer to civilian monitor systems in their daily operations. Examples are operational in Albuquerque, Atlanta, Baltimore, Dallas, Fresno, Houston, Indianapolis, Miami, New York, Pittsburgh, Portland, San Diego, and Toledo.

2. Early civilian review boards were reluctant to find the police guilty of misconduct. In Philadelphia, the internal police-operated board recommended dismissal in 14 percent of its cases during the period that the civilian body did so in only 1 percent (Hudson 1972: 425). Of the 530 cases heard by the Philadelphia civilian review board 1958-1965, only 38 cases resulted in recommendations of disciplinary actions against police officers (President's Commission on Law Enforcement and Administration of Justice 1967b: 201). In New York City, of the 135 cases disposed of by its board during the 1960s, only five resulted in recommendations of disciplinary actions or reprimands (New York Times, March 4, 1967).

The processes developed during the 1980s have shown similar results. The Office of Citizen Complaints in San Francisco sustains only one percent of its investigations against the police (San Francisco Chronicle, May 9, 1990). The Honolulu civilian board sustains 6 percent of its cases (Honolulu Police Commission 1988). The Cleveland civilian board sustains 10 percent of its cases (Cleveland Police Review Board 1991). The Cincinnati board sustains a much higher rate of 23.7 percent of its cases (Cincinnati OMI Annual Report 1990), but this is still lower than the 25 percent of cases sustained by police-operated organizations nationally (Dugan and Breda 1991: 167; compare Pate and Fridell [1993], who report a national average on excessive force cases of 13 percent). A continuing source of information on the work of civilian review boards is the International Association for Civilian Oversight of Law Enforcement, whose corresponding official is based in Evanston, Illinois.

3. Without the rare formalized hearings before the Board of Police Commissioners, the system costs about $500 per complaint. Adding the very expensive hearing, the cost rises to nearly $1,000 per case. This helps explain why Berkeley's system is so expensive. (The Berkeley PRC holds hearings for all cases investigated.)

4. Chief Bishop's determination was manifested, among other ways, by the firing of numerous officers for abuse of force (see Geller and Scott 1992: 278).

5. The numbers are illustrative. In 1989, the Los Angeles Police Department system found 43 percent of its complaints to be "not sustained" (LAPD 1989). The much smaller Richmond, California, department found cases to be not sustained at the rate of 56 percent (Richmond Police Department 1989). In Chicago, the civilian-staffed police department Office of Professional Standards found 81.5 percent of its cases to be not sustained (memorandum to Superintendent of Police from OPS, Jan. 4, 1991; for discussion of OPS, see chapter 12). In New York City, the civilian monitor system reached not sustained findings in 85 percent of its cases (New York City Police Department 1989; for other data on this question, see Pate and Fridell 1993; and for international sustension rates, see chapter 14).

6. We put aside here perennial debates about whether the field of policing qualifies by traditional standards as a profession.

7. Geller (1993), studying police attitudes toward documenting stationhouse interrogations on videotape, discovered that police familiar with this form of monitoring of their conduct found it acceptable and often useful in capturing incriminating evidence in a way that proved convincing in court. Yet officers in departments that had not adopted video documentation techniques found the notion of switching from written or audio documentation to video abhorrent, speculating that it would constitute an oppressive and counterproductive form of monitoring their behavior behind closed interrogation-room doors.

8. Kelling and Kliesmet would argue, presumably, that peer pressure is a still better mechanism for altering rank-and-file conduct; see chapter 10, as well as chapters 1, 4, and 8.

9. Even here the intent of the officer and the degree of harm inflicted has to be weighed, for tight handcuffs can cause serious permanent injuries to wrists and hands.

10. The Berkeley PRC's $600,000 price tag is the cost of civilian review in a city of only 104,000. In Minneapolis, the new civilian board spent over $350,000 in 1991 for a system that held four formal hearings and handled eleven complaints. The Honolulu civilian board, whose budget seems more fiscally conservative, spent over $250,000 on 159 complaints in 1990. In Canada, the Royal Canadian Mounted Police (RCMP) Public Complaints Commission spends over $3 million (U.S.) to monitor 2,400 complaints per year. This commission has formal hearings so infrequently (nine hearings in the past three years) that its spending is virtually all aimed at monitoring police investigations (RCMP 1991). And these monies are *in addition to those spent to support in-house, police-operated systems.*

CHAPTER TWELVE

Toward Justice for All: Procedural Justice and the Review of Citizen Complaints

WAYNE A. KERSTETTER

Many proposals to reform the review of allegations of police misconduct are useful but not sufficient. For example, a *New York Times* editorial assessing the controversy regarding the creation of a wholly civilian panel to review police brutality complaints stated: "The important question is not who does the job but how well, and the key is whether the city upgrades the quality of investigations" (June 29, 1992). The editorial goes on to identify what it perceives to be the central problem: "Complaints often come down to the civilian's word against the police officer's—or a group of officers who refuse to testify against one another. The present review board frequently fails to act because investigators can't decide whom to believe. More aggressive, skilled inquiries could make a difference."

It is hard to argue with the notion that better investigations could make a difference, but a recent study of police excessive force investigations conducted by the Chicago Police Department's Office of Professional Standards suggests that there are limits to the potential for improvement.[1] The Chicago study concluded that the presence of an independent witness (one not connected with the complainant or the police) was the most significant factor in determining the outcome of these investigations (Kerstetter and Van Winkle 1989: 16). The problem is that an independent witness was present in just 16.8 percent of the Chicago cases. Independent probative evidence (either physical or testimonial) that corroborated the complaint was available in only 7.1 percent of the cases. These findings suggest that while improving the quality of investigations is a worthy objective, no matter how good the investigation, substantial numbers of individuals are not going to have their complaints sustained because the evidence required is not available.

The Procedural Justice Effect

Because many citizens will be disappointed with the outcome of their complaint about police use of excessive force, a body of research developed over almost two decades is relevant to efforts to improve the complaint review process. This research shows that if the process by which a decision in a dispute was reached is perceived as fair, even an unsuccessful party will have a more favorable attitude about the outcome. Further, the negative impact that disappointment has on attitudes about the process, the authorities involved, and the social order will be diminished. Research also indicates that this impact on attitudes will increase the likelihood that the individual will obey the law in the future. Researchers have labeled this impact of process on attitudes the *procedural justice effect*.[2]

Twenty-four studies have been conducted to replicate these findings. All have confirmed the effect in part, and only one contradicted it, and that only in part (Lind and Tyler 1988: 67). Other studies suggest that the procedural justice effect operates in other cultures as well (Lind and Tyler 1988: 145). These findings contradict earlier assumptions that people assess their experiences entirely on the basis of what they get out of them. E. Allan Lind and Tom R. Tyler, two of the leaders in this research effort, conclude, "The picture that seems to be emerging is of people much more concerned with the process of their interaction with the law and much less concerned with the outcome than one might have supposed" (Lind and Tyler 1988: 92).[3] This does not mean that people are indifferent to the results of the dispute, but that they will feel better about even a negative result if they perceive the procedures used in reaching a decision as fair. This is true even when the result was very important to the party and when the decision would make a serious difference (Lind and Tyler 1988: 73).

Researchers have attempted to identify the reasons behind the procedural justice effect. Some have suggested that fair procedures are seen as increasing a party's chance of a desired outcome; this is called the instrumental effect of procedures. Other researchers argue that the opportunity to express one's point of view on the issue in dispute is the important factor; this is labeled the value-expressive effect. Lind and Tyler conclude that both effects play a role in producing the procedural justice effect (1988: 100).

There are some limitations to the procedural justice effect. For example, it is apparently less powerful for those who receive positive outcomes, but it is also less important because these people are less likely to be disappointed by the result of the process. Two other limitations are of greater relevance to the review of allegations of police misconduct. A 1986 study by Tyler and McGraw provided some evidence that the disadvantaged place less emphasis on procedural fairness (1986: 42, 115–28). However, Lind and Tyler conclude, "Although the poor care less about procedural justice than do the rich, they still do care about procedural justice more than they care about distributive justice" (1988: 171).

Another relevant limitation may lie in the capacity of social or contextual circumstances to blunt the procedural justice effect. If a person hears others comment on the unfairness of the outcome and this reinforces his or her own feelings, the impact of perceived procedural fairness is diminished (Folger et al. 1979). Similarly, if the context gives rise to doubts about the integrity of the process, the procedural justice effect is diluted (Lind and Lissak 1985). The latter finding emphasizes the importance of the perceived integrity of the decision maker (see also chapter 11).

Further, parties who do not have a direct involvement or participation in the dispute do not experience the procedural justice effect as strongly as those that do. While the impact on these parties is diminished, it does not disappear (Lind and Tyler 1988: 69; Kerstetter and Rasinski 1994). Lind and Tyler have called for additional research on the effect of different roles on procedural justice judgments (Lind and Tyler 1988: 123).

Despite these limitations, the possibility of reducing the discontent of the parties to the dispute justifies giving serious consideration to this psychological phenomenon.

What Makes Procedures Seem Fair?

If procedures matter, the obvious question is *which* procedures are perceived as fair? Procedural justice researchers see people as trying to maximize their personal gain in their interactions with others (Thibaut and Kelley 1959; Tyler 1990: 115). To this end people seek control over decisions that are important to them and resist relinquishing control of these decisions to others. They prefer to negotiate with others rather than have settlements imposed on them. When the conflict between their interests and those of others is such that negotiation is not possible, they will reluctantly yield control over the decision to a third party (Lind and Tyler 1988: 14).

In these situations people prefer to grant only the minimum necessary power to the third party. An important way of retaining as much control as possible is to grant a third party control over the decision but to retain control over the presentation of information on which the decision is based. The research we are reviewing thus distinguishes between *decision control* and *process control.*

Thibaut and Walker, the scholars who first conceptualized the procedural justice effect, contend that procedures that vest process control in those affected by the outcome of the procedure are viewed as more fair than procedures that vest process control in the decision maker (Thibaut and Walker 1978). Subsequent research confirms this view with persons from many different walks of life and in other cultures (Lind and Tyler 1988: 141–45).[4]

Research suggests that a belief by the parties that they have an opportunity to be involved in the decision-making process is the key element in creating a sense of fairness. Specifically, they desire an opportunity to present information and views they believe are relevant to the decision maker and a sense that they have been listened to and that the material they presented was considered (Conley 1988; Tyler 1987c; Tyler 1990: 163).

The opportunity for each side to express its point of view is also seen as having an important educational function for the other side. Thus both sides to the dispute become more informed about what is at stake in the controversy (Tyler 1990: 163).

Adversarial versus Inquisitorial Models of Procedure

A central focus of research has been the relative efficacy of adversarial and inquisitorial procedures in creating a sense of procedural fairness. In the adversarial model, while the decision is controlled by a third party, the collection and presentation of evidence are controlled by the parties to the dispute. The common-law trial familiar to most Americans embodies the principles of the adversarial procedure. In the inquisitorial model both process and decisions are controlled by the third party. Inquisitorial procedures are characteristic of European judicial systems. The relative efficacy of the two models has been compared in a number of respects, including preference of parties to the dispute, opportunity to express one's point of view, contribution to bias reduction, cost, and the perceived versus actual fairness of the resulting procedure.

Experiments in various locales have indicated a clear preference by the parties to the dispute for adversarial procedures (Lind and Tyler 1988: 33–35).[5] This preference was sustained even when the national legal system of respondents was based on the inquisitorial model (Lind and Tyler 1988: 33). The opportunity to control the collection of relevant information and the presentation of that information in the decision-making process (the notion of giving voice to one's perspective) plays an important role in the preference for the adversarial model.

The adversarial and inquisitorial models were evaluated on the basis of their contribution to reduction of bias in the decision-making process. Three types of bias were considered: prior expectancy bias, order effect bias, and party labeling bias. Prior expectancy bias occurs when a decision is made based on expectations derived from past experience with similar but unrelated situations. In the context of allegations of police excessive force, a prior expectancy bias might involve the expectation that persons with prior arrest records are more prone to make false allegations. Experiments conducted with American and French undergraduate students demonstrated that adversarial procedures resulted in a greater objective reduction of prior expectancy bias than did inquisitorial procedures (Thibaut et al. 1972; Thibaut and Walker 1975; Lind et al. 1976; Lind and Tyler 1988: 21).

Order effect bias results from the sequence in which evidence is presented.

Research demonstrates that the procedures normally associated with adversarial hearings came closest to eliminating the impact of order effect bias (Walker et al. 1972; Thibaut and Walker 1975; Lind and Tyler 1988: 22).

Party labeling bias refers to the reduced objectivity of a witness as the result of being identified with one party or the other. A series of experiments that explored the extent and nature of this bias suggest that witnesses, while not omitting unfavorable testimony, worded their testimony in a way that favored the side that called them to testify. The bias involved was substantial. In one experiment, students viewed a slide presentation concerning a barroom fight and then were asked to assume various roles—witnesses for the plaintiff, for the defense, or called by the court. Judges—also played by students—who heard the testimony of witnesses called by the plaintiff attributed 38 percent of the responsibility for the incident under consideration to the plaintiff. Judges who heard the testimony of witnesses called by the court or the defendant (Vidmar and Laird 1983) attributed, respectively, 47 percent and 52 percent of the responsibility to the plaintiff.

In the experiments mentioned above, the witnesses were not cross-examined by opposing counsel, which is the primary defense against party labeling bias and other inaccuracies in an adversarial system. In an earlier study Lind found that the biases inherent in the presentation of both sides canceled each other out in the course of the normal adversarial process (Lind et al. 1983).

The 1983 study by Lind and colleagues is relevant to a concern expressed in the literature that a procedural justice approach in general, and an adversarial process in particular, might increase perceptions of fairness but in fact result in reduced procedural and distributive justice.[6] This could happen either because greater opportunity to express one's views may result in the introduction of more material irrelevant to the decision or because the adversarial process increases the amount of partisan and/or inaccurate information that is presented to the decision maker. Lind's research suggests that the balances built into the adversarial process provide an effective safeguard against these sources of error (Lind and Tyler 1988: 113–14).

One of the strongest arguments against use of adversarial procedures is their cost. The view is widely held that they are more expensive than nonadversarial procedures. Added expense is undesirable in itself and by virtue of the barrier it creates for people of limited means to be adequately represented. When the stakes are too low for contingent fee arrangements to entice private counsel to share the risk, an aggrieved party may go unrepresented.

The perceived expense of an adversarial system is challenged, however, by a line of analysis that uses the notion of "imposition costs." These are seen as the cost of incorrect decisions derived from inaccurate information. The risk of inaccurate information is believed to be greater when the information gathering and presentation are conducted by a third party (Lind and Tyler 1988: 120). While this is an interesting argument, no research is available to support it.

Research demonstrates that enhanced procedural fairness judgments can be attained as the result of brief, informal hearings with relaxed rules of evidence. Such hearings, which allow greater scope for expression of the views by parties, would meet procedural fairness needs and at the same time not unduly increase cost (Lind and Tyler 1988: 121).[7]

Procedural justice studies have identified two additional elements that affect fairness judgments. These are having one's views heard and considered and the neutrality and bias of the decision maker.

Consideration of Views and Neutrality of the Decision Maker

If a party were permitted to express its views but it appeared that those views were not given appropriate consideration, the party's judgment about the fairness of the procedure would likely be hurt and the potential benefits lost. The malaise created by the brief jury deliberations in the O. J. Simpson case illustrates this point. A mechanical decision such as one in which the decision maker obviously simply split the difference between the parties, apparently without attention to the merits of the matter, would also diminish the procedural justice effect. On the other hand, a written or oral explanation of the decision which indicated that both sides of the issue had been considered would enhance the sense of procedural fairness (Lind and Tyler 1988: 106).

Although there is evidence that process control enhances procedural fairness judgments even when the decision maker appears to be biased, the party's belief in the unbiased nature of the decision maker is more likely to lead to a positive interpretation of the outcome (Tyler 1990: 134, 149). Further research regarding the characteristics of decision makers that lead to a belief in their neutrality would prove helpful in this sensitive matter.

In summing up the research, Lind and Tyler state: "Across-the-board endorsement of either the adversary or the inquisitorial procedure run[s] counter to some research results. . . . We believe that as our knowledge of the psychology of procedural justice increases, it will be possible to design novel procedures that perform optimally in the situations to which they are applied. . . . A hybrid procedure can be designed that moderates disputant control over information while allowing sufficient disputant process control to provide opportunity for expression that is critical to perceived fairness" (1988: 117).

The Value and Dignity of the Individual and the Legitimacy of the System

Tom Tyler, in his book *Why People Obey The Law*, suggests that in addition to instrumental and expressive functions, procedure is relevant to another important dimension of human experience: "When people approach authorities, their social standing and feelings of security within the group are on the line. They may have an experience that reaffirms their belief that they are valued, protected members of society who will receive benevolence and consideration from the authorities when they need it; they may also have an experience that makes them feel less valued and protected than they would like to believe" (1990: 175).

If what is at stake for individuals in dispute resolution is a sense of being valued by the social order, what is at stake for the social order is its acceptance as appropriate and trustworthy—in short, its legitimacy in the eyes of its members. Procedural justice research suggests that judgments about fairness, both procedural and distributive, are key determinants of citizen attitudes toward decision makers, the decision-making process and institutions, and the social structure itself. These judgments have important ramifications for the willingness of citizens to obey the law (Tyler 1990: 175).

Lessons for the Review of Allegations of Police Misconduct

This section begins by sketching a general picture of our understanding of the problems involved with the review of allegations of police use of excessive force in order to clarify the context in which the procedural justice effect becomes relevant. It then suggests a number of lessons drawn from procedural justice research which can assist in addressing these problems.

Any system of review of police excessive force allegations will leave a substantial number of complainants disappointed with the result of the investigation. For example, the evidence indicates that civilian review agencies do not substantially alter the outcome of investigations into police misconduct. The experience in Philadelphia (1958), New York (1966), and Berkeley, California (1978), suggests that civilian review is less likely than police internal review to find officers guilty of misconduct and is more lenient in its disciplinary recommendations when it does find them guilty (chapter 11; Perez 1978: 278–79; also see Hudson 1972).

A Vera Institute of Justice study (1988) of New York City data on investigations of police misconduct led two seasoned and judicious observers of the police to conclude: "Making the [review] board independent of the department and adding more civilian investigators won't change the outcome of most investigations, nor is it likely to satisfy more people who file complaints or police officers" (*New York Times,* October 23, 1992: A17).

The study of Chicago's Office of Professional Standards data, discussed earlier, discloses the evidentiary problems inherent in investigations of allegations of police use of excessive force.[8] A central evidentiary problem is the unwillingness of officers to testify against other officers. William Ker Muir's insightful analysis of the moral and legal dilemmas of police officers belies the notion that the reluctance of officers to give evidence to each other can be easily remedied, even by coercive legal process (1977: 197–200).

Beyond these problems, Egon Bittner has alluded to the unavoidable discretion inherent in police use of force (compare chapter 1):

> In sum, the frequently heard talk about the lawful use of force by the police is practically meaningless and, because no one knows what is meant by it, so is the talk about the use of minimum force. Whatever vestigial significance attaches to the term "lawful" use of force is confined to the obvious and unnecessary rule that police officers may not commit crimes of violence. Otherwise, however, the expectation that they may and will use force is left entirely undefined. In fact, the only instruction any policeman ever receives in this respect consists of sermonizing that he should be humane and circumspect, and he must not desist from what he has undertaken merely because its accomplishment may call for coercive means. We might add, at this point, that the troublesome problem of police brutality will not move beyond its present impasse, and the desire to eliminate it will remain an impotent conceit, until this point is fully grasped and unequivocally admitted. In fact, our expectation that policemen will use force, coupled with our refusals to state clearly what we mean by it (aside from sanctimonious homilies), smacks of more than a bit of perversity. (1970: 38)

Whether or not one is willing to accept Bittner's analysis in toto, his insight into the social function of police remains the clearest and most comprehensive statement on the topic: "The role of the police is best understood as a mechanism for the distribution of non-negotiable coercive force employed in accordance with the dictates of an intuitive grasp of situational exigencies" (Bittner 1970: 46). As Michael Lipsky demonstrates in his classic study of public service bureaucracies, such a social role inherently contains nearly insurmountable barriers to full accountability (1980: 16–18, 40–54).

There are real limitations to the effectiveness of any system for the review of allegations of police use of excessive force. These include the inherent evidentiary problems, the patterns disclosed by experience with civilianized investigation of complaints against police, the moral and legal dilemmas of police work and its unavoidable discretion in the use of force, and the barriers to accountability in public service bureaucracies. The limited effectiveness of complaint review systems makes centrally important the possibility that the way a complaint is processed can alleviate the disappointment felt when the result is not what the complainant wishes. In order to capitalize on this fundamental insight, procedural justice research provides at least five lessons regarding ways to increase the likelihood that the complaint review process will be perceived as fair.

The first and most important lesson is that parties to the complaint—both citizen and police—need an opportunity to present to the decision-making authority information they believe relevant and to express their perception of the matter at issue. This point has far-reaching implications for complaint review procedures, most of which currently assign the person claiming to have been victimized by police misconduct the role of a witness in a process controlled by others. The effect of this is to limit the alleged victims' expression of their views of the situation and thus undermine their sense of having been treated fairly.

Second, procedural justice research demonstrates that parties to a dispute prefer adversarial to inquisitorial procedures. And adversarial procedures do appear to be more effective in reducing various biases and producing a more complete picture of the controversy. Concerns about the potential costs of adversarial processes and the possibility that they develop inaccurate information have been met by suggestions of hybrid models (combining features of both adversarial and inquisitorial models) with informal procedures and relaxed rules of evidentiary relevance.

Third, these suggestions underline another potential problem identified by research into the experience of civilian review agencies. Perez (1978), in his study of the Berkeley Civilian Review Board, found a tendency to confuse the adjudication of a complaint about the conduct of a particular officer or officers in a particular incident with a critique of broader issues of departmental policy. Care needs to be taken to minimize the extent to which procedures that offer greater procedural and evidentiary flexibility exacerbate this problem.

Fourth, procedural justice research has implications for the representativeness of the decision-making body. I noted earlier that one of the salient features in producing the procedural fairness effect is the parties' perception that the decision maker is neutral and unbiased.[9] Research indicates that a party's belief that the decision maker is fair increases the chances of a positive interpretation of the outcome (Tyler 1990: 149).

This would seem to be particularly important when the parties are individuals for whom the procedural justice effect is diminished as a result of being poor or living in a social milieu in which cynical comments about the integrity of the process are common. The Chicago study (Kerstetter and Van Winkle 1989) data suggest that a significant proportion of police abuse victims fall into one or both of these categories.[10] For example, 72 percent of victims were minority group members. In order for a procedure to be viewed as neutral and unbiased among this segment of the population, particular care must be taken that the decision-making authority be viewed as fair. Ironically, the opposing party in these cases, the accused police officer(s), also view authority structures with a great deal of cynicism.[11]

In this situation it seems likely that a decision-making authority must include a significant representation of individuals whom each party will view as capable of understanding their point of view. Certainly a decision-making authority composed either entirely of people associated with the police or entirely of people from the part of the community from which most of the complaints arise will not create a perception of fairness among enough of the key interested parties or groups.

To create that perception of fairness, both parties will need to feel that their point of view has been given due consideration—the fifth lesson. Tyler underlines this point: "The most important factor in shaping people's reactions to having process control is their assessment of the degree to which their views are considered by the decision maker. . . . Simply providing structural opportunities to speak is not enough to produce value expressive effects: citizens must also infer that what they say is being considered by the decision maker" (Tyler 1990: 149).

A related implication of procedural justice research pertains to the manner and extent to which decisions are explained. The available research suggests the usefulness of oral or written statements indicating the basis of the decision (Lind and Tyler 1988: 106). Sending the complainant a written notification of the decision with little or no articulation of the reasons underpinning it, as is often done, will not contribute to a perception of "due consideration" of his or her point of view (see chapter 11 for notification procedures used by some agencies).

Procedural justice research suggests a number of lessons for our attempts to provide for satisfactory review of citizen complaints about police behavior:

1. the perceived fairness of the procedure affects attitudes toward outcomes;
2. a substantial opportunity for the parties to provide information and express views is important to the perceived fairness of the procedure;
3. procedures based on the adversarial model which provide parties with significant process control enhance the parties' perception of justice;
4. care must be given to limiting the extent that vesting greater process control in the parties results in the introduction of irrelevant material or in confusing individual liability issues with broader policy and political issues;
5. the credibility of the decision maker affects attitudes toward outcomes—a credible decision maker can make an unfavorable outcome more palatable; and
6. indications that the decision maker gave due consideration to both sides of the dispute make the outcome more acceptable. A written or oral explanation of the decision that provides evidence that the decision maker considered the arguments of both parties enhances a sense of procedural fairness. (Lind and Tyler 1988: 106)

Conclusion

Moving beyond these lessons, the research discussed above suggests the possibility of a more fruitful way of responding to citizens' complaints. Crucial elements here include the likelihood that there will always be a substantial number of unsuccessful complainants, the central importance of an opportunity to express one's viewpoint in the dispute, the tendency to confuse adjudication of a particular complaint with a critique of large policy issues, and the importance of treating all parties with respect and due consideration.

These findings suggest the value of moving away from a judicialized, liability-fixing, punitive model for the review of alleged police abuse of force toward a problem-solving approach (see Kerstetter 1985: 180–82, 197–98; and chapter 1). Such an approach would emphasize reconciliation and compensation for the citizen, when appropriate, and assistance and training for the officer, if necessary. It would also facilitate review and correction of policy or systemic problems in the police department (see Geller and Scott 1992: 279–80, 282, 414–15). Repeated or especially serious misconduct by police officers could be treated by traditional disciplinary methods.[12]

Inherent in this approach is a procedure that seeks to give voice to the perspectives and experience of all parties and to hear and consider their views in formulating a response. It will increase the likelihood that all parties will experience the process as an affirmation of their dignity and worth and as a result enhance the legitimacy of the social order for all concerned.

Suggested Research

At least three issues need immediate research: developing hybrid models, structuring the decision-making authority, and including noninvolved observers.

Procedural justice researchers have expressed the view that elements of adversarial and inquisitorial processes can be combined in ways that are tailored to a particular problem. Research should be undertaken to develop and test appropriate models. Simply relying on traditional models (such as those discussed in chapters 11 and 13) relinquishes the opportunity to utilize for maximum benefit the leads that procedural justice research has provided. Moreover, the variety of models currently in operation provides rich opportunities for research.[13] These studies should include consideration of the reoriented approach suggested above.

How best to structure the decision-making authority in citizen complaint cases is a pressing issue that would benefit from sustained research. The research should focus on the impact of race, institutional and interest affiliation, experience, and personal demeanor on the fairness perceptions of all parties. As with the issue of the tailored procedural models, there currently exists an accumulation of experience that would provide a useful starting point for research.

The impact of various procedures on the perceptions of justice of noninvolved observers needs additional research. In the context of complaints against the police, both community members and police officers who know of but were not involved in an incident are important audiences. Do noninvolved observers react as positively to adversarial procedures, or does the partisanship that is likely to be displayed in such procedures reduce their perceptions of fairness? The procedures adopted should maximize the extent to which these important audiences perceive the process as fair.

The notion that the process by which a complaint is dealt with can improve the attitude of the losing party toward that result is heartening. It is particularly encouraging in an arena where the evidence suggests that complainants will infrequently prevail. The key to this hopeful outcome is to treat all parties and their views, concerns, and interests with respect. This is particularly important for the citizen complainant, but it applies to the accused police officer as well. The procedural justice research reviewed here and the directions for future research provide a path for that endeavor.

NOTES

1. The Office of Professional Standards (OPS) is a part of the Chicago Police Department. Its investigators and supervisors are civilian employees of that department. The study referred to here is based on a random sample of 273 complaints filed with the department in 1985 alleging use of excessive nondeadly force by police officers. These complaints contained a total of 637 excessive force allegations. OPS sustained 6.6 percent of these allegations, exonerated the accused officer(s) in 7.7 percent, judged 18.8 percent unfounded, and failed to reach a conclusion regarding the truth of the allegation in 66.9 percent (Kerstetter and Van Winkle 1989: 22; for additional discussion of OPS, see chapter 11).

2. The research discussed here makes two important distinctions. By procedural justice it means the fairness of the *process* by which decisions are made. Distributive justice relates to the fairness of the *outcome* or *results* of the decision. This literature also distinguishes between subjective and objective justice. Lind and Tyler articulate this difference as "between justice as a subjective, psychological response and justice as a state of affairs" (1988: 3).

3. Much of this chapter is based on Lind and Tyler's *Social Psychology of Procedural Justice* (1988), which summarizes the extensive research on this topic.

4. See studies by Barrett-Howard and Lamm (1986), Leung and Lind (1986), and Leung (1985).

5. Leung's study of Chinese subjects found disputant process control was a positive feature of the adjudicative procedure, but he did not find that the Chinese had a preference for adversary procedures. He hypothesized that this was because the Chinese saw some characteristics of adversary procedure (e.g., conflict) as undesirable. These perceptions counteracted their favorable evaluation of process control (Leung 1985).

6. It is important to recall here the distinction between subjective judgments regarding fairness—either procedural or distributive—and objective judgments.

7. Also see Perez and Muir's discussion (chapter 11) of the costs of different types of police review mechanisms, suggesting that the more expensive methods generally achieve greater legitimacy for the key interest groups.

8. The Office of Professional Standards is staffed by civilians. The data referred to here are reasonably representative of the case experience of any review agency.

9. Bayley (chapter 14) notes that, in at least some of the Australian states, when a complaint about police misconduct is made by a citizen (rather than by a police official), the complaint review board must include a civilian, appointed by the elected police minister.

10. This study distinguishes between people who first notify the Office of Professional Standards of the incident (complainants) and those who were victims of the incident. Sometimes these are the same person. Often, particularly with younger victims, a parent who was not present at the incident will initiate the complaint.

11. Accused police officers have a great deal at stake. Even if their jobs are not threatened, their career interests can be damaged by allegations of excessive force. Given these realities, there will be justified legal and political pressure to ensure that they are treated fairly. Any viable complaint review system must be responsive to these concerns (see also chapter 11).

12. Cheh (chapter 13) cites a Vera Institute of Justice Study (reported in Anderson 1992: A22) in which the Institute discovered that a large percentage of persons who allege they have been mistreated by police do not seek serious punishment for the accused officer(s). Instead, the complainants reportedly would be content with an informal opportunity to discuss the problem with the police and with a simple apology or reprimand of the officer(s).

13. The Cleveland oversight agency provides greater complainant participation than many others. As such, it may provide an interesting research opportunity.

CHAPTER THIRTEEN

Are Lawsuits an Answer to Police Brutality?

MARY M. CHEH

C riminal prosecutions and other kinds of lawsuits have not played a major role in addressing the problem of excessive force by the police. There are many more incidents of police abuse than there are civil lawsuits, and there exists an enormous gap between the number of incidents of police brutality and the number of criminal prosecutions. This phenomenon is partly explained by the inherent limitations on the capacity of any legal system to cure social ills. More pointedly, lawsuits may be especially unsuited to addressing the phenomenon of excessive force and its causes. Commentators agree that comprehensive and enduring solutions to the problems of excessive force lie in proper hiring, training, acculturation, and supervision of police officers; in proper leadership and management of police departments; and in holding police officers accountable to the public (see, e.g., Rudovsky 1992: 493).

Despite the admittedly limited capacity of legal remedies to cure excessive force, the rich potential of civil and criminal responses to this phenomenon has never been fully exploited. Many of the preparatory steps we might take to expand the use of legal remedies, like improved public reporting and meaningful complaint procedures, are, in themselves, means to reduce excessive force incidents.

The main objective of a criminal case is to adjudicate guilt and express societal condemnation of morally culpable individuals. The criminal law is not an effective way to prevent excessive force or to cure systemic misbehavior. Indeed, the use of criminal law to punish police who brutalize, assault, abuse, and even murder citizens represents a failure of preventive measures and, if the misdeeds are widespread, signals the need for immediate and thorough internal reform. The criminal law can proceed only against specific wrongdoers and within very circumscribed procedural forms. Criminal law can punish and, in some instances, deter police brutality, but it cannot of itself force fundamental change in how a department is run, supervised, led, and made accountable. Criminal law's most appropriate application, therefore, is against "bad apples"—individual officers who have committed sanctionable acts.

By contrast, the civil law, because of its greater flexibility and scope, has the potential to serve as the instrument of systemic reform. In adjusting rights and settling wrongs, civil remedies generally offer distinct advantages over criminal sanctions. First, a victim of police misconduct can sue on his or her own behalf and need not await the government's decision to go forward. Second, an injured party need not overcome the heightened procedural protections afforded the criminally accused. For example, a plaintiff can prevail under a preponderance of evidence standard rather than proof beyond a reasonable doubt. Third, although the civil law, like the criminal law, can punish via its potential for imposition of punitive damages, the civil law provides compensation to victims who have been harmed by police misconduct. Recompense is beneficial in itself, and damage awards can spur reform if the costs of misbehavior are high. Fourth, civil lawsuits permit broad discovery of information and may provide a means to uncover police misbehavior and stir public reaction. Finally, the civil law offers various possibilities for framing relief which go beyond punishment or compensation and include remediation. That is, the civil law offers equitable relief, via court injunction and specific orders, that can force a deficient department not only to pay for harm caused but to reform so that the harm is not likely to be repeated.

This chapter describes the civil and criminal remedies currently available to redress incidents of excessive force, and it identifies their inadequacies. The main focus will be on federal causes of action.[1] This chapter presupposes that, even under the best of circumstances, legal remedies will continue to play only a subordinate role. Yet the full potential of these remedies has not been tapped, and the need to do so grows more urgent in the face of inadequate alternative solutions.

What Is Excessive Force and How Much Is There?
Legal Standards, Mixed Messages, and Prevalence

Legal Standards

Under international, constitutional, and model standards, force is legally excessive when it is used for unlawful purposes or when it is used out of proportion to the need. United States constitutional standards, based primarily on the Fourth Amendment, combine these two requirements of lawful purpose and proportionality in a general "reasonableness" test. Reasonableness is determined by the "facts and circumstances of each particular case, including the severity of the crime at issue, whether the suspect poses an immediate threat to the safety of the officers or others, and whether he is actively resisting arrest or attempting to evade arrest by flight" (*Graham v. Connor*, 1989: 396). This case-by-case analysis does not lend itself to categorical rules with the exception of deadly force, which must be limited to cases "where the officer has probable cause to believe that the suspect poses a threat of serious physical harm, either to the officer or others" (*Tennessee v. Garner*, 1985: 11).[2]

The distinction between deadly and nondeadly force may itself be plagued with ambiguity. The meaning of deadly force is often assumed, or simply equated with the use of firearms or other obviously lethal force. Arguably, however, deadly force could include intentional headstrikes with flashlights and batons or the use of dogs in some circumstances.

The definition of nondeadly force is even less clear. For instance, the New Jersey Task Force on the Use of Force in Law Enforcement (1992: 7) concluded that there is a "lack of any common understanding as to what contact—ranging from handcuffing an arrestee in compliance with department policy to physical altercations—should be considered a use of nondeadly force." Pushing, punching, slapping, body blows, chokeholds, and Taser assaults can all be instances of nondeadly force—excessive or appropriate under the circumstances. Some states' criminal codes provide rules regarding the legitimate use of force under provisions of "justification." These standards can be quite detailed and complex and may even be at variance with constitutional norms (ibid.: 104-20). Other standards in the use of force may be too general.

Excessive force as a legal concept is typically too narrow to embrace the wide range of police abuse that citizens complain of (and often refer to as "brutality" or "excessive force"). These complaints cover threats; abusive language; racial slurs; racially and ethnically discriminatory treatment; requiring citizens to assume demeaning positions, without justification, like lying prone in the dirt or submitting to such restraints as hog-tying; unwarranted invasions of the privacy of one's possessions or home; unlawful arrest even without force; and destruction of property. More specific internal standards, including police regulations and codes of ethics, may encompass these actions. Some of these abuses may also be proscribed by civil rights statutes which impose civil and criminal liability for deprivation of constitutional rights, for example, protections against racial discrimination or unlawful searches and seizures. Civil rights statutes can also be employed to hold officers liable for failure to prevent other officers or municipalities from using excessive force against a victim or lying to cover it up. Nevertheless, such abusive police conduct as derogatory comments, overly tight handcuffing, or the exercise of legitimate discretion in a retaliatory way may simply escape the reach of the civil and criminal law.

Ambiguities and Mixed Messages

Because officers must sometimes walk a fine line between duty and excess, minimal fairness would require that, before they are subject to civil or criminal liability for their actions:

- the rules of behavior be clearly, specifically, and consistently set out;
- they receive adequate education and training (including periodic updates), which should include a knowledge of alternatives to the use of force and simulation exercises;
- they subscribe to a code of ethics and receive positive reinforcement for adhering to it; and
- the standards to which they are subject reflect degrees of moral culpability commensurate with the criminal or civil liability they face.

A substantial number of citizen complaints arise out of the use of tactics or weapons which carry an elevated risk of inflicting unnecessary pain and injury and of violating citizens' rights. These include the use of: so-called pain compliance techniques, that is, inflicting pain on demonstrators or others to induce compliance with police orders; chokeholds, Tasers, or stun guns; dogs; and street sweeps or roundups in which large numbers of citizens are encountered, accosted, and detained without lawful justification. When police departments encourage or permit these tactics and tools to be used without carefully defining and limiting the circumstances of their use, the departments may signal approval of or indifference to the use of excessive force.

Police departments can meet the challenges of the streets in different ways. When their rhetoric and tactics are guided by military metaphors, as in the "war on drugs," they invite officers to adopt an "us-against-them" mentality. Often this means the police versus the inner city neighborhood or the housing project or the young males who congregate in certain areas. The very methods of drug enforcement require intrusive actions, including the use of informants, stings, searches, "working the busses and trains," high-profile presence in drug areas (usually in the inner city), and sweeps (again, usually in the inner city). And the police are aware that the drug "war" has led the courts to relax otherwise applicable standards, lessen probable cause requirements, find good faith exceptions to warrant requirements, permit the police to stop travelers meeting loose criteria of drug traffickers, and sustain forfeitures of property and lengthy sentences for drug possession and sale. The not-so-subtle message to the police is to be aggressive, get it done, the ends do justify the means.

The Incidence of Excessive Force

Two general observations concerning the incidence of police use of excessive force have a direct influence on assessing the scope and effectiveness of the criminal and civil law. First, even though the incidence of the use of excessive force is infrequent, in absolute terms and relative to the number of total police-citizen contacts, there are perhaps many more such incidents, including serious ones, than the number redressed by civil suits or criminal prosecutions. Second, whatever the empirical data, the public perceives the incidence of the use of excessive force to be significant and the problem of excessive force to be serious. Both of these observations suggest that any critique of the criminal and civil law must consider ways to make the laws more effective and perceived as more effective. The uncovering and reporting of police violence appear to be necessary first steps.

Criminal Sanctions

Experience demonstrates that the criminal sanction plays only a marginal role in preventing excessive force (see Newman 1978: 449-50).[3] Yet the criminal law must be part of any regime to control the police because criminal abuse may occur, even in the best of departments. And, if excessive force does occur, a criminal prosecution reaffirms the societal condemnation of police lawlessness, strengthens the public's trust and confidence that even the police will be subject to the law, and, if explained and seen as legitimate by other officers, can serve some deterrent and educational purposes.[4]

Criminal Prosecutions under State Law

In all states police can be prosecuted for excessive use of force under generally applicable state laws such as assault, aggravated assault, manslaughter, and murder. In addition, in some states there are civil rights statutes that make unjustifiable use of force by officers a distinct crime. In these latter states an officer can be prosecuted under the specific statute, under the general criminal provisions, or, as happened in the case against the four officers accused of beating Rodney King, under both. Typically, it is also a criminal violation for police officers to file false reports.

There appears to be no comprehensive source of statistics on the number of criminal prosecutions brought against police officers (see chapter 3). Some states (for example, New Jersey) rely on general criminal statutes for officer prosecutions, keep statistics by statute, and do not separate out cases brought against police officers. Other states, whether or not they have a specific statute, simply do not keep relevant data. By all accounts, however, the number of criminal prosecutions brought against police officers each year is quite small (see American Bar Association Project 1972: 151-52; Edwards 1965).[5]

WHY SO FEW PROSECUTIONS? Given the hundreds and perhaps thousands of excessive force incidents that occur each year, some involving quite serious harm, why are there so few criminal prosecutions?

One set of possible explanations arises directly out of the nature of criminal cases. In a criminal prosecution, the accused enjoys many procedural advantages. The government must prove the officer guilty beyond a reasonable doubt; the officer is entitled to counsel and, ordinarily, a trial by a jury; and the officer may refuse to testify. Moreover, in all states it is a complete defense to a charge of excessive force that the officer acted reasonably in the circumstances. It is also a complete defense if the officer reasonably, although mistakenly, believed that the use of force was necessary. States vary concerning criminal liability where an officer mistakenly believes force is necessary but his mistake is reckless or negligent. In such circumstances criminal liability may attach or may be mitigated.

In some cases, the criminal law might appear to be too harsh an instrument to use against a police officer even if he or she did, in fact, use excessive force. In this regard it is useful to note that a high percentage of excessive force claims arise in the context of an arrest, sometimes after a harrowing car chase or in the midst of impending violence or unstable circumstances. Although it might be appealing to let a jury decide, the very use of the criminal law carries a reputational, psychological, and possibly a monetary penalty to the defendant. It may also adversely affect the morale of the other police officers who work in the defendant's department. Therefore, a prosecutor might want to have an especially clear and dramatic case before proceeding. Moreover, the prosecutor's decision not to proceed is generally not reviewable. Citizens may not initiate criminal prosecutions.

The criminal law may also appear to be too blunt an instrument to use against a police officer in some circumstances. Criminal cases have an all-or-nothing quality—either the officer is branded a criminal or he or she is exonerated. In many cases an officer may have misbehaved, but a more measured, constructive response like an administrative sanction, payment of restitution, or retraining is appropriate.[6] Moreover, the criminal law may not permit sufficient distinctions to be made in the degree of culpability of the defendant. For example, in one jurisdiction the criminal statutory options leave no room to distinguish between use of deadly force in circumstances where the officer acted purposefully and where he or she acted recklessly or negligently.

A second explanation for the low number of criminal prosecutions is the reluctance of local and even state authorities to proceed against local officers. The identity of interests between police and prosecutors and the need to maintain good working relationships may color assessments of criminality and the decision whether to prosecute. Government officials may also fail to proceed out of concern that a criminal prosecution could engender or aid a civil damage action against the municipality or the county. The use of special prosecution units or prosecutors may overcome these potential conflicts. Even the simple step of requiring written statements of reasons why prosecutors elected nonprosecution might prove helpful here.

A final explanation is that many jurisdictions lack the underlying complaint and investigative systems necessary to bring cases forward. Many observers cite an inadequate complaint system as a principal reason for failure to address excessive force through criminal or other means (see Rudovsky 1992: 482–88). An inadequate complaint system is not available or not effective, or one that is administered to discourage complaints, compromise them, or cover them up.

Even if there is a viable complaint system, excessive force cases are not necessarily brought to the attention of prosecuting officials, and if they are, it may be at a time when investigation avenues have grown cold or information has been compromised or distorted. In addition to a proper complaint system, most authorities agree that there must also be a system of oversight and accountability outside the department (see, e.g., chapter 11).

Even under the best of circumstances, investigating excessive force cases can be difficult. In many cases the only witnesses will be the victim and the police, and medical data may be inconclusive. If there are other witnesses, they may be reluctant to come forward. Even victims may refuse to proceed, fearing retaliation or feeling unsure of their rights. In addition, the police may cover for one another and file false accounts.

Should there be more excessive force criminal prosecutions? Under current circumstances, it is difficult to know. The experience of lawyers and others close to the issue and the dramatic gap between the number of complaints and the number of prosecutions strongly suggest that criminal acts by the police are being overlooked.[7] Yet even a very low number of criminal prosecutions may be justified if (1) there are procedures in place that permit citizens' complaints to be filed, investigated, and publicly reported; (2) decisions not to prosecute reflect legitimate and informed prosecutorial discretion or grand jury judgment; and (3) cases of low level or ambiguous wrongdoing can be relegated to an effective administrative or managerial remedy. These conditions for justifying a low number of criminal cases are not now prevalent.

WINNING CASES. Even when excessive force prosecutions are brought, they may prove difficult to win. Prosecutors frequently assert that juries are reluctant to convict officers of excessive force except in the clearest of cases and, even then, may ignore the facts and the law. Jurors are naturally sympathetic to an officer, who, after all, became involved in the incident as part of his or her duties. They are reluctant to brand the officer a criminal and find beyond a reasonable doubt that he or she committed a crime. Jurors usually see the victim as unsympathetic, as contributing to the event, or as a criminal who deserved what he or she got. Jurors may worry that a criminal conviction will send the wrong message to other officers, lower morale, or encourage officers to be less aggressive. They may also worry that a convicted officer will face retaliation from prisoners if sent to jail.

Yet criminal cases are brought and are won. For example, the Justice Department brought less than 100 criminal cases out of 8,000 complaints it received. In those cases, however, it recently has had a conviction rate of 60–70 percent (see

Subcommittee Hearings 1991: 6, 10). Although this rate falls below conviction rates for other felonies, it is still significant. Generally 80–90 percent of all criminal felony cases result in a plea disposition prior to trial and, of the cases that go to trial, about 70–80 percent result in convictions (see Maguire and Flanagan 1990: 502–03, table 5.25).

If criminal enforcement is to prove more successful, some innovations might be considered. One idea is to dispense with juries in some cases. Constitutionally a defendant is entitled to a trial by jury in a criminal case, but nonjury trials are ordinarily permitted in petty or misdemeanor cases where the possible sentence does not exceed six months in jail. A trial without a jury is not an option when the crime is particularly brutal or caused death or severe injury. But in close cases, one strategy would be to pursue a misdemeanor rather than a felony prosecution. Even conviction for a petty offense is a criminal conviction—it will carry some punishment and stigma and perhaps trigger internal disciplinary action or termination from the police force.

Another idea is, when possible, to confront the reasons for jury nullification (that is, jury acquittal despite proof of guilt), which occurs in many cases and for many reasons. It is hard to predict the chances that jury nullification will arise in a given case, and harder still to know the precise reasons for it. It is clear that juries expect and require criminal cases against police officers to show dramatically culpable behavior. Special units in prosecutor's offices could develop expertise and experience in handling the distinct problems and strategies that apply to a prosecution for excessive use of force. These special matters include selecting juries, using experts, developing carefully drawn jury instructions, and handling tricky evidentiary issues relating to an officer's prior use of force and the victim's criminal past.

Criminal Prosecutions under Federal Law

There is no specific federal statute that criminalizes police use of excessive force. Rather, broadly written civil rights provisions make it a crime to deprive a person of his or her civil rights under the Constitution or laws of the United States (conspiracy and deprivation of rights under color of law). The use of excessive force may, for example, violate a person's right to be free of an unreasonable search or seizure under the Fourth Amendment, the right to be free of unlawful summary punishment inflicted by officers contrary to the due-process clause of the Fourteenth Amendment, or the right to be free of coerced confessions under due process and the Fifth Amendment protection against self-incrimination.

In response to the acquittal under state law of the officers who beat Rodney King, the Justice Department brought federal civil rights prosecutions against the officers. This federal action raised anew questions about the efficacy and wisdom of using civil rights statutes to redress police use of excessive force and questions about whether the particular statute—18 U.S.C. §242—is well designed for such a task.

The idea of federal prosecution to protect federal rights grew out of the turbulent Reconstruction era following the Civil War. Congress sought strong and sweeping remedies to counter widespread, often government-backed violence against and denial of rights to Southern blacks (see Eisenberg 1991: 3–23; Maslow and Robinson 1953; Lawrence 1992: 26–31). Local and state government officials in the South were not only failing to protect blacks (and white Union supporters) in the exercise of their rights of life, liberty, and property but were actively subverting those rights. State remedies could not possibly be adequate because the states themselves, and their agents, were among the wrongdoers. The precursor of the current section 242 purposefully employed broad language to protect all persons, of any race, against the loss of federal rights under color of law.

The current law provides: "Whoever, under color of any law, statute, ordinance, regulation, or custom, willfully subjects any inhabitant . . . to the deprivation of any rights, privileges, or immunities secured or protected by the Constitution or laws of the United States, or to different punishments, pains, or penalties, on account [of] . . . being an alien, or by reason of his color, or race . . . shall be fined not more than $1,000 or imprisoned not more than one year, or both; and if bodily injury results . . . imprisoned not more than ten years, or both; and if death results . . . any term of years or for life" (18 U.S.C. §242).

This law has come to play a profound and central role in safeguarding basic rights in society. First, a broad-based civil rights statute is a declaration of the importance of those rights—they are primary, not derivative, and they command their own enforcement regime. Second, such a law is an acknowledgement that although local justice can be desirable and empowering, it can also be abusive and corrupt. There are times when the community is powerless to correct official abuse because it has lost effective control or because it acquiesces in or approves of actions against disfavored individuals or groups. Official abuse can take many forms. It can be systematic and widespread or disorganized and sporadic; it can be laced with racism or political favoritism or it can be idiosyncratic or an exercise of bullying. The federal civil rights statute holds out the hope of redress from outside. A third reason that section 242 has achieved such prominence is that, even when the state or local government has tried but failed to punish those who violate state laws and deprive persons of their federal rights, a separate federal prosecution eliminates the real or perceived conflict of interest that may attend state or local prosecution of state or local officers. Finally, a broad-based federal civil rights statute adds that extra measure of insurance that the federal interest will, in fact, be vindicated.

Although there is an understandable tendency to recoil from a double prosecution for the same acts—one by the state for violation of state criminal laws and one by the federal government for violation of the civil rights statute—such a prospect can be confined to manifest miscarriages of justice. A double prosecution is not barred by the constitutional provision against double jeopardy because the state and federal governments are deemed to be different sovereigns entitled to vindicate their respective interests against the defendant (e.g., *Abbate v. United States*, 1959, 359 U.S. 187).

Yet the same difficulties of proving and winning a criminal case against an officer under state law also plague criminal prosecutions under federal civil rights statutes. The investigation may prove as difficult, the witnesses may still refuse to come forward, and the jury may still be unsympathetic to the victim. Similarly, because juries in a federal case will be drawn from essentially the same community as for state prosecutions, it may prove just as difficult to persuade a jury beyond a reasonable doubt that the officer's actions were so unjustified that he or she should be branded a criminal. A new jury may still worry that a convicted officer will face retaliation from prisoners if sent to jail. The new jury may still fear that a conviction will tell other officers that vigorous protection of law-abiding citizens is perilous. Prosecutors and grand juries may never proceed with a case unless it presents a clear and dramatic picture of wrongdoing.

Moreover, federal criminal prosecutions face two further complications. First, they raise delicate issues of federalism (the proper relationship of state authority and control over the police to the federal government and federal courts). Second, in every civil rights case, the prosecutor must prove not only that an officer used excessive force and deprived a victim of a federal right, but also that the officer acted with the "specific intent to deprive a person of a federal right" (*Screws v. United States*, 1945: 104). The Supreme Court has imposed this specific intent requirement in order to avoid striking down the federal civil rights law as too vague.

FEDERALISM AND A MONITORING ROLE FOR THE FEDERAL GOVERNMENT. Federalism concerns have always influenced the interpretation and use of federal civil rights statutes, particularly criminal enforcement. The issue is not, however, one of constitutional authority, for it is established that Congress possesses the necessary constitutional power to adopt a civil rights statute as broad as section 242. Rather, federalism in this regard is a matter of politics, ideology, and prudence. Reasonable minds can and have differed about how extensively, how vigorously, and under what circumstances the federal government should pursue violations of section 242. Congress itself was divided in its view about how radical a revision of federal-state relations was contemplated in the passage of the civil rights laws. And Court interpretation limiting application of the civil rights laws has repeatedly invoked federalism themes.

Through the 1980s and into the 1990s, the policy of the Justice Department has largely avoided the federalism debate because it generally defers to state and local initiative and confines its prosecutions to a limited and discrete set of rights (see Malone 1990: 168 n21).

In testimony before Congress in the wake of the Rodney King beating, John Dunne, then assistant attorney general in the Civil Rights Division of the Department of Justice, described the department's enforcement role in the area of police use of excessive force as a backstop to state and local action. He stated: "The nature of the federal enforcement effort in this area, however, should not be overstated. We are not the front line troops in combatting instances of police abuse. That role properly lies with the internal affairs bureaus of law enforcement agencies and with state and local prosecutors. The federal enforcement program is more of a backstop, if you will, of these others resources" (Subcommittee Hearings, statement of Dunne 1991: 3).

The Justice Department investigates violations of civil rights under section 242 only on receiving a complaint via letters, phone calls, or visits. Of the roughly 8,000 complaints received each year, approximately 3,000 are actually investigated (ibid.: 10). Half of these investigated cases relate to police brutality (ibid.: 4). Very few of the investigated complaints are taken before grand juries for further investigation or indictment (ibid.: 4–6). For example, in 1990 there were 7,960 complaints and 3,050 investigations. Prosecutors filed charges in 33 misdemeanor cases and presented 46 cases to grand juries. The grand juries returned indictments in 30 cases. As noted earlier, of defendants indicted, the Department's conviction rate recently has ranged between 60 and 70 percent.

Theoretically, a federal backstop posture makes good sense and can be viewed as consistent with the general purposes of the civil rights statutes. That is, the law was inspired by a perceived need to act when state and local governments were unwilling to act or were ineffective. A backstop role is both more efficient and potentially more effective. That is the theory. In practice, the central flaw is that an *effective* backup role requires good information and monitoring to know when the backup is needed. The Department of Justice neither monitors or seeks information about police abuses; it awaits complaints. The department does not review the adequacy or reliability of police department internal complaint or review systems. Yet it relies, in part, on reports from police departments to determine whether federal prosecution is warranted in a given case. The Justice Department also does not have a system for identifying trends in police practices and tactics (Skolnick and Fyfe 1993: 211–16).

Active monitoring is the necessary yet missing ingredient of the Justice Department's current policy. Such monitoring should routinely include a review of all deaths and serious bodily injury inflicted by police officers (see Geller and Scott 1992); a review of abuses that appear to be directed disproportionately to political, racial, or other minority communities; a review of broad-based practices, such as pain control techniques used on demonstrators or sweeps of whole neighborhoods for drugs or guns, which result in complaints by or injuries to many victims; a review of repeated complaints against particular officers and particular departments; and a review of complaints which arise where no criminal charges, other than assault on an officer or resisting arrest, are brought against the victim.[8] Such monitoring, of course, presupposes a reporting system that provides true, complete, and accurate information on these matters.

THE SPECIFIC INTENT REQUIREMENT. Due process mandates that criminal laws be drafted with clarity and specificity, so that a person can know what conduct is or is not permissible and so that law enforcement officials cannot arbitrarily pick and choose who is subject to the law. Because the federal civil rights statutes were intentionally drafted in broad language to criminalize the willful deprivation of "any rights, privileges, or immunities secured or protected by the Constitution or laws of the United States," and because the precise content of a federally protected right, especially a constitutional right, may be ambiguous and shift over time, an ordinary citizen might not be able to know, at any particular point, what conduct would amount to a deprivation of a federal right. The law's content is subject to expansion or contraction depending on court interpretation of what is and what is not a constitutional right. Without some confining principle, the dynamic and variable content of constitutional rights would render the statute's standards too vague to give fair notice.

In order to convict a person under section 242, the government must prove that the defendant (1) acted "under color of law," (2) deprived an inhabitant of a state, a territory or the District of Columbia of (3) a constitutional or federal right, and (4) did so willfully. In *Screws v. United States* (1945), the Supreme Court interpreted the willfulness requirement to mean that the government must show that the defendant had the "intent to deprive a person of a right which has been made specific either by the express terms of the Constitution or laws of the United States or by decisions interpreting them."

Commentators have criticized the specific intent requirement as creating a confusing rule which, in any event, does not clarify the vagueness it was meant to resolve (see Lawrence 1992: 9, 90–111; Malone 1990: 191–215). These scholars argue that if a law is written such that an ordinary person reading it could not know what action is prohibited, then it remains a vague law even if a particular person had a specific intention to do an act which, it turns out, violates the law. But this may overstate the case.

The real problem of vagueness here is that the statute incorporates by reference all constitutional and federal rights, including "broad and fluid definitions of due process," and thus sweeps within it "a large body of changing and uncertain law" (*Screws v. United States*, 1945: 95–96). But if that body of rights is confined to constitutional and federal rights that have been made specific and definite, and if the defendant specifically intends to do the act which violates those specific and definite rights, then "he knows or acts in reckless disregard of [the law's] prohibition" (p. 104). A defendant need not be "thinking in constitutional terms" (p. 106).

In this regard the federal civil rights statute may be likened to a number of federal laws that make it a crime for persons regulated by a particular federal agency to violate the rules and regulations of the agency. An agency's rules may be quite extensive, sometimes ambiguous, and they may change over time. If a relevant rule is, however, clear and definite, and if a person is intentionally doing the act prohibited by that rule, then he or she has all of the notice the law would require. Because the individual is regulated by agency rules and because the applicable rule is in fact clear and definite, he or she will be charged with knowing the rule or acting in reckless disregard of its content.

So, too, with police officers. Officers know or should know that citizens have constitutional rights to be free of unreasonable force and violence while confronted by or in the custody of the police. If officers intentionally subject a person to unreasonable force or violence, they have violated the civil rights statute, whether or not they were thinking in constitutional terms.

Although the *Screws* specific intent requirement can be thus explained and justified, commentators are right when they observe that the requirement has confused some courts and has made some prosecutions more difficult. Some courts have imposed the specific intent requirement to mean that the defendant acted with the specific purpose to violate the victim's constitutional rights. Most courts, however, have read the specific intent requirement to be satisfied in police excessive force cases if the defendant purposefully took an action which he or she knew or should have known violated the victim's constitutional rights.

Although many defendants have tried to appeal their cases using the argument that the jury was not properly instructed on specific intent, few have succeeded. It would seem that the main impediment of the specific intent requirement is that it may confuse the jury. The whole notion of thinking of a beating or a murder in terms of a deprivation of a constitutional right, and the necessity for finding a specific intent to violate a constitutional right, may be too elusive for some jurors.

In the kinds of cases which are likely to be brought against police officers under the federal criminal civil rights statute—that is, cases where the police officers' acts were demonstrably excessive, unreasonable, and beyond accepted rules—the specific intent requirement, by itself, should offer little real impediment to bringing the case. Rather, convictions will prove difficult for essentially the same reasons excessive force cases against officers are hard to win in state courts.

Any number of suggestions have been offered to lower the specific intent hurdle, such as it is. The most common suggestion is for Congress to identify and specify the precise constitutional rights it wishes to protect from deprivation. Another idea is to enumerate the distinct types of specific intent that really underlie violation of civil rights. Yet another recommendation is to encourage courts to presume specific intent in some circumstances. One Congressional proposal offered in response to the Rodney King case was to make excessive force a specific federal crime. No action was taken on the idea, and the proposal was dropped from the 1991 crime bill. In view of the limited interest in completely overhauling the civil rights laws and the dwindling or nonexistent interest in enacting a specific civil rights law addressed to the problem of excessive force, the specific intent requirement is likely to remain an element in federal civil rights prosecutions. Working within that requirement, the Department of Justice has demonstrated its ability to prevail in strong cases. Although more resources could be devoted to this effort, such as more special United States Attorney units for these civil rights prosecutions, the law itself appears adequate.

Civil Sanctions

State Law

Most states permit civil lawsuits against police for excessive force. Most actions are brought under such common-law tort doctrines as assault and battery. The elements of these so-called intentional torts mirror those used for such actions against non-police officers. Intent may usually be satisfied by recklessness or even gross negligence.

Use of reasonable force necessary to effect an arrest is a complete defense to most assault and battery actions brought against police. Some degree of force is always allowed to effect the arrest, even when the suspect offers no resistance. For example, handcuffing is almost always allowed, although police internal controls attempt in many jurisdictions to ensure that excessively tight handcuffing is not employed negligently, recklessly, or purposefully. The privilege to use some minimal force to make an arrest is limited by several constraints which apply to federal law enforcement officials and have been largely adopted by the states. First, the force must be objectively reasonable given all the relevant circumstances—subjective good faith is not generally accepted as a defense against use of excessive force in civil suits. Second, deadly force is not permitted to effect an arrest for misdemeanors or nonviolent felonies. In sum, a claim of battery may be negated by showing that, given the class of crime suspected and the alleged resistance offered by the suspect, reasonable force was used.

Officers may also be sued under various negligence theories. Negligence can consist of departures from police department rules and regulations. Under state laws there usually exists no master-servant liability between a police chief and his subordinates. Hence, vicarious liability is usually not imposed on superiors, except where the chief authorized, directed, or ratified the offending actions. Vicarious liability may be established, however, where a supervisor performed or caused the antecedent negligent act, and that act or omission was the proximate cause of the victim/plaintiff's injuries. This type of direct liability suit is usually grounded in negligent appointment, negligent retention, negligent assignment, negligent entrustment, lack of necessary training, and failure to supervise properly.

Liability against the state or municipality may be obtained only where the government waives sovereign immunity. Many states have tort claims statutes that prescribe the circumstances for lawsuits against governmental bodies. States vary on the level of culpability necessary to waive their immunity, making for an uneven doctrine of governmental liability. State's attorneys are often keen to dismiss municipalities and other governmental bodies as named parties because juries are less likely to impose direct monetary liabilities on individual police officers. Evidence of indemnification or insurance is not admissible.

Various states also permit equitable relief against police departments, and some of these suits have proven successful. Yet these lawsuits tend to be massive undertakings that tax the resources of most firms and public interest groups.

Federal Law: Section 1983

In sweeping language, federal law gives all injured persons the right to sue government officials for deprivation of constitutional rights. Title 42 of the United States Code, section 1983 (the Civil Rights Act of 1871) reads: "Every person who, under color of . . . [state law], subjects, or causes to be subjected, any citizen . . . to the deprivation of any right . . . secured by the Constitution and laws, shall be liable to the party injured."

No systematic nationwide data are kept on the number of section 1983 excessive force cases filed against police officers. Particular studies, however, do give a glimpse of the likely numbers. One report stated that the number of civil rights cases filed in federal courts between 1980 and 1986 increased by 56 percent, from 11,485 to 17,875 (see Fisher 1989: 48). When juxtaposed with another report that found that 15 percent of approximately 1,709 lawsuits filed in federal court between 1977 and 1983 alleged police misconduct (ibid.), this translates into approximately 1,700 to 2,600 federal civil rights police misconduct cases filed each year between 1980 and 1986.[9] And the number of cases is apparently on the rise. Del Carmen (1993: 87, 89) speculates that the visibility of the Rodney King incident and other abuse-of-force cases will prompt an increase in the filing of lawsuits against police for misconduct.

Most types of police misconduct, including excessive force claims that may violate the Fourth Amendment, can be the subject of actions under section 1983. There are many advantages for plaintiffs in bringing a section 1983 action to redress excessive police force. Section 1983 actions may be filed as class actions, and prevailing litigants may recover attorney fees, which is a distinct advantage over many state law tort actions, even if plaintiff's recovery is nominal. In addition, due to the Supreme Court's landmark opinion in *Monroe v. Pape* (1961), holding that police officers could be held liable for deprivation of Fourth Amendment rights under the civil rights statute, and *Monell v. Department of Social Services* (1988), holding that municipalities can be held liable for police misconduct if it was pursuant to a policy or custom, section 1983 has become "the primary statutory basis for federal actions seeking to remedy police abuse" (National Lawyers Guild 1992: 2-5).

Of course, plaintiffs must allege violation of constitutional rights, and, while most forms of police excessive force and abuse qualify as a deprivation of constitutional rights, not all will qualify. Some examples of excessive force may be merely negligent, and only a state law claim for negligence may be available. Car chases, for example, often cause injuries giving rise to negligence claims, but ordinarily these are not constitutional violations. If the police intentionally "seize" a suspect, however, as with the use of a roadblock, that sort of activity can be the subject of a section 1983 suit *and* a state law negligence claim.

Many other forms of police abuse have been held actionable under section 1983: false arrest, illegal searches and seizures, denial of persons' free exercise of their First Amendment rights, illegal coercion to obtain a confession, deliberate denial of counsel, and deliberate denial of needed medical care to one in custody. Other causes of action, such as "mere" verbal abuse and harassment, have not been recognized. Still other claims, such as actions for malicious prosecution and failure to provide police protection, have led to conflicting court responses.

For excessive force cases, use of excessive force during an arrest, an investigative stop, or any other action amounting to a "seizure" of the person is actionable under section 1983. (Force used against persons in prison must be analyzed under the more stringent standards applied under the Eighth Amendment protection against cruel and unusual punishment.) The use of excessive force in such circumstances violates the Fourth Amendment. The test for whether force is constitutionally excessive is whether it was "reasonable" under the circumstances. To assess reasonableness, a court must balance the nature and quality of force against the government's interests in using it. Courts must pay "careful attention to the facts and circumstances of each particular case, including the severity of the crime at issue, whether the suspect poses an immediate threat to the safety of the officers or others, and whether he is actively resisting arrest or attempting to evade arrest by flight" (*Graham v. Connor*, 1989: 396).

Furthermore, officers who are present and know police excessive force is occurring have a duty to aid the victim, or they, too, will be liable for violating the victim's constitutional rights.[10] A supervisor may also be liable, whether or not he was on the scene of a beating if, as a supervisor, he did something or failed to do something which was a proximate cause of the violation of plaintiff's rights.

Causation can be difficult to prove but has been found in orders given or not given at the scene of a beating, acquiescence in the misbehavior of subordinates, failure to train in necessary skills, and failure to discipline and reform a violence-prone officer.

A constitutional violation and hence a section 1983 violation can occur even when there is slight injury and even when the force applied was modest. If injuries are slight and force modest, juries may be unsympathetic and unwilling to impose liability. Indeed, whether any particular claim of excessive force will prevail is always hard to predict.

Whether a police officer is permitted to use force, deadly or nondeadly, depends on whether his or her conduct is objectively reasonable, given the totality of circumstances known to the officer at the time he or she acted. This objective analysis makes irrelevant the officer's state of mind, his or her underlying intent, or his or her subjective although mistaken good faith. No malice, evil intent, or specific purpose to violate a constitutional right need be shown. "An officer's evil intentions will not make a Fourth Amendment violation out of an objectively reasonable use of force; nor will an officer's good intentions make an objectively unreasonable use of force constitutional" (*Graham v. Connor*, 1989: 397).

In interpreting the language of section 1983, however, the courts, acting out of considerations of federalism and with self-conscious regard for limiting the use of federal judicial power, have imposed a variety of limitations on section 1983 actions. These limitations include who may sue, what defenses and immunities local officials and governmental entities may rely on, and the kinds of relief available to plaintiffs.

WHO MAY SUE. Only an injured party may sue for a deprivation of constitutional rights, although Federal courts have been receptive to permitting the victim's survivors to sue where police use of force has resulted in death. This is a fairly conventional limitation in civil litigation, but in the context of section 1983 actions, requiring the injured party to sue may actually hamper the ability of some plaintiffs to obtain redress in worthy cases. The problem is that often plaintiffs in police abuse cases are themselves unsavory characters or criminals whose claims of abuse arise while they were committing or about to commit a crime. To meet this difficulty, Federal Appeals Court Judge Jon O. Newman has suggested that legislation be adopted permitting the United States to sue on behalf of an injured civil rights victim (Newman 1978; Newman testimony 1992: 1-2).

Currently, the United States may not sue on behalf of a victim to recover damages, nor, until recently, could the United States sue on behalf of affected citizens generally in order to redress a pattern and practice of police abuse in a particular community. In *United States v. City of Philadelphia* (1980: 199), the Third Circuit Court of Appeals held that, in the absence of specific statutory authority, such pattern or practice suits are impermissible. Congress weighed conferring this authority in the past and adopted a provision in the 1994 Crime Act to permit it.[11] Permitting the federal government to bring excessive force pattern and practice lawsuits is consistent with Congress's authorization of such suits in other civil rights contexts. Congress has, for example, permitted the United States government to bring pattern and practice suits to redress discrimination in voting and housing.

DEFENSES AND IMMUNITIES. A serious deficiency in section 1983 actions lies in the doctrine of qualified immunity or the so-called good-faith defense for officers (quite likely, most police defense attorneys would not concur that this is a weakness in existing law). Under this doctrine a person can defend against liability for denial of a constitutional right by showing he or she had an objectively reasonable good-faith belief that his or her actions were lawful. Some courts have held that the doctrine of qualified immunity applies to excessive-force Fourth Amendment cases, even though finding a violation of the Fourth Amendment already requires that the government prove that the officer acted in an objectively unreasonable manner. Many believe that applying the defense of qualified immunity in excessive force cases confuses jurors and invites them to consider the *subjective* good faith of the officer as a defense.

When encountering the good-faith defense, jurors are first charged that it is a violation of section 1983 if an officer applied force in an objectively unreasonable way. Then they are charged that the officer may defend himself by claiming an objectively reasonable good-faith belief that his actions were lawful. As one senior federal judge explained: "If there is some metaphysical difference between the objective reasonableness that determines whether the officer has acted in violation of the Constitution and the objective reasonableness that determines whether the officer is entitled to the defense of qualified immunity . . . it is safe to say that few jurors understand it, no matter how carefully the trial judge tries to explain it. To most jurors hearing a jury instruction on the defense of qualified immunity, it simply sounds as if the officer should not be found liable if he *thought* [subjectively] he was behaving lawfully, and many jurors will give him the benefit of the doubt on that issue, even if they think his conduct was improper" (Newman 1992: 16; emphasis supplied).

A second deficiency lies in the limited ability of plaintiffs to sue municipalities for harms caused by police excessive force. Under current interpretation of section 1983, plaintiffs may not hold municipalities liable for an officer's actions under a theory of *respondeat superior* (automatically holding the employer or principal responsible for the acts of an employee or agent). Ordinarily, when a government employee injures someone, the employer—the township or the county, for example—is automatically liable for the actions of its employees *as employees.* But in *Monroe v. Pape* (1961), the Supreme Court held that Congress did not intend to recognize *respondeat superior* liability in section 1983; Congress intended only to impose liability on persons who personally deprived another of a constitutional right. The only way liability can be imposed on a municipality or other local governing body is if the municipality maintained a policy or custom that violated the plaintiff's constitutional rights.

The causal connection between a policy or custom and police use of excessive force may be difficult to prove. A single isolated incident of brutality will not be found causally related to the department's policy unless the incident was a "reasonably foreseeable" result of those policies (*Dodd v. City of Norwich,* 1987: 6). Liability has been found where officers act pursuant to an ordinance or written policy, pursuant to unwritten policies where widespread practice would indicate them to be customary, and in the face of acquiescence to patterns of unconstitutional treatment. Liability has also been found for inadequate discipline and inadequate training, though the latter has recently been limited to those cases where failure to train rose to "deliberate indifference" to the constitutional rights of others (see, e.g., *City of Canton v. Harris,* 1989). In addition, liability may be imposed when actions of heads of municipalities and subdivisions in furtherance of their official duties may in themselves be termed policy. Unless the municipality is joined in a lawsuit, juries are often reluctant to impose meaningful damage awards.

LIMITS ON RELIEF. A further deficiency of section 1983 lawsuits, from the perspective of plaintiffs, is the nature and scope of relief permitted. There are significant obstacles to recovery of compensatory and punitive damages, and injunctive relief has effectively become a dead letter.

Compensatory and Punitive Damages
Under section 1983 plaintiffs may recover compensatory damages for any harm caused by the deprivation of constitutional rights. Plaintiffs may also be entitled to punitive damages if the defendants acted willfully, deliberately, maliciously, or with reckless disregard of the defendant's rights. Punitive damages may represent the only basis for recovery where actual harm was minimal. Punitive damages may be recovered, however, only against individual officers and not against the municipality that employs them. The explanation for this difference is a matter of history and statutory interpretation. The Supreme Court has held that, when Congress enacted section 1983 in 1871, it did not intend to abolish municipal immunity from punitive damages.

As mentioned, when individual officers are sued, juries may sometimes be reluctant to impose substantial financial liability or even any liability beyond nominal damages. Jurors may not be told that the municipality routinely reimburses the officer for these awards. And even when the municipality is joined in the suit, a punitive award will not lie against it.

Injunctive Relief

As mentioned, until 1994 the United States government could not bring a civil rights action to enjoin patterns and practices of excessive force, and the scope and effectiveness of such lawsuits has yet to be tested. As an alternative to a government suit, individual plaintiffs could theoretically seek injunctive and other equitable relief. The obstacle here, however, is that the Supreme Court has applied standing requirements so strictly in such cases that, for all practical purposes, they are not viable.

In *Rizzo v. Goode* (1976) the Supreme Court refused injunctive relief requiring a police department to set up formal internal administrative procedures to deal with citizen complaints of police brutality. The Court found that the plaintiff, having shown only twenty instances of abuse in the Philadelphia Police Department, did not have the requisite personal stake to seek an overhaul of police disciplinary procedures. And in *City of Los Angeles v. Lyons* (1983), the Court held that a plaintiff who had been unreasonably subjected to a chokehold could sue for compensatory damage for the harm he actually suffered but that he lacked standing to seek an injunction against use of the practice by the police. The Court set a dramatic and almost impossible threshold for obtaining an injunction in such cases: "Lyons would have had not only to allege that he would have another encounter with the police but also to make the incredible assertion either, (1) that all police officers in Los Angeles always choke any citizen with whom they happen to have an encounter, whether for purposes of arrest, issuing a citation or for questioning or (2) that the City ordered or authorized police officers to act in such a manner" (ibid.: 105–06). The consequence of these cases is that individual plaintiffs do not have effective legal means to enjoin widespread and continuing police violence. (This state of affairs, of course, underscores the importance of police self-control and self-development, discussed so helpfully in chapters 1, 4, and 8.)

PRACTICAL PROBLEMS. In addition to the problems of qualified immunity, limited employer liability, and limitations on relief, section 1983 actions also present substantial practical hurdles for plaintiffs. The entire idea of a lawsuit places the burden of going forward with the victim. The victim may be unaware of his rights or discouraged by or unfamiliar with the bringing of a lawsuit. And, as with criminal cases against police officers, jurors often view the victim unsympathetically. Plaintiffs may also face the dilemma of risking criminal prosecution if they pursue their civil actions. In many jurisdictions, police and prosecutors have followed "the time honored practice of discharging misdemeanant on condition of a release of civil liabilities" (*Hoines v. Barney's Club, Inc.* 1980: 635). That is, in return for dropping a civil action against the police for abuse or the use of excessive force, the government agrees to drop a criminal complaint against the citizen. Frequently the criminal charge arises out of the same circumstances leading to the claim against the police officer; usually the citizen is charged with assault or resisting arrest. In some instances, the criminal charge is filed in order to retaliate against the citizen's complaint and to provide the leverage to extinguish it.

In *Town of Newton v. Rumery* (1987), the Supreme Court declined to view these releases as presumptively invalid or unenforceable in the context of federal civil rights claims against officers. The Court viewed the crucial element as whether or not such agreements were coercive and found that, although they could be, they were not inherently so.[12] The Court would not simply presume that officials would "trump up" a criminal case in order to escape liability or to deter the filing of civil suits. Indeed, it observed that some civil suits are frivolous and the release-dismissal procedure advanced the public interest.

Results of Civil Lawsuits

So great are the gaps in our knowledge about police misconduct litigation that one is left to speculate broadly on their possible effects. As del Carmen (1993: 97) recommends, comprehensive study is needed to elucidate "what percent of cases have been amicably settled and for how much; . . . what percent have been tried and with what outcome; what changes have been made in departmental policies as a direct result of lawsuits; what has been the effect on officer training and morale; what strategies should be adopted to minimize law suits; what are the emerging areas of litigation; and [has] civil liability led to better policing."

COMPENSATION. Lawsuits are frequently inadequate vehicles for compensation because the complexities and protracted nature of litigation may deter the filing of meritorious claims or claims which do not have a high dollar potential. This inadequacy is exacerbated in excessive force cases by juror unwillingness to saddle individual officers with substantial monetary judgments. Some plaintiffs have obtained quite substantial awards. Others get nothing. If an effective system of compensation is to be devised, two avenues of reform are available. They are not mutually exclusive.

First the civil lawsuit, section 1983, can be reformed by permitting plaintiffs to sue municipalities under a *respondeat superior* theory or by permitting the U.S. government to bring damage suits on behalf of plaintiffs.[13] Either or both of these strategies could coax awards out of otherwise reluctant juries. If the officer is not personally at risk or if the plaintiff is not "put on trial," then presumably the issue of compensation will be considered more dispassionately. Second, a system of compensation boards might be established to offer a quick and inexpensive way to compensate for any injuries inflicted by the police (see, e.g., Kolts 1992; see also Kerstetter's recommendation, in chapter 12, of a nonjudicial compensation and reconciliation mechanism). Such a claim system would not preclude a lawsuit but would be available for victims if they chose to enlist it.

PUNISHMENT AND DETERRENCE. Although jurors are not informed of this fact, most civil monetary awards against individual police officers are paid by the government on their behalf. This reimbursement may be embodied in legislation, bargaining agreements, or custom. Nevertheless, it is a rare case where an officer personally feels the financial sting of a judgment. This is not to deny that being a defendant may exact huge personal and emotional costs on officers; the empirical question is what message officers take from this experience. Some observers believe that lawsuits do not make the officer an outcast among his peers or deter future abuses. As far as individual officers are concerned, monetary awards to plaintiffs generally imply no real punishment and offer no real deterrence.

Awards against municipalities may be a different matter. Although many believe that substantial monetary liability has had little or no effect on reforming police practices, the evidence presents a more mixed picture. Lawsuits have affected some policy judgments and forced reexamination of some practices. Walker and Fridell (1989) reported that the Supreme Court's 1985 *Tennessee v. Garner* decision resulted in nearly one-third of the police agencies they surveyed nationwide having to revise their deadly force policies. It appears, however, that the magnitude of the police misbehavior and the consequent magnitude of the judgment awards must be severe before a cause-and-effect relationship is established. The deterrence effect of civil damage lawsuits on municipalities remains, therefore, uncertain and perhaps marginal. It is unclear what magnitude of awards or possible legal exposure would prompt systemic reforms.

REMEDIATION. Civil injunctions and other forms of equitable relief offer the most direct means to require local governments and police departments to reform their practices. It remains unclear whether 1994 legislation granting the federal government authority to bring pattern and practice suits will be a substantial instrument of reform. It seems likely that federal civil suits will be limited to the most egregious of cases and will depend on executive branch willingness to employ this new tool.

Additional legislation will be necessary to permit individual plaintiffs to seek broad-based injunctive relief. Plaintiffs now lack standing to seek such relief except in the most narrow of circumstances. The suggested legislation must create or recognize a new right or interest in being free of "a pattern or practice of conduct by law enforcement officers that deprives persons of rights" (H.R. 3371, 1991), the deprivation of which gives every injured individual the right to obtain equitable relief to eliminate the pattern or practice. This strategy will not necessarily overcome the Supreme Court's standing objection to individual pattern and practice suits, but a similar strategy has worked in other areas of law.

Compared to the government, an individual plaintiff may have a greater incentive to bring a pattern and practice suit. At the same time, pattern and practice suits are typically massive undertakings that may deter all but the most well heeled.

Recommendations

Any recommendations for federal action must be sensitive to the view—expressed by many government officials, police personnel, and commentators—that police reforms are more legitimate, more enduring, and more tailored if pursued on a local level. The national landscape encompasses a wide range of police departments, including many with strong, progressive leaders whose own agendas are more rigorous and more effective in controlling excessive force than anything the federal government could impose from a distance. Yet the lessons of the civil rights struggles, dating from the post–Civil War period until today, show that, in the face of serious deprivations of constitutional rights, the federal government may have to provide the impetus for change.

At least two actions at the national level would both advance the protection of individual rights and be consonant with federalism interests. First, the federal government should mandate (or encourage through conditional grants) a uniform system of complaints and a system for national reporting of complaints about excessive force incidents. These are both the necessary foundation of local awareness (and consequent action) and the essential element for a true federal backstop response, should local authorities fail to act.[14]

Second, the federal government should assist and encourage police departments to design and adopt local external oversight of police department handling of excessive force complaints (the civilian monitor model advocated by Perez and Muir in chapter 11 might be an appropriate mechanism). This effort will provide both the basis for local reform and a more refined foundation for a federal backstop role.

Beyond these recommendations the federal government may also consider a variety of steps to invigorate criminal- and civil-law responses to excessive force incidents. First, even without any legislative action, the executive branch can give excessive force cases a higher criminal prosecution priority. A signal of greater attention can include earmarking more resources and more personnel for the effort. For its part, the legislative branch can strengthen section 1983, including expanding municipal liability and enabling individuals to pursue injunctive relief against systemic excessive force violations.

NOTES

1. For relevant cases and statutes see an earlier, lengthier version of this chapter in Geller and Toch (1995).

2. The Justice Department announced on October 18, 1995, that it had created new guidelines to tighten rules on the use of deadly force by federal agents. In general, an officer may use deadly force if he or she believes that his or her life or the life of another is in imminent danger. The guidelines attempt to identify particular scenarios in which deadly force may or may not be used. For example, deadly force may be used against a fleeing felony suspect if an officer believes the suspect's crime involved serious physical injury or death. But the use of warning shots is expressly forbidden, and officers are directed to use nonlethal force whenever possible (*New York Times*, October 18, 1995, B8).

3. "The criminal sanction will never have significance as a deterrent. Its use is bound to be sporadic at best." Skolnick and Fyfe (1993: 199) explain the limited role of the criminal law by analogizing criminal prosecutions against police officers to criminal prosecutions against other professionals like doctors. In both kinds of cases, they say, "professionals are better situated than lay juries to deal with the sinners among their ranks," and "justice in cases of occupational crime is better served by victims' private civil actions than by public criminal prosecutions."

4. Although criminal prosecutions of police are rare, the criminal law, when it is used, may be used too aggressively in particular instances. If that occurs, a sense of unfairness and loss of morale may defeat the deterrent and educational benefits which might be gained. Indeed, criminal prosecution of one or two officers for abusive acts that are, in fact, widespread may simply reinforce the notion among other officers that the prosecuted few were just unlucky to be caught, improperly singled out, or unfairly punished "for doing their jobs."

5. At the national level, the Justice Department receives about 8,000 police misconduct complaints each year. Three thousand are investigated. Only about fifty of these are presented to a grand jury. At the local level, in Los Angeles, for example, the *Los Angeles Times* reported that, since 1980, the county district attorney, after considering accusations of assaults sent to its office for review, prosecuted officers and deputies in 41 cases of assault but declined to prosecute 278 other cases. About one-half of the 41 cases resulted in convictions (Freed 1991: 1). Meanwhile, in 1990 in Los Angeles alone more than 2,500 complaints of police abuse were recorded by the Police Misconduct Referral Service. Further, Paul Hoffman, director of the American Civil Liberties Union Foundation of Southern California, testified before Congress that, despite hundreds of complaints against Los Angeles police officers, "no one can recall a single instance in which a law enforcement officer in Los Angeles has been prosecuted by the Justice Department" (Subcommittee Hearings, Hoffman testimony 1991: 65). Thus, the federal criminal prosecutions of the LAPD officers who beat Rodney King were highly unusual, particularly in the Los Angeles metropolitan area.

6. Apparently there is considerable potential for using mediation or for a complainant and a police officer to "talk out" an incident, at least where the claimed mistreatment was minor or ambiguous (see chapter 12). The *New York Times* reported on a Vera Institute of Justice study that found that a high number of complainants do not seek serious punishments against officers and would prefer an informal opportunity to seek an officer's apology or reprimand (Anderson 1992: A22).

7. Underenforcement of the criminal law is the norm. If every prosecutor pursued every case in which there was clear evidence of criminal guilt, "the criminal law would be ordered but intolerable" (Breitel 1960).

8. Studies of police abuse frequently find that a very small group of officers is responsible for an overwhelming majority of citizen complaints. For example, the *Boston Globe* reported that statistics in Boston show that 18.8 percent of officers were responsible for

79.4 percent of all complaints and that the 25 officers with the most complaints averaged 85 times as many complaints as the average officer (Murphy 1992: 1; see also chapter 4).

It is unclear whether the 1994 Crime Act provision requiring data collection on excessive force will change federal monitoring policies.

9. If lawsuits in particular jurisdictions parallel federal actions, it again appears that hundreds and perhaps thousands of excessive force civil actions are filed against police officers each year. For instance, in New Jersey, 3,122 state and local tort cases were filed under the New Jersey Tort Claims Act, and 167 were police civil liability suits (Fisher 1989: 56). Although not all civil suits against police officers allege excessive force, the New Jersey study found that the most common claim was assault and battery, followed by false arrest and false imprisonment.

A recent report concerning the Los Angeles County Sheriff's Department looked at 104 excessive force cases settled for more than $20,000 between January 1987 and May 1992; 20 excessive force cases in which verdicts over $20,000 were awarded between July 1988 and May 1992; and 114 settlements and verdicts below $20,000 between January 1989 and May 1992. This review adds up to 238 cases in five and one-half years (triggering a total liability of $33,530,760.85) (Kolts 1992: 25-27). The total involved only excessive force cases against the sheriff's department (not the Los Angeles Police Department or other California authorities), and it did not include cases that were filed but lost or abandoned by plaintiffs for whatever reason. Del Carmen (1993: 89) reports on a U.S. Justice Department study revealing that, in the three-year period ending September 1989, Los Angeles County "settled 61 police misconduct cases for payments ranging from $20,000 to $1.75 million." The City of Los Angeles reportedly paid $11 million in damages for police misconduct in 1990 and $13 million in 1991, with an expected payout in 1992 of $14 million (del Carmen 1993: 89). The City of New York, from 1987 to 1991, paid a reported $44 million in settlement of police misconduct cases (Kappeler 1993; del Carmen 1993); Detroit police cost their city $20 million in payouts during 1990 (Skolnick and Fyfe 1993; del Carmen 1993); and Miami Beach (with approximately 300 police officers) paid $3.5 million as a result of claims against its police from 1986 to 1992 (del Carmen 1993: 89). The author of a 1991 manual on police civil liability speculates that, taking federal and state actions together, as many as 30,000 civil suits may be filed against American police annually for all categories of allegations (Silver 1991).

10. This standing obligation, coupled with the graphic images of inactive bystander officers at the scene of the Rodney King beating, has prompted efforts to devise "intervention" training for police officers (Geller and Scott 1992).

11. The 1994 law allows the Attorney General to bring a civil action for equitable and declaratory relief (no damages) against any governmental authority engaging in a pattern or practice of police conduct that deprives persons of their federal rights (Title XXI, section 210401 [a][b]). The provision is drawn from earlier but unsuccessful efforts to establish this cause of action. For instance, in 1991 Congress had before it a bill to permit pattern and practice suits against law enforcement officials. After passage in the House, the legislation died in the Senate (see Violent Crime Control and Law Enforcement Act of 1991, 102d Cong. 1st Sess.; and see Conf. Rept. To Accompany H.R. 3371, Report 102-405, 102d Cong. 1st Sess. [Nov. 27, 1991]). That bill provided the following: "(a) UNLAWFUL CONDUCT—It shall be unlawful for any governmental authority, or any agent thereof, or any person acting on behalf of a governmental authority, to engage in a pattern or practice of conduct by law enforcement officers that deprives persons of rights, privileges, or immunities, secured or protected by the Constitution or laws of the United States. (b) CIVIL ACTION BY ATTORNEY GENERAL—Whenever the Attorney General has reasonable cause to believe that a violation of paragraph (1) has occurred, the Attorney General, for or in the name of the United States, may in a civil action obtain appropriate equitable and declaratory relief to eliminate the pattern or practice." In July 1992, a Police Accountability Act was introduced in the House of

Representatives to authorize federal government suits over patterns and practices of police misconduct (del Carmen 1993: 95); it, too, failed to attain passage. The 1994 Act, as passed, is identical to the 1991 bill quoted above in this note except that the 1994 law also explicitly mentions in (a) that the government may sue to redress the conduct of "officials or employees of any governmental agency with responsibility for the administration of juvenile justice or the incarceration of juveniles" (Violent Crime Control and Law Enforcement Act of 1994, Title XXI, Subtitle D, Section 210401 [a][b]).

12. The Court emphasized the facts of the particular case before it, that is, that the arrestee was not incarcerated at the time of making the release, that he was represented by a lawyer, and that he made a rational choice to sign the release after reflecting on it for several days.

13. Newman argues that extending liability under *respondeat superior* to constitutional torts will increase the chances that a victim of police abuse will prevail at trial. A suit against the municipality will remove incentives for many jurors to reject a victim's claim in order to protect individual officers from financial hardship. Newman observes that jurors are not told that municipalities frequently indemnify their police officers for damages under section 1983. Thus, when individual officers are the only defendants, they often reject the victim's claim in order to spare the officers. Newman proposes that municipalities or other governmental entities be liable for both compensatory and punitive damages, with punitive damages possibly subject to dollar limits (see Newman 1992: 11-14). Newman also argues that allowing the federal government to sue on behalf of victims of excessive force has a number of advantages. Most important, it would help overcome the problem of the unsympathetic plaintiff. But, in addition, it would send a message to the public that protecting civil rights is a priority for the federal government. It would also allow the talent of the U.S. Attorney's Office and the investigative resources of the FBI to be utilized to combat civil rights violations in the civil as well as the criminal arena (pp. 8-11). Newman's proposal would condition the authority for suit by the federal government with the consent of the victim (p. 19). Finally, if this proposal were implemented along with the *respondeat superior* suggestion, Newman would permit the federal government to sue only the governmental employers and not the individual officer. He maintains that the victim would be adequately compensated by a recovery against the state or municipality alone. A suit by the federal government against the individual officers might be perceived by the jury as an unfair fight and might actually engender undue juror sympathy for the defendants (pp. 19-20).

14. The 1994 Crime Act's direction to the Attorney General to collect data on excessive force may provoke implementation of a uniform and reliable system of reporting.

CHAPTER FOURTEEN

Police Brutality Abroad

DAVID H. BAYLEY

Because the Rodney King incident is so much in mind, police brutality in the United States has become synonymous with unjustified force in the making of an arrest. The British, too, are concerned with this. Arrest-related assaults constitute one of the three major categories of complaints against the police in the United Kingdom (Maguire and Corbett 1991). The other two are driving-related incivility and failure to provide service, neither of which can be considered brutality. The same British study also discovered that most arrest-related assaults took place away from police stations or police cars and usually occurred in confused circumstances where it was not clear who should be arrested. The citizens involved had commonly been drinking. The confusion surrounding such incidents probably explains why 60 percent of people who complained about being assaulted were not subsequently charged with committing an offense. Excessive force in making arrests can extend beyond the use of batons and nightsticks. The police in Queensland, Australia, have been criticized for the use of Mace against Aboriginals and for using chokeholds on unruly people being arrested for minor traffic violations (Criminal Justice Commission 1990–91).

The Forms of Police Brutality

The use of unnecessary force in making arrests is by no means the only form that police brutality takes. Other countries are concerned about very different sorts. At least eight forms can be distinguished, with *arrest-related assaults* being only the first.

2. *Torture.* In the United States this is called the "third degree" and refers to the deliberate application of force to suspects in police detention, usually to elicit information for a criminal investigation or to punish people suspected of criminal activity. In an international survey of torture in the early 1980s, Amnesty Inter-

national concluded that among democratic countries torture did not occur in
Australia, Canada, France, Germany, Great Britain, Japan, the Netherlands, and
Sweden. It did occur, however, in Israel and India. Torture in Israel appeared to
be connected to treatment of Arabs and Palestinians, especially those suspected
of being involved in terrorism. Torture by the police in India is considered an
open secret. Senior police officers, usually retired, have often admitted knowing or
strongly suspecting that it has gone on. A particularly gruesome example occurred
in 1981 in Bihar, India, where officers in one police station blinded twenty-nine
men alleged to be habitual criminals with acid and bicycle spokes.

The Japanese police have been accused of torturing suspects held in police
jails to obtain confessions. After revelations by members of the Tokyo bar, two
international jurists (Etienne Jaudel and Karen Parker) were invited, with the approval of the Japanese government, to investigate the charges. They concluded that
"Japan engages in widespread physical and psychological torture, cruel, inhuman,
and degrading treatment" (Bayley 1991a). The "torture" included prolonged iso-
lation, lack of privacy, interrupted sleep, complete dependence on custodial staff,
even for permission to wash or lie down, lights kept on all night, and irregular and
unannounced interrogations. Force seems rarely to have been applied, but it was
often threatened. Suspects were also denied access to lawyers.

These allegations are part of the larger problem of "substitute prisons." Japanese criminal law requires suspects to be brought before a magistrate within
seventy-two hours of arrest, when charges must be filed or the person set free.
However, judges may authorize two successive ten-day periods of detention at
the request of prosecutors. In effect, Japanese suspects can be held in jail for as
long as twenty-three days, if a judge agrees, during which investigations can continue without charges being filed. During this period police have ready access to
prisoners because, through a loophole in the penal law, they are held in police station lockups rather than prisons run by the Bureau of Corrections (thus the term
"substitute prisons"). In fairness, it should be said that documented cases of abuse
are rare; the Japanese lawyers who made the charges about torture had to work
very hard to come up with even a handful. Clearly, however, abuses have taken
place, and they prompted the Supreme Court to overturn several convictions. My
own conclusion, based on research during the late 1980s and early 1990s, is that
"one does not want to minimize a situation where the potential for impropriety
is both unlimited and secret. The Japanese criminal justice system has power over
suspects that is unique among the world's industrial democracies" (Bayley 1991a).

3. *Deaths in custody.* People who have been arrested sometimes die in police
custody under suspicious circumstances. Because these deaths may be related to
injuries sustained during arrest or from physical punishment inflicted in jail, this
category overlaps the previous two. The Australian government, for example, created a royal commission in 1988 to investigate what was considered to be a dis-

proportionate number of Aboriginal deaths in custody. The investigations led to many changes in the management of prisoners, including the redesign and outfitting of cells and admission of Aboriginal lay visitors to police lockups (Australia, Royal Commission 1991). In Britain, John Mikkelsen died in police custody during the night of July 15–16, 1985, and a coronial inquest blamed the police. After its finding was overturned on appeal, a new inquiry concluded that Mikkelsen had died by "misadventure," and several officers were disciplined (Police Complaints Authority 1986).

4. *Police shootings.* American interest in this issue peaked in the early 1980s, culminating in the Supreme Court's 1985 *Garner* decision that police were not justified in shooting fleeing felony suspects unless there was an imminent danger to the lives of others (Geller and Scott 1992). In the Netherlands during the mid-1980s a blue-ribbon committee investigated the justified and unjustified use of deadly force by the police. Analyzing 1,383 documented cases of shootings by Dutch police, both municipal and state between 1977 and 1986, the committee found that 49 percent had occurred while making arrests, 24 percent were in self-defense, 15 percent were of animals, 6 percent occurred during suspicion stops, 3 percent happened during altercations with suspects, 2 percent were accidents, and less than 1 percent involved people who had escaped from some form of institutional custody (Netherlands, Study Group on Police Violence 1987); for comparable typologies of the circumstances in which American police use deadly force, see Geller and Scott (1992) and Fyfe (1981c).

5. *Police raids.* Accusations have been made in several countries that police have used excessive force, sometimes resulting in death, while raiding premises where illegal activity is suspected or wanted persons are believed to be. This was the case of David Gundy in Sydney, Australia, in 1989, during the police search for a suspected cop-killer. A year later, Darren Brennen, a suspected armed robber, was shot in the face by the Sydney police tactical response group, acting on what turned out to be a false search warrant. Miraculously, Brennen did not die; the robbery charges against him were dropped (*The Bulletin,* August 28, 1990). In Britain, five-year-old John Shorthouse was shot by a West Midlands police officer during an armed raid in 1985 on his parents' home. Although a crown court found the constable who shot the child not guilty, one officer was admonished and three others "given advice" by the chief constable concerning poor planning and execution of the raid (Police Complaints Commission 1986). Finally, in central India, shoot-on-sight orders are commonly issued to heavily armed police tracking rural dacoits (bandits) in the hilly forested areas of Madhya Pradesh and Orissa (Rustumji 1980). Many people are killed this way, not all of them confirmed as dacoits.

6. *Riot and crowd control.* Americans have painful memories of the use of excessive force by police against demonstrators during the tumultuous 1960s and early 1970s. In one notorious case, investigators of police efforts to control dem-

onstrators outside the Democratic National Convention in Chicago in 1968 concluded that there had been a "police riot." In Britain, popular concern with police tactics in handling racial unrest in the Brixton area of London in 1980 led to an official investigation by Lord Scarmon and the issuance of a critical report. The London police were also accused of excessive force in the death of Blair Peach, who, with others, was demonstrating against the fascism of the National Front in 1979. Charges of excessive force surfaced repeatedly during the prolonged coal miners' strike in 1984–85 (Jefferson and Grimshaw 1984). After a riot growing out of the print workers' dispute in Wapping in January 1987, 122 complaints were immediately filed against the police, with another 330 filed later. The director of public prosecutions subsequently brought charges against twenty-six officers for assault, conspiracy to pervert the course of justice, and perjury (Police Complaints Authority 1988).

In India, riots and demonstrations have been a staple of political life since independence was won in 1947 (Bayley 1969, 1983). For this reason Indian police are organized into separate armed and unarmed units, with the bulk of personnel being in the former. Although Indian police have more experience in handling demonstrating crowds than perhaps any police in the world, their actions are so often criticized that they become part of the politics of whatever struggle is going on. For example, in Tamil Nadu State, not a particularly turbulent place by Indian standards, the police opened fire on 103 occasions between 1986 and 1990, all but 16 of those during riot-control operations. Seventy-two civilians were killed and 189 were injured. There were no police deaths, although 302 officers were injured.

7. *Intimidation and revenge.* Occasionally police take justice into their own hands, punishing people without waiting for the less certain actions of courts. Motives vary. In the Bihar blindings police may have been responding to public pressure to "do something" about rural banditry. Some observers have charged that the police were acting in concert with large landowners because the blinded dacoits belonged to low castes who had been agitating for land reform and against the practice of bonded labor. Analysis of data collected in Jamaica, Brazil, and Argentina from April 30, 1990, through June 30, 1991, suggests that police shootings are being used as a form of "social control" (Chevigny 1990). So common are shootings by the police in Brazil that some officers are identified in the media as the "Pistoleiros." In addition, Brazil's notorious death squads, in which off-duty police are believed to participate, have operated for years, their presumed intent being to deter criminal activity by repeat offenders. Chevigny calls this "police vigilantism" (p. 241).

The motivation for brutality may sometimes be revenge. Gary Abdullah was shot by police officers in Melbourne, Australia, in 1989 after being taken into custody for the alleged murder of an officer. An egregious case of revenge occurred in the city of Meerut in the Indian state of Uttar Pradesh in May 1987. After several days of rioting between Muslims and Hindus, a contingent of armed police stormed a Muslim ghetto close to the place where a Hindu man had been killed the previous day. They loaded many men into vans, took them out of town, shot several, and threw their bodies into a canal. The following day armed constabulary went to Malyana, a village outside Meerut, and shot at least ninety persons, according to the state government (*Far Eastern Economic Review* 1987).

8. *Nonphysical brutality.* Not everyone considers brutality to be strictly physical. Like beauty, brutality is in the eye of the beholder. For example, is it brutality when the police apply psychological pressure or threaten to use physical force?

The Complaints Review Board of Quebec distinguishes several categories of misuse of force: verbal abuse and discourtesy, improper use of authority or harassment, illegal searches and seizures, excessive force in making arrests, and unjustified use of firearms. If "brutality" and "misuse of force" are synonymous, then Quebec is defining brutality very broadly (Brodeur 1992; see also discussions of definitional issues in chapters 1, 2, 3, 6, and 8). Similarly, the committee on police complaints in Amsterdam reports that most complaints fit into one of ten categories: rudeness, not being helpful, overreaction, false arrest, misuse of force, painful handcuffing, refusal to take a report, damage to property, refusal by police to identify themselves, and inadequate detention facilities (1990). Which of these should be included in a tally of complaints about police brutality? Misuse of force, of course. But what about handcuffing? Damage to property? Poor detention facilities? Possibly yes in each case, depending on the circumstances.

This review of the forms that brutality takes shows that it is not a simple concept. It covers several quite different police actions, and there is no clear demarcation between brutality and nonbrutality. There is little information nationally or internationally about the proportion of brutality of different kinds. Amsterdam lists complaints under thirty-three headings. Complaints about the use of force comprised 6.4 percent. In Britain in 1979–87, 18 percent of all complaints were about assaults related to arrests (Maguire 1989). In 1989, 28 percent of all complaints against the police outside London were for assault (Maguire and Corbett 1991). In Queensland, Australia, 8.9 percent of complaints in 1990–91 were for harassment, 9.7 percent for assault, and 10.3 percent for incivility and aggressiveness—all three of which might be considered brutality, depending on the circumstances (Criminal Justice Commission 1990–91).[1] In Victoria state in Australia, 43 percent of complaints were about excessive force and demeanor in 1990–91; and in the Northern Territory, 30.3 percent were for assault and aggressive behavior in 1989–90 (Victoria and Northern Territory police 1992).

Not only does concern with brutality focus on different kinds of police conduct from place to place, but concern shifts within countries over time. The United States is a case in point. During the early 1930s, when the Wickersham Commission reported, police brutality connoted the "third degree." In the 1960s it meant excessive force in handling political demonstrations; in the 1970s it referred to unjustified shootings by police; and in the 1990s it brings to mind arrest-related assaults. The comparative study of police brutality requires careful attention to definitions and to the operational inclusions and exclusions that statistical tallies often conceal.

How Much Brutality Occurs?

This most basic question is very difficult to answer (see extended discussion of this question as it applies in the United States in chapter 3). To begin with, few countries care to find out. Information about police brutality internationally depends on the character of governments. Data are readily available for democratic countries, but hardly at all for authoritarian ones. This creates what I shall call the paradox of openness: the best evidence about police brutality comes from countries that probably have the least of it; the least satisfactory information comes from countries that probably have the most of it (compare chapter 3 discussion on interagency comparisons in the United States).

This claim is not merely a democratic conceit, but is supported by the eloquent testimony of the refugees who have fled authoritarian repression of various stripes. It is also substantiated by the careful documentation of groups like Amnesty International and Americas Watch. During the 1980s, for example, Amnesty International found that torture by police occurred primarily in nondemocratic countries, concentrated mostly in Africa, South America, the Middle East, and Southeast Asia (Amnesty International 1984). Authoritarian countries are not called "police states" for nothing (Bayley 1985). The connection between police abuses and the character of government is more than semantic, in the sense that democracy means an absence of repression by official agencies. Cross-national analysis confirms, first, that the enjoyment of human rights is related to levels of economic development and, second, that democracy is related to economic development (Humana 1983; Huntington 1991; Wright 1992; Banks and Textor 1968). It follows that the countries with the least amount of police oppression will be economically developed democracies. This means that most evidence for police brutality in the world will be anecdotal and impressionistic. The only official estimates of its incidence will come from a handful of democratic countries.

As long as we recognize that analysis of official information about police brutality produces a skewed picture of its distribution in the world, it is worthwhile to compare its incidence among democratic countries.[2] The primary source of information about the amount of police brutality comes from tallies of complaints made to official agencies. While my impression is that many police forces keep such records, only a handful of countries keep national totals. These are the countries with centralized police systems, such as Japan, France, and New Zealand.

However, not all democracies with centralized police publish such figures. Japan does not; nor does France. New Zealand does. In the large federal democracies, such as Australia, Canada, Germany, and the United States, national governments do not assemble countrywide data. Constituent police forces collect and publish information about complaints as they please. All Australian state police forces do, as does the Australian Federal Police; many forces in Canada do; some American forces do; no German state forces do. Great Britain is the only country with a noncentralized police system that produces yearly reports on complaints made about its forces.[3] Britain also keeps the most extensive set of historical data on complaints, going back to 1964, with detailed breakdowns by the nature of complaints and their disposition back to 1979. Quebec, Canada has figures dating from 1968. Complaint tallies elsewhere are very recent; few are before 1986.

At the same time, the prospects for comparisons of complaints against the police are improving dramatically because governments are beginning to collect information systematically about their number, nature, and disposition. We are on the verge of an information explosion. Especially commendable efforts are being made in Ontario, Canada; Amsterdam in the Netherlands; and in eight Australian forces.

For a sense of comparative numbers and percentages, here are some figures about the numbers of complaints against the police for assault and excessive force for several foreign police forces. In 1990 in England and Wales, excluding London, 17,409 complaints were filed against 97,223 officers—one complaint for every 5.6 officers. On investigation 2.6 percent of the complaints were substantiated. Almost half of all complaints were about assaults (7,455), and 1.2 percent of those were substantiated (89). Thus, there was one complaint of assault lodged for every thirteen police officers, and one was found to be true for every 1,092 officers (Home Office 1991; Her Majesty's Inspectorate of Constabulary 1991). For the London police, there were 4,371 complaints of all sorts in 1989, or one for every 9.1 officers; 2,328 were for assault, one for every 17.2 officers (*Annual Report* 1990).[4]

In Australia, information about complaints is collected and published by the various state police, as well as the Australia Federal Police, but they are not aggregated for the entire country. In 1990-91 the police of Victoria state recorded one case of assault or excessive force for every 12 officers, with one case substantiated for every 250 officers. In New South Wales, which includes Sydney, there was one complaint of assault for every 15 officers in 1991, with one case substantiated for every 370 officers. In the other Australian states, information is available for the total number of complaints but not for the number substantiated. In South Australia in 1990-91 there was one complaint of assault for every 12.6 officers; in the Northern Territory, there was one complaint of assault or aggressive behavior for every 15.9 officers in 1989-90; in Tasmania in 1990-91, there was one complaint of assault or excessive force for every 16.3 officers; in Queensland in 1990-91, there was one complaint of assault or excessive force for every 38.7 officers; and for the Australian Federal Police in 1990–91, there was one complaint of assault or force for every 37.2 officers.[5]

In Amsterdam in 1990, there were 44 complaints of police misuse of force, or one for every 72.7 officers (Commissie voor de Politieklachten, Amsterdam, 1990). Figures on the proportion substantiated were not given. In New Zealand in 1990–91, there was one complaint of misuse of force for every 30.5 officers; one case was substantiated for every 296 officers.

Finally, in Toronto, Canada, there was one complaint of police brutality for every 17.6 officers during 1990 and in the Quebec Provincial Police there was one of brutality or unjustified force for every 108 officers (Toronto Public Complaints Commissioner; Commission de police du Quebec, *Rapport Annuel* 1990).

These gleanings from police forces on three continents show that rates of complaints about brutality per police officer range from a high of one to twelve in Victoria, Australia, to a low of one to seventy-three in Amsterdam.[6] The rates for substantiated complaints are too sketchy to compare.

There are many reasons for questioning whether figures on the numbers of complaints provide a good indicator of the amount of police brutality, even in democratic countries (see chapters 3 and 11). Complaints are reports made to officials. They are subject to unpredictable differences from place to place, as well as over time, in the convenience of lodging complaints, perceptions of the usefulness of complaining, knowledge of complainants about the law, and accuracy in recording complaints. In addition, there are some unique problems with complaints figures that further undercut their value:

1. A single incident can give rise to multiple complaints, victims, offenders, and infractions. Rules for sorting through these complexities must be established and strictly followed before figures on the number of complaints in one jurisdiction can be compared with another. The British Home Office, for example, has issued guidelines stipulating that cases should be determined by the number of different kinds of misconduct and the number of victims, not by the number of complaints or police officers involved (1985, s. 3.14). The average case has 1.7 complaints, 1.1 complainants, and 2 police officers complained against (Maguire and Corbett 1991). In Toronto in 1990, there were 1.9 allegations of misconduct for every complaint recorded for investigation (Public Complaints Commissioner 1990).

2. Brutality is not a simple category. It can cover assault, excessive force, harassment, intimidation, even rudeness and discourtesy. Decisions about what offenses to include as police brutality vary with those doing the classifying, including outside researchers.

3. Numbers of complaints about brutality mask very different degrees of injury. A single complaint about brutality may arise out of a severe beating, handcuffs fitted too tightly, or unpleasant confinement in a police cell. Complaints

about brutality are not graded for seriousness, as are assaults under criminal codes. An accurate picture of brutality would require classification on such a scale. One police force, in Victoria, Australia, is actually trying to do this, using a twelve-point scale.

4. Complaints about the police can be brought to more than one agency—police, prosecutors, civilian complaint tribunals, ombudspersons, and courts (for the United States, see chapter 11 and 13). It takes hard work to collect them all. In Japan, for example, very few—less than one hundred—complaints are made to the country's 12,000 civil liberties councillors and published each year. Most complaints come directly to the police, and these totals are not published. Failure to include all sources of information about complaints can produce large differences in the perception of brutality between jurisdictions.

5. Recording complaints is not an automatic process. Variations in totals over time or from place to place occur because of differences in judgments about whether reports are trivial, frivolous, or malicious; whether complaints should be conciliated or investigated (see chapter 12); and whether particular complainants are encouraged or warned off. A study of complaint recording in Britain, for example, found that one in three people was dissuaded from making a complaint by mid-ranking officers, sometimes for justifiable reasons, sometimes not (Maguire and Corbett 1989; see also chapter 11). Complaint recording by police agencies, where most complaints are made, is highly responsive to modifications in policy, which sometimes change abruptly in the face of widely publicized incidents. Furthermore, scandals do not always have the same effect on the accuracy of reporting: they may encourage strict counting in some jurisdictions and minimization in others. Thus, the very events that complaints are supposed to represent may directly influence the number of complaints that are recorded, and in unpredictable ways.

6. Complaints magnify the perception of misconduct, as most allegations are found on investigation not to be true. At the same time, using figures on substantiated complaints undercounts the amount of brutality because the process of substantiation is manipulable and unstandardized (see chapter 3). In Britain in 1989, for example, only 3 percent of all complaints were substantiated, while 24 percent were conciliated and 44 percent were "voluntarily" withdrawn (Maguire and Corbett 1991, table 3).[7] Among assault complaints, only 1 percent were substantiated. Moreover, fewer of them were conciliated than other complaints (7 percent versus 24 percent), while many more were voluntarily withdrawn (60 percent versus 44 percent).

In Victoria, Australia, the substantiation rate for assault or excessive force complaints was 5 percent in 1990-91, as opposed to 15 percent for all complaints (Victoria Police, personal communication, 1992). In the Northern Territory in 1989-90, none of the 44 filed complaints for assault were substantiated, as opposed to a general substantiation rate of 7 percent (Northern Territory Police 1992). The substantiation rate for complaints of assault against the Australian Federal Police in 1989–90 was 2.5 percent, as opposed to 12.7 percent for all complaints (Australian Federal Police 1992).

My general conclusion is that figures on complaints as well as substantiated complaints are very unstable, reflecting self-interest on the part of both the police and the public (for further discussion of these issues concerning the United States, see chapters 3 and 11).

In addition to being subject to challenge on methodological grounds, statistics on police brutality complaints, either alleged or substantiated, do not have meaning in themselves. One country may have two, five, or twenty times the complaints as another, but so what? The number of complaints varies with the number of police, which is why the ratio of complaints per police officer was calculated in presenting data on different forces. But the number of complaints may also be affected by the size of the population, in which case the relevant ratio is complaints per citizens rather than complaints per officer. An even more revealing calculation might be the number of complaints compared to the number of contacts police have with people. A lazy police force might not generate as many complaints as an active one. Alternatively, because many brutality complaints occur as a result of arrests, perhaps complaints should be compared to arrest rates or, by extension, crime rates.

Chief Daryl Gates was strongly criticized for appearing to minimize brutality in the Los Angeles Police Department when he said, after the Rodney King beating, that most officers behaved in a completely professional and acceptable manner most of the time. He was undoubtedly right, although what he said may have been politically maladroit. Police brutality is deplorable, but some complaints are inevitable and must be evaluated in terms of what police do. For this reason, the British Police Complaints Authority takes pains to point out each year in its annual report that the conduct of most British officers is beyond reproach.

Furthermore, if it is fair to accept complaints from the public as indicators of improper performance, should not compliments from the public be reported as well, especially if they have been tendered as seriously as complaints? Police agencies often call attention to the number of unsolicited letters they receive praising the work of particular officers. In Britain in 1990, the police received twice as many such commendations from the public and from courts as they did complaints (Home Office 1991). Are these "attaboys," as they are called in the United States, less informative than complaints? Perhaps what is needed is a ratio, even a weighted ratio, of complaints to commendations. One complaint might equal two attaboys. This may sound silly, but it is not. Figures on complaints, if they are to be used at all, must be related to other things. Mark Twain said there were lies, damn lies, and statistics. The remedy is not to abandon numbers, but to use them intelligently and to educate the public to appreciate when that is not being done.

Given these problems of multiple sources, partial data, validity, recording errors, and interpretation, can any estimate be made about the quantity of police brutality? Certainly not on a worldwide basis, and very questionably even within single police forces. Data on reported crime are problematic enough, but it will take a great deal more effort to make complaint collection systems anywhere near as good. The game of science will be difficult to play with respect to the comparison of magnitudes and the analysis of trends in brutality complaints for the foreseeable future.

What Difference Does Brutality Make?

Although the objective incidence of police brutality is hard to document and comparisons among jurisdictions are highly questionable, most countries believe police brutality is a problem at least from time to time. Police brutality seems to be much more than the sum of actions. It is a category of moral concern, a "social fact." That is, it appears to be a problem everywhere regardless of its forms or objective incidence (Gould and Kolb 1964: 654–55). One answer, then, to the question of how serious police brutality is, is that it is as serious as the public believes it to be (chapter 5).

And just as the fear of crime is a problem in itself, so perception of police brutality can be a problem in itself. The fear of crime is thought to affect the use of public places, property values, psychological stress, and the willingness of people to take collective action (Skogan 1990a). Following a similar line of reasoning, the fear of police brutality might affect calls for police service, readiness to assist the police, levels of emotion in police contacts, avoidance of police contact, latent disrespect, repressed anger, and inclination to believe the worst about the police.

Furthermore, the fear of brutality may actually increase the likelihood of brutality occurring, just as the fear of crime may create conditions that encourage the commission of crime. For example, faced with an uncooperative populace, police may resort to sweeps and searches; suspects who flee rather than talk may be more likely to be considered guilty and to be treated roughly; the anger and resentment fed by perceptions of police brutality may encourage protests and collective violence, reinforcing the police belief that only force will work; and belief in the prevalence of brutality may cause people to criticize the police no matter what they do.

Close observers of public opinion in Britain have found a steady decline in respect for the police since the 1950s and attribute it to publicity about corruption and brutality beginning in the 1970s (Reiner 1991a, 1991b; Skogan 1990b).

Only a few studies have asked about people's personal knowledge of the use of force by police. In a survey I conducted in India in 1965, 1.3–22.2 percent of respondents, depending on the locale, knew someone personally who had been struck by the police (Bayley 1969). The Australian Institute of Criminology found in 1987 that 12.1–17 percent of Australians, depending on the state, had personal knowledge of the police using undue force (Australian Institute of Criminology 1988). In London, the Policy Studies Institute reported in the early 1980s that 22 percent of persons who had been arrested said they had been struck or had force used against them. The vast majority, as one might expect, thought the force unjustified (Smith and Gray 1983). The British Crime Survey of 1988 found that only 1.9 percent of the population had tried to make a complaint about the police during the preceding five years. Ten percent said they had been upset by police use of undue force, even though they had not complained. Thirty-six percent reported the police being rude, arrogant, or overbearing (Skogan 1990b).

Minority groups are much more likely to perceive police brutality as a problem. They believe it is more widespread, and they experience it more often (Skogan 1990b; Smith and Gray 1983; Bayley and Mendelsohn 1968). Divergent perceptions of police brutality are part of the dynamics of social stratification in many countries.

In addition to public opinion surveys, judgments about the importance of police brutality can be drawn from its visibility in media coverage, popular culture, politics, and official concern. Again, the paradox of openness arises—brutality will appear more significant in democratic than nondemocratic countries. Concern about police brutality in Britain, for example, was probably most intense between 1975 and 1985. Popular concern was reflected in the findings of the House Select Committee on Race Relations, 1972; creation of the Home Office working group on complaints against the police, 1974; creation of the Police Complaints Commission, 1976; the Scarmon Report on the Brixton disturbances, 1982; and the establishment of the Police Complaints Authority, 1985. Since then criticism has shifted from brutality to misconduct in criminal investigations, in particular the fabrication of evidence.

In Australia, concern with brutality achieved the status of "moral panic" during the late 1980s. It was given extensive coverage by the media, riveting public attention and forcing governments to respond with a host of special inquiries and commissions: the Royal Commission on Aboriginal Deaths in Custody, the National Inquiry into Racist Violence in Australia by the Human Rights and Equal Opportunity Commission of the Government of Australia, the National Violence Commission, and the coronial inquest into police shootings in Victoria.

In Canada, the issue simmered through the 1980s. In Toronto, a Race Relations and Policing Task Force was established in 1988. In 1990–91, however, police brutality gained prominence across the entire country. There were royal commissions on the police use of force in Manitoba and Nova Scotia, official inquiries in Toronto and British Columbia, and public outrage at the death of Marcellus François in Montreal. François was shot in the head after being stopped while in a car. The police had mistaken him for another man. Two thousand police officers demonstrated when their chief publicly criticized the officers involved. Several weeks later a black suspect in another case killed himself on a street in Montreal rather than be arrested.

In Israel the media daily charge the police with using excessive force against Arabs, and the Knesset (parliament) regularly discusses the charges. In April 1991, the world's attention was drawn when Israeli police fired upon unarmed Palestinians throwing rocks at people worshipping at the temple Wall.

The situation in other countries is very different. Popular concern in Japan, despite the revelations about conditions in the "substitute prisons," seems to be small, and there is no crisis of confidence about the police. In the Netherlands, there was a flurry of interest in police shootings during the mid-1980s, but interest died down, especially after the government appointed a commission to investigate police use of force in the preceding decade (Study Group on Police Violence 1987). New Zealand became concerned about police brutality in the early 1980s, mostly in connection with the handling of demonstrations during the tour of the South African rugby team. Today there is little concern.

The lack of correspondence between the objective incidence and the subjective importance of police brutality is undoubtedly traceable, at least in part, to public willingness to excuse or even approve of brutality. The plain fact is that the use of excessive force by the police is not universally condemned. After the Bihar blindings, the chief minister of Bihar said that the blindings had "social sanction" (*The Times* [London], December 7, 1980). Many people were outraged when the state government paid compensation to the blinded victims. Indian police officers tell stories of respectable people asking that suspects arrested for crimes against them be given a bit of "third degree" until they confess. An inspector general of police told me of a high court judge who demanded that his servant, arrested for stealing the family's jewelry, be beaten, despite the fact that the judge had made a name condemning the police for "third degree" methods.

The numerous shootings of suspected criminals and other "undesirable" people in Argentina, Brazil, and Jamaica, which have been called "police executions," are frequently justified by officials, elected politicians, media commentators, and the public generally. As one commentator has noted, the public's sympathy for police excesses "creates a grim world of vengefulness in which persons accused of crime are literally outlaws, subject to execution by everyone, official or private" (Chevigny 1990: 412).

Japan's "substitute prisons" have not become a major issue, in part because the public believes that arrested persons should display contrition and admit their wrongs (Bayley 1991). Although the presumption of innocence is built into Japanese law, it is not strong in popular culture. What the police do is usually accepted as being right. Excuses and justifications by suspects are seen not only as unconvincing but as unseemly. It is entirely proper, therefore, for Japanese investigators to "pressure" suspects to confess as the beginning of social redemption.

The point of all these examples is that the public may excuse in the police what it would excuse in itself. It may, in fact, expect from the police what it would expect from itself. Both public and police frequently blur the distinction between arrest and punishment. The public often agrees with a view attributed to the British police: "Most police officers see it as part of their function to punish, at least in certain circumstances, and this is one of the underlying motivations for their behavior" (Smith and Gray 1983, 2:76).

Viewing police brutality comparatively, one begins to see that its occurrence is a necessary but not a sufficient condition for its being perceived as a problem. The impact of police brutality on public, as well as official, opinion is unpredictable.

What Is Being Done about It?

Efforts to reduce police brutality around the world proceed on two fronts. First, disciplinary supervision over the police may be tightened, often by creating special oversight agencies outside the police (Bayley 1991b, 1991c). Second, police forces may change the way they manage personnel so that brutality is discouraged. These approaches are not mutually exclusive. Here are noteworthy developments on both fronts, based on information drawn primarily from English-speaking democracies.

During the past decade, external supervision of the investigation and discipline of police misconduct has been tightened in many countries. Developments are so varied and so idiosyncratic in detail that they are difficult to compare. The Royal Canadian Mounted Police, for example, added two oversight committees during the 1980s. The director of research and communication explained them to me as follows: "The RCMP External Review Committee and the RCMP Public Complaints Commission are two distinct, independent bodies, both external to the RCMP. The External Review Committee deals with matters internal to the RCMP. The Public Complaints Commission deals with external complaints from the public."[8]

Two distinctions, however, will help in making comparative generalizations. First, responding to complaints of misconduct may be left in the hands of the police or may be given to others outside the police agency. Second, responding to complaints involves two actions—investigating the facts of the allegation and deciding on appropriate punishment if the allegation is found to be true. This double distinction generates the usual four-celled box (see figure 14.1). Police may be

Figure 14.1   Police Disciplinary Procedure in Several Countries

	Police	Nonpolice
Investigation	United States (1) India Japan	(2) Review New Zealand (3) Supervision Victoria State Australian Federal Police Royal Canadian Mounted Police (4) Independent England and Wales
Discipline Action	United States (1) India Japan	(5) Recommendation New South Wales South Australia (6) Independent Ontario Quebec Queensland State

sovereign with respect to both investigation and adjudication or nonpolice may intervene at one or both stages (chapters 11, 12, and 13 discuss the patterns of internal and external review in the United States).

The clear trend during the past ten years has been for those outside the police to play a larger role successively in the investigation of complaints and then in disciplinary hearings. This does not mean that the police automatically cede all authority. Frequently they share responsibility. For example, civilians may review police investigations of misconduct but not undertake investigations themselves. They actually may give specific directions to police investigators but, again, do not substitute their own personnel. As for determining punishment, civilians may be allowed to make recommendations, but the police retain final authority. Finally, civilian authorities may be authorized to take matters out of police hands at either stage.[9]

Figure 14.1 shows these gradations of civilian intrusion with numbers New Zealand created a Police Complaints Authority in 1989 to review all police investigations of complaints. It is also authorized to undertake its own investigations in very serious or controversial cases, but it rarely does so (Quilliam 1992). The model that emerged in Australia during the late 1980s is for civilian oversight, often exercised by an ombudsman specializing in police affairs, to review all investigations, to make suggestions about the course of an investigation when it is deemed necessary, and to take over investigations occasionally "in the public interest" (Goldsmith 1992; Crumpen 1992). Disciplinary decisions on the facts of a case are made by the police, but they may be appealed to the police minister, who is elected. In Victoria, the police commissioner may choose not to hear cases and instead refers them to police boards. A police board is a judicial magistrate in each police division throughout the state. When a complaint about the police is made by a member of the public, as opposed to a government official, the board must include a second civilian appointed by the police minister (Crumpen 1992). New South Wales has a similar system, but differences of opinion about disciplinary action between the ombudsman and commissioner of police must go to a police tribunal, consisting of a district court judge. Appeals from the judge go to the police minister.

In Britain, the Police Complaints Authority (PCA), which was established in 1985, is empowered to "supervise" police investigations of misconduct, which means that it may review and also give directions. The PCA is obligated to review all cases in which there has been a death or serious injury to a civilian. Over the years a three-tier system for handling cases has grown up: (1) informal conciliation by the police in minor complaints; (2) passive review by the PCA of moderately serious complaints; and (3) active intrusion by the PCA into the investigation of a few cases that attract widespread public attention (Maguire and Corbett 1991).

In South Australia, the Police Complaints Authority, a civilian body, may review, supervise, and independently investigate complaints of police misconduct. It may also recommend disciplinary action. If the commissioner of police does not accept its advice, the case is decided by the police minister.

External bodies with investigative oversight may often be less powerful than they appear because of the demanding standard of proof employed. The Police Complaints Authority in Britain, for example, must determine whether complaints are proved beyond a reasonable doubt—the criminal standard—rather than on the preponderance of evidence, the civil standard. The investigating boards of the Ontario Police Complaints Commission, on the other hand, need only "clear and convincing evidence." This makes civilian oversight in Ontario much more threatening to the police than in Britain (see chapter 13 for a review of the effect of different standards of proof in different control systems in the United States).

The British Police Complaints Authority may also displace the police in determining punishments, so it belongs partly in the lower right-hand box of figure 14.1. If the PCA believes that the disciplinary decision of the police is inadequate, it can refer it to disciplinary tribunals composed of the Chief Constable of the force involved plus two PCA members who have not been involved in the investigation (Maguire and Corbett 1992).

Full civilian authority over both investigations and disciplinary actions was created in 1990 in Ontario and Quebec and Queensland state in Australia. The Ontario Police Complaints Commission, an outgrowth of the Toronto Police Complaints Commissioner, has authority over investigations and disciplinary determinations in cases of police misconduct throughout the province. It can take over any investigation, and it can refer disciplinary decisions by the police to three-person boards of inquiry, composed of a lawyer appointed by the attorney general, a nonlawyer appointed by the Police Association, and a nonlawyer appointed by the Association of Municipalities (Ontario Police Services Act 1990; Ontario Ministry of the Solicitor General 1990). The Quebec Ethics Commission may review and independently investigate any complaint against the police throughout the province. Its findings are referred to nonpolice ethics committees, whose decisions about discipline are binding on the police unless an appeal is made to the Provincial Court of Quebec (Brodeur 1992).

The Criminal Justice Commission of Queensland, Australia, which grew out of the celebrated Fitzgerald Commission inquiry into police corruption and misconduct, has power to investigate and impose penalties in any complaint. Reviews and investigations are handled by its Official Misconduct Division. Findings are forwarded to misconduct tribunals, which are also part of the Criminal Justice Commission, and are composed entirely of legally trained civilians.

In sum, during the past decade there has been an extraordinary extension of specialized civilian authority over police discipline in several of the world's developed democracies. Concern about police conduct has been so keenly felt that leaving discipline exclusively in police hands is no longer an acceptable option. In my view, we have reached a watershed: the principle of civilian oversight at both stages of disciplinary proceedings is well on the way to becoming established.

Police management is the second area in which efforts are being made to respond to the problem of police brutality. Some forces, of course, have done very little. Others have been very creative. Their efforts tend to concentrate in the following areas:

1. Reform of procedures for processing complaints and conducting investigations (Britain, Tasmania).
2. Larger, more visible, more expert units for processing and investigating complaints (Victoria, New South Wales).
3. Diversification of recruitment (Vancouver, Toronto).
4. Redesign of training programs to promote cross-cultural understanding and empathy (Quebec, London).
5. Training in nonforceful techniques of dispute resolution (Northern Territory, London).
6. Encouragement of public complaints through active solicitation, simplification of procedures, and retraining of complaints officers (Japan).
7. Development of policy guidelines for activities more likely to generate complaints about brutality, such as the use of deadly force, high-speed motor vehicle chases, and armed raids (Britain, Australia).

In general, the philosophical approach to solving the problem of police brutality seems to be changing. Up to now, brutality and other misconduct were blamed on a few "rotten apples." They were seen as matters of individual deviance. Now brutality is viewed increasingly as a matter of institutional facilitation and organizational responsibility.[10] In other words, it can be corrected if police forces are managed better. While misbehaving individuals must continue to be weeded out, efforts are being made to transform management and institutional culture. The focus of corrective efforts is shifting from individuals to organizations.

Just as brutality is not a problem confined to the countries we know most about—democracies—so, too, solutions are sought to brutality in closed societies as well. The solutions, however, are of an altogether different order. In democratic countries police brutality represents a failure of individual or organizational responsibility. But in authoritarian countries, brutality is often regime-supported. As a result, solutions to brutality become a matter of "high politics," requiring change in regimes and systems of government. Throughout history, rebellions and revolutions have been fueled to varying extents by revulsion to the excesses of the police. The French Revolution, for example, began with the fall of the Bastille, a prison. The crowds clamoring for freedom in Moscow in 1990 converged on Dzerzhinsky Square, named for the founder of the KGB, defaced KGB headquarters, and pulled down Dzerzhinsky's statue. In East Germany, the buildings of Stazi, the secret police, were looted, records seized or destroyed, and Stazi agents went into hiding. Military rule was undermined in Argentina in the 1980s by stories about "desparicidos"—people who had been arrested by the police and were never seen again—and in Chile by tales of the systematic torture of dissidents. The activities of SEVAK, the secret police in Iran, initially cowed but ultimately strengthened the fundamentalist movement that overthrew the shah.

Because police brutality is less visible in authoritarian countries, it may seem to be less of a problem. But appearances are misleading. Police brutality silently but inexorably erodes the foundations of political legitimacy. Efforts to eliminate police brutality exist worldwide. They are overt or subterranean, depending on the character of the political system.

NOTES

1. This information covers April 30, 1990, through June 30, 1991.
2. My sample is further limited by language. My information comes mostly from English-speaking countries.
3. There has been considerable controversy in Britain, stirred by Robert Reiner at the London School of Economics and Political Science, about whether the British police system can properly be characterized as not centralized (Reiner 1988).
4. Data on the proportion substantiated are not available.
5. Information was provided by the police forces of each state.

6. For the latest data on comparable rates for police officers in the United States, see Pate and Fridell (1993); see also chapter 3.

7. These figures are for all England and Wales, including the London Metropolitan Police.

8. This explanation is accurate, but a second (or third) reading and a bit of thinking are needed before it makes sense.

9. This scheme is similar to one proposed by Samuel Walker and Vic W. Bumphus, but with refinements of my own ("Civilian Review of the Police: A National Survey of the 50 Largest Cities, 1991," draft copy, April 1991); see also Kerstetter (1985) and chapter 11.

10. For discussion of pertinent developments in the United States, see chapters 2, 4, 6, and 8.

CHAPTER FIFTEEN

Understanding and Controlling
Police Abuse of Force

WILLIAM A. GELLER and HANS TOCH

O ne of the propositions that has shaped all the chapters in this book is that police agencies must continue to progress and improve. But we also assume that prudent police administrators and other policymakers will want to assess new action initiatives to determine whether the innovations are achieving their intended purposes. Initiatives that worked in one setting and place may need modification in other contexts. Promising ideas that seemed to fall flat elsewhere may succeed under new circumstances for a variety of reasons, including the possibility that previously they were not well implemented and therefore did not have a fair test. Wayne Kerstetter's observation more than a decade ago bears repeating: "With only slight overstatement, one could summarize the history of police experimentation with innovative ideas in one sentence—'We didn't try it, and it didn't work.'"

Change agents cannot expect proof positive of a plausible idea's feasibility under all circumstances before trying it (Schorr 1989; Geller and Swanger 1995). And in deciding whose successes to emulate, public policymakers will want to learn what they can about the various factors that may have produced the desired outcomes. Simple comparisons of variables of interest before and after an intervention may miss the real causes of changes that have been achieved and prompt the diversion of resources to wasteful replications (Tonry 1995: 84).

Defining Excessive Use of Force

This aggregate problem of excessive force is more helpfully defined as a series of subproblems, some of which overlap and sometimes appear together. These subproblems include:

- *any* force when *none* is needed;
- *more* force than is needed;

- *any* force or a *level* of force continuing after the necessity for it has ended;[1]
- knowingly wrongful uses of force;
- well-intentioned mistakes that result in undesired uses of force;
- departmental constraints that needlessly put officers in the position of using more force—and/or using it more often—than otherwise would occur (e.g., problems with training, supervision, deployment, assignment practices, equipment, procedures, and policies precluding use of certain tactics or tools); and
- frequent use of force by particular officers, particular units or departments, even if each instance seems justifiable.

The last subproblem deserves a brief discussion at this juncture lest the critical reader think our concept of problematic police work is so broad that it encompasses even admirable conduct. The officer who uses legitimate force quite often may be a folk hero to many in the organization and the neighborhood but is generally understood by thoughtful, experienced practitioners to be tempting fate. Such an officer risks physical, emotional, legal, financial and other career consequences to himself or herself, loved ones, colleagues, the department and local government, and those on the receiving ends of the officer's uses of force. Moreover, justifiable force may be seen as illegitimate by some in the community, which may fuel future violence directed at officers or failure of citizens to come to the aid of an officer needing assistance.

Thus, if along with the accolades, we can help frequent force users attain the same or superior results with less force, all the better. Showing—not just in words but in deeds—the opportunities to win compliance with lawful requests without resort to physical coercion can position the police as important public educators for communities that wish to resolve conflicts peacefully whenever possible.

Beyond Minimum Standards

However one defines unacceptable police uses of force, as in chapters 1 and 8 and elsewhere (e.g., by Bittner 1970), little progress will be made in upgrading the skill with which police decide whether to use force, what type of force, and how much force to use until we broaden administrative and other inquiries and interventions. Police managers and other overseers now focus primarily on criminal and other grossly substandard officer misbehavior that merits *punitive* responses—some of the unreasonable uses of force depicted in column A of table 15.1.[2] But where punishment is not warranted (e.g., column B), we must learn to provide guidance to help officers continually hone their expertise.

Klockars (chapter 1) calls for such a broadening of focus, to include all police use of force capable of being improved upon in the future. When Klockars's suggestion is understood properly—he recommends punishment only for offi-

Table 15.1   Departmental Attention to Use-of-Force Issues

	Quality of Officer's Decision		
	A Unreasonable	**B** Reasonable	**C** Highly Skilled
1 No force (or very minor force) used	Unreasonable restraint	Justifiable restraint	Commendable restraint
2 Moderate force used (isolated incident)	Abuse of force	Justifiable use of force	Commendable use of force
3 Serious force used (isolated incident)	Abuse of force	Justifiable use of force (guidance to officer)	Commendable use of force
4 Moderate to serious force used frequently	Abuse of force (violence-prone officer and/or departmental problems)	Justifiable use of force (guidance, retraining, departmental changes)	Commendable use of force (departmental, strategic, and/or tactical changes)

Key: Shaded cells represent police conduct that typically receives attention from most police departments. The behavior noted in unshaded cells receives far less consideration.

cers whose conduct is willful, egregious, or repetitive—it becomes less provocative and more commonsensical.[3] When the conduct at issue is lawful and within agency policy but still subject to improvement, talking in terms of opportunities for professional development is less likely to trigger defensive attitudes by officers and their supporters than is employment of such phrases as "excessive force." In Klockars's proposal, the "highly skilled" officers (column C in table 15.1) become the benchmarks against whom other officers should be appraised and whose level of expertise should be the object of professional aspiration.[4] Failure of officers who act reasonably (column B in table 15.1) to succeed in emulating the best in class is not and should not be cause for discipline, any more than one punishes members of a sports team whose work is helpful but not outstanding. But the failure of officers even to try to bring their performance up to superior levels is cause for supervisory concern and remedial assistance. Training, supervision, and other support systems in police departments currently are oriented in too many jurisdictions toward avoiding scandalous, liability-generating, or grossly substandard uses of force by officers. But one would hardly feel comfortable selecting a family doctor whose claim to expertise is a history of avoiding malpractice suits and charges of criminally assaulting other patients; one wants evidence of superior talent, attested to by satisfied customers and admiring peers.

Except for a small number of officers who knowingly and willfully misuse force—and who deserve punishment and separation if the necessary evidence can be compiled—the best results in upgrading the use-of-force decision making and tactical skills of most officers very likely will be obtained through positive incentives rather than through punishment. These incentives include the appeal of officer safety, crime- and disorder-control effectiveness, and building rapport with community members who can help prevent crime.

Explaining Police Abuse of Force

Various influences, parameters, and variables have been shown to affect the use of force and the abuse of force. These influences, parameters, and variables work together in different combinations, and this fact has important implications for desirable lines of research (Ross 1994).

A recommendation that follows once we recognize the complexity of the problem is that research ought to explore the interaction between variables that are usually explored separately—in particular, the relationships of micro-level to macro-level variables. For example, one can ask whether young officers working for a department and city administration in which African Americans enjoy substantial clout would abuse force less frequently than young officers in other jurisdictions.

The best illustration of a relationship between micro- and macro-level variables is the model implicit in the Christopher Commission report (Independent Commission on the Los Angeles Police Department 1991). That model suggests that a strongly enforcement-oriented agency can enhance the proclivity of aggressive officers to engage in proactive exercises that include uses of excessive force. This would mean that within-group rate differences would increase in agencies that espouse a no-holds-barred enforcement philosophy. For instance, the crudeness and cynicism of Mark Fuhrman's testimony in the 1995 O. J. Simpson murder trial seem to have metastasized in the LAPD's macho culture.

One variable illustrated by the Rodney King incident is that of reinforcements that may occur in situations to which groups of officers respond. The presence of other officers on the scene may be an exacerbating influence or—especially if "intervention" training has been administered—may be a calming influence on the individual officer.[5] These notions about responsible "bystanderism" (Staub 1989) and other propositions are researchable and have significance for efforts by police administrators and other public officials to understand patterns of police use and abuse of force. Such propositions are relevant as well to the development of intervention training and other effective control systems.

Another research area that looks promising is that of gender differences in officer responses, given systematic modifications (such as experiments with assignments varying by gender) of organizational constraints. This type of analysis would be an example of proactive organizational experimentation to test a plausible hypothesis: if one creates favorable reinforcing conditions, like greater emphasis in training on the use of interpersonal skills and a reward system that emphasizes successful resolutions of conflicts, female officers might be able to defuse conflict situations even better than male officers or would exercise a tempering influence on male officers. Similar experimental possibilities could be explored with other variables, including familiarity of officers with their beats or the race or ethnicity of the officer assigned to neighborhoods of varying ethnicity.

Estimating the Prevalence of Police Abuse of Force

As argued at some length by Adams (chapter 3) and by Geller and Scott (1992) and others, developing the capacity to estimate how often police use and misuse force is an important part of the foundation for understanding and controlling police-civilian violence (see also Ross 1994). The FBI and others regularly study how often, with what weapons, and (less frequently) why fatal and nonfatal assaults are made against police officers. The objective is the important one of better preparing officers to avert such threats.

Equally necessary is research on abuses of force by police, for such abuses not only harm civilians unjustly but also present the involved officers and their colleagues with career and other risks. Data collected and analyzed regularly will help reveal whether progress is being made over time and whether particular agencies have developed useful approaches that others may wish to emulate. Valid and reliable data on the incidence of police-civilian clashes can also undergird forecasts of future prevalence, which in turn can support strategic investments of resources in training, control systems, deployment, various officer safety and related support programs, community education, and other techniques to forestall the burdens imposed on communities and their police by brutality scandals (Ross 1994).[6] In times of national and local crisis—such as the Rodney King beating, the exposure of former Los Angeles cop Mark Fuhrman's invective and violence; the August 1992 Ruby Ridge, Idaho, shooting of a deputy U.S. marshal and the subsequent killing by federal agents of the son and wife of white supremacist Randy Weaver, or the 1993 Branch Davidian incidents in Waco, Texas, that took the lives of several federal agents and scores of David Koresh's followers—having reliable data on the frequency with which police use force responsibly and the frequency with which they abuse force can help convince those members of the public and of various interest groups who are willing to believe statistics that a notorious misuse of force was a rare exception to an otherwise competent departmental record.

A National Reporting System

One of the leading recommendations by contributors to this volume is the establishment of a reliable, efficient national reporting system (see especially chapter 3). Such a system would have to satisfy a number of requirements, including permitting police to:

1. monitor increases and decreases in their own use of force over time;
2. analyze and evaluate incidents in which force is used;
3. assess the impact of changes in strategy or tactics on the use of force;
4. compare the nature and frequency of use of force in their agency with the use of force in other agencies; and
5. explore organizational, operational, and environmental correlates of the use of force.

In addition, the . . . system would have to:

6. be applicable in agencies of all sizes;
7. contain mechanisms of audit and quality control; and
8. be compatible with practical operational considerations, needs, and limitations. (Klockars 1994: 2)

A national reporting system was mandated by Congress in the 1994 Violent Crime Control and Law Enforcement Act. Under the act, the system is intended "for research and statistical purposes," which include a review of trends. The Attorney General is enjoined to "acquire data about the use of excessive force by law enforcement officers" and to "publish an annual summary of the data" (Title XXI, Subtitle D, Sec. 210402). The availability of a periodic report card about the use of excessive force by law enforcement officers is an enticing prospect, provided we can place statistics into meaningful contexts that help us interpret them. Little is gained if a summary simply records that incident rates have increased in the Northeast but decreased in the Midwest, or that trends differ by size of department.[7] The identification of departments that have experienced increases in incident rates would be especially troublesome if information is not simultaneously available that tells us about factors that might account for the increases. A wide array of factors merits consideration, among them changes in crime rates, a rise in unprovoked assaults on officers,[8] intensification of police enforcement efforts, such as with narcotics crackdowns, variation in procedures for inventorying incidents, sharp increases in the number of sworn personnel,[9] and manifest decreases in sworn strength (Ross 1994: 6–7).[10]

The issue of methodological artifacts is particularly critical. It would be risky to examine trend data before the procedures for gathering and reporting the data have been standardized. Only then can we reasonably ensure that no agency is stigmatized because it has defined excessive force more generously than did other reporting agencies or was more conscientious about encouraging complaints or gathering statistics.

Given the controversy that could attend efforts to implement a national reporting system, however, care must be taken to ensure that questions about data quality and other procedural concerns are not deployed as a subterfuge by persons who oppose a reporting system per se. Those who think they are acting in the best interests of American policing and the public by trying to thwart the acquisition of knowledge about how to reduce police-community tensions do not advance the career interests of good police officers, police morale, or the capacity of communities to forge more trusting, cooperative relationships with their local police.

Although the 1994 Act requires collection and dissemination of data only on police misuse of force ("excessive force"), the Justice Department would be well advised to interpret its mission as one of providing the opportunity for police and other interested parties to get a full and accurate picture of the nature, frequency, and quality of police use-of-force decisions and the consequences of those decisions. This goal would presuppose collecting data on the proper use of police force as well as on the improper use. Only then would police be able to study the complex set of circumstances that surround successful and unsuccessful police tactics so that the infrequent but troublesome incidents involving poor use-of-force tactics can be further reduced.

An early desirable step in the development of a national reporting system on police use and abuse of force would be a conclave of representative departments that could consider details of implementation. Another step would be the provision of resources to make it possible for modestly endowed agencies to gather data called for by the reporting system. Most critically, police representatives should be consulted about what information they would like about other agencies to make sensible comparisons possible.

A use-of-force reporting system should try to cover a wide range of information relating to encounters between officers and civilians and actions taken by departments to reduce unjustifiable conflicts. Intervention-related information can help an agency to demonstrate, for example, that a reform introduced in year A produced a reduction in incident rates in year B. Other contextual information can help show whether any such reduction in year B was accomplished at the expense of other important objectives, such as officer safety, public feelings of security, and crime reporting or victimization rates.

The 1994 crime law specifies that the resulting system should "not contain any information that may reveal the identity of the victim or any law enforcement officer." This prohibition cannot be taken to mean that attributes of conflict participants not be reported, because such data would be essential to the research mission for which the system is created. A reporting system should be able to tell us, among other things, whether suspects were young or mature;[11] whether officers involved in incidents were experienced or inexperienced; whether an incident of apparently precipitous use of force occurred in a geographic area where police had frequently been ambushed or otherwise assaulted; and whether a particular kind of officer was disproportionately involved with a particular type of citizen.[12]

The restriction on data that may disclose the victims' or officers' identities also must not be interpreted to inhibit the acquisition of information relating to types of situations in which conflicts disproportionately arose. Such analyses, when conducted with the active involvement of insightful, experienced practitioners, can be helpful in devising better procedures, training, and other arrangements that improve policing and lessen its risks.

To be of maximal value to the police, a national reporting system must be based on information garnered from different sources. While police departments can supply incident-related data, one needs to draw on census information to describe neighborhoods in which incidents occur. While police can supply arrest data, others must track the dispositions of cases following arrest (at least until such a time when police departments decide that their crime prevention and law enforcement work could benefit from routinely compiling case outcome data and including affected officers in the dissemination loop). A reporting system needed for multilevel research must be omnivorous, multidextrous, and interdisciplinary.

The issues of how much and what sort of standardization of data a national system should require are sensitive ones. This sensitivity implies, among other things, that those expected to use the reporting system must have a hand in shaping, revising, and assessing it.[13] There should be as much standardization as it takes for data from one department to be comparable to those of another. Only a combination of sound theory, careful planning, and trial and error with a commitment to continual improvement will reveal how much standardization is required today and in the future.

Appropriate experts within and outside of departments should explain to the police profession the practical benefits of collecting different kinds of information. For instance, potential impediments to the use of specific police tactics may arise because of actual or apparent abuses of force. Use of stun guns to torture suspects into confessing or use of pepper spray for punishment of a nonresistant arrestee, for example, can remove these devices from the tool kits of all officers in the agency—and in other departments as well. Moreover, deaths following use of pepper spray (oleoresin capsicum) that at first seem linked to the chemical could hinder an agency's continued use of this weapon. Under such circumstances of actual or perceived misuse of force, police could draw on data about the normal, successful, legitimate use of such tactics to convince the public, politicians, and policymakers that the controversial incidents were aberrations or explainable on grounds other than police misconduct. (For instance, some studies suggest that post–pepper-spray deaths are attributable to "positional asphyxia" [Granfield et al. 1994; Connell 1994; *Law Enforcement News* 1995].)

Consulting participating agencies is essential because the categories of data to be included in a national reporting system must be those that the practitioner users of the system find helpful in understanding, defending, and, where needed, correcting their own operations. The financial underwriting of this process is essential, but the real incentive to those who contribute to a reporting system must be that they feel that what they and the nation can thereby learn is of value.

Improving Research Data

All data sources share the limitation that excessive force is an infrequent (hence, a low base rate) problem,[14] but some progress seems feasible in upgrading the quality of data. Improving data sources would enhance not only the quality of research but also the ability of a department to monitor the quality of its policing. Progress in record-keeping could be made both within a given department and on a regional and national basis. In creating centralized information banks, as the federal government was mandated to do in the 1994 Crime Act, it will be necessary also to accommodate the need for desirable local variations arising from policy preferences, research and development interests, union contracts, police officers' bills of rights (Leibig 1994), or other legal obligations. Improvements of records could include the following seven elements, all requiring action by police agencies, with technical assistance as needed from experts on management information systems, records, and other data systems: standardize procedures for the submission of civilian complaints, to make complaint data more valid and more comparable; introduce use-of-force reports where they are not already in place; improve the quality of arrest reports; record and computerize data relating to calls and field contacts so that incident rates can be calculated; ensure that departmental information systems are capable of combining data on incidents, officers, and suspects; devise methods for capturing not only individual-level and incident-level data but also problem-level data; and ensure that agency information systems can identify arrests by offense charged. These kinds of improvements are discussed below in turn.

1. *The standardization of procedures for the submission of civilian complaints, to make complaint data more valid and more comparable.*[15] Submitting complaints can be made easier and more enticing by decentralizing the process and simplifying it. Departments could also agree on publicity designed to invite aggrieved citizens to file complaints. If local police organizations wanted it, federal agencies

or police membership organizations could prepare sample language that police departments, at their discretion, could incorporate in public information campaigns.

As noted in chapter 3, among the reasons to standardize complaint submission procedures is that, as things stand, a community with a low complaint rate can have a high use-of-force department that discourages complaints. And, as noted earlier, a department with a high complaint rate may have relatively few abuses but be fastidious about identifying allegations. These possibilities make it difficult to draw inferences from differences in complaint rates between types of police departments or between different communities when one's excessive force data are confined to citizen complaints (Pate and Fridell 1993).

A related service quality-control issue that should be addressed by policymakers, mostly at local levels, is whether anonymous complaints will be accepted.[16] We believe the best practice (where permitted by law and union contract) is to accept anonymous complaints but to conduct investigations in a way that shows due respect for officers and clear awareness that false complaints can be used tactically by criminals to try to neutralize effective and honorable officers.[17] Police departments or other local government officials might also invest creativity and effort in urging satisfied citizens to "catch and report" officers doing a *good* job. Besides favorable reviews of crime control efforts, one could imagine such an invitation also eliciting citizen reports of officers who used force with commendable skill to avert greater harm and who exercised commendable restraint (see table 15.1).

As innovative procedures are adopted locally for the reception of citizens' complaints, research should ascertain whether the intended objectives are being achieved and whether there are unintended consequences that need to be addressed in future modifications. Research that explores the feasibility of standardized complaint reception procedures (as well as standardized approaches to the classification of complaints received and investigations completed) is an important foundation for developing multijurisdictional and national use-of-force reporting systems that enable responsible interagency comparisons.

2. Some departments have introduced *use-of-force reports,* and others should consider doing so.[18] The wide adoption of a force-reporting procedure would make it possible to conduct surveys that cover the gamut of force used (Ross 1994: 3). Pate and Fridell (1993: 153), for instance, complain that, "because of the lack of mandatory reporting for a number of types of force, a large number of agencies were unable to respond to [their] survey items requesting information regarding the number of times officers used the various types of force during 1991. Further, several agencies supplied data concerning types of force for which reporting was not mandatory. As a result, those data necessarily came from a voluntary subset of officers."

To be useful, such reports should include both narrative and checklist descriptions of encounters that are detailed enough to be coded and classified. To minimize the waste of police officers' valuable time and services, careful thought should be given to devising forms—paperless if possible—asking only for information whose utility can be justified by operational, training, and research and planning necessities. Once officers' reporting obligations are clarified, it would be desirable to find a way to make sure that reports are filed as required (Falcone 1994 reports that suburban Chicago officers underreport vehicle pursuits). Monitoring arrest reports is one possible solution. Others include providing timely and meaningful feedback to employees on the usefulness of their reports. As Multnomah County, Oregon, District Attorney Michael Shrunk put it at a conference in late 1995, for the change agent, "feedback is the breakfast food of champions."

3. *Improvement of the quality of arrest reports* is also desirable. This can be done through additional training, review, and feedback on issues of concern to the reporting officers. Narratives in arrest reports must become richer sources of information where they are currently sparse.[19] Where use-of-force reports are not used, arrest reports should include a requirement to note and describe any deployment of force. Departments might consider providing technical assistance, including transcription facilities for arrest reporting.[20]

4. Ideally, a department should consider *recording and computerizing data relating to calls and field contacts* so that incident rates can be calculated. Such data are also useful in assessments of productivity.[21] Any such police-civilian contact record system should be flexible enough, however, to accommodate the information needs of a department engaged in implementing a community- or problem-oriented policing strategy. The nature, frequency, and impetus for police-civilian contacts often are more varied with such a policing approach than under a more traditional incident-oriented mode of policing.[22]

5. Information systems in use by police departments should contain the capability of *combining data about incidents with officer and suspect characteristics* to allow a focus on problematic patterns. At minimum, arrests ought to be linkable to the shield number of involved officers so that arrest data can be retrieved for individual officers and groups of officers. Suspect-level data would help identify (or refute accusations about) patterns concerning abuse of force against particular civilians or classes of civilians. Such data might also point to categories of individuals who are most likely to challenge police authority or engage officers in physical altercations or patterns of use and abuse of force (and officer endangerment) in the course of addressing crime hot spots, high-rate offenders, or high-rate victims (see, e.g., Bieck et al. 1991: 78–79; Spelman and Eck 1989).

6. Information systems also should have the capability of *identifying arrests by offense charged*. This is particularly crucial for disaggregation purposes. For example, one ought to be able to separate out arrests made for resisting arrest or assault on officers or other charges (e.g., disorderly conduct) that have been found to be associated with use and abuse of force. As discussed by Locke in chapter 6,

prior studies suggest that it is disproportionately in police encounters with persons over less serious offenses that racial considerations may play an inappropriate role in the exercise of discretion to arrest or use force (see also chapter 2).

Problem Officers

Chapter 4 focuses on the violence-prone officer, and particularly on the officer for whom use of excessive force means force used more frequently than expected. Such officers, of course, may both use too much force and use it too often. The first research task that is illustrated in studies by the Christopher Commission is the nomination of problem officers through a procedure which is defensible, in the sense of being valid and reliable.

The most difficult questions to resolve are those that permit us to differentiate officers who must be sanctioned from those who are candidates for retraining (including participatory retraining).[23] The appropriate organizational responses to the range of circumstances depicted in table 15.1 will run the gamut from praise and press conferences honoring heroism to supervisory coaching to peer counseling to formal academy retraining to varying degrees of punishment. Some of the questions that bear on whether to retrain or punish officers are legal and have to do with the adequacy of documenting the charges, level of force used, and other matters.

But research can also inform the selection of various corrective interventions, particularly experimental approaches for "selling" retraining to officers as an employer-provided, skill-building benefit rather than as a minor humiliation meted out when fines, punitive transfers, termination of employment, or other discipline is not warranted. It is also important to experiment with modalities involved in training, variations in assignment, and follow-up and monitoring. Pre-training and post-training inventories of incidents through time series research is critical and must include comparisons with corresponding time series data for officers in equivalent assignments.[24]

Where interventions are targeted solely for officers seen as having behavior problems, it is also desirable to survey nonparticipating officers for knowledge of, and reaction to, interventions. A training effort that is supported by nonparticipants is most likely to have its impact reinforced and least likely to have its effects neutralized through locker-room influences.

Chapter 4 makes a case for peer involvement in retraining and for officer involvement in the research that is associated with retraining (as do other chapters, especially 8 and 10). The recommendation would be that officers participate in research of their own difficulties with violence (through guided self-study), try to invent responses to the problems they believe deserve attention, and evaluate the results of any interventions they can persuade their agencies to deploy. Such an approach affords at least two benefits. First and foremost, it holds considerable promise for reducing abuse-of-force problems. Second, it respects officers' motivations and competencies—a core value of community policing and problem-oriented policing.

This volume does not discuss at any length the nexus between community problem-solving and the reduction of unwanted officer-involved force incidents because there is not sufficient evidence as of the mid-1990s on the operational effects of these promising policing strategies.[25] But unless the central values of community problem-solving are honored in departmental responses to alleged abuse of force, the resulting mixed messages from police administrators will undermine the crime-control and the officer-control and protection objectives which the police departments pursue. Among the operating principles of an organizational culture consistent with community problem-solving are respect for officers' and other citizens' talents, reasonableness, trustworthiness, and need to feel appreciated (Geller and Swanger 1995). Not every police officer and member of the general public deserves such confidence and respect, but police leaders should run their organizations so that officers and communities are given the benefit of the doubt.[26]

Public Opinion and Use of Force

Issues of public opinion are considered in detail in chapter 5. In addition to the prospects for community policing to improve public appraisals of police, other questions deserving research arise concerning public opinion.

- Can reform efforts speak for themselves and percolate into experiences that inspire favorable attitudes? Or is opinion about policing mediated by gatekeepers—the media, politicians, civil rights and civil liberties groups, and others—who must be involved in reform?
- How can print media serve a reform-oriented chief, and what role can television and radio play? (New York-based communications specialist Tony Schwartz offers guidance that many police executives have found novel and practical; see, e.g., Schwartz 1973, 1983.)
- How can an angry community group serve a reform chief who feels captive to a tradition-bound union? (Moore and Stephens 1991a, 1991b)
- How can a reform-minded union capitalize on the support of a reform-minded community group or coalition of groups and the media to overcome the resistance of an antediluvian chief? (see chapter 10 and Schwartz 1983)
- How can progressive managers and progressive unionists collaborate in ways that a cynical public will not dismiss as collusions against the public interest?
- How much carryover is there from such public relations activities as Officers Friendly, police dogs, and "robots" in schools, to unscheduled activities that capture public attention, such as shootings or other injuries of suspects?

- How much carryover is there to potentially controversial incidents from such core public service activities as closing crack houses, catching serial rapists, and solving and preventing other crime and disorder problems?

The reason such questions matter is that the issue of how much enforcement and how much protection people demand is tied to the issue of what means the public accepts in the pursuit of its goals. The ambivalence people express toward oppression that is used in their ostensible defense is a powerful factor to be reckoned with. Strategic police decisions and individual police behavior cannot simply be dictated by public pressures and sentiments,[27] but community policing and problem-oriented policing require sensitivity to public opinion and sharing of the responsibility for decisions and actions by officers and the public. Moreover, although public views arguably are most relevant at the neighborhood level, the media make all members of a community—and, in outrageous or visually tantalizing enough cases, all the world—spectators and consumers of police-civilian encounters, no matter where they take place.

Race and the Use of Force

Why does the use of force by American police invite concerns about racially motivated conduct? Several possible reasons come to mind:

- the historic role of some police departments (and of individual officers in many departments) in enforcing de jure and de facto racism in the United States (Williams and Murphy 1990);
- the use of civil disobedience as a tactic by the civil rights and affiliated social reform movements;
- the fact that much urban crime in America involves members of minority groups as victims and perpetrators;
- the staffing of most police departments predominantly by white officers; and
- the reality that some police employees make racist remarks and a few go so far as to display their bigotry not only in words but in deeds.

Sometimes racial hatred or simple lack of familiarity with another's culture plays a role in police use and misuse of force. Pinning down how often this happens, except in the most unsubtle cases, is difficult to do—at least in a fashion that will be credible across diverse socioeconomic-political groups. Intentionally racist policing probably occurs less often than many people believe, yet it occurs more often than the American body politic can afford to tolerate, given the power of such conduct to trigger both overt riots and the "quiet" riots of despair and alienation observable in many ghetto neighborhoods. O. J. Simpson's acquittal of murder in 1995 drove a wedge between white and black America, and the bravado of detective Mark Fuhrman drove a nail in the coffin of the prosecution's case.

To bolster an environment of racial, cultural, or class insensitivity, an encounter need not even be bigoted in its own right. An illustration is the community's feelings of vulnerability to both the cops and the crackheads expressed in New Orleans after the Kim Groves killing in October 1994 (Nossiter 1994; Marcus 1995). Both the accused officer and the murder victim in the New Orleans case are African-American. But the treatment of lower-class blacks as if they are worthless human beings by anyone wearing a blue uniform feeds pre-existing perceptions that the police are selective in their dedication to serve and protect the public. A steady stream of low-level incivilities, roughness, disrespect, and disregard by police for the fear and criminal victimizations of neighborhood residents corrode a community's capacity to work with police constructively to reduce crime and disorder.

The police in many jurisdictions have made enormous progress over the past several decades in reducing the alienation between their personnel and community residents. But street officers see the gulf between what they *are* accomplishing and what they *might* accomplish if only they (or their colleagues) and minority community residents trusted and understood one another better (Steinhauer 1995; Sexton 1995). Because of the capacity of police use-of-force decisions to contribute positively or negatively to police-community rapport and collaboration against crime, disorder, and fear, police must strive continually for methods that allow them to do their difficult work in a way that maximizes the chances of improving race relations. This is not about being pleasant but about being effective.

In chapter 6, Locke comments, "What may appear as obvious or self-evident [concerning policing and bigotry] can, on careful analysis, turn out to be neither." This, he suggests, "forces those who are not content with unproven answers or unprovable propositions to continue probing the hard questions." Reiner (1992: 478–79), surveying police research in the United Kingdom, argues:

The problem in taking [statistical findings of differential treatment] as unequivocal evidence of discrimination is that the "legally relevant" variables are themselves connected to race. The likelihood of future offending, for instance, is taken as indicated by factors such as single-parent families, unemployed fathers, or being a latchkey child, all of which are themselves correlated with ethnic group. This points to the artificiality of trying to pursue an element of "pure" discrimination. Differential likelihood of offending and of being subject to police prejudice and discrimination are mutually reinforcing aspects of the structural position of groups at the bottom of the socio-economic hierarchy. It is this structural location that is the explanation of a vicious cycle of differential pressures leading to offending and differential risk of apprehension, each confirming the other. . . . The police are reproducers rather than creators of social injustice, though their prejudices may amplify it.

To be sure, some statistical research in the United States has been character-ized as supporting—and may, in fact, support—the proposition that the race of a suspect sometimes contributes to the decision to misuse force. Examples of such analyses include Fyfe's study of the Memphis Police Department and observa-tions on the patterns of offending by some New Orleans police officers (Fyfe 1982; Nossiter 1994).

While the weight of studies to date suggests that police enforcement decisions are not systematically driven by racist sentiments, Worden (chapter 2) found that even after controlling for the effects of various other factors, suspect race helped explain patterns of police use and abuse of force in the jurisdictions examined. For the reasons illuminated by Reiner, Worden does not assert that racist motivations drove these patterns of conduct, but he allows the possibility. If race plays some systematic role, then measures that reduce animosity and ignorance across racial lines—in police-civilian encounters and in society generally—could pay dividends in upgrading decision making by police in potentially violent encounters.

One must also keep in mind, however, that stereotyping can be reciprocal. The officer who intercepts a youth whom he sees as a typical black gang member who is probably engaged in drug trafficking may be seen by the youth as a typical ugly white cop intent on harassing citizens going about their business (see Browning et al. 1994). The officer is adversely reacted to, which confirms his stereotype and results in a decision to arrest (Lundman 1994). This move confirms the youth's worst expectations and causes him to resist arrest, which invites use—and abuse—of force by the police. This experience strengthens prior stereotypes and increases the chance that the next prophecies on all sides also will be self-fulfilling (see Wisby 1995 on Chicago youths' views of police).

The reason it may not be obvious that the composite stereotype held by the officer is a central part of the problem is because law-abiding, middle-class, mi-nority citizens occasionally are abused by officers, and these incidents, due to their visibility and dramatic attributes, are not recognized as being aberrant. We may better help responsible officials take corrective action if we can reveal the extent to which the misuse of force arises out of a sequence of erroneous assumptions by the officer about the civilian. These assumptions often may be grounded more in misperceptions of the civilian's actions and of the circumstances under which he or she is encountered than in the civilian's skin color.

Locke points out in chapter 6 that many minority citizens (among others) will never be convinced by statistical studies that suggest that officers do not discrimi-nate against minority suspects.[28] This may be true even if the studies are superior methodologically—and many, admittedly, are not. If such skepticism is likely to persist, researchers and policymakers would be well advised to regard anti-police sentiment and suspicion as a variable that has a life of its own. A starting place is that the adverse assumptions of minority citizens about police treatment of minority citizens need to be better understood. To what extent are these assumptions based on personal experiences? How much of the resentment is based on publicized examples like that of Rodney King, Malice Green, Kim Groves, or Mark Fuhrman? To what extent are sentiments reinforced by the media or through discussion in groups? What distinctions are drawn between police treatment of suspects and of citizens who are not suspects? To what extent is police behavior seen as a result of an overreadiness to regard people of color as suspects?[29] Is such overreadiness inferred from personal experience or secondhand accounts? Do minorities who are employed by police departments differ appreciably from other minorities in appraisals of officers' readiness to assume criminality based on skin color and other inappropriate factors?

Exploring other questions may afford a fuller understanding of the nature and derivation of viewpoints. How many minority citizens personally know individuals who are engaged in illegal activities? How do they regard these individuals? How many persons of color know individuals who have been victimized by minority-race offenders? How do the citizens feel police should go about locating and apprehending offenders? Do citizens feel that police are overzealous in their pursuit of offenders, insufficiently proactive, or both?

Does one's appraisal of the suitability of zealousness depend on one's prior victimization or particular interest in the outcome of an investigation? Do minority respondents' appraisals vary depending on the extent of "minority empowerment" in the local community? In jurisdictions where the minority citizenry harbors considerable resentment of the police, are attitudes toward the rest of local government the same—and, if not, what factors, such as the inherent obligation of the police to employ coercion, might account for any difference in view?

Studies that explore such questions are bound to find that responses are not homogeneous and that minority citizens are not of one mind in their reactions to police, any more than are other groups. Dialogue designed to reduce misunderstanding and programs designed to defuse tension may have to make provision for the complexity of the resentment that police misbehavior inspires and for divisions of views in minority communities.

One largely unexplored potential resource for helping police develop a comprehensive approach to fostering respect for cultural diversity is the American military. This may seem an ironic suggestion in light of the trend toward policing strategies and styles that are less militaristic (Geller and Swanger 1995). Nevertheless, several observers have noted that the military is one public institution that has made exemplary strides in combating prejudice and discrimination on the basis of race (although accomplishments in dealing with homophobia and sexual harassment seem considerably less impressive). Pulitzer Prize-winning author David K. Shipler (1992), in an opinion piece in the *New York Times*, wrote that the military uses four basic approaches to preventing and remediating racism within its ranks:

Command Commitment. Annual performance appraisals "include a judgment of the officer's or noncom's support for equal opportunity." Personnel have "gradually come to understand that a record of racial slurs and discrimination can derail a career."

Training. The Defense Equal Opportunity Management Institute (DEOMI), located at Patrick Air Force Base in Cocoa Beach, Florida, puts personnel from all branches of the armed forces through intensive multiweek, professionally facilitated encounter groups and workshops to prepare them to serve as Equal Opportunity Advisors in their respective units. In addition, every military recruit gets at least one hour of training on "race relations." This is a reduction from the training time devoted to this subject several years ago, but, as Shipler observes, it is still more than many police officers get.

Complaints and Monitoring. Equal opportunity advisors, after training at DEOMI, both receive complaints about racial and gender bias and proactively visit units throughout the armed services to inquire about the quality of race and gender relations. Shipler reports: "Surveys are done and informal discussions are held to take the temperature of racial tensions. This is practically unknown in police departments."

Promotions and Assignments. According to Shipler, "Although test scores tend to steer blacks toward some specialties like food service and supply, military promotion boards are under orders to strive for representative numbers of people from minority groups and women. The result has been uneven, but it has often meant that whites are supervised by blacks, which breaks down stereotypes" (1992: A15).

In the end, it may be, as Locke suggests in chapter 6, that one of the most productive and practical approaches to reducing the inappropriate influence of race in police use-of-force decisions (and the appearance of this problem) is to pursue essentially race-neutral methods for reducing police-civilian violence. If needless bloodshed can be averted across the spectrum of police encounters, problems of racism and perceptions of racism should also be reduced, because in many jurisdictions people of color represent a disproportionate segment of those with whom the police become engaged in potentially violent situations. Among the promising approaches to stemming police-civilian violence are several types of training initiatives.

Training Approaches

In chapter 8, James Fyfe deals with training as a vehicle for inculcating habits and attitudes that reduce the likelihood of excessive force being used by trainees and by those they influence. Several principles emerge as paramount from that chapter and other work in the field:

- Training must be realistic, nonartificial, and truthful.[30]
- Training must be tailored to the problems officers will encounter in their particular work environments. These problems pertain to: the community being policed; the staffing of the agency and its effects on officer deployment and workload; the reputation of the department for professionalism[31] and for sensitivity to community concerns (as well as the opportunities that reputation creates or forecloses for minimizing uses of physical force by police);[32] the sophistication, accessibility, and suitability of equipment that officers might use to restrain their use of force and other factors.[33]
- Training must guard against unintended messages that reinforce paranoia[34] and other subcultural themes.
- Training must be continuous.

The need for studies that enhance the effectiveness of training and monitor its impact is urgent, given that most conventional training research—which largely gauges academic success or failure or the trainee's feelings about training—does not tell us about the relevance of training to the prevention of violence. Five types of possible studies would be of practical value:

1. Reviews of incidents in which force is used to identify lessons about successful and unsuccessful tactics taught in training. Such lessons could be learned about key decisions that lead to or avert violence.
2. Use of focus groups, observation, and other techniques to compare how identical training content is conveyed using different modalities. Among the modalities worth assessing are live role-play skits, virtual reality simulations, lectures, discussion, self-paced individualized learning as opposed to group sessions, task-oriented training as distinguished from general preparatory training, and field-based rather than academy-based training.
3. Measures of officers' comprehension and retention of training content over time. This line of research could encompass the extent to which training content can be applied to actual situations (critical incidents). It could also study influences of peer pressure and supervision that undermine or bolster the information and skills imparted during training (see Geller and Swanger 1995: 90–94).
4. Measures of attitudes and changes in attitude that are relevant to the deployment of violence (see also chapter 9).
5. Tracking of the performance of trainees who have been variously influenced by training or have been exposed to systematic variations in training content. Such studies could include longitudinal research tracing the impact of "refresher" training or changes in training content instituted at known points in time.

Fyfe also recommends that, in evaluating the effectiveness of violence-reduction training, it is crucial to focus more on what officers subsequently do in the field than on how their potentially violent encounters turn out. "To do otherwise," Fyfe argues, "is to overlook inappropriate conduct until it results in disaster and to discourage officers whose best and most appropriate efforts were unable to prevent violence because of decisions made by their adversaries." Fyfe concludes that the experience of officers can be used and systematized in designing training programs and that experienced officers can also be involved in training research and internal consultation.

Conflict Management Training

Conflict management training enhances officers' oral communication skills as the primary tools for controlling potentially violent people.[35] Naturally, nonviolent tactics will not always work, and police must be competently trained in how and when the panoply of physical coercive techniques should be employed out of necessity.

One popular training program that attempts to strengthen officers' proficiency in staying calm under potentially stressful circumstances and in generating voluntary compliance from difficult people is "verbal judo" (Crime Control Digest 1992; see also Jamieson et al. 1990: 24; Krier 1990; Thompson 1983; Verbal Judo Institute, n.d.; Reyes 1992). Although the "judo" terminology may appeal excessively to officers' combative tendencies, the messages delivered in this training are consistent with the literal translation of the word judo as "the gentle way" (Grossman 1994).

Another promising conflict management tactic entails recognizing and, in appropriate cases (Muir 1977), reducing the fear that officers arouse in suspects. A related point is that citizens need convincing reassurance that they will not be physically retaliated against—especially not by the police (Nossiter 1994)—if they officially report officers who seem out of line.

Tactical conflict management or "violence reduction" exercises have been developed in New York City, Chicago, Dade County (Florida), Tampa, and many other jurisdictions.[36] These teach officers through role playing how to control a potentially violent encounter and how to de-escalate rather than exacerbate tensions between themselves and their clientele. These tactical exercises allow officers safely to experiment with a variety of techniques to reduce the risk of violence in dangerous encounters (see Fyfe 1978, 1989a; Margarita 1980a: 71; Margarita 1980b: 229; Geller 1986). Not all officers will attain the same level of proficiency in violence reduction, but through opportunities to explore their strengths and weaknesses safely, officers will gain a "working knowledge of their skill limitations" (Schofield 1990: 77) and will learn to overcome some deficiencies and to compensate for those they cannot change.

A common theme in many violence-reduction and officer survival training programs is to help officers devise safe ways of approaching the scenes of possible confrontations, making maximum possible use of cover, concealment, communication skills, and other tactics.[37] Fyfe (1989a) has hypothesized that reductions in violence between the police and civilians will come primarily from improvements in officers' *approaches* to (i.e., entry into) potentially violent encounters, rather than from any changes in the officers' actions *during* the encounter (see also Hayden 1981; Scharf and Binder 1983; Bayley and Garofalo 1989: 20). By focusing on officer decisions made prior to arrival in the immediate presence of the subject, trainers and analysts have begun over recent years helpfully to debunk the myth of the "split-second decision." This myth or, as Fyfe has called it, the "split-second syndrome," holds that the only key decisions within the control of most police officers in most potentially violent confrontations will be those that can be made in an instant. While much of the discussion of split-second decisions has centered on averting needless uses of deadly force by police, many principles that have emerged have direct application to the control of nonlethal uses of force as well. The concept of the split-second decision overlooks the string of decisions that an officer can and typically does make—albeit sometimes unconsciously—in advance of any decision to use force. However, officers may be genuinely unaware of choices they are making instinctively, based on their training, or for other reasons. Officers may also not be accustomed to conceptualizing a use-of-force incident as beginning at the moment when it was only a potentially violent encounter.

Among the most important debunking of the myth of the split-second decision is work by Scharf and Binder (1983), who characterized five decision phases in a potential or actual deadly force encounter: anticipation; entry and initial confrontation; dialogue and information exchange; final frame decision; and aftermath (see also Geller 1985a: 157–58). Geller and Scott (1992) have pointed to another phase involving nonlethal tactics between the dialogue/information exchange and final frame decision points. Much more work needs to be done by researchers and innovative police trainers to explore how abuse of force by police can be averted through examination of and experimentation with tactics in pre-confrontation stages of potentially violent police-civilian encounters.

Reiss (1980) recommended involving supervisors in critical decisions that would shape police responses so that decisions to use serious force need not be made in a split second (also see Binder and Scharf 1980: 116–19; Fyfe 1986). Parallel developments concerning the control of high-speed pursuits have occurred in many departments, which have required that supervisors participate, via radio communication, in the decision whether to continue or cease a high-speed chase (see Alpert 1987; Alpert and Anderson 1986; Fyfe 1989b; Alpert and Fridell 1992). Another activity in which there may be potential for violence reduction through supervisory involvement is stakeouts. Some agencies have been criticized for allegedly lying in wait for armed offenders, allowing them to menace or even injure their crime victims, and then engaging the culprits in gunfights as they attempt to flee the scene (see, e.g., Freed 1989; Stolberg 1990; Connelly 1992).[38]

Whether an intervention is called conflict management training, violence-reduction training, or officer-survival training, the purpose is to help officers handle potentially difficult people with appropriate levels of physical force. The anticipated payoff is a reduction in problems that impede effective policing, unjustly harm members of the public, and threaten police careers.

Intervention Training

Another related training development aims to harness peers to help officers who are at risk of losing their self-control. The objective is that the officers at risk regain their composure and avoid using force inappropriately. Sometimes called intervention training, this development has roots in work done over the past several decades by such scholars as Ervin Staub on "bystanderism," a concept that describes the role of spectators to injustice who intervene to attempt to stop it (see, e.g., Staub 1989).[39]

The Rodney King beating on March 3, 1991, provided a powerful stimulus for efforts to design and provide intervention training. In the wake of the incident, the Sacramento Police Department developed simulation training in which the encounter was replicated and officers were guided on how to intervene to stop the swinging batons and gratuitous kicks. On August 27, 1991, the Los Angeles Police Commission amended the department manual to clarify that officers are required "to report and intercede if a colleague is involved in misconduct" (*Crime Control Digest* 1991: 9). Such mandates, to be effective, must be supported by how-to intervention training. This kind of training helps trainable, reasonably proficient officers (column B in table 15.1) to excel (column C). One hopes as well that it can help upgrade deficient work (column A) to proficient and beyond.

Another organization that made some effort to design intervention training is the Joliet, Illinois, police department. There, at the request of then-chief Dennis Nowicki, a mostly first-line officer committee brainstormed how to develop training to help officers help their colleagues in potentially aggravating encounters. When this design task was viewed through the eyes of rank-and-file officers, it was conceived not as a top-down control program but as a buddy system in which officers would help one another to avoid blowing their cool and maybe their careers. A planning challenge considered important was devising methods of nonverbal communication between officers. The point was that, without calling the suspect's (and potential future plaintiff's) attention to the problem that an officer may be on the verge of losing self-control, a colleague could remind the officer to repress his or her aggression.

Intervention training helps achieve several goals: minimizing harm to civilians and officers in potentially violent encounters; protecting officers' careers and police departments' reputations; avoiding civil liability; and promoting long-established legal obligations for officers who witness colleagues' misdeeds to intervene and enforce agency rules and criminal laws prohibiting assault and battery.[40] "It is now well settled law," a police legal advisor has written, "that a police officer who fails to intervene to prevent a constitutional violation may be held liable under 42 U.S.C. section 1983. The leading case followed by every circuit hearing this issue is *Byrd v. Brishke*, 466 F.2d 6 (7th Cir. 1972)" (Spector 1992: 8).

Because the resurgence of administrative interest in intervention training was stimulated by the beatings of Rodney King and others, the facts of *Byrd v. Brishke* are noteworthy. Taken as accurate for purposes of the decision, the plaintiff's allegations were "that he was surrounded by approximately a dozen Chicago police officers and struck repeatedly. Because he could not identify the individual officers who struck him, the plaintiff's theory of liability was that even if the officers didn't participate in the beating, they should be held liable for 'negligently or intentionally failing to protect the plaintiff from others who did violate his rights by beating him in their presence' " (Spector 1992, citing the ruling at p. 10). The court concurred. Later case law has clarified that "an officer's mere presence at the scene of a constitutional violation will not be sufficient to prove liability. The officer must have knowledge of or deliberate indifference to the action that violates constitutional rights. *Masel v. Barrett*, 707 F. Supp. 4 (D.D.C. 1989); *Wilson v. City of Chicago*, 707 F. Supp. 379 (N.D. Ill. 1989). In an excessive force case, an officer will be held liable if he was present when the plaintiff was beaten or knew that such force was being used and failed to stop the officers from using such force. *Peterson v. Dept. of Navy*, 687 F. Supp. 713 (D.N.H. 1988). A plaintiff must also prove that the officer had a realistic opportunity to prevent the use of force" (Spector 1992: 8).

A more recent federal district court decision in Wisconsin underscores earlier case law on the topic. An arresting Milwaukee officer, after transporting an unruly arrestee to the local jail, saw but failed to prevent her partner from beating the prisoner in the jail elevator. She was held liable for ignoring her duty to stop other officers from punishing an individual in her presence (*Diebitz v. Arreola*, 834 F. Supp. 298, 1993; see case description in *National Bulletin on Police Misconduct* 1994a). State courts also have held officers liable for failing to intervene to stop physical abuse of a prisoner by fellow officers (e.g., *Commonwealth v. Adams*, 624 N.E. 2d 102 [Massachusetts, 1994], summarized in *National Bulletin on Police Misconduct* 1994b).

Not only is civil liability a possibility for officer-spectators, but "an officer may be arrested under 18 U.S.C. sections 241 and 242 for failure to prevent a constitutional violation, *United States v. McKenzie*, 798 F.2d 602 (5th Cir. 1985)" (Spector 1992: 8). This was the basis for the federal prosecution of the LAPD sergeant charged with allowing his subordinates to violate Rodney King's civil rights (Reinhold 1992).

Studying and Shaping Police Attitudes about Use of Force

The public and framers of public policy do not always seem to appreciate that police officers are thinking individuals and not robots who can be programmed for unreflective behaviors. Police researchers and administrators must pay attention to the attitudes that officers hold on a variety of issues that affect the propriety of use-of-force decisions.

There are commonalities between research about civilian attitudes toward police use of force (chapter 5) and the studies, discussed by Lester in chapter 9, of police officers' attitudes toward use of force. Studies that compare civilian and officer attitudes using the same scales or other research tools might be devised by the police and civilian participants in "citizens' police academies" and then administered to representative samples of the two populations.

A type of instrument that has proved particularly valuable for research on police attitudes is a critical incident inventory, in which officers are asked how they would respond to a set of hypothetical situations. This approach is helpful because it partly bridges the gap between attitudes toward excessive force in the abstract and behavior on the street. In studying officer attitudes it is also important to explore how relevant attitudes develop over time and what sorts of experiences enter into the formation and modification of attitudes.

Another question that merits attention is whether respondents who favor aggressive tactics differ from other respondents. An example of a finding is that officers who are relatively tolerant of excessive force see more danger in police work, are more oriented toward bread-and-butter issues (see chapter 10), and are more inclined to socialize with colleagues.[41]

An important question is whether officers might be willing to report other officers who use excessive force, or whether they stand ready to take other action that discourages such behavior. A second, related question is whether the justifications for use of excessive force that are offered by perpetrators are accepted by other officers. A third question is what kinds of considerations would officers weigh in deciding whether abuse of force is a serious enough problem to justify violating rank-and-file norms of peer solidarity (such as the "code of silence"). Among other things, officers might consider whether they see a connection between colleagues' mistreatment of suspects and their own future safety in potentially violent encounters. The dangers to officers in subsequent incidents might grow if suspects, enraged or afraid due to stories they have heard about police brutality, become "cop fighters," and if bystanders, who could assist an officer in need (at least by calling 911 for backup), decline to offer such help.

Research could also probe the relative acceptability and effectiveness in reducing police-civilian violence of two divergent procedures: those that ask officers to break the code of silence by identifying coworkers needing assistance and procedures that invite officers to intervene quietly to prevent abusive force without ever officially notifying the organization that a coworker reached the brink of misconduct. Officer estimates of what other officers think about the abuse of force may also be of practical importance because some estimates can discourage officers from expressing their concerns about uses of force in public. The phenomenon is that of pluralistic ignorance, which consists of a liberal majority laboring under the misapprehension that most people's views are hard-bitten and cynical (Toch and Klofas 1984).[42] The possibility of pluralistic ignorance among police is reinforced by the finding in some studies that officers often privately express disdain for perpetrators of excessive force.

Studies can confirm that attitudes toward efforts to control excessive force are independent of attitudes about excessive force. Officers who disdain both excessive force and control measures may view particular control methods as onerous, ineffective, counterproductive, inequitably applied, or a chink in the armor of officer autonomy. Or officers may distrust those who have proposed the controls, such as candidates for local political office.

It is important to enlist officers who disapprove of unprofessional conduct in initiatives to discourage such behavior. To do so, one must find ways of intervening that these officers see as fair and effective. One must also involve the officers in the enactment of the interventions. Sometimes, officers may see methods as meritorious because the rank-and-file were allowed to participate in framing the programs rather than because police managers have struck some inherently ingenious balance among competing interests. The prediction would be that one's degree of participation in or "ownership" of processes and decisions affects one's perception of their legitimacy.

Police Unions and the Police Culture

Many efforts to reduce police abuse of force over the years have proceeded from the articulated or implicit assumption that rank-and-file officers' associations are inherently opposed to interventions that upgrade the quality of police use-of-force decisions. Kelling and Kliesmet in chapter 10 hypothesize that one reason for rank-and-file resistance to change is that unions have a stake in bureaucracy, with its legalistic or authoritarian approach to controlling misbehavior. Moreover, because they are committed to represent or defend members accused of misconduct, it is difficult for unions (and their membership) to collaborate with administrators in addressing use-of-force challenges.

Chapter 10 details responses to a minisurvey suggesting that unions currently advise members to follow rules about use of force, while expressing reservations about the arbitrariness of these rules. The survey also shows that unions complain that officers have no input in the formulation of policy but assert that this organizational problem is not the union's business. Facts such as these about union positions point up logical inconsistencies that plausibly could be addressed through open review and discussion. Police unions have very good reasons (reviewed in chapter 10) to be concerned about abuses of force and to become party to the solution instead of exacerbating the problem of unprofessional conduct.

Among the practical recommendations offered by Kelling and Kliesmet is that modern police departments should resurrect appropriate versions of the Berkeley Police Department's Friday Crab Club. At this weekly meeting, primarily rank-and-file officers and the agency's august chief, August Vollmer, reviewed with candor and a spirit of mutual assistance highlights and lowlights of the police work they had done the prior week. The meeting was a forerunner by several decades of the sort of peer assessment and peer retraining mounted successfully in Oakland in the late 1960s (Toch and Grant 1991). Some police executives whom we briefed on Vollmer's Friday Crab Club expressed enthusiasm about trying a variation on the approach; others voiced skepticism that liability-conscious officers would be willing to relate candidly their successes and difficulties in such a forum. Still other executives were reluctant to emulate Vollmer's empowerment of officers to participate in constantly assessing and revising their work methods.

If a police administrator takes seriously the unleashing of human potential—officers' and civilians'—that lies at the core of community policing and problem-oriented policing, he or she should find little to fear in a group like the Friday Crab Club. Indeed, such a discussion group would be virtually indistinguishable from the rank-and-file staffed "problem advisory groups" established by a number of departments implementing problem-oriented policing (Couper and Lobitz 1991). Concerns about liability exposure—if these are serious—could be addressed by competent police legal advisors.[43] By "competent" we mean lawyers who are equipped to and allowed to play a problem-solving role, helping police executives figure out how to accomplish goals, rather than simply warning about potential obstacles.

The energizing effects of showing officers respect by inviting them to describe what works and what doesn't and to think about ways of improving their policing methods have so much potential to enhance work motivation and to strengthen police service capacity that high priority can justifiably be given to removing administrative or legal barriers that inhibit the development of peer assistance programs (Geller and Swanger 1995).[44]

Administrative Monitoring and Responses to Misconduct

Perez and Muir (chapter 11) cite three attributes—integrity, legitimacy, and learning—that distinguish most defensible procedures for monitoring police misconduct. Integrity involves attainment of intended purposes, legitimacy concerns the review process's reputation among stakeholders, and learning has to do with the impact of the process on future officer conduct. Research can gauge the extent to which a review body demonstrates and enhances these attributes. A quality review system will invite and attract complaints and will investigate them dispassionately and thoroughly. It will also arrive at appropriate and defensible dispositions that are considered just by all interested parties—including complainants, the public, rank-and-file officers, their union leaders, police managers, local government officials, and the media.

Review processes also aim to guide future behavior via externally motivated compliance, officers' internalization of department rules, and effective anticipation and prevention of use-of-force problems.

Surveys that explore learning effects can gauge perceptions of the review process, the behavior that the process reviews, and the officers who are disciplined or retrained. Issues to explore concerning the scope, reputation, and impact of administrative review systems include:

1. whether the systems can address misbehavior that is patterned or habitual, in the sense that some officers have special difficulties, which they manifest over and over again;
2. whether officers who are suspected of using excessive force acquire a good or bad reputation among their peers, supervisors, neighborhood groups, and civil rights and civil liberties organizations;
3. whether the review process is seen as one that distinguishes between good and bad officers;
4. whether disciplining is viewed as discouraging productivity;
5. whether officers who have been disciplined garner sympathy or support from other officers; and
6. whether the process is seen as excessively legalistic or politically tainted.[45]

Other research can include actual behavior inventories, such as changes in arrest patterns following actions of the review body, or changes in the way it operates.

The achievement of a review system's intended goals is the most difficult area to research. This is primarily because assessment may require normative judgments about the quality of monitoring and adjudication procedures and of dispositions. A review process can be partly described by gathering statistics about numbers of complaints; numbers of actions taken (witnesses interviewed, hearings held, etc.); duration of proceedings; energy, person-hours, and expense consumed by the process; and types of disposition. Such inventories can be supplemented with observations and interviews of staff assigned to the monitoring process. However, summaries of findings that rate the process as high or low in integrity presuppose independent criteria of justice, accuracy, and other dimensions of quality that are evaluative in nature. Absent a test of the system using bogus cases of clearly right or wrong conduct, it is difficult to conceive of a methodology for assessing the quality of the system that will avoid the problem of normative judgments. The most defensible way of arriving at such judgments might be to use multidisciplinary expert panels to evaluate the soundness of different review mechanisms. One can also think in terms of minimal standards that cut across reviewing bodies. One prerequisite for any fair and effective system of conduct review is the specification in advance of the performance standards to which employees will be held. This includes reasonably clear policy statements, given meaning through training that relates the policies to the kinds of problems officers will encounter in their daily work.

Part of the reason policy, supervision, monitoring, and other systems have heretofore shown limited effectiveness when directed at lower-level (i.e., non-deadly) uses of force is because such incidents are hard to predefine in policy directives and because transgressions are relatively difficult to establish and document. To counter the detectability challenges involved in dealing with nonlethal force abuses, several contributors to this volume have suggested that departments could experiment with varying degrees of rank-and-file involvement in the monitoring and disciplining process, up to and including the use of peer review panels. This sort of suggestion invites experimentation that includes systematic variation of monitoring and control procedures within and across departments, as well as comparisons of outcomes. Perez and Muir recommend as the best practical approach what they term the civilian monitor system (see also Perez 1994 and Kerstetter 1985). The civilian monitor approach retains the strength of internal investigations and gains public credibility through periodic audits of the quality and integrity of the process by outsiders who are trusted by the community and police alike.

Toward Procedures that Foster Justice for All

In chapter 12, Wayne Kerstetter discusses a procedural justice approach to dispute resolution—treating a complaint of excessive force as a dispute between the complainant and the accused officer(s)—that engages the disputants actively in the presentation of evidence and the understanding of dispositions. The aim of this model of dispute resolution is to maximize the degree to which the disputants see the process as just—and the outcomes as justly derived—regardless of who prevails. Procedural justice research is concerned with complainants, witnesses, accused officers, and so forth and explores the extent to which they see the process as fair and responsive. Such research suggests that active involvement of affected parties enhances the perception of fairness and an approach which fixes the problem rather than the blame can increase satisfaction with the outcome (see also Bianchi 1994). The approach offers opportunities for studies that gauge the reactions of participants to systematic variations in process and outcome.

Given existing variations in procedures used for monitoring police behavior and given the large numbers of administrative complaints filed and their dispositions, a quasi-experimental research design might be used. It would permit follow-up studies in jurisdictions that offer review system participants different opportunities for involvement and that present them with systematically different outcomes. Interviews could take place contemporaneously, which assumes that research teams would have to be fielded on short notice. This instant mobilization strategy has been used in such areas as disaster research. An alternative would be a coordinated, guided self-study model, in which several departments can follow the same procedure (arrived at by consensus) for doing the requisite interviewing.[46]

The potential inherent in procedural justice approaches is to significantly increase citizen satisfaction and officer satisfaction with police complaint review systems (which neither audience generally holds in very high regard), regardless of which party prevails in the adjudicative process. The ripple effect of trust and satisfaction or distrust and hostility spreading from citizen and officer disputants throughout communities and the department deserves attention from police administrators and local government officials. A procedural justice variation on current approaches may help, even if indirectly, to increase citizen trust and the willingness to collaborate with police against neighborhood crime problems. The opposite has been learned as well. Many citizens in New Orleans concluded, after brutality witness Kim Groves was allegedly murdered on orders from the accused officer, that it does not pay to call the police (Nossiter 1994; Marcus 1995).

Studying, Modifying, and Using Legal Remedies

The promise of resolving certain controversies and concerns over police use of force through nonadversarial or relatively informal processes does not, of course, eliminate the need for adequate formal legal remedies when egregious wrongs have been committed. Civil and criminal court remedies are the least desirable and last resort for controlling abuses that will not yield to officer self-control, peer control, supervisory control, and administrative policy and review systems. Still, it is necessary to consider how, for appropriate cases, these formal legal remedies can be used more effectively.

In chapter 13 Cheh deals with the judicial review of police misconduct, noting that "criminal prosecutions and other kinds of lawsuits have not played a major role in addressing the problem of excessive force by the police" (see also Robinson 1992). The precise role that such lawsuits have played—and will continue to play—is open to empirical inquiry. Studies might explore the impact of both specific litigation and litigation (or the threat of litigation) in general. It is almost axiomatic in police circles that policy decisions are heavily driven by concerns about litigation; specifically, many officers ascribe such concerns to their superiors. Police survey research can explore the extent to which litigation and threat of litigation are seen as factors in determining police leadership decisions. It can also examine the extent to which police managers and officers claim to take the threat of litigation into account in arriving at decisions.

Another set of issues meriting research includes whether officers' arrest patterns change in the wake of use-of-force court decisions that apply to their department; whether such rulings have reinforcing effects on rates of complaints; and whether and in what ways the judicial outcomes influence the initiation of additional lawsuits. It may be desirable to classify the court rulings and the litigation experiences on several dimensions: the prevailing party, the severity of any criminal or civil penalty imposed on the losing party, and the "transaction costs" associated with the litigation. Such costs include the duration of litigants' uncertainty over the outcome; litigation expenses; adverse publicity for the litigants and their families, friends, and coworkers; and disruption of normal community and departmental functioning.

The incidence of lawsuits itself may be profitably studied. If the numbers of excessive force complaints generated by different departments are large enough and sufficiently discrepant, it may be possible to isolate correlates of differences in the number (and rate) of initiated suits. But such research cannot be conducted until a means is developed for identifying with reasonable accuracy the number of criminal and civil cases brought against police officers for misuse of force and the array of outcomes in various jurisdictions. The database must also permit calculation of rates for numbers of officers and civilians over time and thus permit sophisticated time series research relating rates of lawsuits to antecedent events and tracking the impact of lawsuits on the police and the community.

Such research could study the value of litigation authorized by federal civil rights statutes (including "pattern and practice" suits permitted under the 1994 Crime Act) to explore and stem police misconduct. One possible effect of such suits might be to promote intervention training, by which officers learn techniques for helping colleagues control their impulses to use improper force. It could also appraise the exercise and impact of a federal "backstop" role, where the Justice Department attempts to stem police abuse of force tolerated by local authorities. If the federal backstop is deployed in cases other than the headline grabbers, however, there must be a national reporting system that reveals, through trends in numbers of complaints and other methods, whether local authorities are taking responsible actions to correct problems that surface in legitimate allegations of abuse.

A sufficiently powerful federal intervention to redress local abuses of force might garner the needed information by, among other techniques, attaching conditions to federal grants.

Any federal remedies—if they are to be of lasting value and not create as many problems as they solve—should be cast as part of a well-conceived, comprehensive program of federal assistance to state and local police agencies. One goal of such a comprehensive support program would be to help police reduce the corrosive effects of abusive officer conduct so that good police and communities can more effectively collaborate against crime, disorder, and fear.

Searching Globally for Insight and Solutions

Efforts by countries other than the United States to reduce the use of excessive force by their police (chapter 14) have included instituting new systems for collecting data about the use of force by officers and new procedures for controlling the problems that involve civilian input. Of particular value may be studies of the design and establishment of democratic policing in newly emerging democracies around the world (Ross 1994). In almost every democratization effort outside this country, the prior tradition of policing was characterized by systematic brutality of a sort that would shock most Americans. Police assassination squads, some employing private citizens as the assassins, are emblematic of the atrocities (Lewis 1995; Chevigny 1995). A collaborative exploration in 1995-96 by the Department of State and the Justice Department's National Institute of Justice into the principles and techniques by which policing fosters—or forestalls—democracy around the globe promises to contribute valuable information.

Despite significant differences in the nature and extent of police misconduct problems in many other countries and in the United States, some of the corrective techniques used by change agents abroad may be instructive to ongoing American professionalization efforts. Offensive practices abroad may be a reminder of how American police and community leaders must not, despite the pressures of a fearful public and guileful politicians, let crime control and fear reduction ends justify antidemocratic means. Finally, the dismal state of affairs elsewhere may be of some solace to those patriotic Americans who, constructively, are frustrated at the pace of progress here and are willing to lend a helping hand.

NOTES

1. The precise moment when force can be de-escalated or ended may be a matter of reasonable professional disagreement and usually will depend on the situation and officer competencies and resources.

2. We use the term *overseers* advisedly. Monitoring behavior is the traditional role of police supervisors and middle managers. Community problem solving and other strategic changes in police roles, missions and methods seek to reduce the counterproductive aspects of the overseer function and strengthen the coaching role for police bosses (see Kelling and Bratton 1993; Geller and Swanger 1995).

3. In an interview, Klockars made clear that the thrust of his proposal is not to expand the scope of punishable police conduct but to expand efforts to help police pursue excellence: "The whole problem in police agencies is that their approach toward the use of force

is largely punitive, largely focused toward keeping police officers from violating those low standards, rather than encouraging them to work in ways that highly skilled police officers do to minimize the use of force" (Rosen 1994: 12).

4. Cell 4C in Table 15.1—the highly skilled officer who frequently is required to use moderate or serious force—represents a talented officer doing the best he or she can under circumstances that necessitate violent interventions. Reducing the frequency of force used in such situations by such officers could require a variety of strategic and/or tactical break-throughs. These innovations may lie in the realms of policy; procedure; deployment; less-than-lethal weaponry; communication skills; incapacitation of offenders whose own criminal violence disproportionately necessitates violence even from very talented officers; and enforceable negotiated agreements to reduce violence between police and organized crime-prone groups such as drug-dealing street gangs.

5. Intervention training is discussed below (see also Geller and Scott 1992: 53, 218, 332–33, 408).

6. Ross (1994: 4–5) argues that useful forecasts of the rate of police-civilian violence can be based on trends in five basic factors accounting for police-civilian interactions. Police engage citizens, proactively or reactively, he notes, in order to "question, help, charge, intimidate, and arrest" them. "It follows that the greater the potential for questioning, helping, charging, intimidating, or arresting, the higher the number and intensity of" what he terms "proactive or reactive violent police-citizen interactions." And, "as the interaction between police officers and citizens moves from questioning to arresting there is a higher probability of" these violent incidents. "Thus, one must identify the factors which will increase these five precipitants if one is to have a reasonable prediction of the future probability of police violence."

7. Related difficulties are manifest in the FBI's annual report *Law Enforcement Officers Killed and Assaulted*. This document provides helpful basic data on the incidence of police victimization but presents only minimal demographic data with which to interpret changing patterns and offers virtually no analysis or guidance on which of several possible interpretations might be the soundest (Geller and Scott 1992). To be fair, the FBI has done separate studies from time to time of the ways in which police are slain, and it has analyzed the available information for ideas to better protect officers, as for example in the 1992 report *Killed in the Line of Duty: A Study of Selected Felonious Killings of Law Enforcement Officers*.

8. Unprovoked assaults might be prompted by street gangs encouraging "cop fight-ing" as part of the gang initiation ritual.

9. Some departments will experience relatively rapid growth of their sworn ranks as a result of the 1994 Crime Act's "100,000 cops on the beat" program. Although a crime-weary nation obviously hopes that great good will be accomplished by the proposed 20 percent enhancement of local police forces, still it must be recognized that, absent proper safeguards, more officers on the beats are more officers available to engage in beatings.

10. Police officers who are demoralized by their department's retrenchment relative to other forces in the region may succumb to frustration and cynicism that in turn leads to intemperate encounters and precipitous or unnecessary resort to coercive methods (Ross 1994: 6–7). *Perceived* understaffing (for there is little validated scientific basis for determin-ing the right number of officers for a given jurisdiction) could also lead to other conditions that might exacerbate abuse-of-force problems. One of these conditions could be official agency adoption of unduly offensive or coercive methods, technologies, and procedures thought to be cost-effective ways of restoring the "tactical edge" to officers outnumbered by criminals (p. 6). Another condition might be increased militancy by unions and other employee associations. While such militancy might be directed at prodding management to accelerate adoption of the kinds of officer safety and other recommendations made here

(see chapter 10), thus far the track record generally has been otherwise, and some believe the prognosis for improvement is bleak (e.g., Ross 1994: 10).

11. Conventional wisdom would suggest that suspects engaged in potentially violent encounters with police will almost invariably be youthful. There have been a number of highly publicized, albeit probably aberrant incidents, in which elderly, possibly deranged or suicidal individuals have been injured in violent confrontations with police. Bennett (1989) predicts that the me-first baby boomers will become the next millennium's "geriatric delinquents," motivated to criminal adventure because at their age they will have nothing to lose (see also Ross 1994: 15). Such predicted changes in the profile of police adversaries underscore the need for a reporting system to document the suspects' ages.

12. Race and ethnicity data on both officers and the civilian participants in use- and abuse-of-force incidents, among other information, are necessary in order to shed more light on the perennially debated question of whether bigotry taints criminal justice decisions. The mandated national reporting system will not end such debates. Accurate information about whether bigoted prejudgments influence police treatment of individuals is necessary both to correct any such problem and to defend the police against false accusations. It would be important that representatives of police management and rank-and-file groups, public interest groups, civil rights and civil liberties organizations, taxpayers' associations, and the appointed and elected local public officials to whom police report be consulted and really listened to during the design phase.

13. If the system is credible and beneficial, senior and middle managers in police agencies around the nation are more likely to insist that their staffs submit complete, accurate, and timely information to the federal data repository. It may also become necessary to link some federal grant funds to compliance with reporting obligations to help ensure a sufficient level of compliance. Given the ability of police abuses of force to undermine a department's best efforts at community policing and problem-oriented policing, there is some conceptual sense in making compliance with the national reporting system a standing condition of the dispersal of federal funds to support adoption and assessment of community policing.

14. The frequency with which police abuse force, perhaps especially lower-level force, varies widely across jurisdictions and neighborhoods within cities. So do perceptions about the propriety of police tactics (see, e.g., Browning et al. 1994). Perceptions of frequency depend also on the vantage point of the observer. One instance of alleged abuse per night in a department of several thousand officers may be diminimus to the statistician and to the officers, but to the internal affairs investigators or the police stationhouse reporter or a police watchdog group or a police chief facing media accusations of tolerating too much police coerciveness, one per night may seem like a lot.

15. Comparability can be further enhanced if departments classify the complaints that are filed in the same fashion, so that force-related complaints can be distinguished from those that relate to other types of issues. Some consequences of not being able routinely to classify complaints against police according to subject matter were illustrated when, under pressure to produce a federal profile of police abuse of force after the Rodney King beating, the Justice Department's Civil Rights Division compiled data on 15,000 complaints received by various Justice Department units over a six-year period (DeParle 1992). An unknown percentage of these complaints were about matters other than police use of excessive force against citizens (e.g., sexual harassment allegations by police employees against one another). For that and other reasons, the Justice Department was placed in the embarrassing position of resisting dissemination of and reliance on its own study, even in dealing with Congressional oversight committees (see chapters 3 and 6 and DeParle 1992).

16. A recent survey indicates that 70 percent of Texas police departments accept anonymous complaints, which are "terminated only if there is insufficient information to pursue the investigation" (Texas Law Enforcement Management 1994: 2).

17. Several NYPD supervisors expressed concern that effective community policing

officers would be undercut by drug dealers and other criminals who knowingly filed false brutality complaints against the officers. According to the supervisors, "the dealers . . . know that an officer's chances of getting desirable assignments in the future, such as assignments to the Organized Crime Bureau, could be damaged by a record of frequent civilian complaints. In addition, it was suggested that dealers also know that commanding officers are held accountable for the number of civilian complaints registered against members of their commands and are anxious, therefore, to hold that number to a minimum" (McElroy et al. 1993: 121–22).

18. Criminologist Geoffrey Alpert (1993), among others, has suggested that it would be advantageous for police departments to call these documents "control of persons" reports rather than use-of- force reports to emphasize that there is a legitimate police objective entailed in appropriate use of force.

19. One way of improving narratives in both arrest and use-of-force reports might be to occasionally get multiple incident descriptions, such as from nonreporting responding officers, witnesses, or arrestees.

20. Since 1985, the St. Louis Metropolitan Police Department, using its Police Incident Reporting System, has enabled officers to submit their arrest reports by telephone to the department's centralized word-processing center. By 1993, approximately 95 percent of arrest and other reports were submitted by officers in this fashion, from phones at crime scenes, at police substations or at district lockups where prisoners are processed (Jones 1993).

21. For example, data about calls for service are critical in assessing outcomes of community problem solving and conventional policing strategies. They are also useful for problem-solving operations, in that they can help define problems to be addressed. Criminal investigations can also benefit from computerized databases.

22. A largely unexplored, potentially researchable question is what the dynamic interrelationships might be amongst community problem-solving efforts, the tactics a department selects in an effort to prevent abuse of force and safeguard officers, and outcomes concerning service delivery, prudential use of force by officers and officer safety. We will comment further on this below.

23. Many officers, police managers and interested parties outside police departments might find the distinction between punishment and mandatory retraining a murky one. This confusion speaks to the necessity of changing police and public views about the value of high-quality training (see chapters 5 and 9) and the positive, nonpunitive opportunities for "lessons-learned" exercises in the wake of unsuccessful—or less successful than desired— police operations.

24. Also valuable would be similar time series studies to compare pre-intervention and post-intervention behavior of officers who are sanctioned but are restored to active duty after they are sanctioned.

25. While there needs to be far more study of the question, an early finding from New York City suggests that officers actively engaged in community policing strategies and tactics used no more force than other officers. This was despite some initial concerns by NYPD supervisors that the growing attachment of Community Patrol Officer Program (CPOP) officers to the residents on their beats would fuel growing frustration over the persistence of problems and provoke officers to use extra-legal methods (with the tacit approval of the community) (Weisburd et al. 1988). Indeed, the preliminary returns suggested that CPOP officers garnered fewer citizen complaints than officers on regular patrol (p. 46 n. 9). It would be useful to explore whether the reduction in complaints was due to better skill in minimizing abuses; better skill in minimizing complaints despite the persistence of abuses; a difference in the type of incidents handled by CPOP and other officers; a more favorable general attitude by citizens toward CPOP officers, causing the citizens to refrain from complaining in specific instances that produce complaints against other officers; or other factors.

26. One of the many specific, practical implications of suggesting that use-of-force

issues be addressed in a fashion consistent with community problem-solving's fundamental principles would apply to departments that espouse—and put into operation—these values in their anti-crime efforts. Such a community policing agency must not behave in ways that are perceived by key stakeholders as diverging from the organization's espoused values. Perhaps the easiest way for a chief to demoralize his or her officers in these stressful circumstances is precipitously to make a scapegoat of the accused officer in order to relieve the external pressure or dismissing as frivolous community claims that the department has abused its authority in the controversial incident. The procedural justice concepts that Kerstetter (chapter 12) recommends be applied to improve current methods used to air and consider complaints against the police might go a long way toward helping departments achieve desirable consistency in their operating principles. We shall discuss the potential value of procedural justice to policing below.

27. Former Santa Ana, California, Police Chief Ray Davis—a hero to many community groups—warned against a "blind pilgrimage to the temples of community control" despite his affinity for grassroots community empowerment (Davis 1985). Many talented organizational leaders, presumably Davis included, would credit their success in reforming their agencies partly to their ability to capitalize on community demands that public servants be held accountable to the public's values and needs (see, e.g., Moore and Stephens 1991a, 1991b; Lappé and DuBois 1994).

28. It is an oversimplification to presume that persons of color will uniformly persist in seeing criminal justice systems as racist. Compare two books by African Americans, for example: *The Myth of a Racist Criminal Justice System* by William Wilbanks (1987) with *Unequal Justice: A Question of Color* by Coramae Richey Mann (1993) (see also discussion in Tonry 1995 and Wilbanks 1993). Consider, as well, the wide range of opinion one finds within the ranks of black police leadership and black judges and prosecutors.

29. Commenting on the fallout of the Rodney King beating and Mark Fuhrman fiasco, Police Chief Jerry Oliver of Richmond, Virginia, in late 1995 declared: "Now police feel what African Americans have long felt—we no longer enjoy a presumption of credibility from the American public."

30. Most training programs that use live "opponents" in role-playing sessions have police personnel assume the roles of the offenders and bystanders. The Tampa police have found that enlisting local actors and other civilian volunteers to play the bystander and suspect roles in police tactical training adds an additional element of realism, without creating offsetting liabilities (Korzeniowski 1990). Geiger et al. (1990) describe the beliefs of FBI personnel about the value of using civilians to assist with certain types of training.

31. We do not use *professionalism* in the sense that Kelling and Kliesmet (chapter 10) use the term to refer to a stage of police evolution. Here, the term is used to reflect high standards of integrity and elements of quality policing.

32. The Detroit Police Department, in the view of Coleman Young when he ran many years ago for his first term as mayor, was sufficiently abusive in dealing with civilians that a standard police device—the common baton or nightstick—was removed from the police tool kit. This left officers with virtually nothing to resort to, other than their wit and their handguns, when they needed to defend themselves and control uncooperative people. The fatal Malice Green beating proved they could also deploy their flashlights as weapons. Above, in highlighting chapter 5 on public opinion, we provide additional discussion of the impact of an agency's general reputation on public acceptance of particular police tactical options.

33. Even the geography and climate of the region have some training and tactical implications. For instance, a violence-reducing weapon such as oleoresin capsicum (pepper spray), to work properly, must be sprayed at a suspect's eyes, nose, and mouth. It may be ineffective outdoors during the winter in a very cold region, where many people wear knitted face masks (Granfield 1993).

34. There is a fair amount of misinformation among officers concerning the hazards of police work. Many officers have exaggerated the dangers of particular types of encounters (e.g., domestic disturbances, non-felony traffic stops and even some types of knife threats) and the prevalence of assaults on officers (see generally, Geller and Scott 1992).

35. Much of the material that follows on conflict management training is from Geller and Scott (1992: 308–33), which contains an extended discussion of these topics and references to numerous publications addressing conflict management training.

36. Korzeniowski (1990) describes the Tampa Police Training Academy's Survival City; Katz (1991) discusses the Los Angeles County Sheriff's Department's Laser Village; Geller and Karales (1981a) describe "The Apartment" constructed at the NYPD's outdoor firing range in the late 1970s; Pledger (1988: 6–7) and Slahor (1992) report on the expansion of the FBI's famed Hogan's Alley to a full-blown Hoganville; Nielsen (1990) describes the Provo, Utah, Police Department's outdoor range replication of actual street circumstances; and Schrader (1988) discusses initiatives in the Anaheim, California, Police Department.

37. A survival course compiled by the U.S. Border Patrol with assistance from Police Executive Research Forum staff and other training experts is premised on strengthening officer skills in utilizing "the five C's—cover, concealment, control, containment, communications" (Smith 1990: 111). Albrecht (1989) has written insightfully about the "contact and cover" method of approaching a potentially dangerous person or scene, in which one officer makes initial contact while the second officer provides cover to protect his or her partner (see also Albrecht and Morrison 1992).

38. The LAPD's Special Investigations Section, "an elite surveillance squad that gathers evidence against dangerous criminals by watching them commit crimes and attempts to arrest them afterward" (Stolberg 1990: A1), was a target of considerable criticism before the department curtailed its activities. The *Los Angeles Times* reported: "Teams of well-armed SIS detectives had, for years, tailed career criminals but often ignored opportunities to prevent armed robberies and burglaries by legitimately arresting suspects beforehand on lesser crimes or outstanding warrants. Instead, records showed, the officers routinely stood by until the suspects they were watching had committed violent crimes. Many suspects were shot when they returned to their getaway cars" (Freed 1989: B1). Between 1967 and June 1990, the SIS reportedly killed more than 25 suspects and wounded another 24 (Stolberg 1990: A1; see also Meyer and Connelly 1992). Granting the benefit of the doubt concerning the motivations and competencies of the members of the SIS, the need to change outcomes by altering strategies illustrates the problem represented by cell 4C in table 15.1. Police have also failed to avert preventable crimes in the hope of catching suspects in the act so that—rather than administering summary execution—they might get the evidence needed to file serious felony charges. Kelling (1991) has criticized the latter approach on the ground that it uses crime victims as "bait to feed the criminal justice system." Under Chief Dennis Nowicki's leadership, the Charlotte-Mecklenburg Police Department in 1995 rose to Kelling's challenge and adopted as the core of its mission statement a commitment to "prevent the next crime."

39. That scholarship explores whether, when, and why individuals, groups, and even entire nations who are bystanders to injustice will intervene in an attempt to restore justice. A chilling example of the problem Staub has studied is the Kitty Genovese murder in New York City in the late 1960s, in which 37 people heard her being killed and did nothing. Schwartz (1973: 145–46) posits reasons for their indifference or inaction based of shifting concepts of the "space" for which one is responsible.

40. Techniques fashioned in private corporate settings under the rubric of compliance programs, designed to "foster compliance with the law by the company's workers" (Herman 1994) so that violations are prevented and punitive responses are obviated, may offer lessons for strengthening police intervention training.

41. It will be interesting to see if, in a department robustly implementing commu-

nity policing, officers' definitions of "partner" tend to expand to the point where residents of an officer's beat are considered professional collaborators and sometimes even personal friends. Still, there may be occasional advantages to the estrangement of recruits from their prior friends and associates that usually accompanies the police socialization process. It is generally believed, for instance, that systematic drug corruption among Latino recruits to the Miami Police Department several years ago arose in part from an overloaded field-training program. Straining under the pressure of a recruit class many times the normal size, the trainers could not sufficiently induct these recruits into the police culture and distance them from some prior associates (suspected of assorted drug-law violations), who enlisted the officers in drug dealing and nonenforcement schemes.

42. The concept may also help explain the oddly wholesale dismissal of crime prevention as a public policy objective in recent speeches by some politicians debating crime-control policy (but compare Herbert 1995 and Alschuler [quoted on book jacket of Tonry 1995]).

43. Some form of confidentiality guarantee would seem to be fundamental if such discussions are to be specific and candid enough to be valuable. Klockars (1994: 3), citing Toch et al. (1975), argues: "Elements of the police subculture [present] such obstacles to candid post-incident assessment that confidential assessments by highly skilled peers [seems] to offer the only reasonable approach."

44. One potential source of legal expertise, beyond that represented by departmental legal advisors and local government corporation counsel (a group that varies widely in professional acumen), might be the American Bar Association. In 1994–95, when the ABA considered whether to attempt to update its *Urban Police Function Standards*, advisors urged the ABA, as a public service, to work to reduce some of the legal barriers that impede police departments from candidly identifying and overcoming their weaknesses concerning use of force and other matters.

45. As officers respond differently to processes they see as legitimate and illegitimate, surveys concerned with learning must also be concerned with legitimacy. A process seen as illegitimate may produce behavior change via reluctant compliance (as opposed to change via internalization). Such change is likely to be of lower magnitude and of shorter duration than the learning produced by a process that is seen as legitimate. A process that is viewed as illegitimate also invites resistance and efforts to circumvent or sabotage its intent.

46. Officers may learn much of value from studying other departments' review systems and doing so from the perspective of a potential citizen user of the systems. Police managers attending a "command college" at the Southwestern Law Enforcement Institute near Dallas, Texas, were sent individually, dressed in civilian clothes, to various Dallas-area police departments simply to inquire what the procedure is for filing a complaint about police work. They found that a substantial percentage of the agencies were unreceptive in various ways (Carlson 1994a). Subtle or unsubtle discouragement of citizens from complaining was highlighted by the Christopher Commission in its review of the Los Angeles Police Department (Independent Commission on the LAPD 1991; see also Nossiter 1994).

Bibliography

Adler, T. (1993). "Separate Gender Norms on Tests Raise Questions." *American Psychological Association Monitor* 24:6.

Adorno, T. W., Else Frenkel-Brunswik, Daniel J. Levinson, and R. Nevitt Sanford. (1950). *The Authoritarian Personality.* New York: Harper and Row.

Alan-Williams, Gregory. (1994). *A Gathering of Heroes: Reflections on Rage and Responsibility—A Memoir of the Los Angeles Riots.* Chicago: Academy Chicago Publishers.

Albrecht, Steven. (1989). "Contact and Cover: One Common-sense Procedure Can Make All the Difference to an Officer's Survival." *Police* (April): 33–36, 69.

———. (1992). *Street Work: The Way to Officer Safety and Survival.* Boulder, Colo.: Paladin Press.

Albrecht, Steven, and John Morrison. (1992). *Contact and Cover: Two-Officer Suspect Control.* Springfield, Ill.: Charles C. Thomas.

Aldrich, John H., and Forrest D. Nelson. (1984). *Linear Probability, Logit, and Probit Models.* Volume 45 of *Quantitative Applications in the Social Sciences.* Beverly Hills, Calif.: Sage.

Alpert, Geoffrey P. (1987). "Questioning Police Pursuits in Urban Areas." *Journal of Police Science and Administration* 15:298–306. Reprinted in Roger G. Dunham and Geoffrey P. Alpert (eds.), *Critical Issues in Policing: Contemporary Readings.* Prospect Heights, Ill.: Waveland Press, 1989.

———. (1989). "Police Use of Deadly Force: The Miami Experience." In Roger G. Dunham and Geoffrey P. Alpert (eds.), *Critical Issues in Policing: Contemporary Readings.* Prospect Heights, Ill.: Waveland.

———. (1993). Presentation to the Criminal Justice Institute, St. Petersburg Junior College, St. Petersburg, Fla. (September 1).

Alpert, Geoffrey P., and Patrick Anderson. (1986). "The Most Deadly Force: Police Pursuits." *Justice Quarterly* 3:1–13.

Alpert, Geoffrey P., and Lorie A. Fridell. (1992). *Police Vehicles and Firearms: Instruments of Deadly Force.* Prospect Heights, Ill.: Waveland.

American Bar Association (ABA). (1970). *Problems and Recommendations in Dis-*

ciplinary Enforcement. Chicago: ABA Committee on Evaluation of Disciplinary Enforcement.

———. (1972). *Project on Standards for Criminal Justice: Standards Relating to the Urban Police Function.* Washington, D.C.

———. (1979). *Urban Police Functions Standards.* Washington, D.C.

American Civil Liberties Union. (1991). *On the Line: Police Brutality and Its Remedies.* New York.

American Civil Liberties Union of Southern California. (1993). *Pepper Spray: A Magic Bullet Under Scrutiny.* Los Angeles.

Americans for Effective Law Enforcement. (1988). *Use-of-Force Tactics and Non-Lethal Weaponry.* Chicago.

Amnesty International. (1984). *Torture in the Eighties.* London: Martin Robinson.

Amsterdam, Committee on Police Complaints. (1990). *Annual Report.*

Anderson v. Creighton. (1987). 483 U.S. 639.

Anderson, David C. (1992). "Making Sense of Civilian Review." *New York Times* (September 29): A22.

———. (1994). "The Crime Funnel: 'Lock 'Em Up' Can't Possibly Cut Crime Much: A Few Cold Facts Show Why." *New York Times Magazine* (June 12): 56–58.

Anderson, K. S. (1991). "National Computer Systems Professional Assessment Services." Letter to L. Morganbesser, Department of Correctional Services, Albany, N.Y. (September 16).

Andrews, P. (1985). "Mellow Attitude Helps Police Gain Stature." *Seattle Times* (August 18): K1, K6.

Arcuri, A. F. (1977). "You Can't Take Fingerprints Off Water: Police Officers' Views Toward 'Cop Television Shows.'" *Human Relations* 3 (1): 237–47.

Arendt, Hannah. (1973). "On Violence." In *Crises of the Republic.* Harmondsworth, England: Penguin.

Associated Press. (1995). "N.Y. Transit Cops Try Guns with Lasers: Dot Beamed on Suspect Could Force Surrender." *Chicago Tribune* (January 8): sec. 1, p. 9.

Australian Institute of Criminology. (1988). "How the Public See the Police: An Australian Survey—II." *Trends and Issues* 15 (October).

Australian Royal Commission on Aboriginal Deaths in Custody. (1991). *National Report.* Canberra: Australian Government Publication Service.

Baker v. Carr. (1962). 369 U.S. 186.

Balch, Robert W. (1972). "The Police Personality: Fact or Fiction?" *Journal of Criminal Law, Criminology, and Police Science* 63:106–19.

Baltzley, D. (1991). "BADGE: Filling the Gap Between Written Tests and Assessment Centers." *Police Chief* 58 (9): 47–50.

Bandura, A. (1986). *Social Foundations of Thought and Action: A Social Cognitive Theory.* Englewood Cliffs, N.J.: Prentice-Hall.

Banks, Arthur S., and Textor, Robert B. (1968). *A Cross-Polity Survey.* Cambridge, Mass.: MIT Press.

Barker, Thomas. (1977). "Peer Group Support for Police Organizational Deviance." *Criminology* 15:353–66.

———. (1978). "An Empirical Study of Police Deviance Other Than Corruption." *Journal of Police Science and Administration* 6 (3): 264–72.

———. (1983). "Rookie Police Officers' Perceptions of Police Occupational Deviance." *Police Studies* 6 (2): 30-38.

Barnhill, W. (1992). "Early Warnings: Identifying Violence-Prone Police Officers." *Washington Post* (August 11): Style section, 5.

Barrett-Howard, E., and H. Lamm. (1986). "Procedural and Distributive Justice: Definitions and Beliefs of West German University Students." Unpublished manuscript, Northwestern University.

Bates v. Jean. (1974). 415 U.S. 651.

Bayley, David H. (1969). *The Police and Political Development in India.* Princeton, N.J.: Princeton University Press.

———. (1983). "Police and Political Order in India." *Asian Survey.*

———. (1985). *Patterns of Policing.* New Brunswick, N.J.: Rutgers University Press.

———. (1986). "The Tactical Choices of Police Patrol Officers." *Journal of Criminal Justice* 14:329-48.

———. (1991a). *Forces of Order: Policing Modern Japan.* Berkeley: University of California Press.

———. (1991b). "Getting Serious About Police Brutality." Draft manuscript.

———. (1991c). Preface to Andrew J. Goldsmith (ed.), *Complaints Against the Police: The Trend to External Review.* Oxford: Clarendon Press.

Bayley, David H., and James Garofalo. (1987). "Patrol Officer Effectiveness in Managing Conflict During Police-Citizen Encounters." In *Report to the New York State Commission on Criminal Justice and the Use of Force* (Vol. III). (May), pp. B1-88. Albany: New York State Commission on Criminal Justice and the Use of Force.

———. (1989). "The Management of Violence by Police Patrol Officers." *Criminology* 27 (1, February): 1-27.

Bayley, David H., and Harold Mendelsohn. (1969). *Minorities and the Police: Confrontation in America.* New York and Glencoe, Ill.: Free Press.

Begans, P. (1985). "Blacks Say Police Routinely Rough Up Suspects." *New York Daily News*/Eyewitness News Poll (February 14).

Bell v. City of Milwaukee. (1984). 746 F.2d 1205 (7th Cir.).

Bennett, G. (1989). *Crime Warps: The Future of Crime in America.* New York: Anchor Books.

Bennett, Richard R., and Theodore Greenstein. (1975). "The Police Personality: A Test of the Predispositional Model." *Journal of Police Science and Administration* 3:439-45.

Benson, Paul. (1981). "Political Alienation and Public Satisfaction of Police Services." *Pacific Sociological Review* 24:45-64.

Berger, Joseph. (1993). "U.S. Studies How Police Use Sprays." *New York Times* (October 16): 25.

Berk, Sarah Fenstermaker, and Donileen R. Loseke. (1980-81). "'Handling' Family Violence: Situational Determinants of Police Arrest in Domestic Disturbances." *Law & Society Review* 15:317-46.

Berkley, George E. (1969). *The Democratic Policeman.* Boston: Beacon Press.

Bianchi, Herman. (1994). *Justice as Sanctuary: Toward a New System of Crime Control.* Bloomington: Indiana University Press.

Bieck, William H., William Spelman, and Thomas J. Sweeney. (1991). "The Patrol

Function." In William A. Geller (ed.), *Local Government Police Management,* pp. 59–95. Washington, D.C.: International City/County Management Association.

Bigham, Steve. (1993). *Attitude and Public Opinion Survey: Reno Police Department-April 1993.* Reno, Nev.: Reno Police Department (May 18).

Binder, Arnold. (1983). "Characteristics of Shooters and Non-Shooters: A Four-City Comparison." Presented at the annual meeting of the American Society of Criminology.

Binder, Arnold, and Lorie Fridell. (1984). "Lethal Force As a Police Response." *Criminal Justice Abstracts* (June): 250–80.

Binder, Arnold, and Peter Scharf. (1980). "The Violent Police-Citizen Encounter." *Annals of the American Academy of Political and Social Science* 452 (November): 111–21.

———. (1982). "Deadly Force in Law Enforcement." *Crime and Delinquency* 28 (7): 1–23.

Bishop, G. F. (1992). *The Greater Cincinnati Survey: Project Report for Cincinnati Police Division.* (Fall). Cincinnati: University of Cincinnati.

Bittner, Egon. (1970). *The Functions of the Police in Modern Society.* Washington, D.C.: U.S. Government Printing Office.

———. (1974). "Florence Nightingale in Pursuit of Willie Sutton: A Theory of Police." In Herbert Jacob (ed.), *The Potential for Reform of Criminal Justice.* Beverly Hills, Calif.: Sage.

———. (1975a). *The Functions of the Police in Modern Society.* 2d ed. New York: Jason Aronson. First published 1970 by National Institutes of Health.

———. (1975b). "The Capacity to Use Force as the Core of the Police Role." In Jerome H. Skolnick and T. C. Gray (eds.), *Police in America,* pp. 61–68. Boston: Little, Brown.

———. (1978). "The Functions of the Police in Modern Society." In Peter K. Manning and John van Maanen (eds.), *Policing: A View from the Streets.* Santa Monica, Calif.: Goodyear.

———. (1980). "The Capacity to Use Force as the Core of the Police Role." In *The Functions of the Police in Modern Society: A Review of Background Factors, Current Practices, and Possible Role Models.* Cambridge, Mass.: Oelgeschlager, Gunn and Hain.

———. (1984). "The Broken Badge: Reuss-Ianni and the Culture of Policing." Book review of *Two Cultures of Policing* by E. Reuss-Ianni, in *American Bar Foundation Research Journal* (1, Winter): 206–213.

———. (1990). *Aspects of Police Work.* Boston: Northeastern University Press.

Black, Algernon D. (1967). *The People and the Police.* New York: McGraw-Hill.

Black, Donald. (1971). "The Social Organization of Arrest." *Stanford Law Review* 23:1087–1111.

———. (1976). *The Behavior of Law.* New York: Academic Press.

———. (1980). *The Manners and Customs of the Police.* New York: Academic Press.

———. (1983). "Crime as Social Control." *American Sociological Review* (February): 34–45.

Black, Donald, and Albert J. Reiss, Jr. (1967). "Patterns of Behavior and Citizen Transactions." In President's Commission on Law Enforcement and Administration of

Justice, *Studies in Crime and Law Enforcement in Major Metropolitan Areas*, Field Studies III, Vol. II, Sec. I. Washington: U.S. Government Printing Office.

Bloch, Peter B., and Deborah Anderson. (1974). *Policewomen on Patrol: Final Report.* Washington, D.C.: Police Foundation.

Block, R. L. (1971). "Fear of Crime and Fear of the Police." *Social Problems* 19 (1): 91–101.

Blumberg, Mark. (1981). "Race and Police Shootings: An Analysis in Two Cities." In James J. Fyfe (ed.), *Contemporary Issues in Law Enforcement.* Beverly Hills, Calif.: Sage.

———. (1982). "The Use of Firearms by Police: The Impact of Individuals, Communities, and Race." Ph.D. diss., State University of New York at Albany.

———. (1986). "Issues and Controversies with Respect to the Use of Deadly Force by Police." In Thomas Barker and David L. Carter (eds.), *Police Deviance.* Cincinnati: Pilgrimage.

———. (1989). "Controlling Police Use of Deadly Force: Assessing Two Decades of Progress." In Roger Dunham and Geoffrey Alpert (eds.), *Critical Issues in Policing: Contemporary Readings.* Prospect Heights, Ill.: Waveland.

———. (1991). "Police Use of Deadly Force: Exploring Some Key Issues." In Thomas Barker and David L. Carter (eds.), *Police Deviance.* Cincinnati: Anderson.

Blumenthal, M. D., R. L. Kahn, F. M. Andrews, and K. B. Head. (1972). *Justifying Violence: Attitudes of American Men.* Ann Arbor: University of Michigan Press.

Boggs, Sarah L., and John F. Galliher. (1975). "Evaluating the Police: A Comparison of Black Street and Household Respondents." *Social Problems* 22 (3): 393–406.

Bolz, Frank, and Edward Hershey. (1979). *Hostage Cop.* New York: Rawson, Wade.

Bonifacio, P. (1991). *The Psychological Effects of Police Work: A Psychodynamic Approach.* New York: Plenum.

Booth, W. (1989). "Strategies for Enhancing Your Assessment Center Performance." *Police Chief* 56 (2): 35–41.

Boston Police Department Management Review Committee. (1981). *Report of the Boston Police Department Management Review Committee.* Boston.

Bouma, D. H. (1973). "Youth Attitudes Toward the Police and Law Enforcement." In J. T. Curran, A. Fowler, and R. H. Ward (eds.), *Police and Law Enforcement* (Vol. 1), pp. 219–38. New York: AMS Press.

Bouza, Anthony V. (1985). "Police Unions: Paper Tigers or Roaring Lions?" In William A. Geller (ed.), *Police Leadership in America: Crisis and Opportunity.* New York: Praeger.

———. (1990). *The Police Mystique: An Insider's Look at Cops, Crime, and the Criminal Justice System.* New York: Plenum Press.

Bowen v. Watkins (1982), 669 F.2d 979 (5th Cir.).

Box, Steven. (1983). *Power, Crime and Mystification.* New York: Tavistock.

Bradburn, N., and S. Sudman. (1988). *Polls and Surveys: Understanding What They Tell Us.* San Francisco: Jossey-Bass.

Brandl, Steven G., James Frank, Robert E. Worden, and Timothy S. Bynum. (1994). "Global and Specific Attitudes Toward the Police: Disentangling the Relationship." *Justice Quarterly* 11 (1, March): 119–34.

Brandon v. Holt (1986), 645 F.Supp. 1261 (W.D. Tenn.).

Brehm, John, and Scott Gates. (1992). "Policing Police Brutality: Evaluation of Principal-Agent Models of Noncooperative Behavior." Paper presented at the annual meeting of the Midwest Political Science Association, April, Chicago.

Breitel, Charles D. (1960). "Controls in Criminal Law Enforcement." *University of Chicago Law Review* 27:427-35.

Brengelmann, J. C. (1982). "Observations Concerning the Development of a New Selective Procedure for Police Recruits." *Schriftenreihe der polizei-fuehrungsakademie* 4:283-91.

Bristow, Allen. (1963). "Police Officer Shootings—A Tactical Evaluation." *Journal of Criminal Law, Criminology, and Police Science* 54:93-95.

Broadaway, F. M. (1974). "Police Misconduct: Positive Alternatives." *Journal of Police Science and Administration* 2 (2): 210-18.

Broderick, John J. (1977). *Police in a Time of Change.* Morristown, N.J.: General Learning Press.

Brodeur, Jean-Claude. (1992). Member of the Complaints Board. Private letter.

Brodsky, S. L., and G. D. Williamson. (1985). "Attitudes of Police Toward Violence." *Psychological Reports* 57:1179-80.

Brooks, T. R. (1965). "Police Brutality?" *New York Times Magazine* (December 5): 60-61, 63, 65-66, 68.

Brown, D. (1991). "Civilian Review of Complaints Against the Police." In Andrew Goldsmith, *Complaints Against the Police.* New York: Oxford.

Brown, Jill I. (1991). "Defining 'Reasonable' Police Conduct: *Graham v. Connor* and Excessive Force During Arrest." *University of California Law Review* 30:1257.

Brown, M. F. (1983). "Shooting Policies: What Patrolmen Think." *Police Chief* 50 (5): 35-37.

———. (1984). "Use of Deadly Force by Patrol Officers." *Journal of Police Science and Administration* 12:133-40.

Brown, Michael K. (1981). *Working the Street: Police Discretion and the Dilemmas of Reform.* New York: Russell Sage Foundation.

Browning, Sandra Lee, Francis T. Cullen, Liqun Cao, Renee Kopache, and Thomas J. Stevenson. (1994). "Race and Getting Hassled by the Police: A Research Note." *Police Studies* 17 (1): 1-11.

Burbeck, E. and A. Furnham. (1985). "Police Officer Selection: A Critical Review of the Literature." *Journal of Police Science and Administration* 13:58-69.

Buros, O. K. (ed.). (1970). *Personality Tests and Reviews.* Highland Park, N.J.: Gryphon Press.

California Peace Officers' Association. (1974). *California Peace Officers' Association News* (March): 25.

Canberra Police Department (New South Wales, Australia). (1994). "Overview Report and Press Release: Canberra People Feel Safer in Their Neighbourhood." (September).

Carlin, Jerome E. (1966). *Lawyer's Ethics: A Survey of the New York City Bar.* New York: Russell Sage.

———. (1968). "Lawyer's Ethics: Formal Controls." In Johnige and Goldman (eds.), *The Federal Judicial System.* Hinsdale, Ill.: Dryden.

Carlson, Dan. (1994a). "Customer Awareness: A Departmental Survey." Unpublished results. Richardson, Tex.: Southwestern Law Enforcement Institute.

———. (1994b). "Michael Josephson to Kick Off Third Annual Ethics Conference." *The Ethics Roll Call: Listening to the Inner Voice* 1 (4, Fall): 1.

Carte, Gene E., and Elaine H. Carte. (1975). *Police Reform in the United States: The Era of August Vollmer, 1905-1932.* Berkeley: University of California Press.

Carter, David L. (1976). "Police Brutality." In A. S. Blumberg and E. Niederhoffer (eds.), *The Ambivalent Force*, pp. 321-30. New York: Holt, Rinehart and Winston.

Cascio, Wayne F. (1977). "Formal Education and Police Officer Performance." *Journal of Police Science and Administration* 5:89-96.

Cashmore, E., and E. McLaughlin. (1991). "Out of Order?" In E. Cashmore and E. McLaughlin (eds.), *Out of Order? Policing Black People*, pp. 10-41. London: Routledge.

Casper, Jonathan D., Tom R. Tyler, and Bonnie Fisher. (1988). "Procedural Justice in Felony Cases." *Law and Society Review* 19:661-701.

Castaneda, Ruben. (1994a). "White House Shooting Proves Fatal: Park Police Defend Decision to Fire." *Washington Post* (December 22): C1.

———. (1994b). "Officer Who Fired Shots Seen Only Briefly on Tape: Homeless Man Raised Knife, Park Police Say." *Washington Post* (December 23): A1.

Center for Law and Social Justice. (1988). *The Problem of Police and Racial Violence.* New York.

Chackerian, R. (1974). "Police Professionalism and Citizen Evaluations: A Preliminary Look." *Public Administration Review* 34 (2): 141-48.

Chaiken, Marcia R., and Jan M. Chaiken. (1984). "Offender Types and Public Policy." *Crime and Delinquency* 30:195-226.

Chandler, E. V., and Jones, C. S. (1979). "Cynicism—An Inevitability of Police Work?" *Journal of Police Science and Administration* 7:65-68.

Chenoweth, J. (1961). "Situational Test: A New Attempt at Assessing Police Candidates." *Journal of Criminal Law and Criminology* 52 (1): 232-39.

Chevigny, Paul B. (1969). *Police Power: Police Abuses in New York City.* New York: Vintage Books (Pantheon).

———. (1990). "Deadly Force as Social Control: Jamaica, Argentina, and Brazil." *Criminal Law Forum* 1 (3, Spring): 389-425.

———. (1995). *Edge of the Knife: Police Violence in the Americas.* New York: Free Press.

Chicago Police Department, Office of Professional Standards. (1991). Internal memorandum (January 4).

Church, G. J. (1992). "The Fire This Time." *Time* 139 (19): 18-25, May 11.

Chusmir, L. H. (1984). "Motivational Need Pattern for Police Officers." *Journal of Police Science and Administration* 12:141-45.

Cincinnati Office of Municipal Investigation. (1990). *Annual Report.* Cincinnati.

City of Canton v. Harris. (1989). 489 U.S. 378.

City of Los Angeles v. Lyons. (1983). 461 U.S. 95.

Civil Rights Act of 1964, Section 703, as amended in Public Law 102-166 (November 21, 1991), 102d Congress.

Civil Rights Cases, The (1883), 109 U.S. 3.

Clark, Ramsey. (1971). *Crime in America.* New York: Simon & Schuster.

Clark, Tom C. (1947). "A Federal Prosecutor Looks at the Civil Rights Statute." *Columbia Law Review* 47:175-85.

Clede, Bill, with Keven Parsons. (1987). *Police Non-lethal Force Manual: Your Choices This Side of Deadly.* Harrisburg, Pa.: Stackpole Books.

Cleveland Police Review Board. (1991). *Report.* Cleveland.

Clifford, F., and D. Ferrell. (1992). "Angelenos Condemn King Verdicts, Rioting Poll Finds." *Albany* (N.Y.) *Times Union* (May 6): A11.

Cochran, Johnnie L., Jr. (1992). Statement of Johnnie L. Cochran, Jr., before the Subcommittee on Civil and Constitutional Rights of the House Committee on the Judiciary, 102d Congress, 1st session (May 4).

Cohen, Bernard, and Jan M. Chaiken. (1972). *Police Background Characteristics and Performance.* New York: Rand.

———. (1973). *Police Background Characteristics and Performance.* Lexington, Mass.: Lexington Books.

Cohen, Howard S., and Michael Feldberg. (1991). Power and Restraint: The Moral Dimension of Police Work. New York: Praeger.

Commission on Accreditation for Law Enforcement Agencies. (1991). *Standards for Law Enforcement Agencies.* Fairfax, Va.

Conference Report to Accompany H.R. 3371. (1991). Report 102–405, 102d Congress, 1st session (November 27).

Conley, John. (1988). "Ethnographic Perspective on Informal Justice: What Litigants Want." Paper presented at the annual meeting of the Law and Society Association, Vail, Colo., June.

Connell, Rich. (1994). "LAPD to Revise Policy on Restraining Suspects." *Los Angeles Times* (May 20): B1, B8.

Connelly, Michael. (1992). "Holdup Victim Testifies in Suit Against Police over Killings: A Night Manager Tells How She Waited for Officers As Robbers Broke into the Restaurant and Threatened Her Life." *Los Angeles Times* (February 26).

Connor, Gregory. (1991). "Use-of-Force Continuum: Phase 2." *Law and Order* (March): 30–32.

Connor, Gregory, and Matthew D. Summers. (1988). *Tactical Neutralization Techniques.* Champaign, Ill.: Snipes.

Cooper, Gerald. (1994). "Evanston Police Department Retreat: Summary of Ideas Discussed and Suggestions Made—Chief Cooper's Closing Remarks." Unpublished document on file with the Evanston Police Department. (February 4–5).

Corbett, M., F. Meyer, R. Baker, and D. Rudoni. (1979). "Conflict, Consensus, and Perceptions of Support Among the Police." *Journal of Police Science and Administration* 7:449–58.

Cordner, Gary W. (1985). "Police Research and Police Policy: Some Propositions About the Production and Use of Knowledge." In William A. Geller (ed.), *Police Leadership in America: Crisis and Opportunity.* New York: Praeger.

———. (1988). "Problem-Oriented Approach to Community-Oriented Policing." In Jack R. Greene and Stephen D. Mastrofski (eds.), *Community Policing: Rhetoric or Reality.* New York: Praeger.

Cornish, D. B., and R. V. Clarke. (1987). "Understanding Crime Displacement." *Criminology* 25:933–47.

Corrigan, R. S., David Lester, and T. Loftus. (1980). "Perception of Danger by Police Officers." *Perceptual and Motor Skills* 50:284.

Couper, David C., and Sabine H. Lobitz. (1991). *Quality Policing: The Madison Experience.* Washington, D.C.: Police Executive Research Forum.

Crawford, T. J. (1973). "Police Overperception of Ghetto Hostility." *Journal of Police Science and Administration* 1:168-74.

Crime Control Digest. (1991). "Revised LAPD Policy Toward Homosexuals Could Lead to Settlement." *Crime Control Digest* (September 9): 8-9.

———. (1992). "Verbal Judo Instructor Course." *Crime Control Digest* (May 18): 8.

———. (1993). "Police Foundation Releases Huge Report on Use of Force: IACP Questions Statistics—Chiefs Ask for a Re-Survey." *Crime Control Digest* (November 29): 1-3.

Criminal Section, United States Department of Justice. (1991). *Police Brutality Study.* Washington, D.C.: U.S. Department of Justice.

Croft, Elizabeth Benz. (1985). "Police Use of Force: An Empirical Analysis." Ph.D. diss., State University of New York at Albany. *Dissertation Abstracts International* 46:2449A. (University Microfilms No. DA8519744).

Croft, Elizabeth Benz, and B. A. Austin. (1987). "Police Use of Force in Rochester and Syracuse, New York, 1984 and 1985." In *Report to the New York State Commission on Criminal Justice and the Use of Force* (Vol. III). (May): C1-C128. Albany: New York State Commission on Criminal Justice and the Use of Force.

Crosby, Andrew. (1979). "The Psychological Examination in Police Selection." *Journal of Police Science and Administration* 7:215-29.

Crumpen, R. D. (1992). Inspector, Internal Investigations Department, Victoria Police. Private letter (February 26).

Cruse, D., and J. Rubin. (1973). "Police Behavior." *Journal of Psychiatry and Law* 1:167-220.

Culver, J. H. (1978). "Television and the Police." *Police Studies* 7:500-05.

Cunneen, Chris. (1991). "The Police Killing of David Gundy." *Aboriginal Law Review* (June).

Cunningham, M. R. (1986). "The Prediction of Employee Violence." *Police Chief* 56:24-26.

Czaja, R., and J. Blair. (1990). "Using Network Sampling in Crime Victimization Surveys." *Journal of Quantitative Criminology* 6:185-206.

Dahl, Robert A. (1967). "The City in the Future of Democracy." *American Political Science Review* 61:953-70.

Daley, R. (1982). "Psychological Screening of Police Candidates." *Police Chief* 49:53-54.

Daly, N. C., and P. J. Morehead. (1992). "Evaluation of Community Policing: Final Report of the Community Survey and Police Department Internal Survey." St. Petersburg, Fla.: St. Petersburg Police Department.

Davis, James R. (1990). "A Comparison of Attitudes Toward the New York City Police." *Journal of Police Science and Administration* 17 (4): 233-43.

Davis, Raymond C. (1985). "Organizing the Community for Improved Policing." In William A. Geller (ed.), *Police Leadership in America: Crisis and Opportunity.* New York: Praeger.

Decker, S. H. (1981). "Citizen Attitudes Toward the Police: A Review of Past Findings and Suggestions for Future Policy." *Journal of Police Science and Administration* 9 (1): 80-87.

———. (1985). "The Police and the Public: Perceptions and Policy Recommendations." In R. J. Homant and D. B. Kennedy (eds.), *Police and Law Enforcement, 1975–1981,* pp. 89–105. New York: AMS Press.

Delattre, Edwin J. (1989). *Character and Cops.* Washington, D.C.: American Enterprise Institute for Public Policy.

———. (1994). *Character and Cops: Ethics in Policing,* 2d ed. Washington, D.C.: American Enterprise Institute for Public Policy.

Del Carmen, Rolando V. (1991). *Civil Liabilities in American Policing.* Englewood Cliffs, N.J.: Prentice-Hall.

———. (1993). "Civil Liabilities in Law Enforcement: Where Are We and Where Should We Go From Here?" *American Journal of Police* 12 (4): 87–99.

DeParle, J. (1992). "To Criticism, U.S. Unveils Report on Police Brutality." *New York Times* (May): A1.

Desmedt, John C. (1984). "Use of Force Paradigm for Law Enforcement. *Journal of Criminal Justice* 12 (2): 170–76.

Dodd v. City of Norwich (1987), 827 F.2d 1 (2d Cir.), *cert. denied,* 484 U.S. 1007 (1988).

Dominick, J. R. (1973). "Crime and Law Enforcement on Prime-Time Television." *Public Opinion Quarterly* 37 (2): 241–50.

———. (1978). "Crime and Law Enforcement in the Mass Media." In C. Winick (ed.), *Deviance and Mass Media,* pp. 105–28. Beverly Hills, Calif.: Sage.

Douglas, Jack, and John Johnson. (1977). *Official Deviance.* New York: Lippincott.

Dugan, John R., and Daniel R. Breda. (1991). "Complaints about Police Officers: A Comparison among Types and Agencies." *Journal of Criminal Justice* 19 (2): 165–71.

Dunham, Roger G., and Geoffrey P. Alpert. (1988). "Neighborhood Differences in Attitudes Toward Policing: Evidence for a Mixed-Strategy Model of Policing in a Multi-Ethnic Setting." *Journal of Criminal Law and Criminology* 79 (2): 504–23.

Dunlap, David W. (1994). "Survey on Slayings of Homosexuals Finds High Violence and Low Arrest Rate." *New York Times* (December 21): A10.

Dunnette, M. D., and S. J. Motowidlo. (1976). *Police Selection and Career Assessment.* Washington, D.C.: U.S. Department of Justice.

Dwyer, W. O., A. C. Graesser, P. L. Hopkinson, and M. B. Lupfer. (1990). "Application of Script Theory to Police Officer's Use of Deadly Force." *Journal of Police Science and Administration* 17:295–301.

Eagan, T. (1992). "Los Angeles' Police Realize They Are No Longer Heroes." *New York Times* (May 11): A1, B6.

Edwards, Richard A. (1965). "Criminal Liability for Unreasonable Search and Seizure." *Virginia Law Review* 41:621–32.

Eisenberg, Theodore. (1991). *Civil Rights Legislation,* 3d ed. Charlottesville, Va.: Michie.

Ellison, K. W. (1985a). "The Job Preview in Police Selection." *Social Action and the Law* 11:74–76.

———. (1985b). "Community Involvement in Police Selection." *Social Action and the Law* 11:77–78.

Ellison, K. W., B. A. Fornelins, and E. A. Giblin. (1985). "The Montclair Police Selection Procedure: A Summary." *Social Action and the Law* 11:69–71.

England, R., and L. Miller. (1989). "Assessing Police Applicants Through Experiential Case Studies." *Police Chief* 56 (4): 115–19.

Facing History and Ourselves. (1994). *Resource Book: Facing History and Ourselves—Holocaust and Human Behavior.* Brookline, Mass.: Facing History and Ourselves National Foundation.

Falcone, David N. (1994). "Police Pursuits and Officer Attitudes: Myths and Realities." *American Journal of Police* 28 (1): 143–56.

Famighetti, Robert (ed.). (1994). *The World Almanac and Book of Facts 1995.* Mahwah, N.J.: Funk & Wagnalls.

Far Eastern Economic Review. (1987). (June 11).

Farmer, Michael T. (1978). *Survey of Police Operational and Administrative Practices 1977.* Washington, D.C.: Police Executive Research Forum.

Federal Bureau of Investigation, Uniform Crime Reports Section. (1992). *Killed in the Line of Duty: A Study of Selected Felonious Killings of Law Enforcement Officers.* Washington, D.C. (September).

Ferdinand, Theodore H., and Elmer G. Luchterhand. (1970). "Inner-City Youth, the Police, the Juvenile Court, and Justice." *Social Problems* 17:510–27.

Fielding, Nigel G. (1988). *Joining Forces: Police Training, Socialization, and Occupational Competence.* London: Routledge.

Fishbein, M., and I. Ajzen. (1975). *Belief, Attitude, Intention, and Behavior.* Reading, Mass.: Addison-Wesley.

Fisher, W. S., S. Kutner, and J. Wheat. (1989). "Civil Liability of New Jersey Police Officers: An Overview." *Criminal Justice Quarterly* 10:45–78.

Fishman, M. (1978). "Crime Waves As Ideology." *Social Problems* 25 (5): 531–43.

Flanagan, Timothy J. (1988). "Public Support and Confidence in the Police: A Multidimensional View of Attitudes Toward Local Police." Paper presented at the annual meeting of the Academy of Criminal Justice Sciences, San Francisco, California (April).

Flanagan, Timothy J., and Kathleen Maguire (eds.). (1992). *Sourcebook of Criminal Justice Statistics—1991.* Washington, D.C.: U.S. Department of Justice, Bureau of Justice Statistics.

Folger, Robert, D. Rosenfield, J. Grove, and L. Corkran. (1979). "Effects of 'Voice' and Peer Opinions on Responses to Inequity." *Journal of Personality and Social Psychology* 37:2253–61.

Foner, P. S. (1975). *History of Black Americans: From Africa to the Emergence of the Cotton Kingdom.* Westport, Conn.: Greenwood Press.

Freed, David. (1989). "Boy's Suit Over Slaying Is Dismissed." *Los Angeles Times* (December 5): B1.

———. (1991). "Police Brutality Claims are Rarely Prosecuted." *Los Angeles Times* (July 7): 1.

Fridell, Lorie. (1989). "Justifiable Use of Measures in Research on Deadly Force." *Journal of Criminal Justice* 17:157–65.

Friedrich, Robert J. (1977). "The Impact of Organizational, Individual, and Situational Factors on Police Behavior." Ph.D. diss., University of Michigan.

———. (1980). "Police Use of Force: Individuals, Situations, and Organizations." *Annals of the American Academy of Political and Social Science* 452 (November): 82–97.

Fyfe, James J. (1978). *Shots Fired: An Examination of New York City Police Firearms Discharges.* Ph.D. diss., State University of New York at Albany.

———. (1979a). "Officer Race and Police Shootings." Paper presented to the annual meeting of the American Society of Criminology, Philadelphia (November).

———. (1979b). "Administrative Interventions on Police Shooting Discretion." *Journal of Criminal Justice* 7:309-23.

———. (1980a). "Geographic Correlates of Police Shooting: A Microanalysis." *Journal of Research in Crime and Delinquency* 17 (1, January): 101-13.

———. (1980b). "Always Prepared: Police Off-Duty Guns." *Annals of the American Academy of Political and Social Science* 452 (November): 72-81.

———. (1981a). "Who Shoots? A Look at Officer Race and Police Shooting." *Journal of Police Science and Administration* 9 (4): 367-82.

———. (1981b). "Race and Extreme Police-Citizen Violence." In R. L. McNeely and Carl E. Pope (eds.), *Race, Crime, and Criminal Justice*. Beverly Hills, Calif.: Sage.

———. (1981c). "Toward a Typology of Police Shootings." In James J. Fyfe (ed.), *Contemporary Issues in Law Enforcement*, pp. 136-51. Newbury Park, Calif.: Sage.

———. (1982). "Blind Justice: Police Shootings in Memphis." *Journal of Criminal Law and Criminology* 73 (2): 707-22.

———. (1986). "The 'Split-Second Syndrome' and Other Determinants of Police Violence." In Anne T. Campbell and John Gibbs (eds.), *Violent Transactions*. New York: Basil Blackwell. Reprinted in Roger G. Dunham and Geoffrey P. Alpert (eds.), *Critical Issues in Policing: Contemporary Readings* (1989). Prospect Heights, Ill.: Waveland Press.

———. (1988a). "Police Use of Deadly Force: Research and Reform." *Justice Quarterly* 5 (June): 165-205.

———. (1988b). *The Metro-Dade Police/Citizen Violence Reduction Project: Final Report*. Washington, D.C.: Police Foundation (June).

———. (1989a). "Police/Citizen Violence Reduction Project." *FBI Law Enforcement Bulletin* 58 (May): 18-25.

———. (1989b). "Controlling Police Vehicle Pursuits." In James J. Fyfe (ed.), *Police Practice in the '90s: Key Management Issues*. Washington, D.C.: International City Management Association.

———. (1989c). "The Split-Second Syndrome and Other Determinants of Police Violence." In Roger G. Dunham and Geoffrey P. Alpert (eds.), *Critical Issues in Policing: Contemporary Readings*. Prospect Heights, Ill.: Waveland. Reprinted from Anne T. Campbell and John Gibbs (eds.), *Violent Transactions*. New York: Basil Blackwell (1986).

———. (1994). Personal conversation with William A. Geller (December 12).

Fyfe, James J., and David Klinger. (forthcoming). *Miami Nice: The Metro-Dade Experiment*.

Galliher, J. F. (1971). "Explanations of Police Behavior: A Critical Review and Analysis." *Sociological Quarterly* 12:308-18.

Gallup, A. M. (1991). "Americans Say Police Brutality Frequent—But Not Locally." *Gallup Poll News Service* 55 (42b).

Gallup Organization. (1988). "*New York Newsday* Stock Market Survey One Year Later." *New York Newsday* (October 9).

———. (1989). "*Newsday* Crime Survey." *New York Newsday* (July).

———. (1991a). "Americans Say Police Brutality Frequent But Most Have Favorable Opinion of Their Local Police." *Gallup Poll Monthly* (March): 53-56.

———. (1991b). *American Public Opinion Index (1980–1990)*. Tallahassee, Fla.: Opinion Research Service.

Gamson, W. A., and J. McEvoy. (1972). "Police Violence and Its Public Support." In J. F. Short and Marvin E. Wolfgang (eds.), *Collective Violence*, pp. 329–42. Chicago: Aldine.

Gardiner, John A. (1969). *Traffic and the Police*. Cambridge, Mass.: Harvard University Press.

Garofalo, James. (1977). *Public Opinion About Crime: The Attitudes of Victims and Nonvictims in Selected Cities*. Washington, D.C.: U.S. Government Printing Office.

———. (1981). "Crime and the Mass Media: A Selective Review of Research." *Journal of Research in Crime and Delinquency* 18 (2): 319–50.

Garrity v. New Jersey. (1967). 385 U.S. 493.

Gates, Daryl F. (1992). *Chief: My Life in the LAPD*. New York: Bantam.

Gavin, J. F., and J. W. Hamilton. (1975). "Selecting Police Using Assessment Center Methodology." *Journal of Police Science and Administration* 3:166–76.

Geller, William A. (1981). "Police Shootings Demystified—The Chicago Study." *Justice Reporter* 6 (1): 1–8.

———. (1982). "Deadly Force: What We Know." *Journal of Police Science and Administration* 10 (2): 151–77.

———. (1985a). "Officer Restraint in the Use of Deadly Force: The Next Frontier in Police Shooting Research." *Journal of Police Science and Administration* 13 (2): 153–71.

———. (ed.). (1985b). *Police Leadership in America: Crisis and Opportunity*. New York: Praeger.

———. (1986). "Crime File: Deadly Force: A Study Guide." Washington, D.C.: National Institute of Justice, U.S. Department of Justice (Companion to NIJ videotape entitled *Deadly Force*, a discussion moderated by James Q. Wilson).

———. (ed.). (1991). *Local Government Police Management* (3d rev. ed.). Washington, D.C.: International City/County Management Association.

———. (1993). "Videotaping Interrogations and Confessions." *National Institute of Justice Research in Brief* (March). Washington, D.C.: NIJ.

———. (1994). Personal communication with William A. Geller, an advisor to the Illinois Criminal Justice Information Authority's police behavior study (March 10).

Geller, William A., and Kevin J. Karales. (1981a). *Split-Second Decisions: Shootings of and by Chicago Police*. Chicago: Chicago Law Enforcement Study Group. Portions reprinted in Harry W. More, Jr. (ed.), *Critical Issues in Law Enforcement* (4th rev. ed.) Cincinnati: Anderson, 1985.

———. (1981b). "Shootings of and by Chicago Police: Uncommon Crises. Part I: Shootings by Chicago Police." *Journal of Criminal Law and Criminology* 72 (4): 1813–66.

———. (1982). "Shootings of and by Chicago Police: Part 2." *Journal of Criminal Law and Criminology* 73 (1): 331–78.

Geller, William A., and Michael S. Scott. (1992). *Deadly Force: What We Know— A Practitioner's Desk-Reference on Police-Involved Shootings*. Washington, D.C.: Police Executive Research Forum.

Geller, William A., and Guy Swanger. (1995). *Managing Innovation in Policing: The*

Untapped Potential of the Middle Manager. Washington, D.C.: Police Executive Research Forum.

Geller, William A., and Hans Toch (eds.). (1995). *And Justice for All: Understanding and Controlling Police Abuse of Force.* Washington, D.C.: Police Executive Research Forum.

Gellhorn, Walter. (1966). *When Americans Complain.* Cambridge, Mass.: Harvard University Press.

Goldberg, L. R. (1993). "The Structure of Phenotypic Personality Traits." *American Psychologist* 48:26-34.

Goldkamp, John. (1976). "Minorities As Victims of Police Shootings: Interpretations of Racial Disproportionality and Police Use of Deadly Force." *Justice System Journal* 2 (2): 169-83.

Goldman, Roger, and Steven Puro. (1987). "Decertification of Police: An Alternative to Traditional Remedies for Police Misconduct." *Hastings Constitutional Law Quarterly* 15 (1, Fall): 45-80.

Goldsmith, Andrew J. (1988). "New Directions in Police Complaints Procedures: Some Conceptual and Comparative Departures." *Police Studies* 11:60-71.

———. (1990). "Taking Police Culture Seriously: Police Discretion and the Limits of Law." *Policing and Society* 1:91-114.

———. (1991a). "External Review and Self-Regulation." In Andrew J. Goldsmith (ed.), *Complaints Against the Police.* New York: Oxford Press.

———, (ed.) (1991b). *Complaints Against the Police.* Oxford: Clarendon Press.

———. (1992). Private letter (March 3).

Goldstein, Herman. (1967). "Administrative Problems in Controlling the Exercise of Police Authority." *Journal of Criminal Law, Criminology, and Police Science* (June): 160-72.

———. (1977). *Policing a Free Society.* Cambridge, Mass.: Ballinger.

———. (1987). "Toward Community-Oriented Policing: Potential, Basic Requirements, and Threshold Questions." *Crime and Delinquency* 33:6-30.

———. (1990). *Problem-Oriented Policing.* New York: McGraw-Hill.

———. (1993). "The New Policing: Confronting Complexity." *National Institute of Justice Research in Brief* (December). Washington, D.C.: NIJ.

Gould, Julius, and William L. Kolb. (1964). *Dictionary of the Social Sciences.* Glencoe, Ill.: Free Press.

Gouldner, Alvin W. (1954). *Patterns of Industrial Bureaucracy.* Glencoe, Ill.: Free Press.

Graber, D. A. (1980). *Crime News and the Public.* New York: Praeger.

Graham v. Connor (1989), 490 U.S. 386; 109 S.Ct. 1865.

Granfield, John. (1993). Comments at a panel on "Technology and Community Safety" at the National Institute of Justice's conference on Community Policing, Arlington, Va. (August 25).

Granfield, John, Jami Onnen, and Charles S. Petty. (1994). "Executive Brief: Pepper Spray and In-Custody Deaths." Alexandria, Va.: International Association of Chiefs of Police (March).

Graves, Franklin R., and Gregory Connor. (1992). "The FLETC (Federal Law Enforcement Training Center) Use-of-Force Model." *Police Chief* (February): 56, 58.

Greene, Jack R., and Stephen D. Mastrofski (eds.). (1988). *Community Policing: Rhetoric or Reality.* New York: Praeger.

Greenwald, J. E. (1976). *Aggression as a Component of Police-Citizen Transactions: Differences between Male and Female Police Officers.* Doctoral Dissertation, City University of New York.

Greenwood, Peter W. (with A. Abrahamse). (1982). *Selective Incapacitation.* Santa Monica, Calif.: Rand Corporation.

Grennan, Sean A. (1987). "Findings on the Role of Officer Gender in Violent Encounters with Citizens." *Journal of Police Science and Administration* 15:78-85.

Gressman, Eugene. (1952). "The Unhappy History of Civil Rights Legislation." *Michigan Law Review* 50:1323-58.

Griswold, David. (1978). "Police Discrimination: An Elusive Question." *Journal of Police Science and Administration* 6 (1): 61-66.

Grossman, Kim. (1994). Conversation between William A. Geller and Officer Kim Grossman of the Evanston (Ill.) Police Department (March 12).

Gruson, Lindsey. (1992). "Syracuse Grapples with Debate over Civilian Review of Police." *New York Times* (August 3): 35.

Guyot, Dorothy. (1991). *Policing as Though People Matter.* Philadelphia: Temple University Press.

Hagglund, C. E. (1984). "Liability of Police Officers and Their Employers." In *Police Civil Liability.* Columbia, Md.: Hanrow Press.

Hahn, Harlan. (1971). "Ghetto Assessments of Police Protection and Authority." *Law and Society Review* 6:183-94.

Hale, D. C. (1989). "Ideology of Police Misbehavior." *Quarterly Journal of Ideology* 13 (2): 59-85.

Hamm, Mark S. (1993). *American Skinheads: The Criminology and Control of Hate Crime.* New York: Praeger.

Hancock, B. W., and C. McClung. (1984). "Abstract-Cognitive Abilities in Police Selection and Organization." *Journal of Police Science and Administration* 12:99-108.

Hanewicz, Wayne B. (1985). "Discretion and Order." In Fred Elliston and Michael Feldberg (eds.), *Moral Issues in Police Work.* Totowa, N.J.: Rowman & Allanheld.

Haney, C., and J. Manzolati. (1981). "Television Criminology: Network Illusions of Criminal Justice Realities." In E. Aronson (ed.), *Readings About the Social Animal,* 3d ed., 125-36. San Francisco: Freeman.

Hanushek, Eric A., and John E. Jackson. (1977). *Statistical Methods for Social Scientists.* New York: Academic Press.

Harris, R. N. (1978). "The Police Academy and the Professional Self-Image." In Peter K. Manning and John van Maanen (eds.), *Policing: A View from the Streets.* Santa Monica, Calif.: Goodyear.

Harvard Law Review. (1977). "Developments in the Law, Section 1983 and Federalism." *Harvard Law Review* 90:1133-61.

Hayden, George A. (1981). "Police Discretion in the Use of Deadly Force: An Empirical Study of Information Usage in Deadly Force Decision Making." *Journal of Police Science and Administration* 9 (1): 102-07.

Haynes, W. Warren, and Joseph L. Massie. (1961). *Management: Analysis, Concepts, and Cases.* Englewood Cliffs, N.J.: Prentice-Hall.

Hazlett, S. O. (1985). "Results of the Selection Procedure." *Social Action and the Law* 11:68.

Heaphy, John F. (1978). *Police Practices: The General Administrative Survey.* Washington, D.C.: Police Foundation.

Hearings Before the Subcommittee on Civil and Constitutional Rights of the House Committee on the Judiciary. (1991). 102d Congress, 1st session (March 20 and April 17).

Hennessey, Michael. (1992). *San Francisco Chronicle* (May 9).

Her Majesty's Inspectorate of Constabulary. (1991). Printout from HMIC database.

Herbert, Bob. (1995). "A Reckless Journey." *New York Times* (January 4): A15.

Herman, Eric. (1994). "Firms Find Compliance Is Not Just for Clients." *Chicago Lawyer: A Publication of the Law Bulletin* (January): 1 and passim.

Hindelang, Michael J. (1974). "The Uniform Crime Reports Revisited," *Journal of Criminal Justice* 2 (1): 1–17.

———. (1976). "With a Little Help from Their Friends: Group Participation in Reported Delinquent Behavior." *British Journal of Criminology* 16:109–25.

Hoerr, John. (1991). "What Should Unions Do?" *Harvard Business Review* (May-June): 30–45.

Hogue, Mark C., Tommie Black, and Robert T. Sigler. (1994). "The Differential Use of Screening Techniques in the Recruitment of Police Officers." *American Journal of Police* 13 (2): 113–24.

Hoines v. Barney's Club, Inc. (1980), 620 P.2d 628 (Cal.).

Home Office. (1991). "Statistics on Police Complaints and Discipline, England and Wales." *Home Office Statistical Bulletin* (June 4).

Honolulu Police Commission. (1988). *Report.* Honolulu.

Horvath, Frank. (1987). "Police Use of Deadly Force: A Description of Selected Characteristics of Intrastate Incidents." *Journal of Police Science and Administration* 15 (3): 226–38.

———. (1993). "Polygraphic Screening of Candidates for Police Work in Large Police Agencies in the United States: A Survey of Practices, Policies, and Evaluative Comments." *American Journal of Police* 12 (4): 67–86.

Houlden, Pauline, Stephen LaTour, Laurens Walker, and John Thibaut. (1978). "Preference for Modes of Dispute Resolution as a Function of Process and Decision Control." *Journal of Experimental Social Psychology* 14:13–30.

H.R. 3371. (1991). 102d Congress, 1st session.

H.R. 5151. (1991). 102d Congress, 1st session.

H.R. Conf. Rep. No. 405. (1991). *Violent Crime and Law Enforcement Act of 1991.* 102d Congress, 1st session.

H.R. Rep. No. 291. (1957). 85th Congress, 1st session.

H.R. Rep. No. 914. (1963). 88th Congress, 1st session.

H.R. Rep. No. 956. (1959). 86th Congress, 1st session.

Huang, Wilson W. S., and Vaughn, Michael S. (1996). "Support and Confidence: Public Attitudes Toward the Police." In Timothy J. Flanagan and Dennis R. Longmire (eds.), *Americans View Crime and Justice: A National Opinion Survey.* Thousand Oaks, Calif.: Sage. Forthcoming.

Hubler, Shawn. (1991). "Grand Jury To Investigate Shootings." *Los Angeles Times* (Sept. 20): B1, B7.

Hudson, James R. (1970). "Police-Citizen Encounters That Lead to Citizen Complaints." *Social Problems* 18 (2, Fall): 179–93.

———. (1972). "Organizational Aspects of Internal and External Review of the Police." *Journal of Criminal Law, Criminology, and Police Science* 63 (3, September): 425–33.

Hudzik, John K. (1978). "College Education for Police: Problems in Measuring Component and Extraneous Variables." *Journal of Criminal Justice* 6:69–81.

Humana, Charles. (1983). *World Human Rights Guide.* London: Hutchinson.

Hunt, Jennifer. (1985). "Police Accounts of Normal Force." *Urban Life: A Journal of Ethnographic Research* 13 (4): 315–41.

Hunter, John C. (1994). "Focus on Use of Force: Pepper Spray." *FBI Law Enforcement Bulletin* (May): 24–26.

Huntington, Samuel. (1991). *The Third Wave: Democratization in the Late Twentieth Century.* Normal: University of Oklahoma Press.

Igarashi, Futaba. (1983). "Crime, Confession and Control in Contemporary Japan." *Law in Context* 2:1–30.

Independent Commission on the Los Angeles Police Department. (1991). *Report of the Independent Commission on the Los Angeles Police Department.* Los Angeles.

Inn, Andres, and Alan C. Wheeler. (1977). "Individual Differences, Situational Constraints, and Police Shooting Incidents." *Journal of Applied Social Psychology* 7:19–26.

International Association of Chiefs of Police. (1990). *Fear: It Kills! A Collection of Papers for Law Enforcement Survival.* Arlington, Va.

Inwald, R. E. (1985). "Administrative, Legal, and Ethical Practices in the Psychological Testing of Law Enforcement Officers." *Journal of Criminal Justice* 13:367–72.

Jamieson, J. P., R. Hull, and P. Battershill. (1990). *Recommendations of the Committee on the Use of Less Than Lethal Force by Police Officers in British Columbia.* Vancouver, Canada: British Columbia Police Commission.

Jefferson, Tony. (1988). "Race, Crime and Policing: Empirical, Theoretical and Methodological Issues." *International Journal of the Sociology of Law* 16 (4): 521–39.

Jefferson, Tony, and Roger Grimshaw. (1984). *Controlling the Constable: Police Accountability in England and Wales.* London: Frederick Muller/Cobden Trust.

Jermier, John M., John W. Slocum, Jr., Louis W. Fry, and Jeannie Gaines. (1991). "Organizational Subcultures in a Soft Bureaucracy: Resistance Behind the Myth and Façade of an Official Culture." *Organization Science* 2:170–94.

Johnson, E. (1983). "Psychological Tests Used in Assessing a Sample of Police and Firefighter Candidates." *Journal of Police Science and Administration* 11 (4): 430–33.

Johnson, K. (1983). "Law Enforcement Selection Practices: The United States and Canada." In I. L. Barak-Glantz and E. H. Johnson (eds.), *Comparative Criminology,* 103–19. Newbury Park, Calif.: Sage.

Johnston, Robert. (1988). "Internal New York City Police Department Report by Chief of Department Johnston to Police Commissioner Benjamin Ward on the Police Encounter at Tompkins Square Park." (August 23).

Jones, J. W. (1982). *Correlates of Police Misconduct: Violence and Alcohol Use on the Job.* London House: Technical Report No. 7.

Jones, Robert. (1993). Conversation with William A. Geller (August 20).

Juris, Hervey A., and Peter Feuille. (1973). *Police Unionism.* Lexington, Mass.: Lexington Books.

Kansas Advisory Committee to the U.S. Commission on Civil Rights. (1980). *Police-Community Relations in the City of Wichita and Sedgwick County.* Kansas City, Kan.

Kappeler, S., and Victor E. Kappeler. (1992). "A Research Note on Section 1983 Claims Against the Police: Cases Before the Federal District Courts in 1990." *American Journal of Police* 11:65–73.

Kappeler, Victor E. (1993). *Critical Issues in Police Civil Liability.* Prospect Heights, Ill.: Waveland Press.

Kappeler, Victor E., Richard D. Sluder, and Geoffrey P. Alpert. (1994a). *Forces of Deviance: Understanding the Dark Side of Policing.* Prospect Heights, Ill.: Waveland.

———. (1994b). "Police Brutality and Abuse of Authority: Making Sense of the Senseless Beating of Rodney King" In Victor E. Kappeler, Richard D. Sluder, and Geoffrey P. Alpert, *Forces of Deviance: Understanding the Dark Side of Policing.* Prospect Heights, Ill.: Waveland.

Kates, Robert C. (1952). "May the Intent to Violate the Federal Civil Rights Statute Be Established By a Presumption?" *Georgetown Law Journal* 40:566–82.

Katz, Jesse. (1991). "Is Training of Deputies for Deadly Clashes Adequate? Despite Extensive Instruction When to Shoot, Critics Say Officers Are Too Quick on the Trigger." *Los Angeles Times* (September 8): A1, A22, A23.

Kelling, George L. (1991). "Crime and Metaphor: Toward a New Concept of Policing." *NY: The City Journal* (Autumn): 65–72.

Kelling, George L., and William Bratton. (1993). "Implementing Community Policing: The Administrative Problem." *Perspectives on Policing* No. 17 (July). Washington, D.C.: National Institute of Justice, and Cambridge, Mass.: Harvard University.

Kelling, George L., and Robert Kliesmet. (1991). "Unions, Participation, and Innovation." Mimeo. Arlington, Va.: International Union of Police Associations.

Kelling, George L., and Mark H. Moore. (1987). "The Evolving Strategy of Policing." *Perspectives on Policing.* Washington, D.C.: National Institute of Justice.

Kelling, George L., Tony Pate, Duane Dieckman, and Charles E. Brown. (1974). *The Kansas City Preventive Patrol Experiment: A Summary Report.* Washington, D.C.: Police Foundation.

Kelling, George L., and James K. Stewart. (1991). "The Evolution of Contemporary Policing." In William A. Geller (ed.), *Local Government Police Management* (3d rev. ed.). Washington, D.C.: International City/County Management Association.

Kent, D. A., and Terry Eisenberg. (1972). "The Selection and Promotion of Police Officers: A Selected Review of Recent Literature." *Police Chief* 39:20–29.

Kerner Commission. *See* National Advisory Commission on Civil Disorders.

Kerstetter, Wayne A. (1985). "Who Disciplines the Police? Who Should?" In William A. Geller (ed.), *Police Leadership in America: Crisis and Opportunity.* New York: Praeger.

Kerstetter, Wayne A., and Kenneth A. Rasinski. (1994). "Opening a Window into Police Internal Affairs: Impact of Procedural Justice Reform on Third Party Attitudes." *Social Justice Research* 7 (2): 107–27.

Kerstetter, Wayne A., and Barrik Van Winkle. (1989). "Evidence in the Investigation of Police Use of Excessive Force in Chicago." Chicago: American Bar Foundation Working Paper No. 9015.

King, Gary. (1989). *Unifying Political Methodology: The Likelihood Theory of Statistical Inference.* Cambridge: Cambridge University Press.

Kirkham, George. (1976). *Signal Zero.* New York: Ballantine.

Kliesmet, Robert B. (1985). "The Chief and the Union: May the Force Be with You." In William A. Geller (ed.), *Police Leadership in America: Crisis and Opportunity.* New York: Praeger.

Klinger, David A. (1992). "Deference or Deviance? A Note on Why 'Hostile' Suspects Are Arrested." Paper presented at the annual meeting of the American Society of Criminology, November 4-7, New Orleans.

———. (1994). "Demeanor or Crime? Why Hostile Citizens Are More Likely To Be Arrested." *Criminology* 32 (3): 475-93.

Klockars, Carl B. (1980). "The Dirty Harry Problem." *Annals of the American Academy of Political and Social Science* 452 (November): 33-47.

———. (1985). *The Idea of Police.* Beverly Hills, Calif.: Sage.

———. (1994). "Reducing Excessive Force: A Draft Program Plan for the National Institute of Justice." April 8 memorandum to NIJ, used with permission of author.

Klockars, Carl B., and William E. Harver. (1992). *The Production and Consumption of Research in Police Agencies in the United States.* A Report to the National Institute of Justice (July).

Klyver, N. (1986). "LAPD's Peer Counseling Program After Three Years." In J. Reese and H. A. Goldstein (eds.), *Psychological Services for Law Enforcement.* Washington, D.C.: U.S. Department of Justice.

Knowles, P., and R. Peterson. (1973). "Measurement of Flexibility in State Police Officers." *Journal of Police Science and Administration* 1 (2): 213-23.

Kobler, Arthur. (1975a). "Police Homicide in a Democracy." *Journal of Social Issues* 31 (1): 163-81.

———. (1975b). "Figures (and Perhaps Some Facts) on Police Killing of Civilians in the United States, 1965-1969." *Journal of Social Issues* 31 (1): 185-91.

Kolpack, B. (1991). "The Assessment Center Approach to Police Officer Selection." *Police Chief* 58 (9): 28-34.

Kolts, James G. (1992). "The Los Angeles County Sheriff's Department." Report presented to the Board of Supervisors of Los Angeles County.

Komarnicki, M., and J. Doble. (1985). *Crime and Corrections: A Review of Public Opinion Data Since 1975.* New York: Public Agenda Foundation.

Korzeniowski, George. (1990). "Survival City." *Law and Order* (October): 30-34.

Kreimer, Seth F. (1988). "Release, Redress, and Police Misconduct: Reflections on Agreements to Waive Civil Rights Actions in Exchange for Dismissal of Criminal Charges." *University of Pennsylvania Law Review* 136:851.

Krier, Beth Ann. (1990). "Copping an Attitude: Ex-Policeman Teaches Officers the Art of Verbal Judo—Reading and Redirecting People." *Los Angeles Times* (May 8): E1 and passim.

Kroes, W. H. (1985). *Society's Victims: The Police.* 2d ed. Springfield, Ill.: Charles C. Thomas.

Lacayo, R. (1992). "Anatomy of an Acquittal." *Time* (May 11): 30-32.

LaFave, Wayne R. and Jerold H. Israel. (1991). *Criminal Procedure*, 2d ed. St. Paul, Minn.: West.

Landis, Jean M., and Lynne Goodstein. (1986). "When Is Justice Fair?" *American Bar Foundation Journal*, 675-708.

Lane, Roger. (1986). *Roots of Violence in Black Philadelphia, 1860-1900.* Cambridge, Mass.: Harvard University Press.

Lappé, Frances Moore, and Paul Martin DuBois. (1994). *The Quickening of America: Rebuilding Our Nation, Remaking Our Lives.* San Francisco: Jossey-Bass.

Lasely, J. R. (1994). "The Impact of the Rodney King Incident on Citizen Attitudes Toward Police." *Policing and Society* 3 (4): 245-55.

LaTour, Stephen. (1978). "Determinants of Participant and Observer Satisfaction with Adversary and Inquisitorial Modes of Adjudication." *Journal of Personality and Social Psychology* 36:1531-45.

LaTour, Stephen, Pauline Houlden, Laurens Walker, and John Thibaut. (1976). "Procedure: Transnational Perspective and Preferences." *Yale Law Journal* 86:258-90.

Law Enforcement News. (1995). "ACLU Seeks Fed Regulation of OC Spray." *Law Enforcement News* (August 20): 5.

Lawrence, Frederick M. (1993). "Civil Rights and Criminal Wrongs: The *Mens Rea* of Federal Civil Rights Crimes." *Tulane Law Review* 67:2113-229.

Lea, Michael, and Laurens Walker. (1979). "Efficient Procedures." *North Carolina Law Review* 57:363-78.

LeBeau, J. L., K. D. Harries, and P. Canter. (1992). "Geography and Policing." In R. Effefson and P. Unsinger (eds.), *Geographic Applications to Law Enforcement.* Springfield, Ill.: Charles C. Thomas.

Leff, Donna R., David L. Protess, and Stephen C. Brooks. (1986). "Crusading Journalism: Changing Public Attitudes and Policymaking Agendas." *Public Opinion Quarterly* 50 (3): 300-15.

Lefkowitz, Joel. (1975). "Psychological Attributes of Policemen: A Review of Research and Opinion." *Journal of Social Issues* 31:3-26.

Leibig, Michael T. (1993). "Police Unions and the Law." *Police Union News* 4 (8, August).

———. (1994). "The IUPA Surveys Nation on the Need for Reform in Police Disciplinary Procedures." *The Law Officer* (IUPA newsletter) 14 (1): 19-21.

Lester, David. (1982). "Civilians Who Kill Police Officers and Police Officers Who Kill Civilians." *Journal of Police Science and Administration* 10:384-87.

———. (1983). "Why Do People Become Police Officers." *Journal of Police Science and Administration* 11:170-74.

———. (1984). "The Use of Deadly Force by Police." *Police Journal* 57:170-71.

Lester, David, and A. F. Arcuri. 1994. "How Did Police Officers View the Rodney King Beating?" *Perceptual & Motor Skills* 79:1382.

Lester, David, A. F. Arcuri, and M. M. Gunn. (1980). "Police Roles, Discretion and Danger." *Perceptual and Motor Skills* 51:318.

Lester, David, and W. Ten Brink. (1985). "Police Solidarity and Tolerance for Police Misbehavior." *Psychological Reports* 57:326.

Leung, Kwok. (1985). "Cross-Cultural Study of Procedural Fairness and Disputing Behavior." Ph.D. diss., University of Illinois.

Leung, Kwok, and E. Allan Lind. (1986). "Procedural Justice and Culture: Effects of Culture, Gender, and Investigator Status on Procedural Preferences." *Journal of Personality and Social Psychology* 50:1134-40.

Levitt, Leonard. (1991). "Too Close for Comfort? DAs Need Cops Too Much to Charge Them, Critics Say." *New York Newsday* (November 15): 7, 30.

Lewis, Anthony. (1995). "Truth and Healing." *New York Times* (January 16): A11.

Lewis, Clare E. (1991). "Police Complaints in Metropolitan Toronto: Perspectives of the Public Complaints Commissioner." In Andrew J. Goldsmith (ed.), *Complaints Against the Police.* New York: Oxford.

Lind, E. Allan. (1975). "The Exercise of Information Influence in Legal Advocacy." *Journal of Applied Social Psychology* 5:127-43.

Lind, E. Allan, and Robin I. Lissak. (1985). "Apparent Impropriety and Procedural Fairness Judgments." *Journal of Experimental Psychology* 21:19-29.

Lind, E. Allan, R. I. Lissak, and D. E. Conlon. (1983). "Decision Control and Process Control Effects on Procedural Justice Judgments." *Journal of Applied Social Psychology* 13:338-50.

Lind, E. Allan, John Thibaut, and Laurens Walker. (1973). "Discovery and Presentation of Evidence in Adversary and Non-adversary Proceeding." *Michigan Law Review* 71:1129-44.

———. (1976). "A Cross-Cultural Comparison of the Effects of Adversary and Non-adversary Processes on Bias in Legal Decision Making." *Virginia Law Review* 62:271-83.

Lind, E. Allan, and Tom R. Tyler. (1988). *The Social Psychology of Procedural Justice.* New York: Plenum Press.

Lipset, S. M., and W. Schneider. (1983). *The Confidence Gap: Business, Labor, and Government in the Public Mind.* New York: Free Press.

Lipsky, Michael. (1980). *Street-Level Bureaucracy: Dilemmas of the Individual in Public Service.* New York: Russell Sage.

Locke, Hubert G. (1967). "Police Brutality and Civilian Review Boards: A Second Look." *Urban Law* 44:625-33.

Lohman, Joseph D., and Gordon Misner. (1966). *The Police in the Community.* Berkeley: University of California Press.

London Metropolitan Police Service. (1990). *Annual Report.*

Lore, R. K., and L. A. Schultz. (1993). "Control of Human Aggression: A Comparative Perspective." *American Psychologist* 48:16-25.

Los Angeles County Sheriff's Department. (1992). *A Response to the Kolts Report.* Los Angeles. (October).

Los Angeles Police Department. (1989). "Internal Affairs Report." Los Angeles.

———. (1991). *Los Angeles Police Department Manual.* I: section 556.40.

Los Angeles Times. (1990). Poll (February 1).

Love, K. G. (1981). "Accurate Evaluation of Police Officer Performance Through the Judgment of Fellow Officers: Fact or Fiction?" *Journal of Police Science and Administration* 9 (2): 143-49.

Lundman, Richard J. (1974). "Routine Police Arrest Practices: A Commonweal Perspective." *Social Problems* 22:127-41.

———. (1994). "Demeanor or Crime? The Midwest City Police-Citizen Encounter Study." *Criminology* 32 (4): 631-56.

MacFarlane, R. I., and Crosby, A. (1976). "Police Officer Discipline: A Study of Experience and Attitude." *Journal of Police Science and Administration* 4:331-39.

Maguire, Kathleen, Anne L. Pastore, and Timothy J. Flanagan (eds.). (1993). *Bureau of Justice Statistics Sourcebook of Criminal Justice Statistics—1992.* Washington, D.C.: U.S. Government Printing Office.

Maguire, M., and C. Corbett. (1989). "Patterns and Profiles of Complaints Against the Police." In Rod Morgan and David J. Smith (eds.), *Coming to Terms with Policing,* chapter 10. London: Routledge.

———. (1991). *A Study of the Police Complaints System.* London: HMSO.

Malone, Edward F. (1990). "Legacy of the Reconstruction: The Vagueness of the Criminal Civil Rights Statutes." *UCLA Law Review* 38:163-222.

Mann, Coramae Richey. (1993). *Unequal Justice: A Question of Color.* Bloomington, Ind.: Indiana University Press.

Manning, Peter K. (1977). *Police Work: The Social Organization of Policing.* Cambridge, Mass.: MIT Press.

———. (1989). "The Police Occupational Culture in Anglo-American Societies." In William G. Bailey (ed.), *Encyclopedia of Police Science.* Dallas: Garland.

Marcus, Frances Frank. (1995). "Overhaul Is Planned for New Orleans Police." *New York Times* (January 16): A8.

Margarita, Mona. (1980a). "Killing the Police: Myths and Motives." *Annals of the American Academy of Political and Social Science* 452 (November): 63-71.

———. (1980b). "Police As Victims of Violence." *Justice System Journal* 5 (Spring): 218-33.

Margolis, R. J. (1970). *Who Will Wear the Badge? A Study of Minority Recruitment Efforts in Protective Services.* A Report of the United States Commission on Civil Rights. Washington, D.C.: U.S. Commission on Civil Rights.

Maslow, Will, and Joseph B. Robinson. (1953). "Civil Rights Legislation and the Fight for Equality, 1862-1952." *University of Chicago Law Review* 20:363-413.

Mastrofski, Stephen D. (1988). "Varieties of Police Governance in Metropolitan America." *Politics and Policy* 8:12-31.

———. (1993). "Eyeing the Doughnut—Community Policing and Progressive Reform. A Review of *Beyond 911: A New Era of Policing.*" *American Journal of Police* 12 (4): 1-17.

Mastrofski, Stephen D., and Roger B. Parks. (1990). "Improving Observational Studies of Police." *Criminology* 28:475-96.

Maxfield, M. G. (1988). "The London Metropolitan Police and Their Clients: Victim and Suspect Attitudes." *Journal of Research in Crime and Delinquency* 25 (2): 188-206.

McCone Commission on the Los Angeles Riots. (1965). *Violence in the City: An End or a Beginning? Report to the Governor* (December 2).

McCoy, Candace. (1984). "Lawsuits Against the Police: What Impact Do They Really Have?" *Criminal Law Bulletin:* 49-56. Reprinted in James J. Fyfe (ed.), (1985), *Police Management Today: Issues and Case Studies,* 55-64. Washington, D.C.: International City/County Management Association.

———. (1987). "Police Legal Liability Is 'Not a Crisis,' Chiefs Say." *Crime Control Digest* 21 (January 19, 3): 1-9.

McCulloch, Jude. (1989). "Armed and Dangerous." *Legal Service Bulletin* 14 (4, August): 171ff.

McDowell, Banks. (1991). *Ethical Conduct and the Professional's Dilemma.* New York: Quorum Books.

McElroy, Jerome E., Colleen A. Cosgrove, and Susan Sadd. (1993). *Community Policing: The CPOP in New York.* Newbury Park, Calif.: Sage.

McIntyre, J. (1967). "Public Attitudes Toward Crime and Law Enforcement." *Annals of the American Academy of Political and Social Science* 374 (November): 37–40.

McKay, Robert, et al. (1972). *Attica—Official Report of the New York State Commission on Attica.* New York: Bantam Books.

McLaughlin, Vance, and Robert Bing. (1989). "Selection, Training, and Discipline of Police Officers." In Kenney, Dennis Jay (ed.), *Police and Policing: Contemporary Issues.* New York: Praeger.

McLeod, J. M., and B. Reeves (1980). "On the Nature of Mass Media Effects." In S. B. Whitney and R. P. Abeles (eds.), *Television and Social Behavior: Beyond Violence and Children,* 17–54. Hillsdale, N.J.: Lawrence Erlbaum.

McNamara, J. H. (1967). "Uncertainties in Police Work: The Relevance of Police Recruits' Background and Training." In David J. Bordua (ed.), *The Police.* New York: Wiley.

Mendez, Gary A., Jr. (1983). "Role of Race and Ethnicity in the Incidence of Police Use of Deadly Force." Unpublished paper prepared on behalf of the National Urban League, New York City. National Criminal Justice Reference Service Microfiche Program.

Meredith, N. (1984). "Attacking the Roots of Police Violence." *Psychology Today* 18:20–26.

Meyer, Marshall W. (1980). "Police Shootings of Minorities: The Case of Los Angeles." *Annals of the American Academy of Political and Social Science* 452:98–110.

Meyers, Michael. (1991). Presentation to the bi-annual conference of the ACLU, Burlington, Vt. (June 24).

Meyrowitz, J. (1985). *No Sense of Place.* New York: Oxford.

Miller, Jon, and Lincoln Fry. (1976). "Reexamining Assumptions About Education and Professionalism in Law Enforcement." *Journal of Police Science and Administration* 4:187–98.

Mills, M. C., and J. G. Stratton. (1982). "The MMPI and the Prediction of Police Job Performance." *FBI Law Enforcement Bulletin* 51 (2, February): 10–15.

Milton, Catherine H., Jeanne W. Halleck, James Lardner, and Gary L. Abrecht. (1977). *Police Use of Deadly Force.* Washington, D.C.: Police Foundation. Portions reprinted in Harry W. More, Jr. (ed.), *Critical Issues in Law Enforcement* (4th rev. ed.) Cincinnati: Anderson.

Milwaukee Mayor's Citizen Commission on Police-Community Relations. (1991). *Report to Mayor John O. Norquist and the Board of Police and Fire Commissioners.* (October 15).

Mirande, A. (1980). "Fear of Crime and Fear of the Police in a Chicano Community." *Sociology and Social Research* 64 (4): 528–41.

Misner, Gordon E. (1972). "The Police and Collective Violence in Contemporary America." In J. F. Short and M. E. Wolfgang (eds.), *Collective Violence,* 343–51. Chicago: Aldine.

Monahan, Jonathan. (1981a). *The Clinical Prediction of Violent Behavior.* Washington, D.C.: U.S. Government Printing Office.

———. (1981b). *Predicting Violent Behavior: An Assessment of Clinical Techniques.* Beverly Hills, Calif.: Sage.

———. (1992). "Mental Disorder and Violent Behavior: Perceptions and Evidence." *American Psychologist* 47:511-21.

Monell v. Department of Social Services (1988), 436 U.S. 658.

Monroe v. Pape (1961), 365 U.S. 167.

Moore, D. W. (1992). *The Superpollsters: How They Measure and Manipulate Public Opinion in America.* New York: Four Walls Eight Windows.

Moore, Mark H., and Darrel W. Stephens. (1991a). *Beyond Command and Control: The Strategic Management of Police Departments.* Washington, D.C.: Police Executive Research Forum.

———. (1991b). "Organization and Management." In William A. Geller (ed.), *Local Government Police Management,* 22-58. Washington, D.C.: International City/County Management Association.

Moran, T. K. (1978). "Toward More Effective Control of Police Discretion: The Co-operative Supervisory Model." *Journal of Police Science and Administration* 6:253-63.

More, H. W., and P. C. Unsinger (eds.). (1987). *Police Managerial Use of Psychology and Psychologist.* Springfield, Ill.: Charles C. Thomas.

Morgan, Gareth. (1986). *Images of Organization.* New York: Sage.

Morris, Norval. (1974). *The Future of Imprisonment.* Chicago: University of Chicago Press.

Morris, Norval, and Gordon Hawkins. (1969). *The Honest Politician's Guide to Crime Control.* Chicago: University of Chicago Press.

Muir, William Ker, Jr. (1977). *Police: Streetcorner Politicians.* Chicago: University of Chicago Press.

Muller, Scott W. (1974). "Legislating Civil Rights: The Role of Sections 241 and 242 in the Revised Criminal Code." *Georgetown Law Journal* 63:203-22.

Murphy, Gerard R. (1986). *Special Care: Improving the Police Response to the Mentally Disabled.* Washington, D.C.: Police Executive Research Forum.

Murphy, Sean P. (1992). "Wave of Abuse Claims Laid to a Few Officers." *Boston Globe* (October 4): 1.

Murty, Komanduri, Julian B. Roebuck, and Joann D. Smith. (1990). "The Image of the Police in Black Atlanta Communities." *Journal of Police Science and Administration* 17 (4): 250-57.

Myrdal, Gunnar. (1944, reprinted 1962). *An American Dilemma.* New York: Harper.

Napper, George. (1985). "Who Disciplines the Police? I Do! A Response to Wayne Kerstetter." In William A. Geller (ed.), *Police Leadership in America: Crisis and Opportunity.* New York: Praeger.

National Advisory Commission on Civil Disorders (Kerner Commission). (1968). *Report.* Washington, D.C.: U.S. Government Printing Office.

National Advisory Commission on Criminal Justice Standards and Goals. (1973). *Police.* Washington, D.C.: U.S. Government Printing Office.

National Association for the Advancement of Colored People, and Criminal Justice

Institute at Harvard Law School. (1995). *Beyond the Rodney King Story.* Boston: Northeastern University Press.

National Bulletin on Police Misconduct. (1994a). "Is Officer Who Witnessed and Failed To Prevent Beating Liable?" *National Bulletin on Police Misconduct* 11 (4, April): 3–4.

———. (1994b). "Officers Fail To Report Injuries Suspect Suffered During Arrest: *Commonwealth v. Adams,* 642 N.E.2d 102 (Massachusetts)." *National Bulletin on Police Misconduct* 11 (6, June): 3–4.

National Center on Police and Community Relations. (1967). *A National Survey of Police and Community Relations.* Washington, D.C.: U.S. Government Printing Office.

National Institute of Justice (NIJ). (1994a). "Oleoresin Capsicum: Pepper Spray as a Force Alternative." Washington, D.C.: NIJ Technology Assessment Program Information Center.

———. (1994b). "Update on NIJ-Sponsored Research: Six New Reports." *National Institute of Justice Research in Brief* (April). Washington, D.C.

National Lawyers Guild. (1992). *Police Misconduct Law and Litigation,* 2d ed. New York: Clark Boardman.

Nelson, Deborah. (1995a). "Cop's Free Rein Costs City Millions: Police Rarely Punished Over Repeated Misconduct Suits." *Chicago Sun-Times* (January 8): 1, 14–16.

———. (1995b). "City Officers Defend Their Record: 'We Were Doing Our Job'." *Chicago Sun-Times* (January 8): 14.

———. (1995c). "City Officers Defend Their Record: 'Desperate Times . . . Call for Desperate Measures'." *Chicago Sun-Times* (January 8): 15.

———. (1995d). "The Price of Police Lawsuits: Payout Often Is Best Defense." *Chicago Sun-Times* (January 8): 16.

———. (1995e). " 'This Can't Be Happening': An Innocent Man's Jailing Shows Price of Bad Arrest." *Chicago Sun-Times* (January 8): 16.

———. (1995f). "Small Group Triggers Large Lawsuits." *Chicago Sun-Times* (January 8): 16.

Netherlands Study Group on Police Violence. (1987). *Use of Violence by the Police.* Amsterdam: Ministry of Justice.

New York City Police Department Civilian Complaint Review Board. (1986). *Nationwide Survey of Civilian Complaint Systems* (January).

New York City Police Department Civilian Complaint Investigative Bureau. (1989). *Annual Report.*

New York Daily News/Eyewitness News Poll. (1985). Untitled poll, data referenced in the American Public Opinion Index (April 29).

New York State Commission on Criminal Justice and the Use of Force. (1987). *Report to the Governor.* Albany, N.Y.

New York Times. (1993). "Two Similar Auto Accidents, Two Very Different Results." *New York Times* (September 8): A20.

New York Times. (1994). "Officer Commits Suicide in Times Square Restaurant." *New York Times* (December 26): A20.

New York Times Poll. (1987). "New York City Race Relations Survey." (March 11). Unpublished data.

Newman, Jon O. (1978). "Suing the Lawbreakers: Proposals To Strengthen the Section 1983 Damage Remedy for Law Enforcers' Misconduct." *Yale Law Journal* 87:447–67.

———. (1992). Statement of Judge Jon O. Newman Before the Subcommittee on Civil and Constitutional Rights of the House Committee on the Judiciary. 102d Congress, 1st session (May 5).

Niederhoffer, Arthur. (1967). *Behind the Shield: The Police in Urban Society.* Garden City, N.Y.: Doubleday.

Niederhoffer, Arthur, and Abraham S. Blumberg. (1970). *The Ambivalent Force: Perspectives on the Police.* Waltham, Mass.: Ginn.

Nielsen, Swen. (1990). "The Need for Replicative Firearms Training." *Police Chief* (November): 36–39.

Northern Territory Police [of Australia]. *Annual Reports.*

Nossiter, Adam. (1994). "Officer Linked to Killing, Shocking Jaded City: New Tale of Corruption in N.O." *New York Times* (December 19): A14.

Novick, Anton (1986–88). Articles in the *Yomiuri Shimbum.*

Nowicki, Dennis E., Gary W. Sykes, and Terry Eisenberg. (1991). "Human Resource Management." In William A. Geller (ed.), *Local Government Police Management.* Washington, D.C.: International City/County Management Association.

O'Brien, J. T. (1978). "Public Attitudes Toward Police." *Journal of Police Science and Administration* 6 (3): 303–10.

O'Hara, K., and K. C. Love. (1987). "Accurate Selection of Police Officials Within Small Municipalities: 'Et Tu Assessment Center?'" *Public Personnel Management* 16:9–14.

Ontario, Ministry of the Solicitor General. (1990). "Background Information to the Police Services Act." Toronto.

Ostrom, E., R. B. Parks, and G. P. Whitaker. (1978). *Patterns of Metropolitan Policing.* Cambridge, Mass.: Ballinger.

Pate, Antony M., and Lorie A. Fridell, with Edwin E. Hamilton. (1993). *Police Use of Force: Official Reports, Citizen Complaints, and Legal Consequences,* Vol. 1. Washington, D.C.: Police Foundation.

Pate, Antony M., Jack W. McCullough, Robert A. Bowers, and Amy Ferrara. (1976). *Kansas City Peer Review Panel: An Evaluation Report.* Washington, D.C.: Midwest Research Institute and Police Foundation.

Peak, Ken, Robert V. Bradshaw, and Ronald W. Glensor. (1992). "Improving Citizen Perceptions of the Police: 'Back to the Basics' with a Community Policing Strategy." *Journal of Criminal Justice* 20:25–40.

Peek, C. W., and G. D. Lowe. (1981). "Race and Attitudes Toward Local Police: Another Look." *Journal of Black Studies* 11 (3): 361–74.

Peirson, Gwynne W. (1978). *Police Use of Deadly Force—Preliminary Report.* Washington, D.C.: U.S. Department of Justice—National Minority Advisory Council on Criminal Justice.

Perez, Douglas W. (1978). "Police Accountability: A Question of Balance." Ph.D. diss., University of California, Berkeley. Ann Arbor: University Microfilms International.

———. (1994). *Common Sense About Police Review.* Philadelphia: Temple University Press.

Perry, I. D. (1987). "Policing Police Misconduct." *Southern-Exposure* 15:31–37.

Petrillo, Lisa. (1990). "When a Cop Shoots, Who Takes a Close Look? Here, Unlike Most Cities, An Outside Probe Rarely Results When Officers Fire." *San Diego Union* (December 21): A1, A10.

Piliavin, Irving, and Scott Briar. (1964). "Police Encounters with Juveniles." *American Journal of Sociology* 70 (September): 206–14.

Pinkele, Carl, and William Louthan. (1985). *Discretion, Justice, and Democracy*. Ames: Iowa State University Press.

Platte, Anthony. (1971). *The Politics of Riot Commissions*. New York: Macmillan.

Pledger, James R. (1988). "Hogan's Alley: The Federal Bureau of Investigation Academy's New Training Complex." *FBI Law Enforcement Bulletin* (December): 5–9.

Pogrebin, M. R., and E. D. Poole. (1988). "Humor in the Briefing Room." *Journal of Contemporary Ethnography* 17:183–210.

Poland, J. M. (1978). "Police Selection Methods and the Prediction of Police Performance." *Journal of Police Science and Administration* 6:374–87.

Police Complaints Authority. (1988). *Annual Report*. London.

Police Executive Research Forum. (1981). *Police Agency Handling of Citizen Complaints: A Model Policy Statement*. Washington, D.C.

Police Foundation. (1981). *The Newark Foot Patrol Experiment*. Washington, D.C.

Pollock, N. L. (1990). "Accounting for Predictions of Dangerousness." *International Journal of Law and Psychiatry* 13:207–15.

Potts, Lee W. (1983). *Responsible Police Administration*. Huntsville: University of Alabama Press.

Powell, Dennis. (1981). "Race, Rank and Police Discretion." *Journal of Police Science and Administration* 9 (4): 383–89.

———. (1990). "A Study of Police Discretion in Six Southern Cities." *Journal of Police Science and Administration* 17 (1): 1–7.

President's Commission on Law Enforcement and Administration of Justice. (1967a). *A National Survey of Police-Community Relations: Field Surveys V*. Washington, D.C.: U.S. Government Printing Office.

———. (1967b). *Task Force Report: The Police*. Washington, D.C.: U.S. Government Printing Office.

———. (1967c). *The Challenge of Crime in a Free Society*. Washington, D.C.: U.S. Government Printing Office.

Price, B. R., and R. Price. (1981). "Police Community Relations: Sex-Conscious Hiring and Professionalism." *Journal of Crime and Justice* 4:48–60.

Primeau, C. C., J. A. Helton, J. C. Baxter, and R. M. Rozelle. (1975). "An Examination of the Conception of the Police Officer Held by Several Social Groups." *Journal of Police Science and Administration* 3 (2): 189–96.

PROMIS Research Project. (1977). *Highlights of Interim Findings and Implications*. Washington, D.C.: Institute for Law and Social Research.

Prothrow-Stith, Deborah, and Michaele Weissman. (1991). *Deadly Consequences: How Violence Is Destroying Our Teenage Population and a Plan to Begin Solving the Problem*. New York: HarperCollins.

Prottas, Jeffrey Manditch. (1978). "The Power of the Street-Level Bureaucrat in Public Service Bureaucracies." *Urban Affairs Quarterly* 13:285–312.

Pugh, G. (1985a). "Situational Tests and Police Selection." *Journal of Police Science and Administration* 13:30-35.

———. (1985b). "The California Psychological Inventory and Police Selection." *Journal of Police Science and Administration* 13:172-77.

———. (1986). "The Good Police Officer: Qualities Roles and Concepts." *Journal of Police Science and Administration* 14 (1): 1-5.

Pynes, Joan E. (1994). "Police Officer Selection Procedures: Speculation on the Future." *American Journal of Police* 13 (2): 103-12.

Queensland Criminal Justice Commission. (1990-91). *Annual Report.*

Quilliam, Peter. (1992). Police Complaints Authority. Private letter (February 14).

Quindlen, A. (1992). "The Good Guys." *New York Times* (February 12).

Rae, S. F. (1940). "Public Opinion Survey." *Public Opinion Quarterly* (March): 75-76.

Rafky, D. M., T. Lawley, and R. Ingram. (1976). "Are Police Recruits Cynical?" *Journal of Police Science and Administration* 4:352-60.

Rankin, Tom. (1990). *New Forms of Work Organization: The Challenge for North American Unions.* Toronto: University of Toronto Press.

Rarick, D. L., J. E. Townsend, and D. A. Boyd. (1973). "Adolescent Perceptions of Police: Actual and As Depicted in TV Drama." *Journalism Quarterly* 50 (3): 438-46.

Rather, Dan. (1992). *48 Hours.* Television program transcript (January 29).

Reeves, Brian A. (1993). "Census of State and Local Law Enforcement Agencies, 1992." *Bureau of Justice Statistics Bulletin.* Washington, D.C.: Bureau of Justice Statistics.

Reiner, Robert. (1985). *Politics and the Police.* New York: St. Martin's Press.

———. (1988). "In the Office of the Chief Constable." *Current Legal Studies* 12:84-103.

———. (1991a). "Policing and Criminal Justice in Great Britain." *Coexistence* 28:107-17.

———. (1991b). "A Much Lower Pedestal." *Policing* 7 (3, Autumn): 225-38.

———. (1992). "Police Research in the United Kingdom: A Critical Review." In Michael Tonry and Norval Morris (eds.), *Modern Policing.* Chicago: University of Chicago Press.

Reinhold, Robert. (1992). "U.S. Jury Indicts Four Police Officers in King Beating: Los Angeles Panel Files Civil Rights Charges." *New York Times* (August 6): A1, A12.

Reiss, Albert J., Jr. (1967). *Studies on Crime and Law Enforcement in Major Metropolitan Areas.* President's Commission on Law Enforcement and Administration of Justice, Field Surveys no. 3. Washington, D.C.: U.S. Government Printing Office.

———. (1968a). "Police Brutality—Answers to Key Questions." *Transaction* 5 (8): 10-19.

———. (1968b). "Stuff and Nonsense about Social Surveys and Observation." In Howard S. Becker et al. (eds.), *Institutions and the Person.* Chicago: Aldine.

———. (1971a). *The Police and the Public.* New Haven: Yale University Press.

———. (1971b). "Systematic Observation of Natural Social Phenomena." In Herbert L. Costner (ed.), *Sociological Methodology 1971.* San Francisco: Jossey-Bass.

———. (1974). "Discretionary Justice." In D. Glaser (ed.), *Handbook of Criminology,* 679-99. Chicago: Rand McNally.

———. (1980). "Controlling Police Use of Deadly Force." *Annals of the American Academy of Political and Social Science* 452 (November): 122-34.

———. (1985). "Shaping and Serving the Community: The Role of the Police Chief

Executive." In William A. Geller (ed.), *Police Leadership in America: Crisis and Opportunity.* New York: Praeger.

———. (1992). "Police Organization in the Twentieth Century." In Michael Tonry and Norval Morris (eds.), *Modern Policing.* Chicago: University of Chicago Press.

Remsberg, Charles. (1986). *The Tactical Edge.* Northbrook, Ill.: Calibre Press.

Renner, K. Edward, and Denice A. Gierach. (1975). "An Approach to the Problem of Excessive Force by Police." *Journal of Police Science and Administration* 3 (4): 377–83.

Reuss-Ianni, Elizabeth. (1983). *Two Cultures of Policing: Street Cops and Management Cops.* New Brunswick, N.J.: Transaction Books.

Reyes, David. (1992). "Police Chiefs Study Training Policy: Many Say King Verdict Stunned Them; They Promise to Implement Outreach Programs Spurred by the Beating." *Los Angeles Times* (May 3): B3, B22.

Richardson, J. F. (1970). *The New York Police: Colonial Times to 1901.* New York: Oxford.

Richmond (Calif.) Police Department. (1989). "Internal Affairs Report." Richmond.

Rizzo v. Goode (1976), 423 U.S. 362.

Robinson, Cyril D. (1992). *Legal Rights, Duties, and Liabilities of Criminal Justice Personnel: History and Analysis.* 2d ed. Springfield, Ill.: Charles C. Thomas.

Rohrlich, T. (1991). "Police Brutality Seen As Common in LA, Poll Shows." *Houston Chronicle* (March 12): 6A.

Rosen, Marie Simonetti. (1994). "A LEN Interview with Prof. Carl Klockars of the University of Delaware." *Law Enforcement News* (April 15): 10–12, 18.

Ross, Jeffrey Ian. (1994). "The Future of Municipal Police Violence in Advanced Industrialized Democracies: Towards a Structural Causal Model." *Police Studies: The International Review of Police Development* 17 (2, Summer): 1–27.

Royal Canadian Mounted Police Public Complaints Commission. (1991). *Annual Report: 1990–91.* Ottawa: Minister of Supply and Services of Canada.

Rudovsky, David. (1992). "Police Abuse: Can the Violence Be Contained?" *Harvard Civil Rights-Civil Liberties Law Review* 27:465–501.

Russell, K. (1976). *Complaints Against the Police: A Sociological View.* Glenfield, Leicester, England: Millek. Rustumiji, K. (1980). "Tour Note 33." (December).

Sabato, L. J. (1991). *Feeding Frenzy: How Attack Journalism Has Transformed American Politics.* New York: Free Press.

St. Clair, James D., et al. (1992). *Report of the Boston Police Department Management Review Committee.* Boston. (January 14).

San Antonio v. Higle (1984), 685 S.W.2d 682 (Tex. Ct. App.).

San Francisco Chronicle (1990) "San Francisco Watchdog Upholds Few Charges." *San Francisco Chronicle* (May 31): 1.

Sauls v. Hutto (1969), 304 F.Supp. 124 (E.D. La.).

Scaglion, R., and R. G. Condon. (1980). "Determinants of Attitudes Toward City Police." *Criminology* 17 (4): 485–94.

Scharf, Peter, and Arnold Binder. (1983). *The Badge and the Bullet: Police Use of Deadly Force.* New York: Praeger.

Schmidt, Wayne W. (1984). "Recent Developments in Police Crime Liability." *Police Civil Liability.* Columbia, Md.: Hanrow Press.

———. (1985). "Section 1983 and the Changing Face of Police Management." In

William A. Geller (ed.), *Police Leadership in America: Crisis and Opportunity*. New York: Praeger.

Schofield, Daniel L. (1990). "Remarks: Legal Issues of Pursuit Driving." *The Police Yearbook 1990.* Arlington, Va.: International Association of Chiefs of Police.

Schorr, Lisbeth Bamberger, with Daniel Schorr. (1989). *Within Our Reach: Breaking the Cycle of Disadvantage.* New York: Anchor/Doubleday.

Schrader, George E. (1988). "Firearms Training/Civil Liability: Is Your Training Documentation Sufficient?" *FBI Law Enforcement Bulletin* 57 (6, June): 1-3.

Schuman, Howard, and Michael P. Johnson. (1976). "Attitudes and Behavior." *Annual Review of Sociology* 2:161-207.

Schur, Edwin M. (1969). *Our Criminal Society.* Englewood Cliffs, N.J.: Prentice-Hall.

Schwartz, Louis B. (1970). "Complaints Against the Police: Experience of the Community Rights Division of the Philadelphia District Attorney's Office." *University of Pennsylvania Law Review* 118:1023-35.

Schwartz, Tony. (1973). *The Responsive Chord: How Radio and TV Manipulate You . . . Who You Vote For . . . What You Buy . . . And How You Think.* Garden City, N.Y.: Anchor/Doubleday.

————. (1983). *Media: The Second God.* Garden City, N.Y.: Anchor/Doubleday.

Scogin, F., and S. Brodsky. (1991). "Fear of Litigation Among Law Enforcement Officers." *American Journal of Police:* 10:41-45.

Screws v. United States (1945), 325 U.S. 91.

Scrivner, Ellen M. (1994a). *The Role of Police Psychology in Controlling Excessive Force.* A National Institute of Justice "Research Report." Washington, D.C.: National Institute of Justice (April).

————. (1994b). "Controlling Police Use of Excessive Force: The Role of the Police Psychologist." A National Institute of Justice *Research in Brief.* Washington, D.C.: National Institute of Justice (October).

————. (1994c). *The Role of Police Psychology in Controlling Excessive Force.* Unpublished report to the National Institute of Justice, summarized in Scrivner (1994b). Full report available through National Criminal Justice Reference Service, Rockville, Md. (report NCJ-146206).

Selznick, Philip. (1966). *TVA and the Grass Roots.* New York: Harper Torchbook.

Sexton, Joe. (1995). "Cold War is Waged in Enclave of Emigrés: In Brighton Beach, the Police and Immigrants from Russia Are Wary." *New York Times* (January 17):A13.

Shah, S. A. (1981). "Dangerousness: Conceptual, Prediction and Public Policy Issues." In J. R. Hays, T. K. Roberts, and K. S. Solway (eds.), *Violence and the Violent Individual.* New York: Spectrum.

Shapiro, Harry H. (1961). "Limitations in Prosecuting Civil Rights Violations." *Cornell Law Quarterly* 46:532-54.

Shawn v. California Department of Beverage Control (1988), 788 F.2d 600 (9th Cir.).

Sheppard, Blair H., and Neil Vidmar. (1980). "Adversary Pretrial Procedures and Testimonial Evidence: Effects of Lawyer's Role and Machiavellianism." *Journal of Personality and Social Psychology* 39:320-32.

Sherman, Lawrence W. (1975). "An Evaluation of Policewomen on Patrol in a Suburban Police Department." *Journal of Police Science and Administration* 3:434-38.

————. (1980a) "Causes of Police Behavior: The Current State of Quantitative Research." *Journal of Research in Crime and Delinquency* 17 (1): 69-100.

————. (1980b) "Perspectives on Police and Violence." *Annals of the American Academy of Political and Social Science* 452 (November): 1–12.

————. (1983). "Reducing Police Gun Use: Critical Events, Administrative Policy, and Organizational Change." In Maurice Punch (ed.), *Control in the Police Organization.* Cambridge, Mass.: MIT Press.

Sherman, Lawrence W., and Mark Blumberg. (1981). "Higher Education and Police Use of Deadly Force." *Journal of Criminal Justice* 9:317–31.

Sherman, Lawrence W., and Anthony V. Bouza. (1991a). "The Best-Laid Plans." In William A. Geller (ed.), *Local Government Police Management,* p. 354. Washington, D.C.: International City/County Management Association.

————. (1991b) "Seizing Opportunities for Reform." In William A. Geller (ed.), *Local Government Police Management,* pp. 358–61. Washington, D.C.: International City/County Management Association.

Sherman, Lawrence W., and Robert W. Langworthy. (1979). "Measuring Homicide by Police Officers." *Journal of Criminal Law and Criminology* 70 (4): 546–60.

Sherwood v. Berry (1984), 856 F.2d 802 (7th Cir.) (*en banc*).

Shipler, David K. (1992). "Khaki, Blue and Blacks." *New York Times* (May 26):A7.

Shortreed, S. C. H. (1989). "An Examination of the Effect of Police Officer's Age at the Time of Employment on Involvement in Misconduct." Master's thesis, Michigan State University.

Silver, I. (1991). *Police Civil Liability.* New York: Matthew Bender.

Skogan, Wesley G. (1990a). *Disorder and Decline.* New York: Free Press.

————. (1990b). *The Police and the Public in England and Wales: A British Crime Survey Report.* London: Home Office, Research and Planning Unit, study no. 117.

————. (1994). "The Impact of Community Policing on Neighborhood Residents: A Cross-Site Analysis." In Dennis P. Rosenbaum (ed.), *The Challenge of Community Policing: Testing the Promises.* Thousand Oaks, Calif.: Sage.

Skogan, Wesley G., Susan Hartnett, Jill DuBois, Justine Lovig, Susan F. Bennett, Paul J. Lavrakas, Arthur Lurigio, Richard Block, and Dennis Rosenbaum. (1994). *Interim Report: Community Policing in Chicago, Year One.* Unpublished report to the Illinois Criminal Justice Information Authority. Chicago.

Skolnick, Jerome H. (1966). *Justice Without Trial: Law Enforcement in a Democratic Society.* New York: Wiley.

————. (1969). *The Politics of Protest.* New York: Simon and Schuster.

————. (1975). *Justice Without Trial: Law Enforcement in Democratic Society.* 2d ed. New York: Wiley.

Skolnick, Jerome H., and David H. Bayley. (1986). *The New Blue Line: Police Innovation in Six American Cities.* New York: Free Press.

Skolnick, Jerome H., and James J. Fyfe. (1993). *Above the Law: Police and the Excessive Use of Force.* New York: Free Press.

Skolnick, Jerome H., and Candace McCoy. (1985). "Police Accountability and the Media." In William A. Geller (ed.), *Police Leadership in America: Crisis and Opportunity,* pp. 103–35. New York: Praeger.

Slahor, Stephenie. (1992). "A New Look to 'Hogan's Alley'." *Law and Order* (March): 29–31.

Smith, Bruce. (1929). "Municipal Police Administration." *Annals of the American Academy of Political and Social Science* 146 (1, November).

Smith, David J., and Jeremy Gray. (1983). *Police and People in London.* Vol. 2, *A Survey of Londoners;* Vol. 3, *A Survey of Police Officers.* London: Policy Studies Institute.

Smith, Douglas A. (1984). "The Organizational Context of Legal Control." *Criminology* 22:19-38.

Smith, Douglas A., and Laura A. Davidson. (1984). "Equity and Discretionary Justice: The Influence of Race on Police Arrest Decisions." *Journal of Criminal Law and Criminology* 75:234-49.

Smith, Douglas A., and Jody R. Klein. (1984). "Police Control of Interpersonal Disputes." *Social Problems* 31:468-81.

Smith, Douglas A., Jody R. Klein, and Christy A. Visher. (1981). "Street-Level Justice: Situational Determinants of Police Arrest Decisions." *Social Problems* 29:167-77.

Smith, P. E., and R. O. Hawkins. (1973). "Victimization, Types of Citizen-Police Contacts, and Attitudes Toward the Police." *Law and Society Review* 8 (1): 135-52.

Smith, Paul M. (1990). "Survival Course for Border Patrol Agents." *Law and Order* (October): 109-13.

Snipes, Jeffrey B., and Stephen D. Mastrofski. (1990). "An Empirical Test of Muir's Typology of Police Officers." *American Journal of Criminal Justice* 14:268-96.

Solomon, Roger M. (1990). "The Dynamics of Fear in Critical Incidents: Implications for Training and Treatment." In International Association of Chiefs of Police (ed.), *Fear: It Kills!—A Collection of Papers for Law Enforcement Survival.* Arlington, Va.: International Association of Chiefs of Police and Bureau of Justice Assistance, U.S. Department of Justice.

Sourcebook of Criminal Justice Statistics 1990. Washington, D.C.: U.S. Government Printing Office.

Sparrow, Malcolm K., Mark H. Moore, and David Kennedy. (1990). *Beyond 911: A New Era for Policing.* New York: Basic Books.

———. (1993). "A Response to Mastrofski." *American Journal of Police* 12 (4): 19-21.

Spector, Elliot B. (1992). "Chief's Counsel: Nonactor Liability—The Duty to Not Look the Other Way." *Police Chief* (April): 8.

Spelman, William, and John E. Eck. (1989). "The Police and Delivery of Local Government Services: A Problem-Oriented Approach." In James J. Fyfe (ed.), *Police Practice in the '90s: Key Management Issues.* Washington, D.C.: International City/County Management Association.

Stahl, David, Frederick Sussman, and Neil Bloomfield. (1966). *The Community and Racial Crisis.* New York: Practicing Law Institute.

State v. Williams (1959), 29 N.J. 27.

Staub, Ervin. (1989). *The Roots of Evil: The Origins of Genocide and Other Group Violence.* Cambridge: Cambridge University Press.

Steinhauer, Jennifer. (1995). "Two Detectives Are Key Players As Deadly Game Goes into Overtime: The Art of Street Talk Is One of the Major Ingredients for Success." *New York Times* (January 16):A12.

Stephens, Darrel W. (1994). "Point of View: Discipline Philosophy." *FBI Law Enforcement Bulletin* 63 (3, March): 20-22.

Stith, Kate. (1990). "The Risk of Legal Error in Criminal Cases: Some Consequences of the Asymmetry in the Right of Appeal." *University of Chicago Law Review* 57:1-61.

Stolberg, Sheryl. (1990). "Six SIS Detectives Cleared in Shooting of Bank Robbers." *Los Angeles Times* (June 8):A1, A38.

Stone, Andrea. (1994). "Man Shot by Park Police Dies: Debate on Deadly Force Lingers On." *USA Today* (December 22): 3A.

Strawbridge, Peter, and Deirdre Strawbridge. (1990). *A Networking Guide to Recruitment, Selection, and Probationary Training of Police Officers in the Major Police Departments of the United States of America.* New York: John Jay College.

Strecher, Victor G. (1991). "Histories and Futures of Policing: Readings and Misreadings of a Pivotal Present." *Police Forum* 1 (1): 1–9.

Sullivan, P. S., Roger G. Dunham, and Geoffrey P. Alpert. (1987). "Attitude Structures of Different Ethnic and Age Groups Concerning Police." *Journal of Criminal Law and Criminology* 78 (1): 177–96.

Sultan, Cynthia, and Peter Cooper. (no date). "Summary of Research on the Police Use of Deadly Force." Washington D.C.: Police Foundation.

Surette, Ray. (1990). "The Media and Criminal Justice Public Policy: Future Prospects." In Ray Surette (ed.), *The Media and Criminal Justice Policy: Recent Research and Social Effects,* pp. 299–312. Springfield, Ill.: Charles C. Thomas.

———. (1992). *Media and Criminal Justice: Images and Realities.* Pacific Grove, Calif.: Brooks/Cole.

Sykes, Gresham, and David Matza. (1957). "Techniques of Neutralization." *American Sociological Review* 22:664–70.

Sykes, Richard E., and Edward E. Brent. (1980). "The Regulation of Interaction by Police: A Systems View of Taking Charge." *Criminology* 18:182–97.

———. (1983). *Policing: A Social Behaviorist Perspective.* New Brunswick, N.J.: Rutgers University Press.

Sykes, Richard E., and John P. Clark. (1975). "A Theory of Deference Exchange in Police-Civilian Encounters." *American Journal of Sociology* 81:584–600.

Takagi, Paul. (1978). "Issues in the Study of Police Use of Deadly Force." National Institute of Justice, National Criminal Justice Reference Service Microfiche Program.

Talbert, T. L. (1974). "A Study of the Police Officer Height Requirement." *Journal of Personnel Management* 3:103–10.

Talley, J. E., and L. D. Hinz. (1990). *Performance Prediction of Public Safety and Law Enforcement Personnel: A Study in Race and Gender Differences and MMPI Subscales.* Springfield, Ill.: Charles C. Thomas.

Teahan, J. E. (1975). "A Longitudinal Study of Attitude Shifts Among Black and White Police Officers." *Journal of Social Issues* 31 (1): 47–56.

Ten Brink, W., and David Lester. (1984). "Reporting Fellow Police Officers for Brutality." *Psychological Reports* 54:36.

Tennessee v. Garner (1985), 471 U.S. 1.

Tennessee Valley Authority v. Hill (1978), 437 U.S. 153.

Terrill, Richard. (1982). "Complaint Procedures: Varieties on the Theme of Civilian Participation." *Journal of Police Science and Administration* 10:4.

———. (1990). "Alternative Perceptions of Independence in Civilian Oversight." *Journal of Police Science and Administration* 17:2.

Terry, Don. (1992). "With Rap, Not Force, 3 Chicago Police Officers Make Progress." *New York Times* (December 4).

Tesser, A., and D. R. Shaffer. (1990). "Attitudes and Attitude Change." *Annual Review of Psychology* 41:479–523.

Texas Law Enforcement Management and Administrative Statistics Program (TELE-MASP). (1994). "Written Policy Directives: Citizen Complaints." *TELEMASP Bulletin* 1 (5): 1–6.

Texas State Teachers Ass'n v. Garland Indep. School Dist. (1989), 489 U.S. 782.

Thibaut, John, and Harold H. Kelley. (1959). *The Social Psychology of Groups.* New York: Wiley.

Thibaut, John, and Laurens Walker. (1975). *Procedural Justice: A Psychological Analysis.* Hillsdale, N.J.: Erlbaum.

———. (1978). "A Theory of Procedure." *California Law Review* 66:541–66.

Thibaut, John, Laurens Walker, Stephens LaTour, and Pauline Houlden. (1974). "Procedural Justice and Fairness." *Stanford Law Review* 26:1271–89.

Thibaut, John, Laurens Walker, and E. Allan Lind. (1972). "Adversary Presentation and Bias in Legal Decision Making." *Harvard Law Review* 86:386–401.

Thomas, W. T., and J. M. Hyman. (1977). "Perceptions of Crime, Fear of Victimization, and Public Perceptions of Police Performance." *Journal of Police Science and Administration* 5 (3): 305–17.

Thompson, George J. (1983). *Verbal Judo: Words for Street Survival.* Springfield, Ill.: Charles C. Thomas.

Thornsted v. Kelly (1988), 858 F.2d 571 (9th Cir.).

Thornton, L. M. (1975). "People and the Police: An Analysis of Factors Associated with Police Evaluation and Support." *Canadian Journal of Sociology* 1 (3): 325–42.

Tifft, L. L. (1974). "The 'Cop Personality' Reconsidered." *Journal of Police Science and Administration* 2:266–78.

THE TIMES. (1980). (December 7): 10. *THE [London] TIMES.*

Titran v. Ackman (1990), 893 F.2d 145 (7th Cir.).

Toch, Hans. (1969). *Violent Men: An Inquiry into the Psychology of Violence.* Chicago: Aldine.

———. (1973). "Cops and Blacks: Warring Minorities." In J. T. Curran, A. Fowler, and R. H. Ward (eds.), *Police and Law Enforcement* 1:243–47. New York: AMS Press.

———. (1977). *Police, Prisons, and the Problem of Violence.* Washington, D.C.: U.S. Department of Health, Education, and Welfare.

———. (1976, 1979) *Peacekeeping: Police, Prisons, and Violence.* Lexington, Mass.: Lexington Books.

———. (1980). "Mobilizing Policing Expertise." *Annals of the American Academy of Political and Social Science* 452 (November): 53–62.

———. (1986). "True to You, Darling in My Fashion: The Notion of Contingent Consistency." In A. Campbell and A. J. J. Gibbs (eds.), *Violent Transactions: The Limits of Personality.* Oxford, England: Basil Blackwell.

———. (1993). "Good Violence and Bad Violence: Self-Presentation of Aggressors Through Accounts and War Stories." In R. Felson and J. T. Tedeschi (eds.), *Aggression and Violence.* Washington, D.C.: American Psychological Association.

Toch, Hans, and J. Douglas Grant. (1991). *Police as Problem Solvers.* New York: Plenum.

Toch, Hans, J. Douglas Grant, and Raymond T. Galvin. (1975). *Agents of Change: A Study in Police Reform.* New York: John Wiley and Sons; Cambridge Mass: Schenkman.

Toch, Hans, and John Klofas. (1994). "Pluralistic Ignorance, Revisited." In G. M.

Stephenson and J. H. Davis (eds.), *Progress in Applied Social Psychology*, Vol. 2. Chichester, England: John Wiley and Sons.

Tonry, Michael. (1995). *Malign Neglect: Race, Crime and Punishment in America.* New York: Oxford.

Toronto, Public Complaints Commissioner. (1990). *Annual Report.*

Town of Newton v. Rumery (1987), 480 U.S. 386.

Trafficante v. Metropolitan Life Ins. Co. (1972), 409 U.S. 205.

Travis, Jeremy. (1994). *Twenty-five Years of Criminal Justice Research: The National Institute of Justice.* Washington, D.C.: National Institute of Justice, U.S. Department of Justice (December).

Trojanowicz, Robert. (1982). *The Flint Experiment.* East Lansing: Michigan State University.

Trojanowicz, Robert, and Bonnie Bucqueroux. (1990). *Community Policing: A Contemporary Perspective.* Cincinnati: Anderson.

Trujillo, Luis. (1981). "Police Use of Deadly Force." *Urban League Review* 6 (1): 71-82.

Tyler, Tom R. (1984). "The Role of Perceived Injustice in Defendant's Evaluation of Their Courtroom Experience." *Law and Society Review* 18:51-74.

———. (1987a) "Conditions Leading to Value Expressive Effects in Judgments of Procedural Justice: A Test of Four Models." *Journal of Personality and Social Psychology* 52:333-44.

———. (1987b). *Why Citizens Follow the Law: Procedural Justice, Legitimacy and Compliance.* Unpublished manuscript, Northwestern University.

———. (1987c). "The Psychology of Dispute Resolution: Implications for the Mediation of Disputes by Third Parties." *Negotiation Journal* 3:367-74.

———. (1988). "What is Procedural Justice?: Criteria Used by Citizens to Assess the Fairness of Legal Procedures." *Law and Society Review* 22:301-55.

———. (1990). *Why People Obey the Law.* New Haven: Yale University Press.

Tyler, Tom R., and Kathleen McGraw. (1986). "Ideology and the Interpretation of Personal Experience: Procedural Justice and Political Quiescence." *Journal of Social Issues* 42:115-28.

Tyler, Tom R., Kenneth A. Rasinski, and N. Spodick. (1985). "The Influence of Voice on Satisfaction with Leaders: Exploring the Meaning of Process Control." *Journal of Personality and Social Psychology* 48:72-81.

Uelman, Gerald F. (1973). "Varieties of Public Policy: A Study of Policy Regarding the Use of Deadly Force in Los Angeles County." *University of Loyola at Los Angeles Law Review* 6:1-65.

Uglow, Steve. (1988). *Policing Liberal Society.* New York: Oxford.

United Nations General Assembly. (1979). *United Nations Code of Conduct for Law Enforcement Officials.* Art. 3.

United States v. City of Philadelphia (1980), 644 F.2d 187 (3d Cir.).

United States v. Fricke (1982), 684 F.2d 1126 (5th Cir.).

United States v. Harrison (1982), 671 F.2d 1159 (8th Cir.), *cert. denied,* 459 U.S. 847 (1982).

United States v. McKenzie, 798 F.2d 602 (5th Cir. 1985)

United States v. Ragsdale (1971), 438 F.2d 21 (5th Cir.), *cert. denied,* 403 U.S. 919 (1971).

United States v. Shafer (1974), 384 F.Supp. 496 (N.D. Ohio).

United States Code. (1992). Title 18, Sections 241, 242, 1341; Title 42, Section 1983.

United States Code Annotated. (1992). Title 42, Sections 1997 *et seq.* Minneapolis: West Publishing.

Urban Studies Center. (1982). *Jefferson County Survey.* Louisville, Ky.: University of Louisville (March).

Urbanya, Kathryn. (1987). "Establishing a Deprivation of a Constitutional Right to Personal Safety Under Section 1983: The Use of Unjustified Force by State Officials in Violation of the Fourth, Eighth, and Fourteenth Amendments." *Albany Law Review* 51:171.

———. (1989). "Problematic Standards of Reasonableness: Qualified Immunity in Section 1983 Actions for a Police Officer's Use of Excessive Force." *Temple University Law Review* 62:61.

U.S. Bureau of the Census. (1952). *Census of Population: 1950, Volume II, Characteristics of the Population, Part 5, California.* Washington, D.C.: U.S. Government Printing Office.

U.S. Commission on Civil Rights. (1966). *To Secure These Rights.* Washington, D.C.: U.S. Government Printing Office.

———. (1981). *Who's Guarding the Guardians?* Washington, D.C.: U.S. Government Printing Office.

U.S. Department of Justice. (1987). *United States Attorneys' Manual.* Clifton, N.J.: Prentice-Hall Law and Business.

———. (1990). *Sourcebook of Criminal Justice Statistics.* Washington, D.C.: National Criminal Justice Information and Statistics Service.

Vala, J., M. Monteiro, and J. Leyens. (1988). "Perception of Violence as a Function of Observer's Ideology and Actor's Group Membership." *British Journal of Social Psychology* 27 (3): 231–37.

Van Maanen, John. (1973). "Observations on the Making of Policemen." *Human Organizations* 32:407–18.

———. (1974). "Working the Street: A Developmental View of Police Behavior." In Herbert Jacob (ed.), *The Potential for Reform of Criminal Justice.* Beverly Hills, Calif.: Sage.

———. (1978). "The Asshole." In Peter K. Manning and John van Maanen (eds.), *Policing: A View From the Streets.* Santa Monica, Calif.: Goodyear.

Vaughn, Jerald R. (1981). "Peer Evaluation in Multi-Dimensional Performance Evaluation: How an Employee Is Perceived by His Fellow Workers May Be As Important As How He Is Perceived by His Supervisors." *Police Chief* 48 (August): 58.

Vaughn, Michael S. (1992). "Problem-Oriented Policing: A Philosophy of Policing for the Twenty-first Century." *Criminal Justice and Behavior* 19 (3): 343–54.

Vera Institute of Justice. (1988). *Processing of Complaints Against Police: The Civilian Complaint Review Board.* New York: Vera Institute of Justice.

Verbal Judo Institute. (no date). "What is Verbal Judo?" Tijeras, N.Mex.

Vidmar, Neil, and N. M. Laird. (1983). "Adversary Social Roles: Their Effects on Witnesses' Communication of Evidence and the Assessment of Adjudicators." *Journal of Personality and Social Psychology* 44:888–98.

Waddington, Peter A. J. (1991). *Strong Arm of the Law.* Oxford, England: Clarendon.

Waddington, Peter A. J., and Q. Braddock. (1991). "Guardians or Bullies? Perceptions of the Police Amongst Adolescent Black, White and Asian Boys." *Policing and Society* 2 (1): 31–45.

Waegel, William B. (1984a). "The Use of Lethal Force by Police: The Complainant." *Journal of Police Science and Administration* 8:247-52.

———. (1984b). "How Police Justify the Use of Deadly Force." *Social Problems* 32:144-55.

Wagner, Allen E. (1980). "Citizen Complaints Against the Police: The Complainant." *Journal of Police Science and Administration* 8 (3): 247-52.

Walker, Daniel. (1968). *Rights in Conflict: The Violent Confrontation of Demonstrators and Police in the Parks and Streets of Chicago During the Week of the Democratic National Convention of 1968. A Report to the National Commission on the Causes and Prevention of Violence.* New York: Bantam.

Walker, Laurens, Stephen LaTour, E. Allan Lind, and John Thibaut. (1974). "Reactions of Participants and Observers to Modes of Adjudication." *Journal of Applied Social Psychology* 4:295-310.

Walker, Laurens, E. Allan Lind, and John Thibaut. (1979). "The Relation Between Procedural and Distributive Justice." *Virginia Law Review* 65:1401-20.

Walker, Laurens, John Thibaut, and Virginia Andreoli. (1972). "Order Presentation at Trial." *Yale Law Journal* 82:216-26.

Walker, R. O. (1982). "Exploratory Investigation of Police Attitudes Toward Violence." *Journal of Police Science and Administration* 10:93-100.

Walker, Samuel. (1992). *The Police in America: An Introduction.* 2d ed. New York: McGraw-Hill.

———. (1994). *Hate Speech: The History of an American Controversy.* Lincoln: University of Nebraska Press.

Walker, Samuel, and Vic W. Bumphus. (1991). "Civilian Review of the Police: A National Survey of the 50 Largest Cities." Unpublished document, University of Nebraska at Omaha, Committee on Research.

Walker, Samuel, and Lorie A. Fridell. (1989). "The Impact of *Tennessee v. Garner* on Deadly Force Policy." Paper presented at the annual meeting of the American Society of Criminology, Reno, Nev., November 10.

Warr, M. (1980). "The Accuracy of Public Beliefs about Crime." *Social Forces* 59 (2): 456-70.

Warren, James. (1992). "Cop Rock: Officers Use Rap Lyrics to Break Down Barriers between Cabrini Residents, Police." *Chicago Sun-Times* (November 15):Sec. 5, p. 2.

Weiler, Paul C. (1990). *Governing the Workplace: The Future of Labor and Employment Law.* Cambridge, Mass.: Harvard University Press.

Weiner, Norman L. (1974). "The Effect of Education on Police Attitudes." *Journal of Criminal Justice* 2:317-28.

Weisburd, David, Jerome McElroy, and Patricia Hardyman. (1988). "Challenges to Supervision in Community Policing: Observations on a Pilot Project." *American Journal of Police* 7:29-50.

Wenk, E. A., J. O. Robison, and G. W. Smith. (1972). "Can Violence be Predicted?" *Crime and Delinquency* 18:393-402.

West, P. (1988). "Investigation of Complaints Against the Police: Summary Report of a National Survey." *American Journal of Police* 7 (2): 101-21.

West, Paul. (no date). "PERF Investigation of Complaints Against Police Survey: Summary Report of Results." Washington, D.C.: Police Executive Research Forum.

West's Annotated California Code. (1992). Cal. Penal Code Section 422.6. Minneapolis: West Publishing.

Westley, William A. (1951). "The Police: A Sociological Study of Law, Custom and Morality." Ph.D. diss., University of Chicago.

———. (1953). "Violence and the Police." *American Journal of Sociology* 59 (1, July): 34–41.

———. (1970). *Violence and the Police: A Sociological Study of Law, Custom, and Morality.* Cambridge, Mass.: MIT Press.

Wharton, V. L. (1965). *The Negro in Mississippi, 1865–1890.* New York: Harper and Row.

Whitaker, Gordon P. (1983). "Police Department Size and the Quality and Cost of Police Services." In Stuart Nagel, Erika Fairchild, and Anthony Champagne (eds.), *The Political Science of Criminal Justice.* Springfield, Ill.: Charles C. Thomas.

Whitaker, Gordon P., Charles David Phillips, and Alissa P. Worden. (1984). "Aggressive Patrol: A Search for Side-effects." *Law & Policy* 6:339–60.

White, A. G. (1987). "Police Management-Recruit Screening: A Selected Bibliography." *Public Administration Series,* bibliography P2372.

White, M. F., and B. A. Menke. (1978). "A Critical Analysis of Surveys on Public Opinions Toward Police Agencies." *Journal of Police Science and Administration* 6 (2): 204–18.

White, Susan O. (1972). "A Perspective on Police Professionalization." *Law & Society Review* 7:61–85.

Wilbanks, William. (1987). *The Myth of a Racist Criminal Justice System.* Monterey, Calif.: Brooks/Cole.

———. (1993). "Opposing View: Drug War Is Not Racist." *USA Today* (July 27): 8A.

Wiley, M. G., and T. L. Hudik. (1974). "Police-Citizen Encounters: A Field Test of Exchange Theory." *Social Problems* 22 (1): 119–27.

Williams, F. P., and C. P. Wagoner. (1992). "Making the Police Proactive: An Impossible Task for Improbable Reasons." *Police Forum* 2 (2): 1–5.

Williams, Hubert, and Patrick V. Murphy. (1990). "The Evolving Strategy of Police: A Minority View." *Perspectives on Policing* Series, No. 13 (January). Washington, D.C.: National Institute of Justice and Kennedy School of Government, Harvard University.

Williams, J. S., C. W. Thomas, and B. K. Singh. (1983). "Situational Use of Police Force: Public Reactions." *American Journal of Police* 3 (1): 37–50.

Willoughby, K. R., and W. R. Blount. (1985). "The Relationship Between Law Enforcement Officer Height, Aggression, and Job Performance." *Journal of Police Science and Administration* 13:225–29.

Wilson v. City of Chicago, 707 F.Supp. 379 (N.D.Ill. 1989)

Wilson, James Q. (1968). *Varieties of Police Behavior: The Management of Law and Order in Eight Communities.* Cambridge, Mass.: Harvard University Press.

———. (1978). "Dilemmas of Police Administration." In Peter K. Manning and John van Maanen (eds.), *Policing: A View from the Street.* Santa Monica, Calif.: Goodyear.

———. (1980). "Police Use of Deadly Force." *FBI Law Enforcement Bulletin* 49 (8): 16–21.

Wilson, James Q., and Barbara Boland. (1978). "The Effect of the Police on Crime." *Law & Society Review* 12:367–90.

Wilson, James Q., and George L. Kelling. (1982). "Police and Neighborhood Safety: Broken Windows." *Atlantic Monthly* 249 (March): 29–38.

Wilson, Orlando W., and Roy McClaren. (1963). *Police Administration.* New York: McGraw-Hill.

Wilt, G. M, and J. D. Bannon. (1976). "Cynicism or Realism: A Critique of Niederhoffer's Research into Police Attitudes." *Journal of Police Science and Administration* 4:38–45.

Winick, C. (1987). "Public Opinion on Police Misuse of Force: A New York Study." *Report to the Governor: Vol. III. Consultant Reports.* Albany: New York State Commission on Criminal Justice and the Use of Force.

Wisby, Gary. (1995). "Cops Fail Youth 'Respect' Test." *Chicago Sun-Times* (January 9): 3.

Wolf, Craig. (1992). "Feeling Betrayed, Police Grow Wary." *New York Times* (July 8): B2.

Wolff, Craig. (1994). "Mayor Vows Investigation of Beating: Troubled by Brutality on Taped S.I. Incident." *New York Times* (May 3):B1, B3.

Wolfgang, Marvin E., R. Figlio, and Thorsten Sellin. (1972). *Delinquency in a Birth Cohort.* Chicago: University of Chicago Press.

Wolfgang, Marvin E., T. P. Thornberry, and R. Figlio. (1987). *From Boy to Man, from Delinquency to Crime.* Chicago: University of Chicago Press.

Wollack, S., J. J. Clancy, and S. Beals. (1973). "The Validation of Entry-Level Law Enforcement Examinations in the States of California and Nevada." Sacramento: Selection Consulting Center.

Wood, B. (1984). *Slavery in Colonial Georgia.* Athens: University of Georgia Press.

Worden, Alissa Pollitz. (1993). "The Attitudes of Women and Men in Policing: Testing Conventional and Contemporary Wisdom." *Criminology* 31:203–41.

Worden, Robert E. (1987). "The Premises of Police Work." Ph.D. diss. *Dissertation Abstracts International* 47A: 3184–85.

———. (1989). "Situational and Attitudinal Explanations of Police Behavior: A Theoretical Reappraisal and Empirical Assessment." *Law & Society Review* 23:667–711.

———. (1990). "A Badge and a Baccalaureate: Policies, Hypotheses, and Further Evidence." *Justice Quarterly* 7:565–92.

———. (in press). "Police Officers' Belief Systems: A Framework for Analysis." *American Journal of Police.*

Worden, Robert E., and Steven G. Brandl. (1990). "Protocol Analysis of Police Decision Making: Toward a Theory of Police Behavior." *American Journal of Criminal Justice* 14:297–318.

Worden, Robert E., and Stephen D. Mastrofski. (1989). "Varieties of Police Subcultures: A Preliminary Analysis." Paper presented at the annual meeting of the Law & Society Association, June 8–11, Madison, Wis.

Worden, Robert E., and Alissa A. Pollitz. (1984). "Police Arrests in Domestic Disturbances: A Further Look." *Law & Society Review* 18:105–19.

Worden, Robert E., and Robin L. Shepard. (1994). "On the Meaning, Measurement, and Estimated Effects of Suspects' Demeanor Toward the Police." Paper presented at the annual meeting of the American Society of Criminology, Miami, Nov. 8–12.

———. (In press). "Demeanor, Crime, and Police Behavior: A Reexamination of the Police Services Study Data." *Criminology* 34.

Wright, Robin. (1992). "Poverty's Long Shadow." *Times Union* (April 29, Section B).

Wycoff, Mary Ann, and Wesley G. Skogan. (1993). *Community Policing in Madison: Quality from the Inside Out: An Evaluation of Implementation and Impact. A Final Summary Report Presented to the National Institute of Justice.* Washington, D.C.: National Institute of Justice, U.S. Department of Justice.

———. (1994). "Community Policing in Madison: An Analysis of Implementation and Impact." In Dennis P. Rosenbaum (ed.), *The Challenge of Community Policing: Testing the Promises.* Thousand Oaks, Calif.: Sage.

Yale Law Journal Project. (1979). "Suing the Police in Federal Court." *Yale Law Journal* 88:781–82.

Young, Warren. (1986). "Investigating Police Misconduct." In Neil Cameron and Warren Young (eds.), *Policing at the Crossroads.* Wellington, New Zealand: Allen and Unwin.

Zamble, E., and P. Annesley. (1987). "Some Determinants of Public Attitudes Toward the Police." *Journal of Police Science and Administration* 15 (4): 285–90.

Zanna, M. P., and J. K. Rempel. (1988). "Attitudes: A New Look at An Old Concept." In D. Bar-Tal and A. Kruglanski (eds.), *The Social Psychology of Knowledge.* New York: Cambridge University Press.

Zevitz, R. G., and R. J. Rettammel. (1990). "Elderly Attitudes about Police Service." *American Journal of Police* 9 (2): 25–39.

Zimbardo, R., C. Havey, and C. Banks. (1975). "Interpersonal Dynamics in a Simulated Prison." *International Journal of Criminology and Penology* 1:69–97.

Zook v. Brown (1989), 865 F.2d 887 (7th Cir.).

Zunno, F. A., and David Lester. (1982). "The Risk of Murder for Police." *International Criminal Police Review* 354:6–8.

Index